KU-731-787

Evan Wright is a contributing editor on *Rolling Stone* magazine. He spent two months living with a platoon of Marine reconnaissance soldiers during the war in Iraq.

GENERATION KILL

o

Living dangerously on the road to
Baghdad with the ultraviolent
Marines of Bravo Company

EVAN WRIGHT

CORGI BOOKS

GENERATION KILL
A CORGI BOOK: 0 552 15189 0

Originally published in Great Britain by Bantam Press,
a division of Transworld Publishers

PRINTING HISTORY
Bantam Press edition published 2004
Corgi edition published 2005

1 3 5 7 9 10 8 6 4 2

Design by Amanda Dewey
Maps by Jeffrey L. Ward

Grateful acknowledgement is made to *Rolling Stone,* where
portions of this book first appeared in a different form.

The second line of the dedication is from Rudyard Kipling's
The Second Jungle Book (1899).

Set in 11/14pt Aldus by
Falcon Oast Graphic Art Ltd.

Corgi Books are published by Transworld Publishers,
61–63 Uxbridge Road, London W5 5SA,
a division of The Random House Group Ltd,
in Australia by Random House Australia (Pty) Ltd,
20 Alfred Street, Milsons Point, Sydney, NSW 2061, Australia,
in New Zealand by Random House New Zealand Ltd,
18 Poland Road, Glenfield, Auckland 10, New Zealand
and in South Africa by Random House (Pty) Ltd,
Endulini, 5a Jubilee Road, Parktown 2193, South Africa.

Printed and bound in Great Britain by
Cox & Wyman Ltd, Reading, Berkshire.

Papers used by Transworld Publishers are natural, recyclable
products made from wood grown in sustainable forests. The
manufacturing processes conform to the environmental
regulations of the country of origin.

TO THE WARRIORS OF HITMAN-2 AND HITMAN-3:

The strength of the Pack is the Wolf.

AUTHOR'S NOTE

○

Because the U.S. Military has partially embraced a conversion to the metric system, Marines measure distances in meters and kilometers, but still use inches and feet and speak of driving in "miles per hour." My account of the invasion retains these inconsistencies, switching between the metric and English systems as the troops did. Keeping track of this is simple: A meter (which equals 39.3 inches) is roughly 10 percent longer than a yard, and a kilometer (which equals 0.6 mile) is just over half a mile.

Some men are identified in this book solely by the nicknames awarded to them by fellow Marines.

GENERATION KILL

○

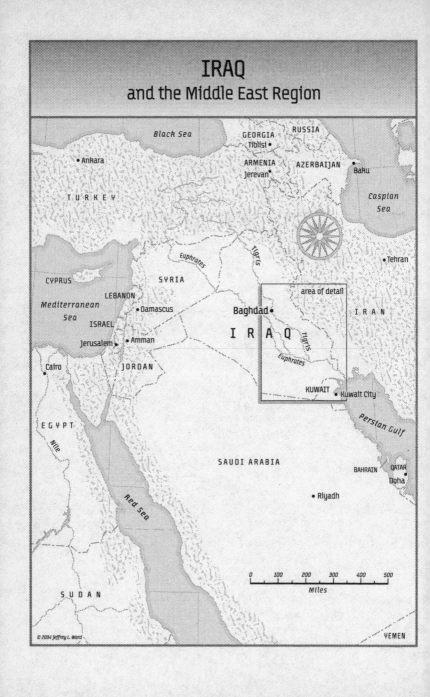

LEADING THE INVASION
First Recon's Movement North into Iraq

Tigris

Al Miqdadiyah

Baqubah

Baghdad

Al Kazimiyah

Euphrates

Salman Pak

Sarabadi

I R A N

Karbala

An Numaniyah

Al Kut

Al Hillah

Al Muwaffaqiyah   Al Hayy

Ad Diwaniyah

Qalat Sukhar

I R A Q

Ar Rifa

Al Samawah   Euphrates   Al Gharraf

Nasiriyah

Tigris

Basra

Safwan

Um Qasr

0   50   100

Miles

Camp
Mathilda

KUWAIT

Kuwait City

Persian Gulf

© 2004 Jeffrey L. Ward

PROLOGUE

○

IT'S ANOTHER IRAQI TOWN, nameless to the Marines racing down the main drag in Humvees, blowing it to pieces. We're flanked on both sides by a jumble of walled, two-story mud-brick buildings, with Iraqi gunmen concealed behind windows, on rooftops and in alleyways, shooting at us with machine guns, AK rifles and the odd rocket-propelled grenade (RPG). Though it's nearly five in the afternoon, a sandstorm has plunged the town into a hellish twilight of murky red dust. Winds howl at fifty miles per hour. The town stinks. Sewers, shattered from a Marine artillery bombardment that ceased moments before we entered, have overflowed, filling the streets with lagoons of human excrement. Flames and smoke pour out of holes blasted through walls of homes and apartment blocks by the Marines' heavy weapons. Bullets, bricks, chunks of buildings, pieces of blown-up light poles and shattered donkey carts splash into the flooded road ahead.

The ambush started when the lead vehicle of Second Platoon—the one I ride in—rounded the first corner into the town. There was a mosque on the left, with a brilliant, cobalt-blue dome. Across from this, in the upper window of a three-story building, a machine gun had opened up. Nearly two dozen rounds ripped into our Humvee almost immediately. Nobody was hit; none of the Marines panicked. They responded by speeding into the gunfire and attacking with their weapons. The four Marines crammed into this Humvee—among the first American troops to cross the border into Iraq—had spent the past week wired on a combination of caffeine, sleep deprivation, tedium and anticipation. For some of them, rolling into an ambush was almost an answered prayer.

Their war began several days ago, as a series of explosions that rumbled across the Kuwaiti desert beginning at about five in the morning of March 20. The Marines, who had been sleeping in holes dug into the sand twenty kilometers south of the border with Iraq, sat up and gazed into the empty expanse, their faces blank as they listened to the distant thundering. They had eagerly awaited the start of war since leaving their base at Camp Pendleton, California, more than six weeks earlier. Spirits couldn't have been higher. Later, when a pair of Cobra helicopter gunships thumped overhead, flying north, presumably on their way to battle, Marines pumped their fists in the air and screamed, "Yeah! Get some!"

Get some! is the unofficial Marine Corps cheer. It's shouted when a brother Marine is struggling to beat his personal best in a fitness run. It punctuates stories told at night about getting laid in whorehouses in Thailand and Australia. It's the cry of exhilaration after firing a burst from a .50-caliber machine gun. *Get some!* expresses, in two simple words, the excitement, the fear, the feelings of power and the erotic-tinged thrill that come from confronting the extreme physical and emotional challenges posed by death, which is, of course, what war is all about.

Nearly every Marine I've met is hoping this war with Iraq will be his chance to get some.

Marines call exaggerated displays of enthusiasm—from shouting *Get some!* to waving American flags to covering their bodies with Marine Corps tattoos—"moto." You won't ever catch Sergeant Brad Colbert, the twenty-eight-year-old commander of the vehicle I ride in, engaging in any moto displays. They call Colbert "The Iceman." Wiry and fair-haired, he makes sarcastic pronouncements in a nasal whine that sounds like comedian David Spade. Though he considers himself a "Marine Corps killer," he's also a nerd who listens to Barry Manilow, Air Supply and practically all the music of the 1980s except rap. He is passionate about gadgets: He collects vintage video-game consoles and wears a massive wristwatch that can only properly be "configured" by plugging it into his PC. He is the last guy you would picture at the tip of the spear of the invasion forces in Iraq.

Now, in the midst of this ambush in a nameless town, Colbert appears utterly calm. He leans out his window in front of me, methodically pumping grenades into nearby buildings with his rifle launcher. The Humvee rocks rhythmically as the main gun on the roof turret, operated by a twenty-three-year-old corporal, thumps out explosive rounds into buildings along the street. The vehicle's machine gunner, a nineteen-year-old Marine who sits to my left, blazes up the town, firing through his window like a drive-by shooter. Nobody speaks.

The fact that the enemy in this town has succeeded in shutting up the driver of this vehicle, Corporal Josh Ray Person, is no mean feat. A twenty-two-year-old from Missouri with a faintly hick accent and a shock of white-blond hair covering his wide, squarish head—his blue eyes are so far apart Marines call him "Hammerhead" or "Goldfish"—Person plans to be a rock star when he gets out of the Corps. The first night of the invasion, he had crossed the Iraqi border, simultaneously entertaining and annoying his fellow Marines by screeching out mocking versions of Avril Lavigne songs. Tweaking on a mix of chewing tobacco, instant coffee crystals, which he consumes dry by the mouthful, and over-the-counter stimulants like ephedra-based Ripped Fuel, Person never stops jabbering. Already he's reached a profound conclusion about this campaign: that the battlefield that is Iraq is filled with "fucking retards." There's the retard commander in the battalion, who took a wrong turn near the border, delaying the invasion by at least an hour. There's another officer, a classic retard, who has spent much of the campaign chasing through the desert to pick up souvenirs—helmets, Republican Guard caps and rifles—thrown down by fleeing Iraqi soldiers. There are the hopeless retards in the battalion-support sections who screwed up the radios and didn't bring enough batteries to operate the Marines' thermal-imaging devices. But in Person's eyes, one retard reigns supreme: Saddam Hussein. "We already kicked his ass once," he says. "Then we let him go, and he spends the next twelve years pissing us off even more. We don't want to be in this shithole country. We don't want to invade it. What a fucking retard."

Now, as enemy gunfire tears into the Humvee, Person hunches purposefully over the wheel and drives. The lives of everyone depend on him. If he's injured or killed and the Humvee stops, even for a moment in this hostile town, odds are good that everyone will be wiped out, not just the Marines in this vehicle, but the nineteen others in the rest of the platoon following behind in their

Humvees. There's no air support from attack jets or helicopters because of the raging sandstorm. The street is filled with rubble, much of it from buildings knocked down by the Marines' heavy weapons. We nearly slam into a blown-up car partially blocking the street. Ambushers drop cables from rooftops, trying to decapitate or knock down the Humvee's turret gunner. Person zigzags and brakes as the cables scrape across the Humvee, one of them striking the turret gunner who pounds on the roof, shouting, "I'm okay!"

At least one Marine in Colbert's Humvee seems ecstatic about being in a life-or-death gunfight. Nineteen-year-old Corporal Harold James Trombley, who sits next to me in the left rear passenger seat, has been waiting all day for permission to fire his machine gun. But no chance. The villagers Colbert's team had encountered had all been friendly until we hit this town. Now Trombley is curled over his weapon, firing away. Every time he gets a possible kill, he yells, "I got one, Sergeant!" Sometimes he adds details: "Hajji in the alley. Zipped him low. I seen his knee explode!"

Midway through the town, there's a lull in enemy gunfire. For an instant, the only sound is wind whistling through the Humvee. Colbert shouts to everyone in the vehicle: "You good? You good?" Everyone's all right. He bursts into laughter. "Holy shit!" he says, shaking his head. "We were fucking lit up!"

Forty-five minutes later the Marines swing pickaxes into the hard desert pan outside of the town, setting up defensive positions. Several gather around their bullet-riddled Humvees, laughing about the day's exploits. Their faces are covered with dust, sand, tar, gun lubricant, tobacco spittle and sewer water from the town. No one's showered or changed out of the bulky chemical-protection suits they've been wearing for ten days. Since all mirrors and reflective surfaces have been stripped from their Humvees to make the vehicles harder to detect, most of the men haven't seen themselves since crossing the border. Their filthy faces seem to make their teeth shine even whiter as they laugh and hug one another.

The platoon's eldest member, thirty-five-year-old Gunnery Sergeant Mike "Gunny" Wynn, walks among the Marines, grabbing their heads and shaking them like you would when playing with a puppy. "All right!" he repeats in his mild Texas accent. "You made it, man!"

"Who's the fucking retard who sent us into that town?" Person asks, spitting a thick stream of tobacco juice, which catches in the wind and mists across the faces of several of his buddies standing nearby. "That sure tops my list of stupid shit we've done."

Trombley is beside himself. "I was just thinking one thing when we drove into that ambush," he enthuses. "Grand Theft Auto: Vice City. I felt like I was living it when I seen the flames coming out of windows, the blown-up car in the street, guys crawling around shooting at us. It was fucking cool."

CULTURALLY, these Marines would be virtually un-recognizable to their forebears in the "Greatest Generation." They are kids raised on hip-hop, Marilyn Manson and Jerry Springer. For them, "motherfucker" is a term of endearment. For some, slain rapper Tupac is an American patriot whose writings are better known than the speeches of Abraham Lincoln. There are tough guys among them who pray to Buddha and quote Eastern philosophies and New Age precepts gleaned from watching Oprah and old kung fu movies. There are former gangbangers, a sprinkling of born-again Christians and quite a few guys who before entering the Corps were daily dope smokers; many of them dream of the day when they get out and are once again united with their beloved bud.

These young men represent what is more or less America's first generation of disposable children. More than half of the guys in the platoon come from broken homes and were raised by absentee, single, working parents. Many are on more intimate terms with video games, reality TV shows and Internet porn than they are with their own parents. Before the "War on Terrorism" began, not a whole lot was expected of this generation other than the hope that those in it would squeak through high school without pulling too many more mass shootings in the manner of Columbine.

But since the 9/11 attacks, the weight of America's "War on Terrorism" has fallen on their shoulders. For many in the platoon, their war started within hours of the Twin Towers falling, when they were loaded onto ships to begin preparing for missions in Afghanistan. They see the invasion of Iraq as simply another campaign in a war without end, which is pretty much what their commanders and their president have already told them. (Some in the military see the "War on Terrorism" merely as an acceleration of the trend that started in the 1990s with Somalia, Haiti, Kosovo: America cementing its role as global enforcer, the world's Dirty Harry.) In Iraq the joke among Marines is "After finishing here, we're going to attack North Korea, and we'll get there by invading Iran, Russia and China."

They are the first generation of young Americans since Vietnam to be sent into an open-ended conflict. Yet if the dominant mythology of that war turns on a generation's loss of innocence—young men reared on *Davy Crockett* waking up to their government's deceits while fighting in Southeast Asian jungles; the nation falling from the grace of Camelot to the shame of Watergate—these young men entered Iraq predisposed toward the idea that the Big Lie is as central to American governance as taxation. This is, after all, the generation that first learned of the significance of the presidency not through an inspiring speech at the Berlin Wall but through a national obsession with semen stains and a White House blow job. Even though their Commander in Chief tells them they are fighting today in Iraq to protect American freedom, few would be shaken to discover that they might actually be leading a grab for oil. In a way, they almost expect to be lied to.

If there's a question that hangs over their heads, it's the same one that has confronted every other generation sent into war: Can these young Americans fight?

As the sky turns from red to brown in the descending dust storm outside the town the Marines have just smashed apart, their platoon commander, a twenty-five-year-old lieutenant named Nathaniel Fick, leans against his Humvee, watching his men laugh. Lieutenant Fick, a Dartmouth graduate who joined the Marines in a fit of idealism, shakes his head, grinning. "I'll say one thing about these guys," he says. "When we take fire, not one of them hesitates to shoot back. In World War Two, when Marines hit the beaches, a surprisingly high percentage of them didn't fire their weapons, even when faced with direct enemy contact. They hesitated. Not these guys. Did you see what they did to that town? They fucking destroyed it. These guys have no problem with killing."

Several Marines from Colbert's vehicle gather around

Corporal Anthony Jacks, a twenty-three-year-old heavy-weapons gunner. Jacks is six foot two, powerfully built, and has a smile made unforgettable by his missing two front teeth (shot out in a BB-gun fight with his brother when he was sixteen). The Marines' nickname for him is "Manimal," not so much in tribute to his size but because of his deep, booming voice, which, when he yells, is oddly reminiscent of a bellowing farm animal. The platoon credits him with pretty much saving everyone's life during the ambush. Of the four heavy-weapons gunners in the platoon, Manimal alone succeeded in destroying the enemy's prime machine-gun position across from the mosque. For several minutes his buddies have been pounding him on the back, recounting his exploits. Howling and laughing, they almost seem like Johnny Knoxville's posse of suburban white homies celebrating one of his more outrageously pointless *Jackass* stunts. "Manimal was a fucking wall of fire!" one of them shouts. "All I seen was him dropping buildings and blowing up telephone poles!"

"Shut up, guys! It ain't funny!" Manimal roars, pounding the side of the Humvee with a massive paw.

He silences his buddies. They look down, some of them suppressing guilty smiles.

"The only reason we're all laughing now is none of us got killed," Manimal lectures them. "That was messed up back there."

It's the first time anyone has seriously raised this possibility: that war is not fun, that it might, in fact, actually suck.

In the coming weeks, it will fall on the men in this platoon and their battalion to lead significant portions of the American invasion of Iraq. They belong to an elite unit, First Reconnaissance Battalion, which includes fewer than 380 Marines. Outfitted with lightly armored or open-top Humvees that resemble oversized dune buggies, they will race ahead of the much larger, better-equipped primary Marine forces in Iraq. Their mission will be to seek out enemy ambushes by literally driving into them.

Major General James Mattis, commander of the First Marine Division—the bulk of the Corps' ground forces in Iraq—would later praise the young men of First Recon for being "critical to the success of the entire campaign." While spearheading the American blitzkrieg in Iraq, they will often operate deep behind enemy lines and far beyond anything they have trained for. They will enter Baghdad as liberating heroes only to witness their astonishing victory crumble into chaos. They will face death every day. They will struggle with fear, confusion, questions over war crimes and leaders whose competence they don't trust. Above all, they will kill a lot of people. A few of those deaths the men will no doubt think about and perhaps regret for the rest of their lives.

ONE

○

MAJOR GENERAL JAMES MATTIS calls the men in First Reconnaissance Battalion "cocky, obnoxious bastards." Recon Marines belong to a distinct military occupational specialty, and there are only about a thousand of them in the entire Marine Corps. They think of themselves, as much as this is possible within the rigid hierarchy of the military, as individualists, as the Marine Corps' cowboys. They evolved as jacks-of-all-trades, trained to move, observe, hunt and kill in any environment—land, sea or air. They are its special forces.

Recon Marines go through much of the same training as do Navy SEALs and Army Special Forces soldiers. They are physical prodigies who can run twelve miles loaded with 150-pound packs, then jump in the ocean and swim several more miles, still wearing their boots and fatigues, and carrying their weapons and packs. They are trained to parachute, scuba dive, snow-shoe, mountain climb and rappel from helicopters. Fewer than 2 percent of all Marines who enter in the Corps are selected for Recon training, and of those chosen, more than half wash out. Even those who make it commonly only do so after suffering bodily injury that borders on the grievous, from shattered legs to broken backs.

Recon Marines are also put through Survival Evasion Resistance Escape school (SERE), a secretive training course where Marines, fighter pilots, Navy SEALs and other military personnel in high-risk jobs are held "captive" in a simulated prisoner-of-war camp in which the student inmates are locked in cages, beaten and subjected to psychological torture overseen by military psychiatrists—all with the intent of training them to stand up to enemy captivity. When Gunny Wynn went through SERE, his "captors," playing on his Texas accent, forced him to wear a Ku Klux Klan hood for several days and pull one of his fellow "inmate" Marines, an African American, around on a leash, treating him as a slave. "They'll think of anything to fuck you up in the head," Gunny Wynn says.

Those who make it through Recon training in one piece, which takes several years to cycle all the way through, are by objective standards the best and toughest in the Marine Corps. Traditionally, their mission is highly specialized. Their training is geared toward stealth— sneaking behind enemy lines in teams of four to six men, observing positions and, above all, avoiding contact with hostile forces.

The one thing they are not trained for is to fight from Humvees, maneuvering in convoys, rushing headlong into enemy positions. This is exactly what they will be doing in Iraq. While the vast majority of the troops will reach Baghdad by swinging west onto modern super-highways and driving, largely unopposed, until they reach the outskirts of the Iraqi capital, Colbert's team in First Recon will get there by fighting its way through some of the crummiest, most treacherous parts of Iraq, usually far ahead of all other American forces. By the end of the campaign, Marines will dub their unit "First Suicide Battalion."

Mattis began hatching his plans for First Recon's unorthodox mission back in November. The General is a small man in his mid-fifties who moves and speaks quickly, with a vowel-mashing speech impediment that gives him a sort of folksy charm. A bold thinker, Mattis's favorite expression is "Doctrine is the last refuge of the unimaginative." On the battlefield, his call sign is "Chaos." His plan for the Marines in Iraq would hinge on disregarding sacred tenets of American military doctrine. His goal was not to shield his Marines from chaos, but to embrace it. No unit would embody this daring philosophy more than First Recon.

In the months leading up to the war on Iraq, battles over doctrine and tactics were still raging within the military. The struggle was primarily between the more cautious "Clinton generals" in the Army, who advocated a methodical invasion with a robust force of several hundred thousand, and Secretary of Defense Donald Rumsfeld and his acolytes, who argued for unleashing a sort of American blitzkrieg on Iraq, using a much smaller invasion force—one that would rely on speed and mobility more than on firepower. Rumsfeld's interest in "maneuver warfare," as the doctrine that emphasizes mobility over firepower is called, predated invasion planning for Iraq. Ever since becoming Secretary of Defense, Rumsfeld had been pushing his vision of a stripped-down, more mobile military force on the Pentagon as part of a sweeping transformation plan.

Mattis and the Marine Corps had been moving in that direction for nearly a decade. The Iraq campaign would showcase the Corps' embrace of maneuver warfare.

Mattis envisioned the Marines' role in Iraq as a rush. While the U.S. Army—all-powerful, slow-moving and cautious—planned its methodical, logistically robust movement up a broad, desert highway, Mattis prepared the Marines for an entirely different campaign. After seizing southern oil facilities within the first forty-eight hours of the war, Mattis planned to immediately send First Recon and a force of some 6,000 Marines into a violent assault through Iraq's Fertile Crescent. Their mission would be to seize the most treacherous route to Baghdad—the roughly 185-kilometer-long, canal-laced urban and agricultural corridor from Nasiriyah to Al Kut.

Saddam had viewed this route, with its almost impenetrable terrain of canals, villages, rickety bridges, hidden tar swamps and dense groves of palm trees, as his not-so-secret weapon in bogging down the Americans. Thousands of Saddam loyalists, both Iraqi regulars and foreign jihadi warriors from Syria, Egypt and Palestinian refugee camps, would hunker down in towns and ambush points along the route. They had excavated thousands of bunkers along the main roads, sown mines and propositioned tens of thousands of weapons. When Saddam famously promised to sink the American invaders into a "quagmire," he was probably thinking of the road from Nasiriyah to Al Kut. It was the worst place in Iraq to send an invading army.

Mattis planned to subvert the quagmire strategy Saddam had planned there by throwing out a basic element of military doctrine: His Marines would assault through the planned route and continue moving without pausing to establish rear security. According to conventional wisdom, invading armies take great pains to secure supply lines to their rear, or they perish. In Mattis's plan, the Marines would never stop charging.

The men in First Recon would be his "shock troops." During key phases of the assault, First Recon would race ahead of the already swift-moving Marine battle forces to throw the Iraqis further off balance. Not only would the Marines in First Recon spearhead the invasion on the ground, they would be at the forefront of a grand American experiment in maneuver warfare. Abstract theories of transforming U.S. military doctrine would come down on their shoulders in the form of sleepless nights and driving into bullets and bombs day after day, often with no idea what their objective was. This experiment would succeed in producing an astonishingly fast invasion. It would also result, in the view of some Marines who witnessed the descent of liberated Baghdad into chaos, in a Pyrrhic victory for a conquering force ill-trained and unequipped to impose order on the country it occupied.

Mattis did not reveal his radical plans for First Recon to its commander, Lieutenant Colonel Stephen Ferrando, until November 2002, a couple of months before the battalion deployed to the Middle East. Ferrando would later tell me, "Major General Mattis's plan went against all our training and doctrine, but I can't tell a general I don't do windows."

At the time of Ferrando's initial planning meetings with Mattis, the battalion possessed neither Humvees nor the heavy weapons that go with them. To the men in First Recon, trained to swim or parachute into enemy territory in small teams, the concept of fighting in columns of up to seventy vehicles, as they would in Iraq, was entirely new. Many didn't even have military operators' licenses for Humvees. The vehicles had to be scrounged from Marine Corps recycling depots and arrived in poor condition. The Marines were given only a few weeks to practice combat maneuvers in the Humvees, and just a few days to practice firing the heavy weapons mounted on them before the invasion.

What made Mattis's selection of First Recon for this daring role in the campaign even more surprising is that he had other units available to him—specifically, Light Armored Reconnaissance (LAR) battalions—which are trained and equipped to fight through enemy ambushes in specialized armored vehicles. When I later ask Mattis why he put First Recon into this unorthodox role, he falls back on what sounds like romantic palaver: "What I look for in the people I want on the battlefield," he says, "are not specific job titles but courage and initiative."

Mattis apparently had such faith in their skills that the Marines in First Recon were kept in the dark as to the nature of their mission in Iraq. Their commanders never told them they would be leading the way through much of the invasion, serving more or less as guinea pigs in the military's experiment with maneuver warfare. Most of the men in First Recon entered the war under the impression that they had been given Humvees to be used as transport vehicles to get them into position to execute conventional, stealthy recon missions on foot. Few imagined the ambush-hunting role they would play in the war. As one of the Marines in First Recon would later put it, "Bunch of psycho officers sent us into shit we never should have gone into. But we came out okay, dog, even though all we was packing was some sac."

TWO

○

THE MARINES OF FIRST RECON have already been living in a Spartan desert camp for six weeks when I first meet them in early March, about a week before the invasion. Their home is a tent city called Camp Mathilda, located in the moonscape desert of northern Kuwait about fifty kilometers below the border with Iraq. The desert here is covered in fine, powdery sand almost like talcum powder. By day it presents an endless vista of off-white tones, both dull and blinding in the harsh sun. Surrounded by barbed wire and armed guards, Mathilda looks like a prison camp. About 5,000 Marines from a variety of units live in hundreds of putty-colored tents encircled by a gravel road, lots filled with hundreds of military vehicles, and rows of shower trailers and diesel-powered generators that fill the air with an incessant growling.

I arrive at about noon on March 11, on a bus from Kuwait City provided by the Marine Corps. I'm the only reporter slated to embed with First Recon. Another was supposed to come as well, but he dropped out after going through mandatory chemical warfare training provided by the Marine Corps in Kuwait City. Marine instructors had scared everyone by talking about nerve gases that, as they put it, will "make you dance the funky chicken until you die"; blistering agents that will make your skin "burst up like Jiffy Pop"; and the risks of suffocating in your gas mask if you vomit. "If it's chunky," an instructor had said, "you won't be able to clear it through the drain tube of your mask. You'll have to swallow it or risk choking on it." It was this last point that got to the other reporter. He suffered an acute attack of sanity in our hotel a few hours later and left the embed program to fly back home.

War fever, at least among reporters, has been running pretty high. Before coming to Kuwait, while staying at the main media hangout hotel by the Navy's port in Bahrain, I'd witnessed two colleagues get into a smackdown in the lobby over the issue of war and peace. A Canadian wire-service reporter, bitterly opposed to the war, knocked down a loudly patriotic American photographer in favor of it. While stunned Arab security guards looked on, the Canadian peacenik clenched the American patriot into a sort of LAPD chokehold and repeatedly slammed his head into the back of a chair. The American was saved from further humiliation only after several tough women from Reuters and AFP waded in and broke apart the one-sided combat.

When I watched the broadcast of Colin Powell making the case for war to the UN, I was aboard a Navy ship in the Gulf with a group of American reporters who cheered whenever Powell enumerated another point building the case for the invasion. They booed when European diplomats presented their rebuttals. Being among reporters here has sometimes felt like the buildup to a big game, Team USA versus The World.

The first Marines I encounter have other issues on their minds. I meet them in a dingy mess tent, a few guys in their late teens or early twenties killing time in the shade before dinner. As soon as I enter, one of them asks me if it's true that J.Lo is dead. Rumors of her death have been circulating through the camp for more than a week. The commanders told the men the story is not true, but one of the Marines I talk to, a twenty-year-old in an infantry unit, pesters me. "Maybe she really did die, but they're not telling us to keep our morale up."

When I tell him the rumor is false, he shakes his head, not quite believing me. You get the idea he's clinging to this drama as something to enliven an otherwise bleak existence. Despite the fact that these Marines are poised to be at the epicenter of a world-changing event, here in the desert without phones or TVs or Internet connections, they seem a million miles away from it.

Everyone is covered in dust. When you walk through the camp, it whooshes up around your boots in clouds like moon dust. Even on days when the wind isn't blowing, it hangs in the air the way dampness does in San Francisco.

Several weeks earlier, the military brought in hundreds of pigeons and chickens, which they placed in cages between the tents to serve as early-warning detectors for gas attacks, as coal miners have used them for centuries. But the desert dust overwhelmed the birds' fragile respiratory systems, killing nearly all of them. The only fauna thriving here are the rats that live under the plywood floorboards of the tents and come out at night to scamper around the slumbering Marines.

Every twenty-four hours the temperature fluctuates by up to fifty degrees, with frigid nights in the upper thirties turning into blazing days in the upper eighties. Throughout the day, you're either shivering or sweating. The sun is so intense that steel objects, such as machine-gun barrels, when left out in it for any period of time, become so hot they can be picked up only by using towels like oven mitts.

By early March the desert sandstorms known as "shamals" have begun. Shamal winds gust at up to fifty miles an hour, sometimes blowing over the twenty-meter-long platoon tents Marines sleep in, shredding apart the canvas and burying them in several feet of sand. It's no wonder the chickens couldn't hack it. The Marines who've been here for weeks have runny noses and inflamed eyes from the constant dust. A lot of them walk around with rags wrapped around their faces to keep the dust out, but it doesn't seem to do any good. Several develop walking pneumonia even before the invasion begins.

Of the thousands of troops in the camp, the Recon Marines are easy to spot. Unlike infantry jarheads who work out in olive-drab shirts and shorts, Recon Marines appear on the gravel running track in all-black physical-training uniforms, a distinctive look augmented with black watch caps they don two hours before sunset. All day long, despite the shamal winds and choking dust, you see them practicing martial arts in the sand, or running on the gravel track, wearing combat boots, loaded down with weapons and packs weighing more than 100 pounds. Whenever a Recon Marine runs past on the track, carrying a particularly crushing load, his buddies pump their fists in the air and scream "Get some!"

Recon Marines take pride in enduring the hostile conditions. One of the first guys I meet in the battalion brags, "We're like America's little pit bull. They beat it, starve it, mistreat it, and once in a while they let it out to attack somebody."

In my first couple of days at the camp I'm placed in a tent with officers. I can't tell anybody apart; they all look the same in their desert camouflage fatigues. Most of the officers seem to be square-jawed, blue-eyed white guys in their mid to late twenties. The initial reason I strike up an acquaintance with Lt. Fick, commander of the platoon I end up spending the war with, is he's easily recognizable. Though he's twenty-five, he has a loping, adolescent stride you can spot from a hundred meters away. He's one of fifty men who introduce themselves to me during my first twenty-four hours at the camp, but he's the only one I'm able to call by name on my way to the mess tent and ask if I can join him for dinner.

Dinners are served on trays in a cafeteria line staffed by South Asian laborers. As we move through the line, Fick informs me that for a couple of weeks running, the only entrée served has been mushy, gray chicken pieces. He speculates these might be remnants of the doomed camp chickens. Fick has one of those laughs involving a momentary loss of control that causes him to pitch forward like someone knocked him on the back of the head.

He is six foot two with light-brown hair and the pleasant, clear-eyed looks of a former altar boy, which he is. The son of a successful Baltimore attorney father and a social-worker mother, Fick admits, "My family had a *Leave It to Beaver* quality." He entered Dartmouth intending to study pre-med, but in his sophomore year he was inspired to consider the military when he took a class conducted by a charismatic former Special Forces soldier who'd served in Vietnam. Fick ended up double-majoring in political science and classics, then attended the Marine Corps' Officer Candidates School. Two years after graduating in 1999, he found himself a Marine second lieutenant on a landing craft delivering humanitarian supplies to war-torn East Timor. "I had a boatload of food rations and boxes of brand-new ThighMasters," he says.

"We were delivering exercise devices for the oppressed, starving people of East Timor." He throws his head forward, laughing.

The absurdities of the military amuse Fick. A few weeks after 9/11, he led an infantry platoon on a clandestine helicopter mission into Pakistan to retrieve a Black Hawk downed by the Afghan border. After that, Fick and his men were among the first Marines to seize the ground in southern Afghanistan at Camp Rhino. When he returned home after weeks of living in frozen fighting holes, the Marines sent him a bill for five hundred dollars, charging him for the food rations he'd consumed during his combat deployment. He says, "We had a saying about the military in Afghanistan: 'The incompetent leading the unwilling to do the unnecessary.' "

Despite his cavalier humor, Fick finished at the top of his class in Officer Candidates School and near the top of the Marine Corps' tough Basic Reconnaissance Course. He is also something of a closet idealist. His motivation for joining the Marines is a belief about which he is quietly passionate. "At Dartmouth, there was a sense that an ROTC program, which the school did not have, would militarize the campus," he explains. "They have it backward. ROTC programs at Ivy League campuses would liberalize the military. That can only be good for this country."

During our first meal together, he explains the breakdown of First Recon. The 374 Marines in First Recon Battalion are spread among four companies—Alpha, Bravo, Charlie and an auxiliary Headquarters and Support company. Alpha, Bravo and Charlie are the front-line combat companies containing the battalion's 160 actual Recon Marines. The rest of the battalion's personnel fill support positions. Fick commands Bravo

Company's Second Platoon. He's held the position for less than a year, having entered First Recon after his return from Afghanistan.

Platoons are the basic building block of each company. There are twenty-one enlisted Marines in each platoon, as well as a commander and a medical corpsman (who is an enlisted man provided by the Navy). Enlisted Marines—that is, those who are not officers—function within a complex web of hierarchy. Privates answer to corporals, and corporals to sergeants. Above sergeants there are staff sergeants, gunnery sergeants, first sergeants, master gunnery sergeants and sergeant majors. Above them all are officers.

Yet, as Fick explains, due to the traditional role of First Recon, in which small teams ordinarily function independently behind enemy lines, the men who are most trusted within a platoon are often the enlisted team leaders. Each platoon is divided into three teams, each led by one man, usually a sergeant. These men, like Colbert in Fick's platoon, often have more training and experience than the officers commanding them.

"The men naturally look up to someone like Colbert," Fick says. "He's been in the reconnaissance community for years. If you walk in here as an officer and start throwing your weight around based on rank alone, enlisted men will look at you like you've got a dick growing out of your forehead. You have to earn their respect."

First Recon, according to Fick, contains a heightened level of tensions between officers and enlisted men. "This unit fosters initiative and individual thinking. These guys are independent operators. That's great ninety-nine percent of the time. But the flip side is they don't play well with others."

Despite the frictions, Fick believes in the men he

commands. "I have the best platoon," he says repeatedly. Away from his men, Fick cannot talk about them without smiling.

It's because of his enthusiasm that I decide to join his platoon for the war. Initially, the battalion had planned for me to spend the invasion riding with the support company in the rear. But in exchange for handing over my satellite phone—severing all contact with the outside world—First Recon's commander, Lt. Col. Ferrando, allows me to move in with Bravo Second Platoon and ride with its Team One, led by Colbert.

IT'S AFTER DARK when Fick pushes me through the entrance to his platoon's tent to introduce me to his men. Forty-two enlisted Marines sleep here, those from Bravo's Second and Third platoons. It's lit with bare fluorescent light tubes suspended from the tent poles, which turn everyone's skin a different shade of chartreuse. The floor of loose plywood sheeting is piled with crates of rations, gear and weapons, which the men sleep between in cramped rows. In the small amount of open space, two Marines circle in flip-flops, sparring with their bare hands. One guy is in the corner, dealing cards to himself, doing push-ups according to their face values; he does the whole deck a couple of times a day. Others, a couple of whom have black eyes and scraped noses from their constant martial-arts fighting, recline on the floor studying invasion maps or reading dog-eared copies of Sun Tzu, Elmore Leonard, Steven Pressfield's Greek military-historical novel *Gates of Fire*, and *Hustler*.

Before Fick makes his introduction, a couple of Marines stand nearby carrying on a loud reminiscence about great chicks they knew in high school. "Everybody called her

One Pound," a Marine in this group is saying. "A pretty little Asian girl. Her eyes were so small and tight you could have blindfolded her with dental floss. We called her One Pound 'cause she always looked like she'd just smoked a pound of weed."

Fick clears his throat. He is younger than some of the sergeants he commands, and when he addresses the men, he often lowers his voice to a more mature and authoritative-sounding register. He introduces me in this official, Marine-officer voice, then leaves.

One of the first men to greet me is Navy Hospitalman Second Class Robert Timothy "Doc" Bryan, the twenty-nine-year-old medical corpsman. A tall redhead with narrow features, he approaches with a tight grin and shakes my hand. "So you came here for a war, huh? You like war?" He continues to squeeze my hand, then puts his face about eight inches from mine and stares with unblinking, electric-blue eyes. His smile begins to twitch. "I hope you have fun in this war, reporter."

He releases my hand and smacks my shoulder. "I'm just fucking with you, that's all. No harm." He walks off, laughing.

Several others break into laughter with him. Doc Bryan, I later find out, is always pissed off at something, if not the presence of a reporter, then incompetent military leaders or the barbarity of war. He's a self-made man, son of a steamfitter from a small town outside of Philadelphia, the first in his family to attend college. He attended Lock Haven University, then the University of Pennsylvania on a football scholarship while he earned a master's in education. In his younger days, Doc Bryan had a lot of ambient rage he used to burn off in weekend bar fights. "I'm always angry," he later tells me. "I was born that way. I'm an asshole."

A diesel generator drones somewhere outside. The tent reeks of farts, sweat and the sickeningly sweet funk of fungal feet. Everyone walks around in skivvies, scratching their balls.

Vigorous public ball scratching is common in the combat-arms side of the Marine Corps, even among high-level officers in the midst of briefings. The gesture is defiantly male, as is much of the vernacular of the Marine Corps itself. Not only do officers and enlisted men take pride in their profanity—the first time I meet First Recon's battalion commander, he tells me the other reporter who dropped out probably did so because he writes for a "fucking queer magazine"—the technical jargon of the Corps is rich with off-color lingo. The term "donkey dick," for example, is used to describe at least three different pieces of Marine equipment: a type of fuel spout, a radio antenna and a mortar-tube cleaning brush.

Recon Marines will proudly tell you that if you look up their official Military Occupational Specialty in a Marine Corps manual, their job title is listed as "Reconnaissance Man." Theirs is one of the few remaining fields in the military closed to women. For many, becoming a Recon Marine represents one of the last all-male adventures left in America. Among them, few virtues are celebrated more than being hard—having stronger muscles, being a better fighter, being more able to withstand pain and privation. They refer to extra comforts—foam sleeping pads, sweaters, even cold medicine—as "snivel gear," and relentlessly mock those who bring it as pussies.

Nor do the men have any CD or DVD players, Game Boys or any similar entertainment devices. They were forbidden to bring such distracting items to the Middle East. They are young Americans unplugged. Their only entertainment is talking, reading and playing cards or chess. There's a chessboard set up in the center of the tent, where a company tournament has been going on for six weeks now.

At night they fight constantly. They judo-flip each other headfirst into the plywood floor of the tent. They strong-arm their buddies into headlocks and punch bruises into each other's ribs. They lie in wait for one another in the shadows and leap out swinging Ka-Bar knives, flecking their buddies' rib cages with little nicks from the knife tips, or dragging their blades lightly across a victim's throat, playfully simulating a clean kill. They do it to keep each other in shape; they do it for fun; they do it to establish dominance.

The top dogs in the platoon are the team leaders. You can immediately pick out these guys just by the way they move among the men. They have a swagger, a magnetism that pulls the other guys to them like rock stars. In this tent the three most revered are Sergeants Kocher, Patrick and Colbert. The three of them served on a Recon team together in Afghanistan under the leadership of Colbert.

Sergeants Eric Kocher and Larry Shawn Patrick are the more obvious alphas of the pack. Kocher is thickly muscled and aspires to become a professional bodybuilder. Though technically he's part of Bravo Third Platoon, he spends much of his time in Second Platoon's section. He tells dirty stories that make everyone howl, but he has the kind of eyes that never seem to smile, even when the rest of his face is laughing. Though he is twenty-three, he projects such focused intensity he seems at least a decade older.

Patrick, a twenty-eight-year-old from a small mountain town in North Carolina, speaks with a mild Southern accent and has the gentle manners that go with it. With brown hair and blue eyes that have faint lines at the corners that crinkle when he smiles, he has a kindly, almost hangdog appearance. His fellow Marines call him "Pappy," and behind his back they speak of him in the most reverential terms. "You'd never think it to look at him," a Marine tells me, "but Pappy is straight up the coldest killer in the platoon. If you saw him on the street back in the civilian world, you'd just think he's the most average Joe out there. That's why he's so dangerous."

Colbert, the platoon's top team leader, is in charge of Team One. The year before, he was awarded a Navy Commendation for helping to take out an enemy missile battery in Afghanistan. He greets me with a formal handshake and a crisp salutation: "Welcome aboard. I hope your time with us is enjoyable and productive."

His politeness is so exacting it almost makes him come off like a prick. Everything about him is neat, orderly and crisp, in keeping with his Iceman nickname. Colbert is decidedly not one of the big ball-scratchers in the platoon. There is about him an air of Victorian rectitude. He grew up in an ultramodern 1970s house designed by his father, an architect. There was shag carpet in a conversation pit. One of his fondest memories, he later tells me, is that before cocktail parties, his parents would let him prepare the carpet with a special rake. Colbert is a walking encyclopedia of radio frequencies and encryption protocols, and can tell you the exact details of just about any weapon in the U.S. or Iraqi arsenal. He once nearly purchased a surplus British tank, even arranged a loan through his credit union, but backed out only when he realized that just parking it might run afoul of zoning laws in his home state, the "Communist Republic of California."

Beneath his formal manners, there is another side to Colbert's personality. His back is tattooed in a garish wash of color depicting a Louis Royo illustration of a warrior princess babe from *Heavy Metal* magazine. He pays nearly $5,000 a year in auto-motorcycle insurance due to outrageous speeding tickets. He routinely drives his Yamaha R1 racing bike at 150 miles per hour on southern California's freeways, and his previous racing bike was rigged with model rocket engines by the exhaust pipe to shoot flames when he wanted to "scare the bejesus out of commuters." He admits to a deep-rooted but controlled rebellious streak that was responsible for his parents sending him to military academy when he was in high school. His life, he says, is driven by a simple philosophy: "You don't want to ever show fear or back down, because you don't want to be embarrassed in front of the pack."

He holds sway over the other men not through physical power or personal magnetism but through sheer force of skill, determination and a barely concealed sense of superiority. During mountain warfare training, he's legendary for having ascended the final thousand meters of Mt. Shasta on a broken ankle, carrying 150 pounds of gear. Where other Marines speak of the special bonds of kinship between them, the mystical brotherhood formed in the crucible of shared hardship, Colbert shuns the crowd. He spends as much time as he can alone in his corner of the tent, engrossed in a military laptop, study-ing invasion maps and satellite imagery. While his brother Marines cavort and laugh around him, Colbert says, "I would never socialize with any of these people if we weren't in the Marines."

There is, of course, a widespread though usually unvoiced public perception that the military is a refuge for the socioeconomic dregs of society, people driven in by lack of jobs or paucity of social skills. Fick observes, "A lot of the people I went to school with at Dartmouth look down on the type of people who are in the Marine Corps."

But if you examine the backgrounds of the average enlisted men in First Recon, the picture is a little more complicated. There's no shortage of guys who came in to escape life in street gangs, sometimes with a little nudge from a local prosecutor. A Marine talking about his alcoholic dad or his crackhead mom does not raise eyebrows. But at the same time, you're just as likely to run into Marines who joined fresh out of prep school, or who turned down math or swim scholarships at universities. The most "boot" (inexperienced) private in Second Platoon is a nineteen-year-old who rejected an appointment at Annapolis in favor of becoming an enlisted Marine. The machine gunner in Team Three is from a well-to-do Oakland Hills, California, family and has a sister at Harvard.

What unites them is an almost reckless desire to test themselves in the most extreme circumstances. In many respects the life they have chosen is a complete rejection of the hyped, consumerist American dream as it is dished out in reality TV shows and pop-song lyrics. They've chosen asceticism over consumption. Instead of celebrating their individualism, they've subjugated theirs to the collective will of an institution. Their highest aspiration is self-sacrifice over self-preservation.

There is idealism about their endeavor, but at the same time the whole point of their training is to commit the ultimate taboo: to kill. Their culture revels in this. At the end of team briefings, Marines put their hands together and shout, "Kill!" In keeping with the spirit of transgression, they also mock some of the most delicate social conventions in America. The Hispanics in the platoon refer to the white guys as "cracker-ass fucks," the whites refer to them as "muds" and to Spanish as "dirty spic talk," and they are the best of friends.

Person, the aspiring rock star who serves as the driver and radio operator for Colbert's team, is among those whose feelings about the Corps seem almost conflicted. From Nevada, Missouri, a small town where "NASCAR is sort of like a state religion," he was proudly raised working-poor by his mother. "We lived in a trailer for a few years on my grandpa's farm, and I'd get one pair of shoes a year from Wal-Mart." Person was a pudgy kid in high school, didn't play sports, was on the debate team and played any musical instrument—from guitar to saxophone to piano—he could get his hands on.

Becoming a Marine was a 180-degree turn for him. "I'd planned to go to Vanderbilt on a scholarship and study philosophy," he says. "But I had an epiphany one day. I wanted to do my life for a while, rather than think it." Like Colbert, he's a veteran of Afghanistan and professes absolute support of this war. Yet it often seems as if the driving force behind this formerly pudgy, nonathletic kid's decision to enter the Corps and join one of its most elite, macho units was to mock it and everything around him.

Tonight, he entertains his fellow troops by pacing the tent, reading letters aloud sent by schoolchildren to boost morale. He opens one from a girl who writes that she is praying for world peace. He throws it down. "Hey, little tyke," Person shouts. "What does this say on my shirt? 'U.S. Marine!' I wasn't born on some hippie-faggot commune. I'm a death-dealing killer. In my free time I do push-ups until my knuckles bleed. Then I sharpen my knife."

Doc Bryan leaps up, brandishing a *Hustler*. "Check this out," he says.

"I already seen that," a Marine says. "Pictures of those chicks pissing."

"No, listen to this." Doc Bryan paces the tent reading an editorial by Larry Flynt damning the coming war as a grab for oil. "He is a very cognizant man," Doc Bryan concludes. "Gents, this is a very cognizant way of explaining what we are all doing here. We're going to be fighting a war for oil."

Nobody seems to care much about the point he's making. In a weird way, external facts about the looming war don't really seem that important to these guys. The dominant feature of their lives is simply the fact that they are all together, which they enjoy tremendously. Being around them is reminiscent of being a thirteen-year-old at a weekend sleepover with all of your very best friends in the world. Only this weekend goes on indefinitely, perpetually nurturing the mystical bonds, the warrior dreams.

There is an undeniable Peter Pan quality to the military. A Marine psychiatrist attached to the First Division says, "The whole structure of the military is designed to mature young men to function responsibly while at the same time preserving their adolescent sense of invulnerability."

Most Marines can remember the exact moment they decided to enlist. A lot of them were sparked by a specific TV commercial. In it, a cartoonish Arthurian hero slays a fire-breathing dragon, then promptly morphs into a Marine in dress blues standing at attention with a silver sword at his side.

Sergeant Rudy Reyes, thirty-one, the platoon's best martial-arts fighter (whom the other men continually jump and ambush in order to test themselves against his superior skills), describes his passion for the Marine Corps in terms that blend New Age mysticism with the spirit of comic-book adventure. "I joined the Marines for idealism and romance," he says. "Idealism because it's so hard. The Marine Corps is a wonderful tool of self-enlightenment. Discipline erases all preconceived notions, and the pain becomes a medium of self-discovery. That's the idealistic side. The romance comes in because we are a small band of hard motherfuckers, trained to go behind enemy lines against forces twenty or forty times bigger than us. And brother, if that ain't romantic, I don't know what is."

My first night with the platoon, Reyes says, "You're lucky to be here, brother. We are the baddest, most tight-knit niggas in the battalion."

Just before lights out, a private approaches me and says, in polite, respectful tones, "Sir, I'll get you a place to sleep."

He leads me to the wall of ponchos dividing the tent between Second and Third platoons, and widens a space between a machine gun and a stack of military rations boxes for me to spread out my sleeping bag. Only after the lights go off do I learn that I have been placed in the walkway used by the Third Platoon Marines when they go out to the latrines at night. Semi-naked burly guys in boots or flip-flops traipse over my head all night long. My placement here, the Marines later tell me, was their way of welcoming me. Later, I know they're starting to warm to me when guys start jumping on my neck and sticking the tips of Ka-Bars into my ribs.

FOR THE MARINES at Camp Mathilda, the first tangible sign that the war might actually be happening soon comes in the form of Pizza Hut delivery cars that stream into the camp all the way from Kuwait City on the night of March 16. As the South Asian franchise workers haggle with

Marines outside the cars, selling the pies for twenty or ten bucks apiece, Fick grimly observes, "I think we can take this as the clearest indication yet that we're getting ready to roll out for the invasion. They don't just feed Marines pizza for no reason."

Just after dawn on the morning of March 17, the Marines are told they have four hours to load their Humvees and trucks to pull out for a forward staging area near the Iraqi border. The men in Second Platoon clear out the tent in near silence. By eight o'clock temperatures have already reached the upper eighties. The heat is compounded by the fact that everyone has been ordered into their bulky chemical-protection suits. They lug weapons, rucksacks and crates of ammunition with sweat pouring from their faces. Everyone moves about in a feverish dream state.

By nine o'clock, First Recon's convoy of some seventy Humvees and trucks have been loaded and maneuvered into position in the sand. The 300 or so enlisted Marines line up for formation. A battalion master sergeant struts in front of the troops and shouts, "Anybody who doesn't want to be here, raise your hand."

Laughter swells from the ranks.

"Good," the sergeant continues. "You are going to be in the biggest show on the planet."

When formation ends, Marines jump up and down, laughing and throwing each other around in the dust. Two different men run past me, shouting exactly the same phrase, "This is like Christmas!"

Their enthusiasm for the rollout doesn't necessarily mean everyone's a warmonger. A Marine explains the peculiar logic of troops getting ready for combat. "The sooner the war starts," he says, "the sooner we go home."

I make my last call before turning in my satellite phone

to the battalion commander. The phone was provided by my editor to keep him updated on my movements, but I decide to call my girlfriend in Los Angeles instead. I'm not allowed to tell her we're leaving the camp. She says that everyone at home is expecting the war to start any day. People in Los Angeles are panicking. Her friends are driving to a cabin at Lake Arrowhead to wait out the war in safety. It seems unreal to me. I suppress the urge to ask her if J.Lo is dead.

THREE

○

FIRST RECON'S CONVOY pulls out from the gates of Camp Mathilda at noon on March 17 under an unusually clear, dust-free blue sky. The Marines' objective is a staging area about twenty kilometers south of the Iraqi border, where they will be in position to punch into Iraq on a few hours' notice. They have no orders yet to begin the invasion, but this is the last step. This maneuver is the battalion-wide equivalent of cocking a loaded pistol and aiming it at someone's head.

Tens of thousands of other American and British troops are on the same path this afternoon. As soon as First Recon's convoy pulls onto the "highway"—a narrow, rutted asphalt lane surrounded by open desert—we become snarled in traffic. Some 150,000 coalition troops are camped nearby, and it looks as if all of them have poured onto the same highway at once. Thousands of vehicles—Humvees, tanks and trucks—fill the road in a jam that snakes across the desert for thirty kilometers.

Traversing this portion of the Kuwait desert, you begin to get a sense of the scale of the undertaking. We crawl past fenced lots in which thousands of tanker trucks, tractor-trailers and pieces of construction machinery are parked, waiting to roll into Iraq on the heels of the combat units. There are supply depots covering acres of sand with mountains of munitions, oil drums and rations crates. Lying beside the road are steel pipe sections that military construction crews are welding together into a pipeline to supply fuel and water to the invasion force as it goes north. It all has the feel of a monumental industrial enterprise. Somehow all these pieces are being put together—the people and the equipment—to function as one large machine. Though at the small-unit level all I see is the friction among the moving parts—Marines shouting at other vehicles to get out of the way, guys jumping out to hurriedly piss by the road, people taking wrong turns—the machine works. It will roll across 580 kilometers to Baghdad. It will knock down buildings, smash cars and tanks, put holes in people, shred limbs, cut children apart. There's no denying it. For certain tasks, the machine put together in this desert is a very good one.

Colbert's team digs into its position in the staging area after midnight. The moon overhead is so bright it looks almost like someone is shining a flashlight on us. It's taken nearly fourteen hours to reach this spot of open desert. The battalion's seventy-odd vehicles fan out across a couple of kilometers, with the Humvees facing north, their guns oriented toward Iraq. Marines move through the moonlit gloom with pickaxes and shovels, digging "Ranger graves"—shallow, one-man sleeping holes designed to protect their occupants from shrapnel in the event of an Iraqi attack. Then the Marines stretch "cammie nets"—camouflage netting—over their vehicles to make them harder to spot.

Temperatures have plunged into the lower forties. In their haste to pack up in the morning, many Marines had buried fleece vests and other warming "snivel gear" in the bottoms of their rucksacks. Some left this behind altogether. While Colbert's team digs into their position, Marines who'd been so jubilant in the morning start bitching, primarily to amuse themselves.

Jacks, the giant gunner in Second Platoon's team whom everyone calls Manimal, walks over to Colbert, whining, "I'm sick of this war."

"It hasn't even started yet, you pussy," Colbert says.

"It's fucking cold out here," Manimal says.

"You can't be cold," Colbert says. "You're a killer."

"Yeah, but I didn't pack no snivel gear," Manimal says. "You got a fleece I can borrow till the war's over?"

A LOW-INTENSITY DUST STORM starts sometime before dawn on the first morning at the staging area. Sleeping in open holes, you wake up with your face covered in powder. The wind moans continually. By sunrise it looks like we are in a snowstorm. Marines gather underneath the cammie netting draped over their vehicles, repacking gear, cleaning weapons, waiting. Their commanders tell the men the war will probably start on the twenty-second or twenty-third.

Colbert sits upright in his Ranger grave, filling his rifle magazines with bullets, peering out at the opaqueness of the desert—the dusty winds blowing past the cammie nets—and says, "It almost feels like we're at the bottom of the ocean."

Colbert's specialty within the platoon is deep-sea diving. He's trained to lead his team through miles of ocean and penetrate coastal defenses. Despite the years he's spent on training missions in the water, he confesses to me that the deep sea terrifies him. "The scariest thing for me is to open my eyes under the ocean, especially at night," he says. "I'm scared every time I do it." He adds, "That's probably why I love diving."

Colbert tells me his feelings about the upcoming venture are similar. As a professional warrior, politics and ideology don't really enter into his thoughts about why he is here in the desert, waiting to invade a country. "I'm not so idealistic that I subscribe to good versus evil. We haven't had a war like that since World War II. Why are we here now? I guess it's to remove this guy from power. I'm not opposed to it, and I wasn't going to miss it." For him, it's a grand personal challenge. "We're going into the great unknown," he says. "Scary, isn't it?" he adds, smiling brightly. "I can't wait."

AN HOUR BEFORE DAWN on March 20, the Marines in the staging area are awakened by the thundering of distant artillery. It confuses everyone because the night before, commanders in First Recon told the men the invasion wouldn't start for a couple more days. Colbert keeps a small shortwave radio in his Humvee, and I join him in the gray morning light while he tunes in the BBC. They announce that the Americans have bombed Baghdad—in what we later learn was a failed attempt to hit Saddam. The explosions we hear in the desert are American strikes on Iraqi positions just over the border. Colbert clicks off the radio. He looks up with a grave expression. It's probably how he looks when he opens his eyes under the ocean for the first time on a dive. "Well," he says. "We kicked the hornet's nest. Now we better kill all the fucking hornets."

At about ten in the morning, Fick gathers the platoon for a briefing. This is held, as all future ones will be, around the hood of his Humvee. It's one of those weird desert days, chilly in the shade, blazing hot in the sun. All Marines now wear full battle gear—bulky chemical-protection suits, Kevlar helmets and flak vests, which have ceramic plates in the front and back to stop AK-rifle rounds, and utility vests covered in hooks and straps for carrying rifle cartridges, grenades and radios. All of this weighs about sixty pounds and gives the Marines a puffed-out appearance, like partially inflated Michelin Men. They jostle together, leaning on each other's shoulders, trying to get as close as possible to Fick.

"This is our forty-eighth day in the field," Fick says. "And last night President Bush started the war. We can expect to roll out of here tonight."

He allows a tense smile. He, like everyone else, seems to be wrestling with excitement and a profound awareness of the seriousness of this situation. "You're being called on to kill," he says. "You're going to be shot at. The Iraqis will try to fuck you up. Don't be a trusting American. Leave that at the border. Think like a devious motherfucker. Be suspicious. Be aggressive."

The Marines have drilled for weeks, studying the Rules of Engagement (ROE). The ROE lay out all the conditions regarding when a Marine may or may not fire on Iraqis. The problem is, some Iraqi soldiers will presumably change out of their uniforms and fight in civilian clothes. Others will remain in uniform but surrender. There might be some in uniform surrendering, and others in uniform fighting. On top of this, large segments of the civilian populace are expected to be armed with AKs, so these armed but not hostile civilians will be mixed up with enemy fighters dressed in civilian clothes. Therefore, the usual battlefield rules—shoot guys wearing enemy uniforms; shoot guys with weapons—don't apply. What the ROE boil down to is that if the Marines come across a bunch of armed Iraqis, they generally can't shoot them unless the Iraqis shoot at them first.

Fick has two big concerns about the ROE, which he brought up to me earlier in private. "If we kill civilians, we're going to turn the populace against us and lose the war. But I don't want to lose Marines because the ROE have taken away their aggressiveness."

Fick repeats a mantra, echoed by every commander throughout the Corps. "You will be held accountable for the facts not as they are in hindsight but as they appeared to you at the time. If, in your mind, you fire to protect yourself, you are doing the right thing. It doesn't matter if later on we find out you wiped out a family of unarmed civilians. All we are accountable for are the facts as they appear to us at the time."

Following Fick's talk, Gunny Wynn addresses the men. Gunny Wynn serves as Fick's loyal executive. He is thirty-five, making him the oldest man in the platoon. He's also among the more experienced men in the platoon. In Somalia he headed a sniper team and scored numerous confirmed kills, a fact that alone gives him instant macho credibility with his Marines. He has a lean coyote's physique and speaks with a rangy Texas accent.

Gunny Wynn describes himself as a "staunch conservative" who's never smoked marijuana. With his chiseled face and Texas accent, he fits the image, yet he likes to point out, "I'm not one of those guys driving around waving Texas flags. It's just the place I'm from." He almost never barks at the men the way platoon sergeants do in movies. His conservatism boils down to a rigid adherence to his own personal code. "The most important part of my job," he tells me, "is to care about my men." His leadership philosophy is based on "building confidence in my men by respecting them." He and Fick function not so much like autocrats but like parents. At times, Gunny Wynn almost seems like a worried den mother, whose role is to soften the more aggressive messages Fick gives the men.

His guidance for handling the ROE is almost the polar opposite of Fick's. "I spent five months in Somalia, and we got a lot of good kills out there," he says. He gazes at the men, not blinking, letting his credibility as a sniper-killer sink in. "But we let a lot more bad guys get away than we killed, and that's okay. Don't fucking waste a mother or some kid. Don't fire into a crowd. Those people north of here have been oppressed for years. They're just like us. Don't hurt them, even if you can justify it later under our ROE."

Gunny Wynn's gentle talk is interrupted by the sound of Marines screaming across the desert, "Gas! Gas! Gas!"

Everyone freezes for an instant. In the distance we see Marines in gas masks flagging us. They stand with their arms extended out, bending their elbows and tapping their shoulders—universal sign language for a gas attack. In their bug-eyed, black masks, they resemble insects.

FOUR

○

WITH EXPLOSIONS BOOMING in the distance and now frenzied shouts of a gas attack, it's the first time I feel like I'm in a war. While the nonexistence of Saddam's weapons of mass destruction has almost become a bad joke in the wake of the invasion, on the morning of March 20, just south of the Iraqi border, with the bombing having begun, threat of a chemical attack is foremost on everyone's mind. It's one of the biggest fears among Marines.

The chemical-protection suits everyone wears are called MOPPs (which stands for Mission Oriented Protective Posture, but in military parlance, MOPP has become the name of the suit itself). On the outside they look like ordinary fatigues, though extra-bulky ones. Due to a supply fuckup, Marines have been issued MOPPs in dark forest-green camouflage, which makes them extra-conspicuous targets in the desert. MOPPs come in two pieces: pants, held up by suspenders, and a hooded jacket. They are fabric on the outside. On the inside they are lined with a plastic mesh that feels like the surface of a scouring sponge and is embedded with carbon powder, a barrier to most chemical agents. They are hot, stiff and scratchy, and have the bulk of wearing a ski suit after you have fallen into a lake.

They are always soaking wet on the inside, from sweat. Not only is the suit itself hot, but on top of it everyone wears the added sixty pounds of flak vests, ceramic plates and utility harnesses. One of the dumbest features of the MOPPs issued to Marines is that they don't have flies, so to go to the bathroom, a Marine has to remove his utility harness, his flak vest and his MOPP jacket in order to pull down his suspenders and lower his pants. Obviously, in a chemical environment they would have to poop or piss in their pants. Marines tried to get Depends diapers to wear underneath the MOPPs, but most were unable to.

To try to cool things down, a lot of Marines are "free-balling" in their MOPPs, going buck naked in them, but the scouring-pad liners make this an extremely un-comfortable option.

MOPP boots are the coup de grâce to making the whole ensemble a torturous experience. These are rubber galoshes worn on top of Marine combat boots. The rubber boots must be worn with the rest of the MOPP at all times, even when Marines sleep at night. They are so clammy and sweaty and wobbly that at every step you take it feels like your boots are stuffed full of dead fish.

In a gas attack, there's a specific order in which Marines are trained to seal up their MOPPs. The very first thing you're supposed to do is shut your eyes and stop breath-ing. Then, with your eyes closed, within the next nine seconds, you're supposed to dig your mask out of the carrying bag strapped to your leg and put it on your head, making sure you have a good seal around your face. Then you can open your eyes and start breathing.

The bag the mask comes in is loaded with all kinds of other vital junk, too. Squeezed up next to the mask are

Cipro packets (for battling Anthrax), charcoal pads (for neutralizing those nasty skin-blistering agents) and seven autoinjector syringes, each about half the size of a turkey baster. Three of these contain nerve antidotes, three more contain antidotes to the antidotes (since they are themselves toxic) and the seventh contains Valium. Marines are trained to use the antidotes on themselves. The Valium is there to be used on a buddy, in case he's already too far gone from a nerve-agent attack—it will prevent him from twitching and flopping around as badly while he dies. It won't save him, but it will probably improve the morale of everyone else nearby.

The problem with gas-mask kits is that when you reach in and grab the mask—in a panic, not breathing and with your eyes squeezed shut—all the autoinjectors tend to fly out. In my spare time over the past two weeks I've been practicing putting my mask on and have gotten reasonably good at it.

Now, in this alert, I throw it on in under nine seconds. The first breath is scary. When I open my eyes, I imagine that I might see spastic Marines suffering from nerve-agent exposure, that my hands and ears and other parts of my body still exposed will start burning and my skin will start popping off. But it's all good. I see the other Marines by Fick's vehicle, with their masks on, now calmly sealing up their MOPPs, closing everything up with snaps, Velcro and drawstrings. Then everyone puts on giant rubber kitchen gloves.

I manage to get it all put together about as quickly as the Marines nearby. We stand around looking at each other through the warping, fish-eye lenses of our gas masks. I can't conceal my feeling of triumph. Not only am I glad that I don't seem to be showing any symptoms of exposure to gas, but I'm also not a little proud that I've gotten fully MOPPed up without panicking. Unlike these Marines, I haven't spent the last few years of my life in wars or training exercises with bombs going off, jumping out of airplanes and helicopters. In my civilian world at home in Los Angeles, half the people I know are on anti-depressants or anti–panic attack drugs because they can't handle the stress of a mean boss or a crowd at the 7-Eleven when buying a Slurpee. That's my world, and it wouldn't have surprised me if, thrust into this one, in the first moments of what we all believe to be a real gas attack, I'd just flipped out and started autoinjecting myself with Valium.

No doubt, some of the Marines expected this of me as well. Ever since the platoon showed its hospitality by putting me in the walkway of their tent the first night I arrived, some have let it be known that they regard reporters as "pussy faggot lefties," wimps who can't hold up to the rigors of combat. But I've passed this test with flying colors.

Only when we're trudging back to Colbert's vehicle, everyone in full MOPP, do I realize I made a critical error while donning my mask.

One of the bad habits I picked up covering the military is "dipping"—chewing tobacco. Smokeless tobacco is the universal drug of American fighting men (and women, too, in integrated units). You don't actually chew dip. Instead, you pinch a wad about half the size of a golf ball and shove it under your front lower lip. In the process of destroying your gums and teeth, it also wallops you with a nicotine buzz that makes filterless Camels seem like candy cigarettes.

Dip's only side effect is that it causes you to salivate like a rabid dog. You constantly expectorate thick streams of brown goo. And this is my problem now. Right before the gas alert I had put a fat dip in my lip. It always makes you a little bit nauseated. Now I have this reservoir of spittle building in my mouth. There's a drain tube in my mask, but I fear the slimy mass of spit and tobacco will clog it.

I drop into the sand by Colbert's vehicle. Other Marines are sitting around nearby. I lie back and swallow the plug of tobacco, hoping nobody notices in case I become really sick or start acting strangely.

According to military chemical-weapons experts, these are the symptoms of exposure to toxic agents:

1. Unexplained runny nose
2. Sudden headache
3. Sudden drooling
4. Difficulty seeing; dimness of vision
5. Tightness of throat
6. Localized sweating
7. Nausea

I immediately cycle through all of these symptoms as the plug slides down my throat. I fight the urge to throw up, ever mindful of warnings we have received about the dangers of "chunky vomit." As the waves of nausea subside, I become aware of a new sensation: wind blowing inside my pant legs. When the Marines issued my MOPP, I had complained to the sergeant who gave it to me that it looked kind of small. She had dismissed this as another example of a prima-donna reporter's whining, and had told me, "The suit fits good." But fully tied up, there's about an inch gap between my pant legs and my boot tops, and this is not good.

The culprit is my suit's g-string—a strap that you take from behind the jacket, pull between your legs and snap in the front. It's designed to keep the jacket snugly sealed over the pants. Mine is so tight that it has jammed my pants up my crack and is letting air in over my boots.

I lie back and try unsnapping the g-string, but it's stuck. The harder I pull—my fingers extra clumsy in my rubber clown gloves—the tighter it gets. Marines seem not to notice as I sit back in the sand, struggling with the g-string. My lenses start to fog from my heavy breathing. Then I glimpse a gas-masked figure leering over me. It's Corporal Gabriel Garza, a heavy-weapons gunner on Colbert's team.

In the platoon, Garza, twenty-two, is something of a cipher. He wears Coke bottle–lens glasses and a blue bandanna around his neck, which his grandmother, who raised him, gave him for good luck. She is an aloe picker in south Texas, and Garza always grins when he mentions her. "She used to beat me with a two-by-four when I was bad," he says. "That's 'cause she cares about me." Garza has a round head and is not particularly tall or imposing, yet he is one of the strongest Marines in the platoon. According to his buddies, he can bench-press ten repetitions of 300-pound free weights. He works out constantly. Every night at Mathilda he would follow his dinner with a glass of salt water and lemon wedges, or oranges rolled in salt. When I asked him what the point of his unusual diet was, he said, "It makes you tougher." He seldom talks, but frequently, while sitting alone, will suddenly begin shaking with quiet laughter, the only sound a whistling from his nose. Everyone in the platoon likes him. They call him the "Zen Master." But when they compliment him on his physical power, he just shrugs and says, "It's nothing. I've got retard strength."

Now he's standing over me, turning his head to his side in a quizzical gesture. Another feature of gas masks is that you can't really talk through them; nor can you hear too well through the MOPP hood. We try to carry on a conversation. It sounds like the parents in a Charlie Brown cartoon: *wa wa wa.* I gesture to the g-string now twisting my testicles, and Garza immediately unsheathes a pair of Leatherman pliers he carries on his vest and looms over me. I lie back, my legs spread as if I'm about to undergo a gynecological exam, and Garza delicately nestles the plier tips against my balls and clasps the g-string. When he rips it off, he tears a dime-size hole in the front of my MOPP, rendering the whole thing useless.

A few minutes later, pulling my mask off after they sound the all-clear, I'm greeted with a rush of cold air and laughter.

"I just performed testicle surgery on the reporter," Garza brags.

The funny thing is, all the Marines who've been stand-offish the past week are suddenly pounding me on the back, bruising my ribs with affectionate punches. "You've got brown shit all over your chin," one of them says, brushing tobacco juice off my face with his sleeve. I seem to have gained acceptance by making a total jackass of myself.

The comedy session near Colbert's Humvee is cut short when Marines down the line shout, "Scud! Scud! Scud!"

Everyone MOPPs up again. This time, expecting missiles, we dive into a large pit—deeper than the Ranger graves we've dug—which Colbert's team excavated next to his vehicle. The way to avoid flying shrapnel from a missile detonating nearby is to get as close to the ground as possible, though you have to turn sideways because the mask ventilator protrudes several inches from the front of your face. Waiting for what presumably will be some sort of explosion, your breathing becomes rapid. Underneath the MOPP hood and mask, every internal sound is magnified. With each breath, you hear the mask ventilator apparatus clicking and wheezing like a hospital life-support system. Due to the odd acoustics of the MOPP suit, little grains of sand rolling down the side of your hood sound like bombs. What the MOPP basically does is encase you in your own private panic attack.

I'm directly across from Person. Our faces are inches apart. His chest rises up and down quickly. He's breathing rapidly, too, which makes me feel better. Maybe I'm not the only one panicking.

Eventually you get bored of lying in the hole, and you want to look over the edges and see what's happening. I edge up a little, looking for birds. If they're flying, it means there's no gas.

There's a series of explosions in the distance. Different from the blasts earlier. These are drawn-out sounds— *gagoon, gagoon*—followed by a series of sharp bangs. Then it's silent.

After the all-clear ten minutes later, Gunny Wynn walks over, grim yet excited. "That was a no-shit Scud attack," he tells the men.

"I guess this really is war," Colbert says.

"What's a Scud?" Garza asks.

Gunny Wynn smiles. "It's a missile, Garza, a pretty big one. They can load them with chemicals if they want."

Garza ponders this for a moment, then smiles. "That's awesome. I just lived through a Scud attack."

Later, Fick finds out the sounds we heard were not Scuds. While some Scuds were launched toward Kuwait City, out here in the desert, the Iraqis are firing Silkworm antiship missiles, one of which, according to Fick, landed 200 meters from First Marine Expeditionary Force head-quarters south of us.

There are several more gas and missile alerts through-out the afternoon. Between them the Marines congregate under the shade of their Humvee cammie nets, recleaning all their weapons, linking individual machine-gun rounds into belts and talking. Sitting in little clumps, passing the weapons and gear back and forth while doing the intricate finger work, it almost looks like a ladies' sewing circle. No one talks much about the invasion they are supposed to launch in a few hours. If anything, their focus on routine humor and bullshitting is almost more determined than ever in the face of the impending assault.

The most flamboyant figure in Second Platoon is Reyes, the Marine on Team Two who on my first night in their tent talked about the romantic idealism of being in the Corps. This afternoon he sits beneath his team's cammie netting, cleaning his rifle, dressed in an out-rageous camouflage overcoat his fellow Marines call his "Chicken Suit." Tufts of multicolored fabric hang off the arms and shoulders like feathers. He wears a similarly peacockish cover on his helmet, the ensemble comple-mented with heavy-duty orange goggles that somehow manage to look stylish. They call them his "J.Lo glasses."

Reyes has the insanely muscular body of a fantasy Hollywood action hero. Before joining the Marines, he lived in a dojo, competed nationally in kung fu and tai chi tournaments, and fought in exhibitions with the Chinese national team. He is the battalion's best martial artist, one of its strongest men, and seemingly one of the gayest. Though he is not gay in the sense of sexual orientation—Reyes, after all, is married—he is at least a highly evolved tough guy in touch with a well-developed feminine side. With his imposing build, dark, Mexican-American features and yet skin so pale it's almost porcelain, he is a striking figure. His fellow Marines call him "Fruity Rudy," because he is so beautiful.

"It doesn't mean you're gay if you think Rudy's hot. He's just so beautiful," Person explains. "We all think he's hot."

While the other Marines spent their free time at Mathilda poring over porn and gun magazines, Reyes read self-affirming articles in Oprah's magazine, waxed his legs and chest and conducted afternoon yoga classes. His father was a Marine, but when he was three the family split apart due to drug problems. According to Reyes, a close relative of his who was a drug-addicted cop used to bust prostitutes and bring them home to baby-sit him and his brother. Reyes wound up in boys' homes in Kansas City. "Those boys' homes were gladiator academies," Reyes says. "Darwin was living and breathing strong. I was twelve years old and seventy pounds. I had older men making sexual advances on me. I was preyed upon by bigger, stronger people. I was always the new guy in a shitty neighborhood in a shitty school. I was inspired by Spider-Man, Speed Racer and Bruce Lee. I decided to become a warrior."

Reyes adds, "I have very low self-esteem. I need to empower myself daily through physical training and spirituality. I identify with redemption stories like The Color Purple. I love the journey of a woman from weak and less-than to someone who is fully realized."

This day, on the eve of invading Iraq, Reyes is concerned about his body. "I am going to hell out here," he says, handing a belt of machine-gun rounds to Manimal, his teammate. "I eat terribly in the field."

"We've had plenty of chow," Manimal says.

"Back home I only eat sushi and vegetables," Reyes counters. "The food we eat here is garbage, that awful

American diet. Someday, I think Sheree and I will live in San Francisco," he says, referring to his wife of five years.

"What's so great about San Francisco?" Manimal asks.

"There's no fat people there," Reyes answers. "And Chinese martial arts are very much a part of the culture there."

"Why would you give a fuck if there are fat people where you live?" Manimal laughs. "People are people."

"I want to live in a place where people care about themselves."

"Jesus Christ, Rudy," Colbert says, slipping in under the cammie net. "When are you going to realize you're fucking gay? When we're on libo," he says, referring to liberty port calls Marines make around the world, "you wear Banana Republic Daisy Duke shorts, and now you're rolling into battle with your goddamn chicken suit and J.Lo glasses. You dress like a pimp queen."

"Brother, I wear clothes that are body-conscious, but I don't dress like no goddamn pimp queen. I've got too much respect for myself." Reyes howls with laughter. He and Colbert tap knuckles after a successful exchange of put-downs.

ABOUT TWO HOURS before sunset, First Recon's commander, Lt. Col. Ferrando, gathers his men for a final briefing. In the chain of command, Ferrando is at the top of the battalion. As officers go, platoon commanders like Fick are at the bottom. Each platoon commander answers to his respective company commander, and each of these—the commanders for Alpha, Bravo and Charlie—answer to Ferrando. For all practical purposes, within the battalion, Ferrando is God. In war, especially, his authority is absolute.

Every Marine is indoctrinated with a simple saying that clearly states the Corps' priority in achieving its aims in war: "Mission accomplishment, then troop welfare." One thing about the Marine Corps is it doesn't bullshit the troops about their place in the scheme of things. The responsibility of deciding when their lives might become expendable for the sake of a mission falls on Ferrando.

Ferrando's command post out in the field is a small black tent set up by a movable antenna farm of seven-meter towers held up with guy lines and stakes. It looks like the deck rigging of a sailing ship washed up on the desert. About a hundred of his officers and senior enlisted men and team leaders gather by his command post. Ferrando is forty-two, thin, with a narrow head and eyes slightly close together. But the thing you notice about him is his voice—a dry, whispered rasp. Seven years ago his vocal cords were removed after a bout with throat cancer. Because of his distinctive voice, his call sign is "Godfather."

Even standing fifteen meters back from him in the open desert with wind whipping through your ears, Ferrando's croaking whisper carries. It's kind of creepy. It sounds like someone with his lips pressed to your ear speaking directly into it, clear as Satan's whisper to Eve.

"Good news," Ferrando rasps to the men. He arches his eyebrows, not really smiling but still making a sort of happy face. "The BBC reported we struck Baghdad. The outcome of this war has already been determined. Iraq will go down." He gazes out at the rows of Marines standing before him, bulked up with their MOPP suits, toting their weapons. "If you bump into an Iraqi who wants to fight, you will kick his fucking ass."

Marines generally love this kind of tough talk from their commanders. The men in the crowd grin and nod enthusiastically. But then Ferrando loses some of them. He turns from the excitement of impending combat to the topic that often seems to obsess him more than anything: the Marines' personal grooming. "I don't know when we are going to get to the Euphrates," he says, "but we will, and when we cross the Euphrates all mustaches will come off. That is the rule. Make sure your men shave their mustaches." It's an adage among officers that "a bitching Marine is a happy Marine." By this standard, no officer makes the Marines in First Recon happier than Ferrando. Since assuming command of the battalion about eighteen months earlier, Ferrando has shown a relentless obsession with what he calls the "Grooming Standard"—his insistence that even in the field his troops maintain regulation haircuts, proper shaves and meticulously neat uniforms.

In traditional deployments, such as Colbert's tour in the Afghan War, Recon teams go into the field without their commanders. Ferrando and others at the top stay behind at Camp Pendleton. Usually the highest-ranking authority in the field during a Recon mission is the team leader.

Some of the tension in the battalion that Fick alluded to when I first met him at Camp Mathilda stems from the fact that due to Maj. Gen. Mattis's unorthodox plan to employ First Recon in Iraq as a unified, mobile fighting force, Ferrando and other senior commanders are now for the first time accompanying Recon Marines into the field. This stress is compounded by Ferrando's singular obsession with maintaining the Grooming Standard.

Experienced team leaders in Bravo Company—like Colbert and Kocher—think they did a fine job in Afghanistan without always keeping their shirts tucked in and wearing color-coordinated running uniforms as

Ferrando made them do at Mathilda. Kocher complains, "Out here we have a pile of captains, gunnery sergeants and staff sergeants with us that can't do jack shit. They don't even know how to refuel vehicles, get us batteries. All they do is make us get haircuts and shaves."

For his part, Ferrando seems bent on stamping out the uniquely individualistic nature of Recon Marines. "These men who don't like the Grooming Standard probably don't belong in the Recon community," he told me earlier. "They are the ones who gravitated here because of the myth that as Recon Marines they would become cowboys, exempt from standards everyone else in the Corps maintains."

One of his senior enlisted men, tasked with enforcing the Grooming Standard, is more blunt. "These Marines are incorrectable [sic]," he tells me. "They are cocky. They are not as good as they think they are."

The hostility is mutual. To some Marines their battalion commander's obsession with appearances makes him seem like a careerist out of touch with the men he leads. "The problem is, higher-ups like Ferrando aren't warriors, they're Marine Corps politicians," a Marine in Second Platoon gripes. "They're terrified some general's going to walk over here and see someone running around with his shirt untucked."

Prior to commanding First Recon, Ferrando was the parade commander at the Marine Corps' headquarters in Washington, D.C., a position he himself admits is "the most ceremonial billet in the Corps." He has never been deployed in combat before, and while his job turns on his ability to inspire and lead several hundred young men, he admits, "My temper and personality are not suited for today's youth."

Away from his men, Ferrando displays a dry humor.

When I ask him about his cancer—if he ever smoked, chewed tobacco or had other bad habits—he tells me he was a runner and a fitness nut, then adds, smiling, "I guess I'm just lucky." At Camp Mathilda, Ferrando spent much of his time agonizing over the ROE, perfecting ways to strike a balance between protecting his Marines and not harming civilians. He also sincerely believes the Grooming Standard will give his men better odds of surviving in combat. "Discipline in all its forms enhances the survivability of troops," he tells me.

Despite his virtues, he has a tough time getting these across to his Marines. Fick says, "I respect Lieutenant Colonel Ferrando, but for some reason he's been unable to inspire trust in the men."

Following his prewar invasion briefing this afternoon, Colbert expresses disappointment in his commander. Walking back from the briefing, even Colbert, who seldom complains, says, "Why would he bring up mustaches tonight of all nights?" He shakes his head, laughing. The order for Marines to shave their mustaches at the Euphrates originated with Mattis, not Ferrando. But what bugs Colbert is Ferrando's timing. "We're getting ready to invade a country, and this is what our commander talks to us about? Mustaches?"

JUST BEFORE THE SUN DROPS, Colbert and his team pull down the cammie nets from their vehicle and prepare to move out. The wind has died down, and it looks like it's going to be a clear night for the invasion. Nearby, the battalion chaplain, Navy Lieutenant Commander Christopher Bodley, walks among the platoons, offering final prayers. Bodley is a tall, dark-skinned African American with a gentle manner and a high, melodious voice. Though several Marines in Colbert's Second Platoon profess religious beliefs, they treat the chaplain with the polite disinterest you'd show a door-to-door vacuum-cleaner salesman.

"Uh, oh. Here he comes," Colbert says, glimpsing the chaplain traipsing across the sand with a smile, a Bible and a Marine bodyguard toting an assault rifle. "Another nuisance to waste my time."

Manimal walks over, shooting the chaplain suspicious glances. "Back at Mathilda I went to a service to get communion, but the priest gave a fucking moto speech on why we are fighting this war. It was fucking bullshit."

Fifty meters from Colbert's vehicle, the chaplain gathers a small crowd of faithful in the sand. A huge, lumbering, bald Marine gunnery sergeant removes his helmet, kneels and reads Psalm 91. Then the chaplain delivers a sermon. Marines call themselves "Devil Dogs"—according to lore, German soldiers in World War I nicknamed them this, "Tuffen Hunds," in grudging praise of their tenacity—and the chaplain incorporates this into his sermons. "They nickname you Devil Dogs," he tells his flock. "But Jesus was the original Devil Dog. He faced evil, and he beat it. Jesus is the Devil Dog you will want on your side going into battle."

By Colbert's Humvee, a twenty-year-old redheaded corporal jumps up as more helicopters fly north. "Get some!" he screams. Then he adds, "They kill hundreds of people, those pilots. I would have loved to have flown the plane that dropped the bomb on Japan. A couple dudes killed hundreds of thousands. That fucking rules! Yeah!"

FIVE

○

AT SEVEN O'CLOCK on the night of March 20, the Marines in First Recon are ordered into their vehicles, to load their rifles and drop belts of ammo into the feed trays of their machine guns and to prepare to move out. At this time, more than 25,000 Marines, 20,000 British troops and 30,000 U.S. Army soldiers in the northern Kuwait desert are all doing the same. The 242-kilometer-long Iraqi border with Kuwait is fortified with fences, minefields and seven-meter-high earthen berms. On the other side there are some 50,000 Iraqi troops equipped with more than 1,000 tanks and other types of armor.

The booming we've heard since the morning has been the American bombardment of Iraqi positions near the border. According to officers I've spoken to, Marine intelligence personnel hacked into the computer of the Iraqi general in command of forces there, and Maj. Gen. Mattis has been personally e-mailing him, urging him to surrender. But the Iraqis have not. They have spent the day firing artillery intermittently and ineffectively toward American units in the desert. Earlier in the morning, Iraqi soldiers were observed out in the open by the border, laying more mines.

In a couple of hours, Marine and Army engineers in armored units are going to race up to the border, supported by heavy American artillery, rocket and aerial bombardment, and blow breaches through the berms. The U.S. Army's Third Infantry Division will push north to a broad superhighway that goes for nearly 600 kilometers all the way to Baghdad, then travel on it largely un-opposed until coming to within about 150 kilometers of the capital.

The Marines and British forces will be in a race the moment they blast through the berms. Their objectives are to reach and secure the oil facilities and ports around Rumaylah, Basra and Um Qasr some seventy kilometers to the east of the border crossing. The American fear is that the Iraqis will begin blowing up these oil and port facilities, causing an environmental disaster. Coalition forces hope to secure them within the first forty-eight hours of the invasion.

First Recon will enter the breach at the border follow-ing mechanized Marine elements. But while they cut to the east toward Basra, First Recon will race ninety kilo-meters north, on its own, to secure a bridge over the Euphrates. The biggest concern for First Recon after crossing the border is that the battalion will be operating solo. Unlike the Army and other Marine units that include thousands of troops, armored vehicles and heavy artillery guns all moving together, First Recon's 374 Marines in Humvees and trucks will move alone on a trek through open desert believed to contain tens of thousands of Iraqi soldiers. While most enemy forces are expected to scatter, even a few rogue Iraqi tanks with crews willing to fight could wreak havoc on First Recon.

The point of Mattis's plan to send First Recon ahead of his main battle forces is that this battalion will be among the fastest on the battlefield. As beat-up as First Recon's Humvees are, they are quicker than tanks and, due to their small numbers, they can outmaneuver large concentrations of enemy forces. According to the doctrine of maneuver warfare, their relative speed, not their meager firepower, is their primary weapon. True to his radio call sign, "Chaos," Mattis will use First Recon as his main agent for causing disorder on the battlefield by sending the Recon Marines into places where no one is expecting them. At this time in the invasion, none of the enlisted men in First Recon fully understand that this is the plan. They think they are embarking on a fairly conventional recon mission to seize a remote bridge on the Euphrates. Many believe they will have no role in the invasion following this mission.

AT ABOUT EIGHT-THIRTY on the night of the twentieth, engineers in Marine Regimental Combat Team Five (one of the three regimental forces, each composed of about 6,000 troops, that belong to the First Division) begin blasting breach holes through the berms at the Iraqi border. An hour later, at First Recon's staging area twenty kilometers south, the Marines are told to start their engines.

The four Marines in Colbert's vehicle have already been sitting inside in total darkness, waiting for a few hours, when they receive the order.

"So we're going to go invade a country," Person says cheerily as he hits the ignition.

"I bet gas prices will be lower," says Trombley, who sits to my left in the backseat.

Adding to the natural stimulation everyone feels at starting an invasion, quite a few Marines have begun eating Nescafé instant coffee crystals straight from foil packets and popping ephedra and other over-the-counter go pills for what is expected to be an all-night mission. Everyone's already tired. They've been up since four or five in the morning, when the explosions started in the desert, and they spent the day diving in and out of holes during all the gas-attack and Scud alerts.

Unlike the Humvees used by elite Army units, which have armor and air-conditioning, most of First Recon's Humvees don't even have doors or roofs. Some teams modified them by welding in extra racks for ammo and removing windshields so they can fire their rifles through them. The Humvees are so stuffed full of weapons and supplies, the men hang their rucksacks filled with personal gear on the sides of the vehicles. One Marine observes that the Humvees look like the truck driven by the Clampetts in *The Beverly Hillbillies.* Given the age and battered condition of the vehicles when they arrived, it's a little like the Marines who will be leading the invasion in them are entering a Formula One race in demolition derby cars.

Colbert's place in the Humvee is the front passenger seat directly in front of me. His personal weapon is an M-4 rifle, the shortened version of the M-16. His M-4 also has an auxiliary tube below the barrel, called a 203, which is a single-shot grenade launcher. He keeps this between his knees. "Let's go, Person," he says. "We're on the move."

The Humvee lurches forward, banging and creaking. Garza, who earlier in the day helped me wrestle free from my MOPP suit, stands on a raised metal platform in the center of the vehicle between the seats. His boots, legs and ass are constantly in everyone's face as he swivels around in the turret, manning the MK-19 automatic grenade launcher on the roof.

Each Humvee is equipped with either a .50-caliber machine gun or an MK-19 (usually referred to as a "Mark-19"). The .50-cal, as the machine gun is called, is a heavy weapon, with a barrel about a meter long, that fires steel-penetrating rounds that will rip apart cars or trucks a kilometer away but won't do much against a tank. The Mark-19, which resembles one of those machines that fire tennis balls on a practice court, launches grenades at a rate of about one per second. These grenade rounds also have an effective range of about a kilometer. The heavy weapons can devastate infantry on the ground, destroy bunkers and wreck mud-brick or cement structures in Iraqi towns, but they're not really meant to stop tanks or take on large mechanized forces.

Despite the imposing size Humvees appear to have when you see civilian versions on the streets, there's barely any room inside Colbert's. Everyone is bulked up with their helmets, vests, MOPP suits and rubber boots. The vehicle is crammed with boxes of military food rations, several five-gallon cans of water, extra diesel fuel, more than 300 grenades, a few thousand rounds of rifle and machine-gun ammunition, special smoke and thermite incendiary grenades, several pounds of C-4 plastic explosive, claymore mines, a bale of concertina wire, cammie nets, a spare tire, extra parts, fluids and filters for the engine, a tool set, bolt cutters, map books, bags of ropes, a fire extinguisher, five rucksacks of personal gear, chemlites, several hundred extra batteries for the portable radios, shovels, a pickax, a sledgehammer and, suspended by parachute cord from the rear interior roof, an AT-4 antitank missile, which continually bangs against the back of my helmet.

It is pitch black inside and out. For obvious reasons, nobody uses headlights during an invasion. All mirrors have been removed. You can barely see over the dashboard, since the center console is stacked with three radios, each about the size of an old VCR.

Both Person and Colbert have radio transceivers clipped to their helmets to communicate with vehicles in the platoon, as well as with the battalion and with pilots when there is air cover. It's arguable that comms—radio communications—are as important to a team's survival as its weapons. But comms seldom work as they should.

Dust, magnetism and sun spots all interfere with the radios constantly. In addition, the radios in the various battalion networks rely on encryption codes that constantly need to be loaded and synchronized. The system is prone to bad connections, dead batteries, software crashes and, as Person explains, "retards in the battalion who keep changing the frequencies without telling us." Even in the best of times, the radios blink out. Colbert and Person often end up shouting the same commands and queries into their microphones until the signals go through.

Luckily, Person is something of a genius when it comes to radios. The reason he's on Colbert's team is that despite his constant mockery of everything, Colbert considers him one of the most competent Marines in the platoon. He has voluminous knowledge of encryption protocols and a sixth sense for how to hot-wire bum radios, often by unplugging all the cables and licking the sockets, all while driving in the darkness. Teams in other platoons whose radio operators aren't as skilled sometimes resort to leaning out their doors and shouting.

Moving in a pitch-black vehicle, bobbing over a rutted desert, unable to see much outside the window except the occasional blob shape of another vehicle, is disorienting, like sitting backward on a train or being in an elevator that drops unexpectedly. You have the nagging sense that you're about to run into something.

Person sees through the darkness with a set of night-vision goggles (NVGs) clipped over the front of his helmet. NVGs, which weigh a couple of pounds, consist of two lenses that cover each eye, then bend into a barrel that protrudes about five inches. The whole thing looks like a crazy monocular scope you look through during an exam at the eye doctor. They provide a foggy, greenish display of the road ahead, with no depth perception—it's hard to tell if a vehicle is ten feet or fifty feet in front of you, or if a black shape in the road is a barrel or a hole. If a light flashes, from a fire by the road, a bomb exploding or oncoming headlights, the wearer of NVGs is temporarily blinded.

Since there are no mirrors or rear window on the Humvee, in order to back up or make a sharp turn, Person shouts up to Garza, who stands in the turret wearing his own set of NVGs, to ask him what's there. Because the Humvee's diesel is loud, the wind is always blowing, the radios are crackling in and out and there are more and more explosions as we near the border, just keeping the Humvee in the convoy requires continual shouting from everyone inside.

Person, like many other Marines in First Recon, has practiced driving a Humvee at night with NVGs only a few times. Nor does he have a military operating license for a Humvee. There are right now some 75,000 soldiers and Marines in thousands of vehicles converging on a handful of breaches in the berms at the border. There is as much traffic rolling as there is on sections of the San Diego Freeway at rush hour, only it's dark and everyone's in tanks and heavily armed Humvees. It's a wonder the whole invasion doesn't end in a gigantic pileup by

the border. Most of the drivers are amped-up nineteen-
and twenty-year-olds, wrestling with the same problems
Person has—the limitations of NVGs, screwy comms and
orders that change constantly.

All of this is happening beneath a sky that has turned
pink, red and orange from the ferocious bombardment
being unleashed on Iraqi border positions ten to twenty
kilometers in front of us. Rockets and artillery shells
fly overhead, filling the air with a cacophony of
strange sounds—whistling, rumbling; some rockets
make a sizzling sound. The horizon flashes as they
impact.

"This is the shit," Person says as he takes in the
destruction in his NVGs, which are exponentially in-
tensifying every flash. "I wish I had some shrooms."

"Yeah, it's the shiznit," Colbert says. "Now, watch the
fucking vehicle in front of you."

With the effects of all the legal stimulants he's taking
starting to show, Person begins to babble, a disembodied
voice coming from beneath his helmet and NVGs. "I'll tell
you why we're invading. Fucking NAMBLA," he says,
referring to the North American Man/Boy Love
Association. "Places like Thailand where they go to fuck
children and shit, it's drying up. We're opening up Iraq for
a whole new supply of children."

"Halt the vehicle, Person," Colbert says, passing on an
order from the radio. "We're stopping for a few minutes."

"NAMBLA's infiltrated First Recon," Person continues,
after bringing the vehicle to a stop. "There's a guy in
Third Platoon, he's going to be collecting photographs of
all the children and sending them back to NAMBLA HQ.
Back at Pendleton he volunteers at a daycare center. He
goes around collecting all the turds from the five-year-
olds and puts them into Copenhagen tins. Out here

everyone thinks he's dipping, but it's not tobacco. It's dookie from five-year-olds."

"Shut up, Person," Colbert orders.

Next to me, Trombley breaks the silence, speaking in low tones. "I wonder if she's ever killed anyone," Trombley says, stroking the barrel of the SAW machine gun, which he holds on his lap, pointed out the window. The SAW, which stands for "squad automatic weapon," is a portable machine gun capable of firing up to 1,000 rounds per minute. Ammunition comes in 200-round belts, which are several feet long. They fit into a drum beneath the barrel of the SAW, but Trombley likes to take the belts out of the drums and drape them around his neck like Rambo, which provokes sharp rebukes from Colbert whenever he catches him.

Trombley, who at nineteen is the youngest member of the team, is a thin, dark-haired and slightly pale kid from Farwell, Michigan. He speaks in a soft yet deeply resonant voice that doesn't quite fit his boyish face. One of his eyes is bright red from an infection caused by the continual dust storms. He has spent the past couple of days trying to hide it so he doesn't get pulled from the team. Technically, he is a "paper Recon Marine" because he has not yet completed the Basic Reconnaissance Course. He also hasn't quite yet gelled with the rest of the platoon. In bull sessions they subtly ignore him, talking over and around him when he's sitting among them. He accepts it silently, without backing down, studying his fellow Marines intently with his furtive, inflamed eye.

But it's not just his youth and inexperience that keep Trombley on the outside, it's also his relative immaturity—caressing his weapon and talking to it, wearing his ammo belts around his neck. Other Marines make fun of him for his B-movie antics. They're also suspicious of his tall tales. He claims, for example, that his father was a CIA operative, that most of the men in the Trombley family died mysterious, violent deaths, the details of which are vague and always shifting with each telling. He looks forward to combat as "one of those fantasy things you always hoped would really happen." In December, a month before his deployment, Trombley got married. (His bride's father, he says, couldn't attend the wedding, because he died in a "gunfire incident" a while before.) He spends his idle moments writing down lists of possible names for the sons he hopes to have when he gets home. "It's up to me to carry on the Trombley name," he says.

Despite other Marines' reservations about Trombley, Colbert feels he has the potential to be a good Marine. Colbert is always instructing him—teaching him how to use different communications equipment, how best to keep his gun clean. Trombley is an attentive pupil, almost a teacher's pet at times, and goes out of his way to quietly perform little favors for the entire team, like refilling everyone's canteens each day.

Through some unspoken arrangement, Trombley has decided that since I am the only civilian in the group, I'm even lower on the totem pole than he is. "Good chance we'll run over a mine," he says in the darkness. "Don't worry, there's ways to survive. Soon as you hear the blast, curl up like a little bitch." He nudges me with his elbow. "You can curl up like a little bitch, can't you?"

FIRST RECON SPENDS SEVERAL HOURS halting and starting, zigzagging back and forth just south of the border beneath the fiery, rocket-streaked sky. Light from burning oil facilities set ablaze by Iraqis near Rumaylah begin to create a false dawn. Higher-ups in the division keep ordering First Recon to move toward different breach points in the border.

At four in the morning, the battalion finally receives definitive orders about which breach to enter. But the men in Bravo are further delayed when their company commander takes a wrong turn in the darkness. The commander who makes this error is a man the men call "Encino Man," after the movie of the same title about a hapless caveman who thaws out and comes to life in modern-day Southern California. The men nicknamed this officer Encino Man not only because of his Neanderthal features but also because of his perpetual air of tongue-tied befuddlement. A former college football star now in his early thirties, Encino Man is reputed to have a hard time articulating the simplest of orders. Encino Man's thickly browed face often bears a pleasant smile, which makes him well enough liked by the men. But they don't altogether trust him as a commander (he serves as Fick's immediate superior), because he seems to be, in their eyes, something of a dimwit. Encino Man is one of those senior officers who never would have deployed on a traditional Recon mission. Prior to taking command of Bravo Company, he was an intelligence analyst.

Although the Corps rates him as a fit commander and he has an admirable service record, fellow officers have expressed their alarm to me over Encino Man's seeming inability to understand the basics, like reading a map. One officer says to me, "We came out of a briefing once, after we'd been looking at a map for an hour, studying one town on it, and he came up to me and asked, 'What was the name of that place? Can you show me where it is on the map?' I was like, 'What reality was this guy in during the previous briefing?' "

A few hours before the invasion, Encino Man had covered over the side windows of his command vehicle with duct tape. He believed this would mask light seeping out from a computer screen in his vehicle, making it "extratactical"—harder to spot by enemy forces. Unfortunately, the covered windows seem to have interfered with his already questionable navigation abilities.

While we sit, pulled over by a desert trail, waiting for the battalion to "unfuck" itself in the wake of Encino Man's blunder, Colbert observes, "The fucking idiot. If the enemy's going to spot you, they'll see the light coming through the windshield. You can't tape that up." He shakes his head. "This is the man leading me into battle."

"Fucking dumbass," Person agrees.

The sky begins to lighten. We're stopped in a no-man's-land a few kilometers south of the border. Convoys of armored vehicles race past. Having now been up for twenty-four hours, watching others enter Iraq ahead of them sours the mood of Colbert's team.

He and Person spot a Marine, whom they both know and despise, taking a leak outside the Humvee. "That's that fucking pussy," Person says. "He was crying when we left Camp Pendleton." He adds in a pitying baby voice, "He didn't want to go to Iraq."

Colbert looks at him. "When we were at the airport flying out here he lost his gear. He was trying to get out of coming here."

"Yeah," Person says. "He was at the airport on the phones, calling senators and stuff to try to get them to pull strings. Fucking pussy wimp."

"A scared little bitch," Colbert says. He and Person stare together at the Marine they deem cowardly, bonding in their mutual contempt. The judgment of the pack is relentless and unmerciful.

At about seven in the morning on March 21, the battalion is ordered into the breach. The early-morning light glares through the smudged windshield. The earthen berms, seven meters high, loom ahead. Beyond, black smoke from oil fires seems to fold over the horizon like a blanket. We enter the breach zone, small mountains of sand, littered with scraps of metal piled on either side. Beside me, Trombley slumps over his SAW, snoring.

"Wake up, Trombley," Colbert says. "You're missing the invasion."

SIX

○

COLBERT'S FIRST IMPRESSION of Iraq is that it looks like "fucking Tijuana." We've pulled onto a two-lane asphalt road rolling through a border town north of the breach. There's a row of shops on one side—cinder-block structures with colorful hand-painted signs and steel shutters pulled over their fronts, with a smashed-up Toyota truck pushed off on the side of the road, probably by a tank. It's ghostville.

All of the major Marine combat forces are racing east or hugging the border, leaving no other friendly combat forces in First Recon's area of operation. The battalion pushes north in a single-file line alone on unpaved trails through what has become open, almost lunar desert, periodically dotted with mud huts, small flocks of sheep and clusters of starved-looking, stick-figure cattle grazing on scrub brush. Once in a while you see wrecked vehicles: burnt-out tanks and car frames, perhaps left over from the first Gulf War. Plumes of smoke clog the horizon to the east from the oil fires in Rumaylah.

At the small-unit level, everyone's survival boils down to simple human observation. Each Marine in the vehicle is charged with watching a specific sector. To my left,

Trombley keeps his SAW machine gun trained out his window. In front of me, Colbert rides leaning into the scope of his M-4 pointed out the passenger window on the right. The Humvees are vulnerable to small arms—AK rifles, RPGs and light machine guns from up to about 600 meters distant, and heavier weapons beyond this range. With each vehicle's main gun—the Mark-19 grenade launcher or the .50-cal machine gun—accurate to about 1,000 meters, the goal is to identify and destroy any hostile threats before they come within range of the Humvee.

The Marines chatter constantly, calling out everything they see in the surrounding desert—a pipe 300 meters off that could be the barrel of a gun, a shepherd in the distance whose staff could be an AK—while passing binoculars back and forth, and trading information with the other Humvee teams over the radio.

Berms are the dominant feature of Iraq, whether here in the southern desert or in the greener farmlands north of the Euphrates. Berms are man-made piles of sand or earth, ranging in height from a couple of meters to a couple of stories. They are built on the sides of the dry canals, which are scratched throughout the desert. They are built as walls, to contain pastures, to demarcate grazing lands, as windbreaks or as military fortifications. They go in all directions. People have been digging berms here pretty much continually for the past 5,000 years.

The newest berms, which seem to have been excavated in the past few months, hide deep bulldozed pits called revetments, intended to conceal tanks. Every few hundred meters along the berms in some stretches of the desert there are two-meter-high conical towers capped with sandbags, to serve as machine-gun nests. All fortifications appear to have been abandoned.

Colbert's team passes through them warily. Small groups of hostile forces could be concealed anywhere. In addition, Fick keeps passing down reports he's receiving from higher-ups in the battalion—rumors of stray Iraqi tank units allegedly operating somewhere in the desert. But no one sees any signs of tanks or hostile forces.

Instead, the Marines begin having their first up-close encounters with Iraqis—small groups of shepherds and women in black robes outside square mud huts. A woman with something in her hands pops out from behind one of the huts a hundred meters back from the trail we're on.

Colbert shouts up to Garza on the main gun. "Garza! Woman in black. What's she doing?"

The Mark-19 fills the Humvee with a clattering sound as Garza swivels the gun toward the woman. "She's carrying a bag in her hands," he shouts from the turret. "No weapons."

A moment later Garza shouts. "Hey!"

Colbert tenses on his M-4, pressing his eye against the scope. "Talk to me, Garza. What is it?"

"I just waved at an Iraqi and he waved back at me. That was cool."

"Good, Garza," Colbert says. "Keep making friends. As long as they're not doing anything where we have to shoot them."

"Hey, it's ten in the morning!" says Person, yelling at two farmers dressed in robes in the distance. "Don't you think you ought to change out of your pajamas?"

BY LATE AFTERNOON First Recon has pushed fifty kilometers into Iraq, becoming the northernmost Marine unit in the country. Now no one has slept for thirty-six hours. It's in the upper eighties outside, and cramped in the Humvee in plastic-lined MOPPs and rubber boots, everyone's face drips sweat. Between calling out potential targets, Colbert and Person stay awake by screeching pop songs—Avril Lavigne's "I'm with You" and "Skater Boy"—deliberately massacring them at the tops of their lungs.

Marines supplement their diets of caffeine, dip and ephedra (technically banned in the Corps, but liberally consumed) with candy and junk food. Military rations, called "meals ready to eat" (MREs), come in brown plastic bags about three quarters of the size of a phone book. Each contains a main meal like spaghetti, stew or "chunked and formed" meat patties in a foil pouch. You heat these pouches by shoving them inside a plastic bag with chemicals in it. When you add water, the chemicals immediately boil, emitting noxious and (according to warnings on the package) explosive fumes. The main entrées are prepared through a mysterious desiccation process. Even though your meat patty might be swimming in juices, when you bite into it, it's dry and crumbly and brings to mind chewing on a kitchen sponge. In flush times like now, at the start of the invasion, when every Marine is rationed three MREs a day, most push aside the main meals and eat the extras. In addition to entrées, MREs are loaded with junk food—pound cakes, brownies, "Toaster Oven Pastries" (identical to Pop-Tarts), cookies, Skittles, M&M's, Tootsie Rolls, Charms hard candies, Combos cheese-filled pretzels, and powdered grape-drink mix and cocoa powder, which Marines eat straight out of the packages, like the instant coffee.

The process of tearing through an MRE and picking out the goodies is called "ratfucking." Colbert's team maintains a ratfuck bag in their Humvee for all the discarded MRE entrées, saving them for a rainy day.

Though at times throughout the advance north, Colbert's vehicle goes on point for the entire battalion, placing its occupants at the very tip of the Coalition invasion, as the heat and fatigue delirium sets in, the undertaking sometimes feels like a family road trip. Colbert is the stern father figure. Person is like the mom, the communicator, trying to anticipate his needs, keeping spirits up with his cheerful banter. Garza and Trombley are the children, happily munching candy, eager to please their dad.

As team leader, Colbert controls every aspect of his men's lives, down to their bodily functions.

"Trombley," Colbert shouts, leaning over his rifle, watching his sector. "Are you drinking water?"

"Yes, Sergeant."

"Are you pissing?"

"At our last halt, Sergeant."

"Was it clear?"

"Yes, Sergeant."

"Good."

A COUPLE OF HOURS before sundown, battalion radios explode with chatter. Several teams in our convoy spot a pair of new-looking white SUVs traveling along an adjacent trail at a high rate of speed. The trucks are marked with red circles on the doors and are loaded with clean-shaven young Arab men armed with AK rifles. The Recon Marines request permission to stage a "snatch mission" on the trucks—to go after them, grab the occupants and find out who they are. The request is denied. The vehicles are allowed to pass. The Marines are infuriated. Later, they'll find out the armed men who ride in civilian trucks, especially those with markings on the side, are Fedayeen—paramilitary guerrilla fighters. At this stage in the campaign, top U.S. commanders are concerned only with fighting regular Iraqi forces, defeating them en masse as they did in the first Gulf War. It will take a few days before American commanders realize their most dangerous opponents are the Fedayeen, who are gearing up to fight them in a guerrilla war. So for now, the Marines are ordered to simply let these guys pass right by them.

At this point in the day, the Marines in Colbert's vehicle are pretty much in the dark as to what they're doing. They've been pushing north for hours, but they're not heading in the right direction to begin the mission they have all trained for: seizing the bridge on the Euphrates.

Colbert tries to tune in the BBC during a brief halt. The BBC will emerge as the best source of information on the invasion in which the Marines are participating—even Battalion Commander Lt. Col. Ferrando relies on it. But during this stop, reception is too spotty to pick up any news. "I have no intel, no big picture," Colbert tells his team.

Fick approaches the vehicle and tells Colbert that the battalion isn't going to the bridge tonight. Instead, everyone will be heading to an elevated train track at a place called Burayyat An Rataw. He has no idea why.

The desert leading up to the tracks is littered with industrial trash—shredded tires, old fence posts, wrecked machinery, wild dogs and, every thirty meters it seems, a lone rubber flip-flop. Person calls each one out, " 'Nother flip-flop. 'Nother dude walking around somewhere with one sandal on."

"Shut the fuck up, Person," Colbert says.

"You know what happens when you get out of the

Marine Corps," Person continues. "You get your brains back."

"I mean it, Person. Shut your goddamn piehole."

At times, the two of them bicker like an old married couple. Being a rank lower than Colbert, Person can never directly express anger to him, but on occasions when Colbert is too harsh and Person's feelings are hurt, his driving becomes erratic. There are sudden turns, and the brakes are hit for no reason. It will happen even in combat situations, with Colbert suddenly in the role of wooing his driver back with retractions and apologies.

But late this afternoon, nearing the tracks, Colbert doesn't have the patience to play games. He's wrestling with profound disappointment. Since the night I met him he'd been talking about how excited he was to carry out this bridge-seizure mission. His platoon and his team had been slated to lead the way to the bridge for the entire battalion. Colbert was going to be one of the first Americans to reach the Euphrates. Back at Camp Mathilda, he had told me that this task was going to be "the recon mission of a lifetime." But now it's off.

We stop in the chalk-white desert about a kilometer south of the railroad tracks at Burayyat An Rataw. They run east-west along an elevated roadbed that stretches as far as the eye can see. We are now approximately seventy kilometers north of the border. The next-closest American unit is more than thirty kilometers away. First Recon is very much alone here. Earlier in the day, there were some overflights from Cobras, but there's no air cover now.

Like a lot of civilians whose memories of the first Gulf War were shaped by gee-whiz Pentagon camera footage shown on CNN of U.S. bombs and missiles striking Iraqi targets with pinpoint accuracy, I had assumed that American spy planes and satellites could see everything on the ground. But in this war, an intelligence officer in the First Marine Division tells me, "We think we know where about seventy percent of Saddam's armor and weapons are. That still leaves thirty percent that's an unknown, which is a lot." Dust and cloud cover inhibit the ability of spy planes and satellites to see on the ground, as do berms, huts and revetments. "Part of First Recon's job," the intel officer tells me, "is to uncover ground. Despite all the high-tech assets we have, the world is blank until you put people on the ground."

On the ground here, the first and last lines of defense are these Marines, who haven't slept all night. They can spot approaching hostile units from a kilometer or two out, which will only give them a few minutes to prepare. Not much time if it's a sizable force.

Colbert's team and the rest in the platoon are ordered to cover their Humvee in cammie nets and dig in facing the tracks. The battalion spreads out in a defensive perimeter across a couple of kilometers. Fick tells the men their job is to observe the tracks tonight, but not even he knows what they're really supposed to be looking for, or why they're doing it.

It amazes me, as the only civilian among them, how little these guys actually know at times about what they're doing or what the future holds. But the more time you spend with a combat unit, the more you realize nobody cares too much about what they're told is going to be happening in the near future because orders change constantly anyway. Besides that, most Marines' minds are occupied with the minutiae of survival in the present, scanning the vista in this land they've just invaded, searching for signs of the enemy.

Still, some of the men are deeply disappointed by the apparent cancellation of the bridge mission. "No mission?" Garza asks. He steps down from the Humvee turret after spending approximately eighteen hours there—through the night and much of the day under a blazing sun. "I'll be mad if we don't get in this war."

"Missions are always getting fragged," Colbert says, resigned. "The mission isn't important. Just doing your job is."

His team spends forty minutes digging Ranger graves about 800 meters from the elevated train tracks. The desert pan is so hard here, where a few inches beneath the sandy topsoil it's interlaced with vestigial coral from the era when this was underwater (specifically, as part of the Persian Gulf, which used to be a sea covering all of Kuwait and southern Iraq), that every inch has to be hacked away with pickaxes, the blades sparking with each blow to the stoney crust. As soon as we are finished, the battalion orders everyone to move forward to within thirty meters of the tracks.

"The dirt will be better where we're going," Colbert reassures his weary men.

But the dirt is the same. We chop a new set of graves as oil fires some twenty-five kilometers distant compete with the sunset. With the sun dropping, the temperature plummets and sweat-drenched MOPPs now feel like they're lined with ice, not merely hard plastic. The Marines cover the Humvee in cammie nets. Half the Marines go on watch; the other half settle in for two hours of sleep.

Sleep is a sketchy proposition. Marines are not permitted to take their MOPP suits or boots off, even at night. They crawl into the Ranger graves fully dressed, with their weapons and gas masks at their sides. Some wrap themselves in ponchos. Others sleep inside "bivy sacks"—zippered pouches that have an uncanny resemblance to body bags.

After dark, the oil fires make the night sky flicker like it's illuminated by a broken fluorescent light. American planes fly overhead, too high to be seen, but they throw out flares to repel missiles, which flash like lightning. One thing about war I've learned: It produces amazingly colorful night skies.

Trombley, now on watch, spots wild dogs. "I'm going to leave some food out by my hole tonight," he says. "I'm going to shoot me a dog."

"No, you're not, Trombley," Colbert says, his voice rising from his Ranger grave. "No one's shooting any dogs in Iraq."

IT RAINS AFTER MIDNIGHT, turning my Ranger grave into a mud pit. Temperatures have dropped into the forties. Everyone is awake, shivering cold but excited. Clumps of Iraqi soldiers—six to twenty at a time—walk along the elevated tracks in front of us. The railroad line runs from Basra to Nasiriyah. The soldiers, we later find out, are deserters who've apparently walked from Basra, about seventy kilometers east of this position, and are heading toward Nasiriyah, the next-nearest sizable city, about a hundred kilometers northwest of here.

The Marines watch the Iraqis through NVGs and night-vision rifle scopes. "Nobody shoot," Colbert says. "They're not here to fight."

Sergeant Steven Lovell, one of Colbert's fellow team leaders in the platoon, walks over to consult with him. Lovell, a twenty-six-year-old who grew up on a dairy farm outside Williamsport, Pennsylvania, has a bow-legged farmer's gait and a sly, rural wit. Before joining the Corps he attended college to study chemical engineering, but found he didn't like being around the "eggheads" on campus. "See how they're walking all jacked-up, sore foot?" he says, pointing at the Iraqis. "They're in a bad way."

After sunrise, Bravo Company's two platoons are sent over the tracks to snatch groups of surrendering Iraqis. By nine o'clock, it's already becoming a hot day. The work of stopping and searching all the enemy soldiers is stressful and tedious.

The Iraqis stream along the tracks and a canal that runs behind them. The Marines set up positions to intercept them, and the Iraqis walk right into them with their arms up. Then the Marines herd them into groups, put them on the ground and search them. Quite a few of the Iraqis carry miniature Tabasco bottles and candies—from MREs—which means they've already been captured, fed and let go by other American forces. Most seem eager to surrender again, hoping to get more food and water. They're dressed in a combination of military uniforms and civilian clothes. Behind them there's a trail of discarded Iraqi fatigues and AK rifles.

Over the course of the morning, the Marines grab about 200 of them, putting them down and searching each one. There are so many Iraqis coming, the Marines wave off dozens, perhaps hundreds more, who cut a wide swath around them and continue on their way.

Through a Marine translator, the Iraqis say they've come from units in Basra and started fleeing two days ago as soon as the American bombardment began. They say because they surrendered, they are being hunted and executed by Fedayeen death squads east of here, and ask for protection. Many carry colorful slips of paper dropped by American planes promising them safety in return for surrendering.

Several of the men claim they worked in special units

in charge of launching chemical-filled missiles. They say they were moving these missiles just a few days ago, getting ready to launch them. These men have atropine injectors, used to counteract nerve agents, which normally would be carried by those handling such chemicals. One of the more baffling aspects of the invasion is that the Marines will encounter numerous Iraqis, both soldiers and civilians, who claim to have firsthand knowledge of chemical weapons. At times, Marines will speculate that Iraqis are fabricating these stories in an attempt to curry favor by telling the Americans what they want to hear. But farther north, they will encounter village elders who seem quite sincere, pleading with the Marines to remove weapons stocks they believe Saddam's military buried near their farms, which they fear are poisoning their water. Given the fact that no such weapons have been found, you get the idea Saddam or someone in his government created the myth to keep the people and the military in awe of his power.

The surrendered soldiers are a wretched lot. While most are in their early twenties and look decently fed, quite a few don't have shoes and have swollen, bleeding feet. Doc Bryan, the corpsman, treats more than a dozen who have infected sores, dysentery and fevers. Even the healthiest are severely dehydrated. Some are old men. As a group, they seem dazed and numb as they accept the water and humanitarian rations the Marines hand out. A couple of them are crying. I walk among rows of them, offering anyone who wants one a Marlboro Red. Quite a few decline, patting their chests and coughing. Some say in halting English, "I'm sick." Apparently, the continual dust of southern Iraq gets to them, too.

Several Marines pass around a photo pulled from the wallet of a surrendered Iraqi. Most of the Iraqis have ordinary pictures of families—children, wives, parents. But one guy has a picture of himself holding hands with another man. Both wear gaudy, effeminate-looking Western shirts, and one seems to have makeup on. The Marines can't believe they've captured a gay Iraqi soldier.

But the funny thing is, most of the Marines passing the photo around aren't making the homo jokes they usually make among themselves. Some of them just look at it, shaking their heads. After spending several hours with the surrendered Iraqis, the Marines seem taken aback, almost depressed by their misery. A Marine staff sergeant can't get over the fact that so many are attempting to make a 170-kilometer trek through the open desert with rags tied to their feet and antifreeze jugs filled with water. "I knew from the first war they'd surrender," he says. "But I didn't expect how beaten down they'd be. I wish we could do more for them, give them more water."

"We're not the Red Crescent society," Colbert says. "We barely have enough for ourselves."

ON WHAT IS ONLY their second day in Iraq, the Marines in Bravo Company's Third Platoon have concluded that their platoon commander has lost the plot. The men in Bravo's Second and Third platoons are extremely close. Not only did they share the same tent in Kuwait, but here in the field the two platoons are usually right next to each other. Unlike the men in Second Platoon who universally respect, if not adore their commander, Lt. Fick, the men in Third Platoon view their platoon commander as a buffoon. While he is a highly rated Marine Corps officer, with stellar fitness reports, some of his men have mockingly nicknamed him "Captain America."

When you first meet Captain America, he's a likable

enough guy. At Camp Mathilda, when he still had a mustache, he bore an uncanny resemblance to Matt Dillon's roguishly charming con-artist character in *There's Something About Mary*. Captain America is thirty-one years old, married, and has a somewhat colorful past of having worked as a bodyguard for rock stars when he was in college. If he corners you, he'll talk your ear off about all the wild times he had doing security for bands like U2, Depeche Mode and Duran Duran. His men feel he uses these stories as a pathetic attempt to impress them, and besides, half of them have never heard of Duran Duran.

Twenty-four hours ago, when the invasion started, Captain America revealed another side of himself, which further eroded his standing among his men. He's prone to hysterics. Before crossing the border, he ran up to his men's Humvees parked in the staging area and began shouting, "We're in the shit now! It's war!" All morning since the Iraqi army deserters first appeared by the railroad tracks, Captain America has been getting on the radio, shouting, "Enemy! Enemy! Enemy!"

While it's perfectly fine for officers to shout dramatically in movies, in the Marines it's frowned upon. As First Recon's commander, Lt. Col. Ferrando, will later say in an apparent reference to Captain America, "An officer's job is to throw water on a fire, not gasoline."

One of Captain America's team leaders, twenty-three-year-old Sergeant John Moreno, says, "Something twisted in him the night we crossed into Iraq. He gets on the radio and starts shouting about how we're going to take on Iraqi tanks. We didn't see any tanks. It's embarrassing for us."

While rolling up to the train tracks yesterday, Captain America provoked Colbert's wrath for leading his men on a treasure hunt for discarded Iraqi helmets. "We're in an area suspected to have mines, and the most obvious thing to booby-trap is a helmet lying on the ground," Colbert fumed. "It's completely unprofessional."

Now, while the Marines search and interrogate the surrendered Iraqis, Captain America draws the ire of his top team leader, Kocher. The sergeant and his men are guarding several Iraqis not far from Colbert's team when a wild dog pops over a berm, barking and snarling. Behind them, Captain America races up, shouting, "Wild dog! Shoot it!"

Kocher quietly tells his men, "Don't shoot." Instead, they open up a beef-and-mushroom MRE dinner and lure the dog, who gratefully eats and is soon allowing the Marines to pet him. It's a small act, but by making it, Kocher directly contradicts his commander. "I don't care who he is," says Kocher. "The guy can turn the smallest situation into chaos. We're surrounded by Iraqis, some with weapons nearby. Some we haven't grabbed yet. If my men start lighting up a dog, the Iraqis might panic, other Marines might open fire. Anything could happen."

Before First Recon's campaign is over, Captain America will lose control of his platoon when he is temporarily relieved of command. Already, some of his men are beginning to fantasize about his death. "All it takes is one dumb guy in charge to ruin everything," says one of them. "Every time he steps out of the vehicle, I pray he gets shot."

A WHILE AFTER THIRD PLATOON'S dog incident, First Recon's commander orders the Marines to begin releasing the Iraqis. Prior to the war, Maj. Gen. Mattis had told reporters that surrendered enemy prisoners "will be funneled to the rear as soon as possible. Some people get their heart back after surrendering and want to fight again, so we want to get them out of the way as quickly as possible."

But First Recon doesn't have the resources to ship the hundreds of Iraqis surrendering by the tracks back to rear units. The battalion's support company trucks only have room to transport about seventy of them.

Under the Geneva Convention (articles 13 and 20), once you've accepted the surrender of enemy forces you are obligated to provide food, water and medical attention, and to take "all suitable precautions to ensure their safety during evacuation." Here, those provisions are dispensed with through a simple expedient. The Iraqis taken by the Marines are unsurrendered and sent packing.

Unfortunately for the Iraqis, First Recon's commander orders his Marines to tell these men who have just walked some seventy kilometers from Basra to go back the way they came. (From the American standpoint, a wise order, given the fact that these Iraqi soldiers had been heading to Nasiriyah, where in a few days the Marines will first confront urban war.) The prisoners are unhappy with this news. They have been saying all morning that Fedayeen death squads where they have come from have been capping their friends. And the Marines have dismantled and tossed all of their weapons into a nearby canal so they can't defend themselves. Several wave the slips of paper promising safe passage if they surrendered. But most are too exhausted to protest and start the trek back toward the Fedayeen death squads.

Person and I sit in the Humvee, eating cheese Combo snacks, watching the Iraqis limp back along the tracks.

"That's fucked," Person says. "Isn't it weird to look at those Iraqis and know that some of them are probably going to die in the next few hours?"

SEVEN

○

LATE IN THE AFTERNOON on March 22, First Recon leaves the railroad tracks at Burayyat An Rataw and pushes northwest to take up a new position along a canal. Fewer than forty-eight hours have elapsed since the invaders blew through the breaches at the border. After a few light skirmishes, Marine and British forces have captured the key oil facilities around Basra. Now, approximately 20,000 Marines in the First Division are heading west, then north onto highways that will take them into central Iraq.

First Recon's job this early evening is to move about fifteen kilometers north of the route on which the bulk of the First Division will be rolling. The battalion is to set up along a waterway and watch for Iraqi forces to make sure that they don't drop down unexpectedly and attack the First Division on the highway.

Colbert's team drives along a winding canal, watching for enemy forces, while Person discusses the band he formed after high school, Me or Society. A heavy-metal rap group, his band once opened for Limp Bizkit at a show in Kansas City. "We sucked, but so did they," Person says. "The only difference is, they became famous right after we played together. I became a Marine."

Colbert brings up a mutual friend in the battalion who listens to death metal and hangs out in vampire clubs in Hollywood.

"You remember that time he went out dressed in diapers and a gas mask?" Person says, laughing appreciatively.

Trombley, who seldom jumps into conversations between Colbert and Person, can't hide his disgust. "That's sick. Can you believe we're defending people's freedom to do that?"

Colbert corrects him, delivering a sharp civics lesson. "No, Trombley. That's good that people have the freedom to do that. We're even defending people like Corporal Person, too."

The land is fertile along the canal. There are scruffy pastures, as well as little hamlets, each consisting of two or three mud huts bunched together. "Keep your eyes on the swivel," Colbert reminds his chatty team. "This is backcountry."

But villagers who come out by the trail greet the Marines with smiles. A teenage boy and girl walk ahead on the trail, holding hands.

"Kind of cute," Colbert observes. "Don't shoot them, Garza," he adds.

As they roll past the hand-holding teens, Colbert and Person wave at them and start singing the South Park version of "Loving You," with the lyrics "Loving you is easy 'cause you're bare-chested."

We bump onto a set of rail tracks and follow them toward a narrow bridge across the canal. The battalion has chosen a train bridge as its crossing point over the canal. According to Colbert, spy planes have observed the train bridge for several days, and everyone is reasonably sure that no freight trains will appear around the bend on the other side. The Humvee jiggles so intensely on the rail-road ties, it feels like someone is sawing my teeth. We pull onto the bridge. It's about seventy-five meters long and just wide enough for the Humvee. I look out my window and see pebbles kicked up by the tires tumble into the water five meters below.

"Just think how easy it would be to drive off the edge right now," Person says.

"Yeah," Colbert says. "You could have an epileptic fit, a bee could sting you or one of your zits could explode."

"That's why I popped them all this morning, so we would be safe."

WE REACH THE OBSERVATION POSITION by the canal after dark. Lights twinkle from a town several kilometers west. Obviously, electricity still works in parts of Iraq. When the Humvee stops, we hear crickets and frogs. The place seems untouched by war. Colbert's team sets up in line with the platoon along a low berm running in front of the canal. The men prepare for another chilly, sleepless night. Through their night optics they observe villagers moving around huts a few hundred meters away on the other side of the canal. Iraqi armored forces are suspected of being on the move somewhere beyond the villages. At about nine o'clock, orange flashes burst on the horizon several kilometers northeast of the canal. U.S. warplanes are bombing targets.

Greater numbers of Iraqis appear on the other side of the canal—bunches of them moving—and the Marines judge them to be military deserters fleeing the American bombing. But some Marines grow edgy.

A few vehicles down the line from Colbert's, Doc Bryan is nearly shot by a nervous Marine, a senior enlisted man.

Doc Bryan rides with Lovell's Team Three. He is crouching by his team's vehicle, observing the village on the other side, when he feels a burning sensation in his eyeball. It takes him a moment to figure out: Someone is pointing an infrared-laser aiming device from a rifle into the side of his eye. The laser's invisible, but he feels its heat. Just as Doc Bryan turns, a senior enlisted Marine tramps out of the darkness, aiming his rifle at him, cursing. "Jesus, I thought you guys were enemy," the senior enlisted man says. "I almost shot you."

The senior enlisted man, a company operations chief, tells Doc Bryan he had trained his weapon on him and almost fired, believing he was an enemy infiltrator.

In the layers of bullshit Recon Marines feel they labor under in the battalion, this company ops chief is nearly at the top with Captain America and Encino Man. They call him "Casey Kasem," because of his warm, gravelly voice, which over the radios sounds like that of the old rock DJ.

In his late thirties, lean and dark-haired, Casey Kasem usually rides with Encino Man. Casey Kasem's job is to ensure that the Marines have enough supplies—fuel, water and batteries for their night optics. Like Encino Man, he's one of those rear-echelon men in a support position, who ordinarily wouldn't have deployed with the Recon Marines.

One of the things that burn everyone up about Casey Kasem is the fact that for whatever reason there are not enough batteries or adequate rechargers to operate the platoon's only PAS-13 thermal-imaging device. Unlike their NVGs, which amplify existing light, the PAS-13 uses heat and can see through dust and foliage. The PAS-13 gives the platoon a critical advantage and means of survival in night operations, but the platoon only has enough batteries to operate it for a couple of hours each night. Within a few days, when they are at the height of their operations in ambush country, the men will sometimes go whole nights without any batteries at all for their PAS-13, and in at least one instance, this deficiency will nearly kill them.

Adding insult to injury, while there are not enough batteries for the Marines' critical night-fighting gear, Casey Kasem did have the presence of mind to bring along a personal video camera. He is constantly sticking it in everyone's face as part of his effort to make a war documentary that he hopes to sell after the invasion. "He's just another king-size jackass making life more dangerous for us," Doc Bryan says.

Tonight Casey Kasem is highly agitated because he and Encino Man have concluded that "enemy infiltrators" have moved into the Marines' position and are preparing an attack.

"Over there. Enemy infiltrators," he tells Doc Bryan, pointing toward the village he and others on the team have been watching.

While Doc Bryan is not technically a Marine, he is a product of the Navy's most elite special-warfare training and could have chosen to have been placed with either Navy SEALs or a Marine Recon unit. Doc Bryan, who arguably has better combat training than many Recon Marines, is supremely confident of his judgment. "That's a village," Doc Bryan says.

"No. Over there," Casey Kasem whispers excitedly, pointing along the canal. "Looks like a squad-size group of Iraqis, maybe an RPG hunter-killer team observing us."

"Those are fucking rocks," Doc Bryan says. "They're not moving."

"Not moving," Casey Kasem says, "because those are the most disciplined Iraqis we've seen so far."

Casey Kasem sounds the alert up and down the line. Marines are pushed out with weapons and optics to observe the Iraqi "squad." Only at first light do the Marines definitively prove to Casey Kasem that the "disciplined Iraqis" are indeed rocks.

Through the heightened alert, Colbert spends the night calming his team. When Garza takes the watch on the Humvee's Mark-19, Colbert tells him, "Garza, please make sure you don't shoot the civilians on the other side of the canal. We are the invading army. We must be magnanimous."

"Magna-nous?" Garza asks. "What the fuck does that mean?"

"Lofty and kinglike," Colbert tells him.

"Sure," Garza says after a moment's consideration. "I'm a nice guy."

EIGHT

○

THE MARINES ARE ALMOST EUPHORIC the next morning, March 23, when Fick briefs them on the next leg of the invasion. He doesn't know for sure yet where they are going, but higher-ups in the battalion have insisted that today is the day all men must shave off their mustaches. "Given the Battalion Commander's previous order regarding mustaches, I think we can all take this as a clear indication that we're crossing the Euphrates soon," he tells his men just after sunrise.

Later, after they've refueled the Humvees, Fick issues specific orders. "Our objective is a town called Nasiriyah, a crossing point on the Euphrates. The word is the Army passed through it twenty-four hours ago and declared it 'secure.'"

At the time Fick is delivering his sunny assessment on conditions at Nasiriyah, an Army maintenance unit has just been ambushed outside of town, about four hours earlier, sustaining numerous casualties.

(Fick later speculates that the optimistic assessment he was given on the state of Nasiriyah stemmed from a foul-up fairly typical of military communications, which can take on the aspect of a game of telephone. "The Marine

106

Corps had been expecting the Iraqis to blow the bridges in Nasiriyah," he explains. "Someone probably reported that the bridges were 'intact,' and this got changed to 'the bridges are secure,' to 'the whole town is secure.' ")

Colbert's team pulls back from the canal with the rest of the battalion and drops onto a freeway, bound for Nasiriyah. They join several thousand U.S. military vehicles driving north at forty-five miles per hour, which in military convoys is lightning speed. "Look at this, gents," Colbert says. "The First Marine Division out of Camp Pendleton rolling with impunity on Saddam's highways."

It's a bright, clear day. No dust at all. Several hundred Iraqi children line the highway, shouting gleefully. "Yes, we are the conquering heroes," Colbert says.

Everyone's spirits are up. Colbert seems to have gotten over his disappointment at the scrubbing of his team's bridge mission. The sense is that this campaign is unfolding like the last Gulf War, an Iraqi rout in battle followed by an American race to gobble up abandoned territory as swiftly as possible.

"As soon as we capture Baghdad," Person says, "Lee Greenwood is going to parachute in singing 'I'm Proud to Be an American.'"

"Watch it," Colbert says. "You know the rule."

One of the cardinal rules of Colbert's Humvee is that no one is permitted to make any references to country music. He claims that the mere mention of country, which he deems "the Special Olympics of music," makes him physically ill.

Along the highway, they pass columns of tanks and other vehicles emblazoned with American flags or moto slogans such as "Angry American" or "Get Some." Person spots a Humvee with the 9/11 catchphrase "Let's Roll!" stenciled on the side.

"I hate that cheesy patriotic bullshit," Person says. He mentions Aaron Tippin's "Where the Stars and Stripes and the Eagles Fly," then scoffs, "Like how he sings those country white-trash images. 'Where eagles fly.' Fuck! They fly in Canada, too. Like they don't fly there? My mom tried to play me that song when I came home from Afghanistan. I was like, 'Fuck, no, Mom. I'm a Marine. I don't need to fly a little flag on my car to show I'm patriotic.' "

"That song is straight homosexual country music, Special Olympics–gay," Colbert says.

By noon the battalion cuts off the freeway to Route 7, a two-lane blacktop road leading into Nasiriyah. Within an hour Colbert's team is mired in a massive traffic jam. We stop about twenty kilometers south of Nasiriyah, amidst several thousand Marine vehicles bunched up on the highway. We are parked beside approximately 200 tractor-trailers hauling bulldozers, pontoon sections and other equipment for building bridges. Among these are numerous dump trucks hauling gravel. One has to marvel at the might—or hubris—of a military force that invades a sand- and rock-strewn country but brings its own gravel.

UNBEKNOWNST TO THE MARINES stopped on the highway on this lazy afternoon, twenty kilometers ahead of them the American military is experiencing its first setback of the war. Marine units are bogged down in a series of firefights in and around Nasiriyah. A city of about 400,000, Nasiriyah lies just north of a key bridge over the Euphrates. (The bridge First Recon originally planned to seize is located in a remote area far east of Nasiriyah; that mission was called off in part because planners erroneously believed the bridge over Nasiriyah was wide open for the taking.) Several hundred Marines from a unit dubbed "Task Force Tarawa" attempted to cross the bridge into the city earlier in the day, and are now pinned down by several thousand Fedayeen guerrilla fighters around the bridge and inside the city.

Nasiriyah marks the spot where the terrain in Iraq changes dramatically. At Nasiriyah, the desert land, watered by the Euphrates, turns almost tropical in places. There are dense palm groves, fields of tall grass, even rice paddies. These predominate south of the bridge, where Marines from Task Force Tarawa are dug in taking heavy machine-gun, mortar, artillery, RPG and AK fire.

The fighting in Nasiriyah started at about three in the morning after an Army maintenance convoy that had been rolling on the superhighway far south of the city took a wrong turn onto Route 7 and drove toward the town. The soldiers in this unit, including most famously Private First Class Jessica Lynch, had no navigation equipment and poor maps. They were ambushed a few kilometers outside Nasiriyah, with eleven killed, six captured and five missing.

A few hours later, after dawn, the Marines from Task Force Tarawa, which includes a total of about 5,000 troops, arrived. Their original mission had been to secure the bridge and the route through Nasiriyah for other Marine forces, which would then move through the city and continue north. But having received word of the ambushed soldiers—and seeing with their own eyes the blown-up, burned Army vehicles from the maintenance units smoldering by the side of the road—the Marines from Task Force Tarawa began a search-and-rescue mission. They pushed up to within a kilometer of the bridge aboard lightly armored vehicles and dismounted into the surrounding fields—a patchwork of dried mudflats, berms, grass and palm trees. While the Marines called out, yelling for any American soldiers to show themselves, they started to take rifle and machine-gun fire from surrounding huts and berms. They also heard American voices calling out to them. They found nine soldiers, several of them wounded, from the lost convoy hiding in the foliage, and rescued them.

Still taking sporadic enemy fire, the Marines in Task Force Tarawa regrouped on the highway and prepared to roll onto the bridge into Nasiriyah. They started before noon, about the time First Recon pushed up Route 7 and became mired in the military traffic jam twenty kilometers south of them.

The lead Marines in Task Force Tarawa crossed onto the bridge into Nasiriyah aboard tanks and Amtracs. Amtracs are ungainly, tracked vehicles designed to swim over the ocean as well as drive on land, but are not really designed for heavy combat. Each holds roughly twenty Marines. About a dozen vehicles made it across the bridge, then cut east, hoping to find a route bypassing the center of Nasiriyah.

But the tanks quickly ran into one of the worst features of Iraqi cities: unpaved streets running with open sewer water. They bogged down in the muck, unable to move any farther.

More Amtracs, containing a total of about 150 Marines, raced across the bridge and drove straight into the heart of the city. Central Nasiriyah is a warren of two- to four-story brick and concrete structures, most of them surrounded by walls. As the Marines sped into the center of the town, they began to take hostile fire. Iraqis dressed in civilian clothes, hiding behind walls and windows of the buildings lining both sides of the streets, fired AK rifles, machine guns and RPGs into the Amtracs. The Marines continued on and had made it three kilometers into the heart of Nasiriyah when an Amtrac was hit by an RPG, wounding several. The column pressed ahead to seize a canal bridge on the north side of the city.

Additional Amtracs attempted to cross the Euphrates but were attacked by Iraqis dug in on all sides. Marines jumped out and fanned into the surrounding terrain to fight them. Some tried to call in fire support from Marine mortar units, but their radios went down. Three Marines were killed and four wounded in the first moments of fighting.

Then Army A-10 attack jets, sent in to support them, appeared in the sky, swooped down and began strafing Marines. How the A-10 pilots, flying low, mistook Marines for hostile forces is one of those mysteries of battle. The A-10s' strafing runs shredded Amtracs and killed as many as ten Marines.

As the firefight intensified by the bridge, Task Force Tarawa pushed more Amtracs forward to evacuate the wounded. One was blown to pieces when an enemy round penetrated the armor and detonated the stocks of ammunition inside, killing the Marines in the rear of the vehicle.

By the end of the afternoon on March 23, pockets of Marines from Task Force Tarawa are cut off along several kilometers of the route into and through Nasiriyah. Eighteen Marines are dead, four are missing and more than seventy are wounded.

TWENTY KILOMETERS SOUTH of the fighting, the mood on the highway is almost festive. It's a clear, warm afternoon, with dazzling blue skies. No one knows about the firefights ahead or the Marines dying. Though all afternoon we've seen Cobras and "casevac"—casualty evacuation—helicopters shuttling back and forth toward Nasiriyah. Marines who haven't slept or stopped moving in days loll about in the shade of Humvees and trucks stopped on the road, dozing with their flak jackets off. Others lie in the sun, MOPP suits partially opened, heads back, trying to soak up rays.

There are nearly 10,000 Marines parked on the road, as well as a sprinkling of British troops who appear to be lost. Everyone defecates and pisses out in the open beside the highway. Taking a shit is always a big production in a war zone. There's the MOPP suit to contend with, and no one wants to walk too far from the road for fear of stepping on a land mine, since these are known to be scattered haphazardly beside Iraqi highways. In the civilian world, of course, utmost care is taken to perform bodily functions in private. Public defecation is an act of shame, or even insanity. In a war zone, it's the opposite. You don't want to wander off by yourself. You could get shot by enemy snipers, or by Marines when you're coming back into friendly lines. So everyone just squats in the open a few meters from the road, often perching on empty wooden grenade crates used as portable "shitters." Trash from thousands of discarded MRE packs litters the area. With everyone lounging around, eating, sleeping, sunning, pooping, it looks like some weird combat version of an outdoor rock festival.

Shepherds, undaunted by the American military might amassed on the highway, walk through the lines. Flocks of sheep and herds of goats zigzag between the rows of tanks, trucks and Marines. Only a few Marines notice. They point at the animals and laugh. Collectively, they seem lulled into a sense of security by the sheer volume of troops and equipment jumbled on the road. No one is up on the vehicle guns. Few, if any, are on watch.

Colbert returns from taking a dump, and Trombley, whom Colbert has relentlessly pestered about drinking enough water to maintain clear urine, turns the tables on him.

"Have a good dump, Sergeant?" Trombley asks.

"Excellent," Colbert answers. "Shit my brains out. Not too hard, not too runny."

"That sucks when it's runny and you have to wipe fifty times," Trombley says conversationally.

"I'm not talking about that." Colbert assumes his stern teacher's voice. "If it's too hard or too soft, something's not right. You might have a problem."

"It should be a little acid," Person says, offering his own medical opinion. "And burn a little when it comes out."

"Maybe on your little bitch asshole from all the cock that's been stuffed up it," Colbert snaps.

Hearing this exchange, another Marine in the platoon says, "Man, the Marines are so homoerotic. That's all we talk about. Have you guys ever realized how homoerotic this whole thing is?"

Just before sundown, Marine artillery batteries, dug in a few kilometers ahead, begin to pound the city. As darkness falls, Colbert's team excavates Ranger graves by the Humvee. The ground trembles as a column of massive M1A1 tanks rolls past, a few feet from where the Marines are resting. Out of the darkness, someone shouts, "Hey, if you lay down with your cock on the ground, it feels good."

I WAKE UP AT DAWN on March 24 to the sound of a pickax thudding into the ground near my sleeping hole. Near me, a sergeant in Second Platoon named Antonio Espera excavates a pit, sweat rolling off his face even though it's a chilly morning. "I'm fucking ashamed, dog," he says, huffing as he swings the pickax. "When we left Afghanistan we didn't leave a speck of Americana behind."

Espera gestures to the trash-strewn road. "I was trained Marines don't litter."

His rage at the garbage—thousands of brown plastic wrappers and green foil pouches from MREs lying along the highway—has made him irrational. He's digging a trash pit, when there are half a dozen sleeping holes, soon to be vacated, which could serve the same purpose. But he continues digging at a furious pace.

With his shaved head and deep-set eyes, Espera is one of the scariest-looking Marines in the platoon. Technically, he serves as Colbert's assistant team leader, though in actuality he commands a separate Humvee. Espera's crew of four Marines always rolls directly behind or beside Colbert's, and he is one of Colbert's closest friends in the platoon. The two men could hardly be more opposite. Espera, thirty, grew up in Riverside, California, and was, by his own account, truly a "bad mother-fucker"—participating in all the violent pastimes available to a young Latino from a broken home and raised partially in state facilities. He was serving in an infantry platoon when he and Colbert met a few years earlier. Somehow they struck up a friendship, which on the face of it is odd. Colbert, with his Nordic features and upper-middle-class background, is also among those who frequently engage in routine racial humor, referring to the Spanish language as "dirty spic talk." Espera, who's part Native American, part Mexican and a quarter German, frequently rails about the dominance of America's "white masters" and the genocide of his Indian ancestors. But describing his friendship with Colbert, Espera says, "Inside we're both the same: violent warriors. Only he fights with his mind, and I fight with my strength." For his part, Colbert says that when he met Espera he was impressed by his "maturity, dedication and toughness." Even though Espera is not yet a Recon Marine, Colbert pulled strings to bring him into the elite battalion to serve as his assistant team leader.

This morning, despite the ongoing boom of artillery and rumors now spreading among the ranks of a bloody fight taking place up the road, Espera and several other Marines in the platoon seem to be suffering from a low-grade case of invaders' guilt. "Imagine how we must look to these people," he says, disgustedly kicking a pile of trash into his freshly dug pit.

There is a cluster of mud-hut homes about thirty meters across from the platoon's position by the road. Old ladies in black robes and scarves stand in front of the homes, staring at the pale, white ass of a Marine. He's naked from the waist down, taking a dump in their front yard.

A Marine on Espera's team who's helping him pick up the trash gestures toward this odd scene and says, "Can you imagine if this was reversed, and some army came into suburbia and was crapping in everyone's front lawns? It's fucking wild."

Colbert tunes in the BBC. The men receive the first hard reports of the heavy fighting in Nasiriyah, of Americans being captured, of mass casualties among the Marines.

None of the younger Marines listening to the reports shows much reaction. But the news hits Gunny Wynn, the platoon sergeant, hard.

"I can't fucking believe it," he says. "How did so many Marines get hit?"

Doc Bryan rants, "Marines are dying up the road, and we're sitting back here with our thumbs up our asses."

A while later, Doc Bryan's prayers are answered. At twelve-thirty on the afternoon of the twenty-fourth, a somber Fick gathers his team leaders for a briefing. "In approximately one hour, we are going to bust north to the bridge at the Euphrates," he says. "Change in the ROE: Anyone with a weapon is declared hostile. If it's a woman walking away from you with a weapon on her back, shoot her. If there is an armed Iraqi out there, shoot him. I don't care if you hit him with a forty-millimeter grenade in the chest."

When he finishes, Espera says, "Sir, we're going to go home to a mess after we start wasting these villages. People aren't going to like that."

"I know," Fick says. "We now risk losing the PR war. Fighting in urban terrain is exactly what Saddam wanted us to do."

Fick has no clear idea what First Recon will be doing at the bridge. The word he's been given from his commander is that his platoon is going to serve as a quick reaction force to rush into the city and evacuate Marines that are wounded there. But the details he has on this mission are sketchy. He's not even certain of what route they're going to be taking through the city, or even what their destination will be once they get there.

After his briefing, Fick does what he often does in a difficult situation: He turns to Colbert for advice. When I first met Fick and heard him extol the intelligence and character of his men, I had wondered if this was just lip service. But I've found in the past few days of the invasion that whenever there's a problem—a life-and-death one, such as this mission—Fick always turns to his men for guidance. Now he and Colbert and other team leaders spread out maps of Nasiriyah on the hood of his Humvee and try to figure out where in the hell they might be going. There are several routes through the city (which is spread across approximately sixteen square kilometers), and they have no idea which their mission into the city will take.

Meanwhile, Espera gathers men from his team and Colbert's and passes on the briefing Fick just delivered on the change in the ROE. He summarizes Fick's briefing like this: "You see a motherfucker through a window with an AK, cap his ass." But then he warns the men, "Don't get buck fever like Casey Kasem did the other night at the canal. You cap an old lady sweeping her porch, 'cause you think her broom is a weapon, it's on all of us."

THE REASON FIRST RECON and all the rest of the Marines have been waiting on the highway south of Nasiriyah for twenty-four hours and now are venturing out with orders that are unclear is that their leaders aren't quite sure what to do. Ever since lead elements of Task Force Tarawa were unexpectedly chewed apart and stopped in their advance through the city yesterday, Marine commanders have been waffling.

The point of taking Nasiriyah and its bridge is clear enough. The city is a gateway into central Iraq. From the start, Maj. Gen. Mattis's invasion plan has hinged on sending a substantial Marine force through central Iraq on a route that stretches for 185 kilometers from Nasiriyah in the south to Al Kut in the north. Al Kut sits on the Tigris and commands key bridges that the invading force will need to cross in order to reach Baghdad.

The land between Nasiriyah and Al Kut is historically known as the Fertile Crescent or Mesopotamia, which is

Greek for "land between two rivers"—the Euphrates and the Tigris. Mesopotamia has been inhabited for more than 5,000 years. Its terrain is a starkly contrasting patchwork of barren desert and lush, tropical growth, all interlaced with canals. It was here that humankind first invented the wheel, the written word and algebra. Some biblical scholars believe that Mesopotamia was the site of the Garden of Eden.

Mattis's plan is to invade it with a Regimental Combat Team—designated as RCT-1—a force of about 6,000 Marines. First Recon will serve as RCT-1's advance element. His objectives are twofold: to pin down large numbers of Republican Guard forces in and around Al Kut (thereby preventing them from defending Baghdad to the west), and to secure Al Kut's main bridge over the Tigris.

Meanwhile, Mattis's two other Regimental Combat Teams, totaling about 13,000 Marines, will move toward Baghdad on western highways through open desert, much as the Army has been doing since crossing the border. By dividing his forces, Mattis hopes that at least one set of them will be able to seize passable bridges over the Tigris (which the western highways also cross). The problem he's facing on March 24 is that for more than a day now, RCT-1 has been hesitating on the outskirts of Nasiriyah.

The Marines of Task Force Tarawa, engaged inside the city and south of it in fields by the bridge over the Euphrates, only pushed into Nasiriyah in order to secure the route for RCT-1 and First Recon to use on their advance north. While the Marines in Task Force Tarawa who entered the city suffered heavy losses the day before, the continual American bombardment of Nasiriyah by artillery, attack jets and helicopters has prevented enemy forces from massing on them. They have not retreated and remain in place in Nasiriyah.

Unfortunately, the commander of RCT-1, Colonel Joe Dowdy, whose forces have been stopped on the highway south of the city, along with First Recon's, for the past twenty-four hours, has been unable to obtain a clear picture of what's going on in the city with Task Force Tarawa. It's another one of those combat situations that's hard for a civilian, who might think of the U.S. military as an all-seeing, all-powerful, high-tech entity, to comprehend. While Dowdy is only a few kilometers south of the bridge and Task Force Tarawa's positions, his radios can't communicate with their radios. Task Force Tarawa, based out of Camp Lejeune in South Carolina, uses different encryption codes from those used by Dowdy's forces, which came from Camp Pendleton. West Coast Marines can't communicate with East Coast Marines.

For the past twenty-four hours, Dowdy has been wavering, alternately planning to send his 6,000 Marines straight through the city or to bypass it and use a distant crossing point, or even to send some through and hold others back. Unlike First Recon's commander, whose obsession with mustaches and the Grooming Standard alienates his men, Dowdy is a wildly popular figure in his regiment. With his burly physique and bulldog face, he fits the image of a Marine Corps commander and delivers rousing speeches peppered with verse from Shakespeare and Kipling. But at Nasiriyah he meets his downfall. It seems he simply can't make up his mind (and within a few days Mattis will take the nearly unprecedented step of removing Dowdy from command, probably as a result of this delay).

As of noon on March 24, Dowdy's latest scheme is to push First Recon ahead of RCT-1 and have them join elements of Task Force Tarawa still fighting on the southern side of the bridge. After this, he intends to drive

RCT-1 through the city and use First Recon as a quick-reaction force to rush into the city and rescue any of his Marines who are wounded in the initial assault.

NINE

○

At one o'clock on the afternoon of March 24, the Marines in First Recon climb into their vehicles and pull them onto the highway south of Nasiriyah. The winds are picking up. Yesterday's clear skies have turned gray. The road is clogged with thousands of military vehicles, but they have pulled to the side, forming a one-lane channel through the congestion.

Colbert's team settles into the Humvee and Person begins punching the dashboard and cursing. Someone higher up in the company changed radio frequencies without telling him, and now he can't use them. It's the first time I've ever seen him lose control in earnest.

Colbert calms him. "It's okay. We'll fix it. Everyone's just nervous because we lost a lot this morning," he says, referring to the news of Marine casualties.

At one-thirty p.m. First Recon's convoy of seventy vehicles starts moving on the highway toward the bridge at Nasiriyah. Given the heavy casualties sustained by Marines at the bridge during the past twenty-four hours, it's a reasonable assessment that everyone in the vehicle has a better-than-average chance of getting killed or injured this afternoon.

It's about twenty kilometers to the bridge. The funny thing I notice between all the vehicles lined up on the road is that all the trash dropped by the Marines in the preceding twenty-four hours, which Espera had been railing about earlier in the morning, has been picked up.

The air is heavy with that fog of fine, powdery dust—familiar from Camp Mathilda but which we hadn't seen a lot of until today. Cobras clatter directly overhead. They circle First Recon's convoy, nosing down through the barren scrubland on either side of the road, hunting for enemy shooters. Before long, we are on our own. The helicopters are called off because fuel is short.

Then we clear the last of the vehicles in RCT-1's convoy. A Marine standing by the road pumps his fist as Colbert's vehicle drives past and shouts, "Get some!"

No one says anything in the vehicle.

We drive into a no-man's-land. A burning fuel depot to our right spews fire and smoke. Garbage is strewn on either side of the road as far as the eye can see. It appears that we're driving straight through the town trash dump, with shredded plastic bags littering the area like confetti after a parade. The convoy slows to a crawl, and the Humvee fills with a black cloud of flies.

"Now, this looks like Tijuana," says Person.

"And this time I get to do what I've always wanted to do in T.J.," Colbert adds. "Burn it to the ground."

There is a series of thunderous, tooth-rattling explosions directly to the vehicle's right. A Marine artillery battery is set up in a field next to the road, firing into Nasiriyah. The 155mm guns in the row have six-meter-long barrels spouting flames and black smoke with each shot. We draw even with them, then move ahead. It's a strange sensation feeling those massive guns firing behind you. Marines who so scrupulously picked up all their litter this morning are now bombing the shit out of the city.

Up ahead are wrecked U.S. military vehicles, a burned-up Dragon Wagon military transport truck, a mangled Humvee. The windshield is riddled with bullet holes. We pass a few meters from the Humvee, close enough to see pools of brown fluid—probably blood—spilled on the ground by the doors.

We drive into an increasing gloom. The hundreds if not thousands of artillery rounds and bombs poured onto the city in the past twenty-four hours have kicked up a localized dust storm over the road. Visibility drops to a few kilometers.

"Small-arms fire to the rear," Colbert says, passing word from the battalion radio. No one reacts. It's like a weather bulletin.

"Car coming at twelve o'clock!" someone shouts. Weapons clatter as everyone readies to shoot it.

A white Toyota passenger car with orange fenders—the markings of an Iraqi taxicab—zooms out of the black cloud ahead, toward First Recon's convoy, where, no doubt, up and down the line hundreds of Marines take aim to shoot it.

"No weapons! No weapons!" gunners shout in Colbert's Humvee, meaning they don't see any weapons in the cab.

The cab squeezes past Colbert's Humvee and continues down the line. A taxi driving into a convoy of heavily armed Marines during a firefight and artillery bombardment seems insane. The stereotype of the reckless Arab cabdriver in New York City pops into my mind. Later, Marines figure out that cabs are used by Fedayeen to move through their lines and observe or to ferry troops.

They're also used by car bombers. And they're used by civilians to evacuate the wounded.

Ever more powerful blasts boom outside the Humvee. We pass a succession of desiccated farmsteads—crude, square huts made of mud, with starved-looking livestock in front. Locals sit outside like spectators lining a parade route. A woman walks by the road with a basket on her head, oblivious to the explosions.

We reach the bridge over the Euphrates. Marines from Task Force Tarawa are spread out on both sides of the road in fields and dense palm groves. Rifles crack intermittently, with occasional bursts from machine guns. They've been dug in here for twenty-four hours now and are still taking fire from Iraqi gunmen farther out in the fields.

The bridge is a long, broad concrete structure. It spans nearly a kilometer and arches up gracefully toward the middle. The guardrails on both sides are twisted and riddled with bullet holes. The dust and smoke are so dense it's like being in a snowstorm. We can't even make out the city on the other side of the bridge. The span simply disappears into a gray cloud bank.

After fifteen minutes of solid tension inside the Humvee, Person cannot repress the urge to make a goofy remark. He turns to Colbert, smiling. "Hey, you think I have enough driving hours now to get my Humvee license?"

First Recon's column cuts off the road at the causeway where the bridge starts. We take a left down a dirt trail and drive below the bridge to the banks of the Euphrates. There we finally glimpse Nasiriyah on the other side. The front of the city is a jumble of irregularly shaped two- and three-story structures. Iraqi towns are characterized by uniform dullness of color, buildings constructed somewhat haphazardly out of mud bricks or from cinder blocks covered in stucco. Everything is the shade of earth, of the dust that hangs in the air. Through the haze, the buildings appear as a series of dim, slanted outlines, like a row of crooked teeth.

To our immediate right, a dozen or so Marines from Task Force Tarawa sit between the bridge pilings beneath the elevated roadway. Some are stretched out, sleeping, despite the steady blasts of Marine artillery landing in the city on the opposite riverbank. One of the Marines sits upright, puffing on a fat cigar. His face is black with grime. He stares expressionlessly at Colbert's Humvee. No moto greeting of *Get some!* from him.

First Recon's Alpha and Charlie companies set up along the bank of the river, facing the city. Bravo pulls back about seventy-five meters from the river's edge.

The whole maneuver—driving seventy-five meters from the riverbank—takes about fifteen minutes. The ten Humvees in Bravo Company's two platoons run into about twenty trucks from the battalion's Support and Headquarters Company, which are trying to drive into a field farther back from the bridge. The Humvees drive around like clown cars as everyone shouts over the radios or out their windows to direct traffic. Finally, Colbert's Humvee stops next to the road leading onto the bridge. There's no clear order of what Bravo is doing here yet.

Colbert can't get over the lush greenery of the palm groves and fields around us. After two months in the desert, it's jarring to suddenly have arrived in Mesopotamia's fertile surroundings on the outskirts of the Garden of Eden. Even as Marine artillery rounds blow it to smithereens, Colbert keeps repeating, "Look at these fucking trees."

An enemy mortar explodes nearby. A mortar blast is

different from artillery. You hear the blast as an artillery shell is fired, then the sound of it whizzing through the sky, followed by the boom as it hits. Mortars come out of nowhere. There's no warning, just a blast, and a column of black smoke where it hits. If they're close you feel a sharp increase in the air pressure. The sonic vibrations make the hairs on your body tingle, and your teeth feel numb for an instant.

Another mortar bangs outside. Person smiles. "You know that feeling before a debate when you gotta piss and you've got that weird feeling in your stomach, then you go in and kick ass?" he says. "I don't have that feeling now."

A machine gun rattles up on the riverbank.

"Stand by for shit to get stupid," Person says, sounding merely annoyed.

SEVENTY-FIVE METERS in front of us are the men in First Recon's Alpha and Charlie companies, spread across the southern banks of the Euphrates. They form a line stretching for nearly a kilometer from the bridge on their eastern side to grassy fields on the west. The men begin taking sporadic sniper fire from Nasiriyah. As enemy shots crackle in the air, the Marines take cover behind low, dried mud berms, then scan the city, which rises one hundred meters distant on the opposite riverbank, through rifle scopes and binoculars. They search the thousands of windows and crevices and alleys for signs of enemy shooters.

The procedure when you're getting shot at by rifles or machine guns is pretty straightforward. The Marines all hunt for muzzle flashes. If a gun is pointed toward you, even if the shooter is concealed behind a wall or berm, its flash will generally be visible. Every time an enemy gunman takes a shot, he momentarily reveals his position.

The men in Alpha and Charlie companies spot muzzle flashes coming from windows of apartments 250 meters or so across the river. But in their first twenty minutes at the riverfront, the Marines fire very few shots. There are civilians moving about in the streets of the city. Even during this low-intensity gun battle, some even stand still, trying to observe the Marines aiming at them.

The strangest, most unsettling spectacle Marines see, however, is that of armed men who dart across alleys, moving from building to building, clutching women in front of them for cover. The first time it happens, Marines shout, "Man with a weapon!"

Despite the newly aggressive ROEs, Marines down the line shout, "I'm not shooting! There's women."

One of the Marines witnessing this is the commander of Alpha Company, Captain Bryan Patterson, whose Humvee command post is set fifty meters back from the riverfront. Patterson, thirty-two, is from Indianapolis, Indiana, and is a graduate of the U.S. Naval Academy. With his medium build and dark hair he tends to keep a tad longer than regulation, he looks not a day over twenty-four.

Until this afternoon Patterson has always wondered how he would react under fire. Though he's been in the Marines his entire adult life and before joining First Recon he commanded an infantry platoon, he's never been in combat.

Now several mortars impact within 150 meters of his position. Patterson gets on his radio and calls the battalion. His fear is that these might actually be "friendly" mortars dropped by Marines, not aware that

First Recon has moved up to the western side of the bridge. Several minutes later, the battalion radios back that these are definitely not Marine mortars.

While Patterson stands there out in the open by his Humvee, talking on the radio, the area around him is raked with enemy gunfire. Marines taking cover behind surrounding berms look up to see if their commander is hit and burst into laughter. Patterson seems oblivious to the shooting and keeps talking on the radio, periodically tilting his head back, gulping down Skittles from an MRE.

Whatever indefinable qualities make a good commanding officer, Patterson has them. Unlike Encino Man and Captain America in Bravo Company, Patterson's men speak of him in the highest terms. Patterson hardly fits the image of the swaggering, barrel-chested Marine Corps officer. He is one of the most unassuming characters you could ever meet, almost shy. He admits, "I can't give gladiatorial speeches to my men." His reasons for going to the Naval Academy and becoming a Marine couldn't be more prosaic. "I didn't know what I wanted to do with my life," he says. His view of being an officer is devoid of romance. "As company commander, I'm like a midlevel manager at any corporation."

His views on the war are equally temperate. "There is not a good thing that comes out of war," he tells me later on. "I'm not going to pretend I'm this great American savior in Iraq. We didn't come here to liberate. We came to look out for our interests. That we are here is good. But if to liberate them means putting a Starbucks and a McDonald's on every street corner, is that liberation? But I have to justify this to myself. It's Saddam's fault." Still, he says, "the protestors have a lot of valid points. War sucks."

The reason his men look up to him is probably very simple. Aside from the fact that he's calm and articulate, Patterson respects them. His Marines came to the Middle East on a ship, and behind the backs of his men, Patterson often says, "I could have fallen overboard and they would do fine without me."

Now, he and his men come under increasing fire at the riverbank. His Marines spot an anti-aircraft artillery (AAA) battery shooting at them from across the river. AAA guns fire large-caliber rounds from multiple barrels, like extremely high-powered machine guns. They are designed to shred aircraft flying thousands of meters overhead, but in Iraq, gunmen point the barrels down and aim them at ground targets, such as Marines. Their fire is devastating, and this one, about a kilometer and a half down the riverbank, is beyond the effective range of the heaviest weapons possessed by the Marines in First Recon.

Patterson and his men notice some Marines from Task Force Tarawa a couple hundred meters away. Among them is a Javelin team.

The Javelin is basically a big, honking, shoulder-fired missile for blowing up tanks. Patterson brings the Javelin crew forward. Within minutes they fire a missile into the AAA battery across the river. Patterson watches through his binoculars as a direct hit from the Javelin blows up the AAA battery, setting off numerous secondary explosions as nearby stocks of munitions cook off. He estimates the one strike takes out three to five Iraqis who'd been manning the AAA guns. "It felt good to get revenge for the Marines from Task Force Tarawa killed in Nasiriyah," Patterson later admits.

Now, directly across the river, every Iraqi with an AK or machine gun seems to open up on First Recon's position.

Apparently, the Javelin strike alerted everyone in the city with a gun to the Marines' presence here. Taking concentrated enemy fire, the men in Alpha and Charlie lose their inhibitions about possibly shooting women in the city. Up and down the line, just about every rifle, machine gun and grenade launcher roars to life. For about sixty seconds they savage the city, pouring thousands of rounds into it. Patterson later says of this first burst of wild, fairly indiscriminate fire, "They all had to pop their cherries."

IN THE STORM OF SHOOTING set off by Alpha's attack on the AAA gun, enemy fire rakes the area around Colbert's Humvee, seventy-five meters back from the riverfront. Bravo Second Platoon occupies slightly elevated ground behind Alpha's position, but luckily most of the Iraqi fire seems to be wildly high. A row of palm trees between us and the riverbank shivers as rounds rip through fronds and send puffs of smoke off the trunks. Incoming rounds, I notice as I crouch down to the ground beside Colbert's vehicle, make a zinging sound, just as they do in Bugs Bunny cartoons.

Initially, Marines in Bravo stand outside their vehicles, milling around with stupid smiles on their faces. Several are giggling. It's like everyone just stepped onto the set of a war movie. One of First Recon's seniormost enlisted men struts past, shouting, "Gotta love this shit! We're in the middle of it now, boys!" He sounds like the emcee at a pro-wrestling smackdown. "It is on!"

This senior enlisted man, in his mid-forties, is one of those thickly built, slightly overweight guys whose fat just makes him look even more threatening than he is. His job is to be the grand enforcer of discipline within the enlisted ranks, to be sort of a professional dickhead.

Fairly or unfairly, the Marines' nickname for him is the "Coward of Khafji."

Khafji, a small Saudi Arabian town south of the Kuwait border, was the setting of one of the earliest battles of the first Gulf War. In the official version, Iraqi mechanized units, probing for American weaknesses, dropped into Khafji, surprising advance Marine units occupying the town, kicking off a forty-eight-hour battle to extricate the Americans.

According to several enlisted men and officers in First Recon, the battle of Khafji was actually triggered by several Marines who veered into the town to make phone calls to their families and girlfriends at home. As incredible as this sounds, it's true that in the current war, Marines, such as Colbert, carry international calling codes, which can be used on Iraqi landlines to dial out to Marine satellite phones. Recon units are trained, if they're cut off behind enemy lines and their radios are down, to break into Iraqi homes or offices and dial their units' satellite phones.

In the legend circulating through First Recon, the senior enlisted man they've nicknamed the "Coward of Khafji," then a sergeant in another unit, was among those who led the charge on Khafji's available phones. Marines were frantically dialing home when several noticed a sizable force of Iraqi soldiers occupying a nearby building. As the story goes, the "Coward of Khafji" jumped into a Humvee and fled the town. He later told his fellow troops he had fled in the interest of saving a "water bull" (storage tank) attached to the rear of his Humvee and preventing it from falling into Iraqi hands. (When I ask him about the veracity of this story, he denies it happened that way but refuses to provide any details.) Whatever the truth, the Coward of Khafji name has stuck.

Now, as the Coward of Khafji walks past Colbert's vehicle amid the rising gunfire, Person leans out the window and shouts, "Hey, where's your Humvee? Isn't it time for you to get out of here?"

Luckily for Person, the gunfire is increasing. The Coward of Khafji, who possesses a mighty authority to punish men within the battalion, doesn't hear him.

A volley of enemy mortars explodes in the surrounding fields. Machine-gun fire, which previously seemed to be only coming in from the north—the direction of the city—now erupts on all sides. Currently, Second Platoon faces the river to the north. The Humvees in the platoon are pushed up beside the elevated causeway leading onto the bridge. Around us are open, dried mudflats. These extend fifty to seventy meters north toward the river, and to the west and south of us. Beyond the mudflats are fields of dry, bent grass. Several dozen Marines from Task Force Tarawa are spread out in these fields, lying prone on the ground, firing at Iraqis and outlying buildings.

Several hundred additional Marines from Task Force Tarawa are also directly across the roadway from us in a sunken field to the east. This field, perhaps a kilometer square, has high-tension power lines running through it and is bounded by a thick forest of palms and a scattering of buildings. One of these buildings, a small two-story hospital, contains Fedayeen, who have been targeting Marines in the field all afternoon. More Fedayeen have been shooting from the palm grove.

In the past few moments, heavy fire from First Recon's Marines in Alpha and Charlie has been joined by shooting from the thousand or so Marines in Task Force Tarawa to our east, west and south. It sounds as if dozens of weapons are now firing on all sides. It's as loud, and nearly as steady, as the sound of a river rushing over a dam. One thing you can say about intense weapons fire, it sounds like it ought to. It's an extremely angry noise.

When I jump down, face-first into the dirt, I twist my head to the side and see the palm trees overhead shiver from multiple rounds hitting them. I also see that the grass in the field to my left is waving from the effects of low, grazing machine-gun fire. The fire is outbound, and though I can't see the weapon, I can see a ghost of black smoke rising above what is probably the barrel. It's my hope that most of the fire I'm hearing is outbound, from Marines. I would hate to think it's from Iraqis massing to overrun our position.

But in my first experience at being in the midst of heavy gunfire—from machine guns to mortars to Marine artillery still slamming into the city over our heads—I feel surprisingly calm. While the Marines might possess that "adolescent sense of invulnerability," I have the more adult handicap of having always lived in denial. It's a problem for which I've attended therapy sessions and self-help groups in an effort to overcome, originally at the urging of a now ex-wife. But I find that in a pitched fire-fight, denial serves one very well. I simply refuse to believe anyone's going to shoot me.

This is not to say I'm not scared. In fact, I'm so scared I feel not completely in my body. It's become a thing—heavy and cumbersome—I'm keeping as close to the ground as possible, trying to take care of it as best I can, even though I don't feel all the way in it. As I squeeze flat against the earth, so do the Marines around me in Second Platoon. Guys who'd been laughing and joking a few moments earlier drop down and embrace the earth. I look up and see Espera five meters in front of me, cursing and wiggling, trying to pull down his MOPP suit. Espera makes no show of trying to laugh off his fear. He's wrestling his penis out of his pants so he can take a leak while lying on his side. "I don't want to fucking piss on myself," he grunts.

The Marines took a combat-stress class before the war. An instructor told them that 25 percent of them can expect to lose control of their bladders or bowels when they take fire. Fearing one of these embarrassing accidents, when the bullets start flying they piss and shit frantically whenever they can.

The guy on my other side is Pappy, the team leader they all look up to as "the coldest killer in the battalion." Since my arrival with the platoon, he's been one of the most hesitant to talk to me. Early on at Camp Mathilda, he had said in his polite, North Carolina accent, "It's nothing personal, but I just don't have good feelings about reporters."

Now he catches my eye and flashes a smile. He seems neither giddy, as are some of the others, nor terrified. But he looks a lot older, suddenly, as if the lines around his eyes have deepened in the hour since we drove up here.

"How are you doing?" I ask.

"I'm not like some of these younger Marines, eager to get some," Pappy says. "I'd be just as happy if they ordered us to turn around right now and we drove back to Mathilda. Just the same, I want to be with these guys so I can do what I can to help them live."

I ask him what the hell we're doing here waiting around by the entrance to the bridge while the bombs fall. I can't figure out why Bravo company is up high by the road, where the men are exposed, yet can't fire their weapons for fear of hitting Marines in surrounding fields.

Pappy's response is sobering. "Our job is to kamikaze

into the city and collect casualties," he says. "We're just waiting for the order to go."

"How many casualties are there?" I ask.

"Casualties?" he says. "They're not there yet. We're the reaction force for an attack that's coming across the bridge. RCT-1 is going to be moving up here any minute and crossing the bridge. We're going in during the fight to pick up the wounded."

It's the first time anyone has told me anything about this mission that I'm accompanying them on. I don't know why, but the idea of waiting around for casualties that don't exist yet strikes me as more macabre than the idea of actual casualties.

Yet despite how much it sucks here, it's kind of exciting, too. I had almost looked down on the Marines' shows of moto, the way they shouted *Get some!* and acted so excited about being in a fight. But the fact is, there's a definite sense of exhilaration every time there's an explosion and you're still there afterward. There's another kind of exhilaration, too. Everyone is side by side, facing the same big fear: death. Usually, death is pushed to the fringes in the civilian world. Most people face their end pretty much alone, with a few family members if they are lucky. Here, the Marines face death together, in their youth. If anyone dies, he will do so surrounded by the very best friends he believes he will ever have.

As mortars continue to explode around us, I watch Garza pick through an MRE. He takes out a packet of Charms candies and hurls it into the gunfire. Marines view Charms as almost infernal talismans. A few days earlier, in the Humvee, Garza saw me pull Charms out of my MRE pack. His eyes lighted up and he offered me a highly prized bag of Combos cheese pretzels for my candies. He didn't explain why. I thought he just really liked Charms until he threw the pack he'd just traded me out the window. "We don't allow Charms anywhere in our Humvee," Person said in a rare show of absolute seriousness. "That's right," Colbert said, cinching it. "They're fucking bad luck."

The heavy gunfire tapers off. Mortars still explode every couple of minutes, but everyone rises from the ground. Lying in the dirt becomes tedious. In a way it also becomes more terrifying because you can't see what's going on around you.

Now when there's a boom, most people just drop to one knee. One Marine in another platoon has developed a fierce stutter. "P-p-p-pass m-my b-b-binoculars," he spits out. His buddies exchange looks but say nothing to him. Not far away, an officer who took cover beneath a Humvee won't come out. Marines don't laugh at this, either. (Some are disturbed by this act of perceived cowardice in one of their leaders and later seek counselling.)

Colbert seems to blossom under extreme duress. He goes into full Iceman mode, becoming extra calm, alert and focused even when everyone's just standing around waiting for another blast.

Marines tear into their MREs. They eat a lot during lulls in firefights. Most just squeeze main meals—like the pressed, crumbly steaks and chicken patties—directly from the foil pouches into their mouths.

Then a new sound erupts nearby—a rapid-fire thunking. Everyone drops to the ground except Colbert. He remains upright, eating. "Those are ours, gents," he says between bites. Colbert informs the Marines flattened in the dirt that the "thunking" was unmistakably the sound of Marine Bushmaster weapons. No need to worry.

F-18 fighter-attack jets rip through the sky and drop

low just 200 meters or so over our heads. Marines call these "moto passes." The jets fly too high and too fast to be much help hunting down small human targets on the ground, but their dramatic appearances are intended to boost morale.

While we sit around eating, there's a massive explosion overhead just on the other side of the causeway. Cables from high-tension electric towers snap and bounce above us, struck by a friendly artillery round, intended for Nasiriyah. It happens too quickly for anyone to duck. Shrapnel bangs into Pappy's Humvee, but no one is hit.

Marines thirty meters across the road from us are not so lucky. We hear screams of "Corpsman!" I stand up and see one injured Marine staggering in circles. The errant round sprayed six Marines from another unit with shrapnel. Two are later reported to have been killed from wounds sustained in this incident.

CLOSER TO THE RIVER, Patterson's men are also experiencing the chaos of fire from all directions. Patterson pushes some of his men farther west and south into surrounding fields. He's concerned that outlying farm structures might conceal enemy gunmen.

Corporal Cody Scott, a twenty-year-old from Midland, Texas, leads a team out from Alpha's Second Platoon to clear a building. Scott joined the Marines over his mother's objections on his eighteenth birthday, and is a big guy with the slow-moving gravity of someone much older. The night before, while paused on the highway south of Nasiriyah, Scott took the time to record his thoughts in his diary: "I feel that the military—leading men into battle—is my calling. Some people are artists, some musicians; I was born a warrior. Since I was young

I've felt drawn to the warrior society. This war, as of yet, is not a bloody one. The opposition is slim. Our minions are rolling in with such force that the enemy is laying down without a fight. The people of this country live like rats. Hopefully, these people will lead a better life because of what we're doing."

Now leading his team—"a ragtag mishmash of men," as he calls them in his diary—on their first combat mission is a chance to fulfill all his dreams. They follow the berm of a small canal, running north-south. Their objective is a hut about 150 meters away. As they bound toward it, an Iraqi man pops out of the field in front of them. Scott and his men raise their weapons to shoot him, but the Iraqi is unarmed. He gestures to them, speaking in Arabic. Scott fears it's a trap. Maybe he's there to lead them into an ambush.

But before he can take any action, three mortars explode nearby on the western side of the structure. The Iraqi disappears as Scott and his men take cover. Then rounds slam into the ground all around them. Scott's men try shooting. His M-4 jams on a double feed—two rounds stuck in the chamber—and a SAW gunner's weapon also malfunctions, popping off just one round at a time. Another gunner on his team succeeds in laying down a steady bead of fire.

About this time they notice that all the red tracers streaming in at them are coming from the west, where Marines from Task Force Tarawa are hunkered down. The mini-firefight is Marines shooting at Marines.

Scott's men stop shooting, as do the Marines firing at them in the distance. In his diary that night, Scott writes a considerably more concise and less florid entry than his previous ones: "Combat was not what I expected. How we all made it out without a scratch is beyond me."

* * *

IN ADDITION TO THE PROBLEM of friendly fire, Patterson's Alpha Company snipers on the riverfront are dealing with the ambiguities of guerrilla war, not covered in the Marine Rules of Engagement. The ROE under which the Marines operate are quite naturally based on the assumption that legitimate targets are people armed with weapons. The problem is Iraqis dressed in civilian clothes who are armed not with guns but with cell phones, walkie-talkies and binoculars. These men, it is believed by the Marines, are serving as forward observers for the mortars being dropped into their positions.

Mortars are a weapon of choice for the Iraqis. A mortar is a rocket-propelled bomb that is launched from a tube that's about a meter long. The mortar rocket itself is about the size and shape of a bowling pin. It fires out of the tube almost straight up, then arcs down and explodes—anywhere from one to six kilometers away. Even the smaller mortars used by the Iraqis will, when they hit, scoop out about a meter-wide hole in the ground and spray shrapnel for twenty-five meters in all directions. A direct hit from a mortar can disable the biggest American tank, or blow the fuck out of a Humvee.

Since mortars are small and light, they can be moved around easily and fired from rooftops, trenches, alleys, even from the backs of pickup trucks. Even better from the enemy's standpoint, you can't tell which direction they're being fired from. They might be five kilometers away in a trench behind a house or an apartment block.

But since mortar crews are so far away and usually out of sight, they rely on forward observers. These characters tend to hang out near Marine positions with binoculars, cell phones or radios. They watch where the mortars are landing and call back to the guys shooting them to tell them how to adjust their fire. Those who appear to be observers in Nasiriyah are unarmed, dressed in civilian clothes and blend in with the population.

During the first hour by the river, Marine snipers had to request permission up the chain of command to get "cleared hot" to shoot suspected forward observers. Killing unarmed civilians is a dicey issue, but eventually the Marine snipers are given permission to take out Iraqis with binoculars or cell phones on the other side of the river.

Marine snipers work in two-man teams, a shooter and a spotter. One of the best teams in Alpha Company is led by thirty-nine-year-old Sergeant Ken Sutherby, originally from Michigan. Sutherby looks and talks exactly the way you'd expect a Marine sniper to. He is tall and gaunt, with unblinking, pale-blue eyes, and speaks in a dry, almost airless voice. His laconic mannerisms are no doubt reinforced by the fact that Sutherby is slightly hearing impaired. He carefully scrutinizes anyone speaking to him in case he misses a word. When you get to know him, he emerges as something of a character, like a vaguely improbable figure in an Elmore Leonard crime novel.

Sutherby has been in and out of the Marine Corps since the age of nineteen. Between his years as a rifleman and sniper, he's worked as a car repo man in his hometown of Detroit, as a bodyguard for members of the Saudi royal family in Beverly Hills, and most recently, again as a bodyguard, this time for Suge Knight, the hip-hop mogul and convicted felon behind Death Row Records. Sutherby rejoined the Marines this last time because "it's more stable than working in the civilian world."

Beneath it all, Sutherby is basically a family man. He

and his wife have four kids of their own and provide foster care to as many abused and neglected children. "I enjoy my family," he says. In fact, he calls his M-40 sniper rifle "Lila," which stands for "Little Angel," his nickname for his youngest daughter.

Sutherby and Lila get their first kill at about three o'clock in the afternoon. While nearby Marines in Alpha pour fire into buildings and windows across the river, where they think there are enemy gunmen, Sutherby and his spotter observe an Iraqi man in what they describe as "black pajamas," behaving suspiciously in an alley. He's about 400 yards distant (for some reason, while the rest of the Corps is metric, snipers still do everything in yards), and he seems to be watching the Marines through a pair of binoculars.

Sutherby and his spotter crouch behind a low brick wall. He props Lila on a sandbag for stabilization and watches the Iraqi in black pajamas for a good ten minutes. Every time mortars boom on the Marines' side of the river, the Iraqi steps out in the alley. On his last trip out, Sutherby takes a chest shot.

Sutherby seldom gets to see the results of his work. As soon as he takes the shot, the recoil jiggles his scope, blurring his vision. But his spotter, a twenty-two-year-old, Corporal David Raby from Nashville, Tennessee, sees the man go down. A minute later another Iraqi steps into the same alley with a pair of binoculars, perhaps even those from the man Sutherby just shot. He takes out the second guy with another chest shot.

After another hour, Sutherby and Raby see a man in an alley who has binoculars and a cell phone or radio. He is 500 yards away, and more careful than the first two. He appears every fifteen minutes or so, popping his head out from around a corner. Sutherby and Raby are forced to wait half an hour until the guy lingers long enough to get a clean shot. By this time, Sutherby's eyes are fatigued. He rests on Lila's stock, with his eyelids closed, until Raby says, "Sutherby! You see him?"

Sutherby opens his eyes and kills the man. It's a perfect head shot. In fact, Sutherby has the rare satisfaction of seeing the kill. The man's hands jerk up to his face while he tumbles forward.

Sutherby doesn't think about much in the way of philosophical or spiritual matters when he's killing people. The only things going through his mind are "shot geometry, yardage, wind." After his third kill, however, he does take pleasure in noting a marked decline in enemy mortar fire.

BY FOUR IN THE AFTERNOON, the smoke and dust are so thick, our position by the bridge at Nasiriyah is engulfed in a sort of permanent twilight. Finally, after being absent for the past two hours, helicopter gunships—both Cobras and Hueys—show up. They nose down over a palm grove across the road, taking passes with rockets and machine guns, spitting out white smoke trails and red tracer streaks. Fireballs bloom from the trees below. The 20mm machine guns fired by the Cobras are beyond loud—you can feel the buzzing sound they make deep in your chest. The Hueys, which are shaped like tadpoles, fire lighter machine guns operated by door gunners. You've seen Hueys in just about every Vietnam War movie ever made, as they were a staple of the U.S. military in that conflict. Seeing them now, flying over the flaming palm grove, it suddenly feels like we've stumbled onto the set of *Apocalypse Now*.

As if on cue, Person leans out the window of his

Humvee and starts singing a Creedence Clearwater Revival song, a Vietnam anthem. Then he stops abruptly. "This war will need its own theme music," he tells me. "That fag Justin Timberlake will make a soundtrack for it," he says. Then adds with disgust, "I just read that all these pussy pop stars like Justin Timberlake and Britney Spears were going to make an antiwar song. When I become a pop star, I'm just going to make pro-war songs."

One of the helicopters fires a TOW missile. Flames splash up from the trees. For the first time today, Marines in First Recon punch their fists into the sky and scream "Get some!" The helicopters continue to vomit destruction.

Even Pappy, grim all day, smiles watching the helicopters. "I used to get a kind of semi-chubb when Cobras went past," he says. "After today, seeing those birds overhead makes me so hard I could hammer nails."

In the midst of this, I look up and see a shivering, dazed dog wandering through the smoke on the road. A red rag is tied around his neck, indicating that he must belong to someone.

Fick still has no word on RCT-1's pending assault through the city. Enemy gunfire has dropped off. All we hear now is the continued booming of Marine artillery. Military ambulances are now parked across the street, picking up wounded from the field. A Humvee with loudspeakers crawls through the gloom along the edge of the palm grove, blaring surrender messages in Arabic. In the field there's a lone captured enemy fighter, dressed in rags, sitting on his knees, hands bound behind his back. A half dozen Marines stand around him with their rifles pointed at his chest.

Colbert's team pulls back to a reed fence, edging the field to the south. We dig holes. As I labor over mine,

"Fruity Rudy" Reyes comes up behind me and pats my shoulder. The guy is so strong his fingertips feel like ball-peen hammers drumming into me. "Work it, brother," he says. "All it takes is a little consistency every day to build those muscles."

Reyes is relentlessly cheerful and bright in a way that brings to mind the host of a morning talk show. Adding to this impression, he is the platoon's unofficial fitness guru, always ready with a helpful bromide. As I continue to huff and wheeze, he adds, "You know what the best workout machine is? The human body."

Later, as we sit in the mud eating more MREs, a dirt-covered Marine from Task Force Tarawa walks out from the field. He stops in front of us, looking vaguely shell-shocked.

"How's it going, buddy?" Colbert asks.

"They shot one of my Marines in the stomach out there." He gestures toward the field. "We fired back. Blew a donkey's head off. We didn't see nothing else."

"Buddy, you need anything—food, water?" Colbert asks.

"It's all good, bro." He wanders off.

AT SUNSET FIRST RECON remains at the bridge. The whole reason the battalion came here was to serve as a quick-reaction force when RCT-1's massive convoy crossed the bridge and entered the city. But RCT-1's commander, Col. Dowdy, who has been flip-flopping for the past thirty hours on how and when to enter the city, continues wrestling with indecision. Instead of sending the whole convoy through in the afternoon as he'd planned, a couple of hours earlier he sent a small force of Marines dashing through the city in special, high-speed armored vehicles. They reported meeting almost no resistance as they sped through to the other side of the city, where they are now waiting.

Despite some reports of light resistance in Nasiriyah, the Marines in Task Force Tarawa who entered the city the day before remain in their original positions, still under enemy attack. Their situation is so tenuous, they haven't yet retrieved the dead Marines still lying in shot-up Amtracs. Still taking heavy fire, their commander is asking Dowdy to loan him fourteen M1A1 tanks to reinforce their positions. It's a situation common in combat: Two different sets of Marines operating in the same city a couple of kilometers apart are reporting radically different conditions.

After receiving a visit from Lieutenant General James Conway (Maj. Gen. Mattis's boss, commander of the entire First Marine Expeditionary Force in the Middle East), who urges him to take action, Dowdy finally decides he will send RCT-1 through Nasiriyah at midnight. First Recon is ordered back from the bridge. Their mission to serve as a quick-reaction force has been scrubbed. The six hours they spent at the bridge under fire was basically a waste of time (though Marines in Alpha and Charlie did take out perhaps two dozen or more hostile fighters, as well as the AAA battery). First Recon will now roll through Nasiriyah sometime after midnight, simply as part of the convoy with RCT-1.

TEN

○

IT'S AFTER DARK and growing cold when First Recon pulls back from the bridge at the Euphrates River on the evening of March 24. Its convoy of seventy vehicles rolls south four kilometers from the bridge. They stop on the highway and maneuver into the single-file marching order they will take into the city. Everybody turns off their engines and waits.

When I get out of Colbert's vehicle, I smell the town trash dump we noticed earlier in the day. A bombed oil-tank storage facility blazes in the night sky about 300 meters in front of us. Marines wander out of the vehicles in high spirits. No one says so, but I think everyone's pretty happy they didn't have to do the reaction-force mission into the city.

First Recon's Alpha Company Marines killed, by their most conservative estimates, at least ten Iraqis across the river. Some of these killer Marines come up to Colbert's vehicle to regale his team with exploits of their slaughter, bragging about one kill in particular, a fat Fedayeen in a bright orange shirt. He was one of those guys with a cell phone or radio. He kept stepping out the front door of a building directly across the river, then popping back inside. More than a dozen Marines, armed with an assortment of rifles, machine guns and grenade launchers, had been watching him, waiting to get cleared hot to shoot. When they finally did and the fat man stepped out his front door again, he was literally blown to pieces. "We shredded him," one of Colbert's Marine buddies says. "We fucking redecorated downtown Nasiriyah."

It's not just bragging. When Marines talk about the violence they wreak, there's an almost giddy shame, an uneasy exultation in having committed society's ultimate taboo and having done it with state sanction.

"Well, good on you," Colbert says to his friends.

Person shares an observation about his own reaction to combat. He stands by the road, pissing. "Man, I pulled my trousers down and it smells like hot dick," he says. "That sweaty hot-cock smell. I kind of smell like I just had sex."

The lighthearted mood is broken when headlights appear in the darkness. It's now about nine o'clock at night. Three civilian vans, coming from the direction of Nasiriyah, bear down on First Recon's position on the road. Initially, Marines just sit around gabbing and joking, paying them no mind.

By now, rumors have swirled through the ranks that yesterday in Nasiriyah Iraqi forces faked surrendering—came out with white flags, then opened up on the Marines. These stories are passed by officers and picked up by the media. Later, some units that were supposedly attacked in this manner deny this ever happened. But the legends of these devious tactics, along with tales of Jessica Lynch's alleged mutilation and rape, gain wide credence.

Despite these fears, nobody lifts a finger to stop the approaching vans. It's extremely difficult to maintain a combat mind-set twenty-four hours a day. After being under fire for six hours at the bridge, Marines just want to goof off and revel in the triumphs of having killed and survived.

Fick runs up to remind them they are invaders in a hostile land. "Stop these fucking vehicles!" he yells.

Marines leap up, weapons clattering, and surround the vans.

The dome lights are on in the rear van. I see a man curled over in the backseat in a fetal position. He's covered in blood-soaked rags.

A translator is brought up. He speaks to the driver of one of the vans, then tells Fick that the vans are filled with doctors and wounded civilians. They can't get to hospitals in Nasiriyah, so they're driving south looking for one.

Fick radios the battalion requesting permission to send the vans south down the highway. Permission is granted, but it's a futile exercise. The Marine convoy these vans are attempting to drive through stretches for twenty or more kilometers. Since all the units are on different comms, it's impossible to pass word to them to allow these vans through. In the best-case scenario, the vans will be repeatedly stopped and won't reach a hospital for a day or two. In the worst case, they will be shot up by nervous Marines.

"It sucks," Fick says as we watch the vans creep off south through the Marine convoy. "This is what happens in war. For all we know, those wounded were the same guys shooting at us all day. They can't use the hospital up the road, because Iraqis were using it to fire on Marines."

But Fick has other concerns. In a couple of hours his men will roll through the city. Marines have dubbed the route through Nasiriyah "sniper alley," though within a few weeks the same nickname will apply to any street in an Iraqi town.

Colbert briefs his team inside the Humvee. "The last

friendly units that went through there were taking RPGs from the rooftops," he says. "I want the Mark-19 ranged high. Trombley, anything that moves on the left that looks like a weapon, shoot it."

"Gee, I hope I get to run over somebody at least," Person says, growing petulant. As the driver, he doesn't have easy access to his weapon. This fact bugs him. "I'm one of the best marksmen here. I can shoot people, too."

Colbert tells him to shut up. "Look," he tells his team. "There's nothing to worry about. Everyone just do your job. We're going to have a lot of ass rolling in front of us."

"Ass" in the Marine Corps refers to heavily armed units, such as tanks. The Marines have been told that some armored elements of RCT-1 will move through the city ahead of them.

Espera, who drives behind Colbert with his team in a Humvee with no roof or doors on it, is worried. "I can understand a mission to assault a city, but to run a gauntlet through it?" he says, leaning into Colbert's window. "I hope these generals know what they're doing."

AT MIDNIGHT, Espera and I share a last cigarette. Marines, unable to sleep, stand around by their Humvees wrapped in ponchos to ward off the bitter cold, some of them jumping in place to warm up. Espera and I climb under a Humvee to conceal the light of the cigarette and lie on our backs, passing it back and forth.

Espera reenlisted in the Marines on his way back from Afghanistan. While there, he and his squad of Marines spent forty-five days living in a three-meter-deep hole somewhere in the desert. The only action they saw occurred on the night their perimeter was overrun by camels. Espera and his men opened up on them with machine guns. "After three weeks out there, no sleep, living in those holes, I was fucking hallucinating," he explains. "We thought those camels were fucking Hajjis coming over the wire. When we lit those motherfuckers up, it was fucking raining camel meat. It was a mess, dog. Motherfuckers even did a story on it in the *L.A. Times.*"

Now Espera admits he sometimes regrets reenlisting. "To come to this motherfucker?" He adds, "I've been so up and down today. I guess this is how a woman feels."

Though Espera takes pride in being a "violent warrior," the philosophical implications weigh on him. "I asked a priest if it's okay to kill people in war," he tells me. "He said it's okay as long as you don't enjoy it. Before we crossed into Iraq, I fucking hated Arabs. I don't know why. I never saw too many in Afghanistan. But as soon as we got here, it's just gone. I just feel sorry for them. I miss my little girl. Dog, I don't want to kill nobody's children."

No one's sleeping in Colbert's Humvee, either. When I get back in, Trombley once again talks about his hopes of having a son with his new young bride when he returns home.

"Never have kids, Corporal," Colbert lectures. "One kid will cost you three hundred thousand dollars. You should never have gotten married. It's always a mistake." Colbert often proclaims the futility of marriage. "Women will always cost you money, but marriage is the most expensive way to go. If you want to pay for it, Trombley, go to Australia. For a hundred bucks, you can order a whore over the phone. Half an hour later, she arrives at your door, fresh and hot, like a pizza."

Despite his bitter proclamations about women, if you catch Colbert during an unguarded moment, he'll admit that he once loved a girl who jilted him, a junior-high-school sweetheart whom he dated on and off for ten years and was even engaged to until she left him to marry one of his closest buddies. "And we're still all friends," he says, sounding almost mad about it. "They're one of those couples that likes to takes pictures of themselves doing all the fun things they do and hang them up all over their goddamn house. Sometimes I just go over there and look at the pictures of my ex-fiancée doing all those fun things I used to do with her. It's nice having friends."

I watch the artillery streak through the sky toward Nasiriyah. Marine howitzers have been pounding the city for about thirty-six hours now. Each 155mm projectile they fire weighs about 100 pounds. There are several different types, but two are most commonly employed in Iraq: high-explosive (HE) rounds to blast through steel and concrete; and dual-purpose improved conventional munitions (DPICM) rounds, which burst overhead, dispersing dozens of grenade-size bomblets intended to shred people below.

The bulk of those flying into Nasiriyah are HE rounds. A single HE round can knock down a small building, send a car flying ten meters into the air, or blast a four-meter-wide crater in the ground. They spray shrapnel in a burst that's considered lethal within a fifty-meter radius and has a high probability of maiming anyone within an additional 150 meters.

The Marines' artillery guns have a range of thirty kilometers. But even in the best of circumstances, artillery fire is an imprecise art. Rounds can veer off by twenty meters or more, as we witnessed today when one burst overhead. Despite the improvements in munitions and the use of computers and radar to help target them, the basic principles of artillery haven't changed much since Napoleon's time.

For some reason reporters and antiwar groups concerned about collateral damage in war seldom pay much attention to artillery. The beauty of aircraft, coupled with their high-tech destructive power, captures the imagination. From a news standpoint, jets flying through the sky make for much more dramatic footage than images of cannons parked in the mud, intermittently belching puffs of smoke.

But the fact is, the Marines rely much more on artillery bombardment than on aircraft dropping precision-guided munitions. During our thirty-six hours outside Nasiriyah they have already lobbed an estimated 2,000 rounds into the city. The impact of this shelling on its 400,000 residents must be devastating.

It's not the first time the citizens of Nasiriyah have been screwed by the Americans. On February 15, 1991, during the first Gulf War, George H. W. Bush gave a speech at the UN in which he urged "the Iraqi people to take matters into their own hands and force Saddam Hussein, the dictator, to step aside." The U.S. military also dropped thousands of leaflets on the country, urging the same. Few heeded this call more than the citizens of Nasiriyah. While the Iraqi army was routed in Kuwait, the mostly Shia populace of Nasiriyah led a coup against Baathist leaders controlling the city. When Saddam's armed forces subsequently came in to put down the uprising, they did so with the tacit approval of the Americans, who allowed them to use helicopters against the rebels. (The American administration at the time didn't want to see Iraq torn apart by rebellion; Bush's call for an overthrow of the government had merely been a ploy to tie up Iraq's armed forces while the U.S. military prepared to battle them in Kuwait.) After the resistance was quashed in Nasiriyah, months of bloody reprisals followed, in which thousands of its citizens are believed to have been killed.

In this war Marine intelligence analysts will later estimate that their advance into Nasiriyah was stopped by between 3,000 and 5,000 Saddam loyalists. Despite America's dazzling high-tech capabilities—the Marines move through Nasiriyah by blasting it to hell.

As a reporter watching this bombardment from Colbert's Humvee, knowing we will be rolling through Nasiriyah soon, I feel relief every time I see another round burning through the sky. Each one, I imagine, ups the odds of surviving.

At three in the morning, Gunny Wynn pokes his head in Colbert's window. We were supposed to move a couple of hours ago. But things are always delayed. "We're going at dawn," he says.

"That's fucking asinine," Colbert says. "Moving under cover of darkness is our primary advantage."

Gunny Wynn attempts to reassure him. "One thing we saw in Somalia was no matter how hard the fighting, gunmen usually sleep between four and eight. They just conk out, like clockwork. So we should be okay."

Colbert spends his final sleepless moments in the darkness, fantasizing about all the custom gear he should have brought for his Humvee—extra power inverters to charge the batteries of his thermal nightscope, a better shortwave radio to tune in the BBC, a CD player.

"We could hook up speakers and play music to fuck with the Iraqis," Person says.

"We could drive through Nasiriyah playing Metallica," Trombley adds.

"Fuck that," Person says. "We'd play GG Allin."

"Who the fuck is GG Allin?" Colbert asks.

"Like, this original punk-rock dude," Person says. "He believes murder should be legalized. You should be able to kill people you hate. He's fucking cool."

No one points out that this concept already seems to be the prevailing one in greater Nasiriyah.

ELEVEN

○

ON THE MORNING of March 25, the men in First Recon, most of whom have been up all night in anticipation of entering the hostile city, are finally told to start their engines. Colbert's Humvee rolls toward the bridge at about six-thirty in the morning. The smoke has cleared, but it's an overcast day. Just before the causeway onto the bridge, we pass Marines in gas masks standing by the side of the road. They gesture for us to don our masks, indicating there's a gas attack.

"You have got to be kidding me," Colbert says. He points out the window. "There's birds flying. Fuck it. We're not putting on our masks."

We drive onto the bridge. The guardrails on either side are bent and tattered. There are piles of empty brass shell casings and discarded steel ammo boxes on both sides. But aside from these signs of combat, it just looks like your average concrete bridge. I'm amazed that with all the gunfire—especially mortars and artillery—it wasn't hit. The Euphrates below is a flat ribbon of gray.

On the other side we pass several blown-up Amtracs. Marine rucksacks are scattered on the road, with clothes, bedrolls, and bloody scraps of battle dressing. Nearby are puddles of fluorescent pink engine coolant from destroyed vehicles.

The city ahead is about six kilometers across, a sprawling metropolis of mud brick and cinder block. Smoke curls from collapsed structures. Homes facing the road are pockmarked and cratered. Cobras fly overhead, spitting machine-gun fire into buildings on both sides of us. We see no civilians, just dogs roaming the ruins.

Nobody talks in Colbert's vehicle. Reports fly over the radio that other vehicles in First Recon's convoy are coming under fire. Then we halt on the northern end of Nasiriyah. We are surrounded by shattered gray buildings, set back about fifty meters on either side of the road. The things you look at are the thousands of gaps everywhere—windows, alleys, doorways, parapets on the roofs—to see if there are any muzzle flashes. You seldom see the guys actually doing the shooting. They hide behind walls, sticking the gun barrels over the edges to fire. All you see is a little flame spouting from the shadows. Colbert leans into his rifle scope, scanning the buildings. "Stay frosty, gents," he says.

We are stopped because Alpha Company has halted in order to pick up a wounded Marine from Task Force Tarawa with a bullet in his leg. The best they can do is put the Marine's stretcher on top of the Humvee. While attempting to load him, snipers in rubbled buildings on both sides of the road begin firing into the convoy. They concentrate their fire on Recon's support trucks. The driver of one takes a bullet in the chest, but it's stopped by his interceptor vest. An RPG round zooms over the nose of another support truck and explodes nearby. The Marines in the support trucks, derisively referred to as POGs (People Other than Grunts) by Colbert and others in the frontline units, begin launching Mark-19 grenades into a nearby building. Then a Cobra slices low and fires its machine gun directly over the heads of the men on the trucks.

SOME IN THE BATTALION are glad to come under fire and have a chance to shoot back. Few more so than the battalion's executive officer (XO), Major Todd Eckloff. Thirty-five years old, he grew up in Enumclaw, Washington, about an hour outside Seattle. He decided to become a Marine at the age of five. He says, "My grand-mother was big on patriotism and military books and songs." She helped raise him, and Eckloff grew up singing the Marines' Hymn the way other kids do nursery rhymes. When he was just a toddler, his grandmother participated in an adopt-a-soldier program, serving dinners for Vietnam vets in their home. Eckloff still remembers the first time he met a Marine. "I was with my grandmother at the South Center Mall, and coming toward us was a Marine in his dress blues. That's when I knew what I wanted to be. I was a dork about becoming a Marine." Eckloff adds, "In high school I had a license plate that said 'First Recon.'"

But since graduating from Virginia Military Institute and joining the Marines more than a decade ago, Eckloff has never had a chance to enjoy combat. He was deployed late to the Gulf War and simply "guarded shit," then served uneventfully in the Balkans. Finally in his dream unit, First Recon, Eckloff nevertheless has one of the most frustrating billets. "As XO, my job is really to do nothing but take over if the battalion commander is shot."

Now under fire in the convoy, he at last has his oppor-tunity to taste combat. He rides in a supply truck, but in his mind, as he later tells me, "It's cool, because I'm able to shoot my weapon out of the window."

Eckloff carries a Benelli automatic twelve-gauge shotgun. As rounds pop off outside, he slides it out the window and blasts an Iraqi fifteen meters away in an alley. He sees him disappear in a "big cloud of pink." The next instant he spots another guy running on a balcony area and gives him several blasts. Eckloff is certain he hit him. "My aim is good," he says.

Later, after I interview him and others riding in the support units, I tally that these Marines claim altogether to have killed between five and fifteen Iraqis during several minutes of shooting in Nasiriyah. It's a high number given the fact that during six hours of sometimes extremely heavy gun battle by the bridge yesterday the commander of Alpha Company believes his unit of eighty Marines got somewhere between ten and twenty kills.

Kocher, the team leader in Bravo's Third Platoon, doubts there was much of a gun battle through Nasiriyah. "A lot of this was just some officers and POGs who think it's cool to be out here shooting up buildings," he says.

Kocher tells me this just after we've cleared Nasiriyah's outer limits. Initially, I dismiss his opinion as Recon Marine snobbery. The fact is, Recon's Support and Headquarters elements did come under fire in Nasiriyah. At the same time, there are some in the battalion—a very small number of men—who seem to develop a penchant for driving through towns and countryside firing wildly out of their vehicles.

FIRST RECON remains on Route 7 after leaving Nasiriyah. The Marines will take this road, two lanes of unmarked asphalt, all the way to Al Kut. Aside from the berms rippling a meter or two above the surface of the land, central Iraq tends to be as flat as Kansas. Route 7 parallels the Gharraf River (which the Marines refer to as a "canal") connecting the Euphrates in the south with the Tigris in the north.

While traveling on paved roads, First Recon rolls in a single-file convoy, vehicles spaced roughly twenty-five meters apart. The average convoy speed out of Nasiriyah is about twenty miles an hour, though we tend to stop every ten minutes or so. Currently, other units from RCT-1, convoys of fifty to two hundred, are advancing on the same road, or pulled off beside it, with Marines dismounted in fields firing at targets—huts or berms—in the distance. These forces, along with First Recon, are the first Americans to invade this portion of Iraq.

Just north of Nasiriyah, we pass through a light industrial zone of cement factories, machine shops and yards full of tractors and excavating equipment. It almost looks like the outskirts of a Midwestern farm town, except for all the dead bodies. Corpses are scattered along the edges of the road. Most are men, enemy fighters, some with RPG launchers still in their hands, rounds scattered nearby. A few hours earlier, just before dawn, while the Light Armored Reconnaissance (LAR) units Col. Dowdy sent through the city the previous afternoon had been parked out here waiting for First Recon and the rest of the RCT-1 to clear Nasiriyah and catch up with them, waves of two- and three-man RPG teams had come out of the surrounding fields and industrial buildings to attack them. Few ever got off a shot.

LAR units ride in eight-wheeled amphibious, black-armored vehicles that resemble upside-down bathtubs. Each has a Bushmaster 25mm rapid-fire canon mounted in a top turret. Unlike the open turret in a Humvee, which requires a man standing in it to fire the weapon, the Bushmasters are fully enclosed. They resemble small tank guns and are operated by a crewman sitting below inside the vehicle, controlling the weapon with a sort of joystick. Not only do the Bushmasters lay down devastating fire—hundreds of explosive, armor-penetrating rounds per minute—but the guns are also linked to Forward-Looking Infrared Radar scopes, which combine both thermal imaging and light amplification to easily pick out targets 1,000 meters distant in the darkness, well beyond the effective range of Iraqi RPGs and AKs. When the Iraqi RPG teams attempted to assault them in the hours before dawn on the road north of Nasiriyah, the LAR units decimated them, killing an estimated 400 to 500. Because it was dark, many of the Iraqis kept coming out of the fields, apparently unaware that their comrades were being cut to pieces all around them.

Corpses of the Iraqi attackers who fell in the road have been run over repeatedly by tracked vehicles. They are flattened, with their entrails squished out. Marines in First Recon nickname one corpse Tomato Man, because from a distance he looks like a smashed crate of tomatoes in the road. There are shot-up cars and trucks with bodies hanging over the edges. We pass a bus, smashed and burned, with charred human remains sitting upright in some windows. There's a man in the road with no head and a dead little girl, too, about three or four, lying on her back. She's wearing a dress and has no legs.

Twenty-one-year-old Lance Corporal Jeffrey Carazales from Cuero, Texas, has a profound realization as he cruises through the destruction at the wheel of a Humvee in Bravo's Third Platoon. "Everything in life is overrated except death. All that shit goes out the window—college, nice cars, pussy. I just don't want to end up looking like that dude who looks like a box of smashed tomatoes."

* * *

COLBERT HAS his own problems. His radio is on the same network with Bravo's Third Platoon under the command of Captain America. All morning Captain America has been tying up the network shouting that his vehicle is coming under fire. "I am so sick of him spazzing out," Colbert yells, throwing down his headset. "He's running over rocks and reporting it's enemy fire."

The enlisted Marines riding with Captain America are becoming alarmed. Several days ago, back at the railroad tracks, he picked up weapons discarded by the surrendering Iraqis, among them a small East German machine gun. Now, rolling north of Nasiriyah, he's begun firing out the window of his Humvee, even when nobody else in his platoon sees any enemy threats.

While driving past an Iraqi home with an unoccupied Chevy Suburban parked in front, he sprays it with machine-gun fire.

One of the enlisted men in his vehicle challenges him. "What are you shooting at?" he asks him.

"The enemy uses SUVs all the time," he answers. "Any chance to take one out, I will."

The Marines don't necessarily disagree with his logic. It's the random unexpectedness of his firing. They are trained to call in targets over the radio, not just to verify them but to alert everyone else. Marines aren't just supposed to run around the countryside shooting guns out the window. One of the Marines who ride in the Humvee with him concludes, "The guy doesn't know what he's doing."

BUT WHATEVER FAULTS emerge among some commanders and enlisted Marines, everything about racing up a highway in a country you're invading is baffling. You pass three dead men by the road, surrounded by weapons, then shepherds in the field behind them waving and smiling. There's a car with a dead woman shot in the backseat—no hint why Marines or helicopters shot her—followed by a burned-up SUV packed with AAA guns in the rear. Many houses we pass have white flags hanging over their front doors, which Marines take to be surrender flags. Then we pass homes with black flags on them. The radios up and down the battalion come to life. Everyone wants to know, are these special flags used to signal enemy fighters? Marines train their weapons on homes flying black flags until word is passed down the net that these are flown by Shia households.

Marines in Alpha Company spot a BM-21, an Iraqi mobile rocket launcher, moving toward First Recon's convoy. The battalion halts and calls in an air strike on it.

While they're waiting, two men pop up from a berm in the field beside Colbert's vehicle and take off running. Marines train their guns in on them to shoot, but neither of them have weapons, so they let them go.

Gunny Wynn spots two men lying down in another berm about 300 meters distant. One seems to be holding something in his hands that glints—binoculars or a gun sight. Pappy and Reyes, who serve as one of the platoon's sniper teams, set up by the road, with Reyes spotting.

They observe the two men for about ten minutes. An object continues to glint in one of the men's hands. Pappy is cleared hot to take him out and fires a single shot. Pappy doesn't dwell much on the details of his kill. When I ask him about it a short while later, he says, "The man dropped down and did not come up."

For his part in the killing, Reyes says, "I pray I'm

making the right decisions. My fate is all in the Tao I've tried to live by."

WHILE WE REMAIN HALTED, waiting for the air strike on the Iraqi rocket launcher, Corporal Michael Saucier from First Recon's Charlie Company is helping pull road security on the convoy. Saucier, a twenty-year-old from Savage, Minnesota, operates a .50-caliber heavy machine gun and is one of several young Christians in the battalion. In bull sessions with other Recon Marines, he freely talks about his belief in "God, Jesus, the whole nine yards." At the same time, he's not really a big Bible-thumper. He counts among his closest friends one of the most profane nonbelievers in the battalion, and plans, when he gets out of the Corps, to go with him on a "Fear and Loathing" tour of Europe. Despite his relaxed attitudes about doctrine—Saucier believes "Christianity should be about sincerity, not a bunch of rules and denominations"—he's come to war covered in kick-ass Christian tattoos. There's a cross on his back, a dove on one leg, and the face of Jesus adorns his chest.

When the convoy stops for a "short halt"—typically one expected to last less than twenty minutes—the vehicles split into two columns. They park on both sides of the road, with the rear wheels of the Humvees in the dirt, the front wheels on the pavement, all of them facing the road at a forty-five-degree angle. The parking maneuver is called a "herringbone." At both ends of the herringboned convoy, two Humvees pull ahead of the others, park side by side in each lane of the road and face out, orienting their main guns forward to stop traffic from approaching. The procedure for stopping vehicles is for the .50-cal gunners on the Humvees to cart their weapons up and fire warning shots high over approaching cars.

Saucier is on his team's .50-cal, mounted in the center of their open-top Humvee, when he and other Marines see a passenger car about 350 meters down the road "acting funny." The car stops, and four clean-cut young men step out of a nearby field and approach it.

Of all the little clues Marines are hunting for to determine whether the people and objects in this alien environment are hostile or benign, some facts begin to emerge: Fighters tend to be clean-cut or have mustaches, and farmers usually have beards. The four young men Saucier observes walking up to the car are all clean-cut. They get into the car, and it begins to drive toward Saucier's Humvee.

Rules have changed since last night when Marines allowed three civilian vans to roll through their lines unchallenged. Now Marines are under orders to keep all civilian traffic at least 200 meters from their convoy.

Saucier aims his .50-cal high over the passenger car now approaching and thunks off several warning shots, sending bright tracers coursing over it. The car keeps coming.

"Light it up!" Marines shout nearby.

Saucier rips a ten-second burst, riddling the car with 100 armor-piercing incendiary rounds. The vehicle bursts into flames about 150 meters away, then rocks up and down as secondary explosions erupt inside. Nobody gets out.

Saucier and the other team members who also fired have just killed five men. The day before, by the Euphrates, Saucier fired into buildings in the city where he saw muzzle flashes, but he never saw any people. This is the first time he has seen a bunch of guys, then helped kill them.

Saucier stares at the burning car as explosions continue to burst inside, and he is relieved. "It means they must have been carrying weapons in there," he concludes. "Those must have been bad guys."

AFTER CHARLIE COMPANY destroys the white car, the battalion resumes its advance.

Bravo's Third Platoon pushes in front of us and immediately comes under fire from a sniper hidden somewhere in a gas station. Marines saturate the suspected sniper position with fire and continue north. While they roll, Captain America spots an Iraqi man running through the field outside his window and cuts him down with his East German machine gun.

After being up all night, then experiencing the adrenaline-fueled ride through Nasiriyah, the morning has a dreamy quality. Charred or colorfully mashed-up people along the road just add to the surreal impression. The mood in Colbert's Humvee is eerily relaxed.

Next to me, Trombley opens up an MRE and furtively pulls out a pack of Charms. "Keep it a secret," he says. In full violation of Colbert's ironclad no-Charms-because-Charms-are-bad-luck policy, he unwraps the candies and stuffs them into his mouth.

TWELVE

○

By ten in the morning on March 25, First Recon has covered about twenty kilometers since passing through Nasiriyah. Neither Lt. Fick nor the Marines in Second Platoon knows what they are doing here on Route 7. Maj. Gen. Mattis's grand scheme of sending the 6,000-strong RCT-1 from Nasiriyah to Al Kut—now about 165 kilometers north of here—is completely unknown to the men in the platoon.

Right now the only order the men are operating under is to turn off Route 7 onto a dirt trail winding through an area of dry canals. The trail loosely parallels Route 7, runs for about ten kilometers through a series of small villages and ends outside a town called Al Gharraf (named for the canal). At this point most Marines don't even know the name of the town, or if it indeed is their final destination for the day. While the 6,000 troops in RCT-1 will continue on Route 7, the 374 Marines in lightly armed First Recon will be invading this little chunk of Mesopotamia all by themselves.

Another essential piece of information the Marines in the battalion haven't been given is that the purpose of driving onto this trail is to draw enemy fire. Today marks their first day of serving as ambush bait in central Iraq. They will spend most of the next ten days moving north, either on Route 7 or on parallel dirt trails, frequently ten to twenty-five kilometers ahead of RCT-1, trying to scare enemy forces into attacking. The rationale makes sense when it's explained to me by Mattis after the invasion: The small force races up back roads ahead of the big force rolling behind on the main road. The enemy orients their troops and weapons on the small force (not realizing it's the small one), and the big force hits them where they're not looking for it. It's a trick that works best when you're going up against an army like Iraq's, which has no air assets and bad communications and will have a tough time figuring out that the small force is just a decoy. I admire the plan when Mattis and others explain it to me. And in a way, I'm glad I didn't know about it in advance, because it would have been scarier to remain with Second Platoon. Perhaps this is why they didn't tell the Marines in the platoon about this plan either.

Colbert's Humvee is in on point for the company when we make the turn off Route 7. There's a dead man lying in a ditch at the junction. Two hundred meters past the corpse, there's a farmhouse with a family out front, waving as we drive by. At the next house, two old ladies in black whoop and clap. A bunch of bearded men shout, "Good! Good! Good!" The Marines wave back. In the span of a few minutes, they have gone from kill-anyone-that-looks-dangerous mode to smiling and waving as if they're on a float in the Rose Bowl parade.

A kilometer or so onto the trail, we are surrounded by lush fields of grain, then small hamlets nestled beneath palm groves. Rays of sunlight poke through the clouds, turning the dust in the air silver. Fick's impression is that the "whole place tingles." And not in a bad way. More villagers run out from their homes, cheering. Grinning fathers hoist up their babies By one house, teenage girls in maroon dresses sneak out from behind a wall. Defying tradition, their heads are uncovered, displaying pretty faces and long black hair. They jump up and down, laughing and waving at the Marines.

"Damn! Those girls are hot," Person says.

"Look alert," Colbert warns.

The road dwindles to a single, rutted lane. We crawl along at a couple of miles per hour, then stop. Several boys, about nine or ten, scramble up from a dry creek bed on our right. They come within about five meters of the Humvee and start yelling, "Hello, America!" Some of them put their hands to their mouths, begging for food.

Colbert tries to ignore them. One of the kids, however, stares him down. He makes clownish faces at Colbert, trying to make him laugh.

"Fuck it," Colbert says. "Break out the humrats," he says, referring to humanitarian rations. "Let's feed the ankle-biters."

We throw several bright yellow humrat packs out the window. As kids run up to grab them, Colbert says, "You're welcome. Vote Republican." He gazes at them, now yelling and fighting each other for the humrat packs, and adds, "I really thank God I was born American. I mean, seriously, it's something I lose sleep over."

By now, a shamal dust storm has begun to brew. Obliteration of sunlight in a true shamal, as this one is, is nearly complete. A typical Iraqi shamal produces a dust cloud that extends three to six kilometers from the Earth's surface into the upper atmosphere. The sky turns brown or red or yellow, depending on the complexion of the dust. Our sky is the color of bile—brown tinged with yellow. Winds now gust up to fifty miles an hour. We hear thunder.

First Recon's convoy becomes twisted up on the back trails winding through the hamlets and palm groves. One set of vehicles takes a wrong turn. A bridge indicated on the map turns out not to exist. A couple of the battalion's seven-ton trucks nearly tumble into a dry canal when the roadway gives out. It takes about an hour for the convoy to "unfuck" itself. When it does, Bravo Company, which had been in the lead, ends up at the rear. The battalion convoy is cut in two, with Alpha, Charlie and Headquarters in front, and Bravo a few kilometers back.

Colbert's vehicle creeps forward, hugging the edge of a dry canal. Here the canal is about seven meters deep and an equal distance across. The Humvee is squeezed between a two-meter-high berm on the left and the canal on the right. We're on a donkey path, on the verge of slipping into the canal. We find out from the battalion radio that RCT-1, moving several kilometers west of here on the highway, is in contact with suspected Republican Guard units.

We round a bend. A village directly across from us on the other side of the dry canal looks like something out of a Sergio Leone Western. Tumbleweed blows past crude adobe huts. One of them has a peaked roof and arches in the entrance, making it resemble a small Spanish church. Villagers stream south (against the direction in which we are moving) on the opposite side of the canal. There are dozens of them—women carrying bundles on their heads, children and old ladies pulling handcarts loaded with household goods. Whereas an hour earlier villagers had been waving and smiling, the demeanor of these people is radically different. Most avoid eye contact with us. Some on the other side of the canal break into a run when they see us approach. Watching them go, Colbert concludes, "These people are fleeing."

On our side of the canal, an Iraqi man walks briskly past Bravo Company's first sergeant and gives him the thumbs-down, indicating trouble ahead. Then a villager tells a Marine translator that they are fleeing because enemy forces are preparing for an attack in the town north of here.

Inside Colbert's vehicle we hear the news of a possible attack over the radio while watching the continued exodus of villagers. Black clouds roll overhead. Lightning flashes. The winds are so strong now, the palm fronds on the surrounding trees have flipped backward. We're riding directly into the wind. Colbert shakes his head, laughing. "Could it look any worse than this? Every sign is telling us something bad is going to happen."

Moments later, gunfire erupts ahead. The five Humvees from Bravo's Third Platoon are directly in front of us, squeezed onto the donkey trail in a single-file column. The weird Spanish-looking village remains beside us across the canal on our right. To the left over a berm, there's a small cluster of two-story adobe huts, with palm trees growing between them. Unseen people inside this mini-hamlet seem to be shooting at Third Platoon.

We stop. More rifle shots crackle.

"There's incoming rounds to our rear," Person says, sounding almost bored as he passes on a report from the radio.

"Damn it," says Colbert. "I have to take a shit."

Instead, Colbert picks up a 40mm grenade, kisses the nose of it and slides it into the 203 launcher on his rifle. He opens the door and climbs up the embankment on the left to observe the homes on the other side. He signals for all the Marines to come out of the vehicle and join him. Marines from other vehicles fire into the hamlet with rifles, machine guns and Mark-19s. There are about forty-five seconds of popping and booming, then it stops.

"They say we're taking fire from those huts," Colbert says, eyeing the hamlet through binoculars. "I see no targets."

"There's people poking their heads out behind a palm tree!" another Marine on the berm shouts.

Trombley lies next to Colbert with his SAW poised to fire. "Should I light 'em up?" he asks Colbert.

"No, not yet, Trombley. Those are civilians."

ALPHA AND CHARLIE COMPANIES are currently about two kilometers ahead of us on the same trail on the outskirts of the town where locals have warned of an enemy attack. The Marines are surrounded by open fields on the right and a row of huts and two-story houses about 300 meters back from them on the left. As the lead Humvees in Alpha (who are at the front of the battalion) draw alongside these structures, they come under heavy machine-gun and AK fire. Then enemy mortars burst in the fields to the right.

The lead troops in Alpha immediately dismount and take cover behind a meter-high, mud-brick wall on the left side of the road. The fire is coming from the village structures a few hundred meters beyond this wall.

The main road into Al Gharraf is about 300 meters farther ahead of them. Though the sky has darkened from the gathering sandstorm, the cobalt-blue dome of a mosque is visible ahead, rising over the town. It's about the only color that can be seen anywhere.

Behind Alpha on the same trail, the Marines in Charlie Company come under fire. Saucier, the .50-cal gunner with Jesus tattooed on his chest, is among those taking cover. Everyone is crouched low, frantically looking around, trying to figure out where the shooting is coming from. Saucier, however, becomes distracted. A couple hundred meters away there's a woman in black walking through the field. The winds are so powerful she leans into them, her robe billowing behind her. She's using both hands to drag a large child—maybe a six- or seven-year-old boy—across the berms. The kid has obviously been shot or wounded—Saucier thinks from an enemy mortar burst, since several of these hit near where the woman had been walking. He observes her for several seconds, then struggles to turn away and refocus on his own survival. "You can't dwell on this stuff here," he later says. "But I'll definitely take it home with me."

Capt. Patterson believes there are at least two dozen enemy fighters holed up in the huts to the left, firing on his men. The Marines saturate the area with heavy-weapons fire, but they can't silence the enemy machine guns, which have everyone pinned down.

He makes the difficult decision of calling in an artillery strike on the huts. Any artillery strike within 600 meters of your position is called "danger close," given the wide kill radius of artillery shells. With the huts 300 meters away, Patterson is almost calling in a strike on top of his own men. But on their own, they can't get past them.

Since Alpha is spread across a couple hundred meters, not all the men get the word that there is a danger-close artillery strike on its way. Corporal John Burris, a twenty-one-year-old in Alpha Second Platoon, is among those kept in the dark.

Burris is one of those guys who could have done any number of things besides join the Marine Corps. His family owns a construction equipment and supply company in Tulsa, Oklahoma. "My family goes to college and then joins the family business," Burris says. A talented swimmer, he was offered scholarships at several universities, but opted for the Marines. His choice of the military didn't stem from any special patriotic urge. He wanted to buck family tradition, and besides, he was worried he'd party too hard in college. Even in full battle fatigue, toting his rifle, Burris barely looks old enough to drive, an impression that is added to by his perpetually cheerful disposition. For him, the whole campaign so far has been an oddly slapstick affair. Yesterday, by the Euphrates, he was ordered to advance on a suspected enemy gun position and drop a 203 round into it, but when he jumped up and ran toward it, he tripped and cut his face open on his rifle stock. In the midst of all the shooting, his fellow Marines fell over laughing.

Now, as the first danger-close artillery rounds scream in and burst over the nearby field, Burris pops his head over the berm. He thinks it's enemy fire, and his first instinct is to get up and see where it's coming from. A piece of shrapnel thuds into the ground behind him. Someone yells at him to get the fuck down. He rolls over, laughing, while the artillery strike of twelve DPICM cluster munitions saturates enemy positions with nearly 600 mini-bombs. The Iraqi guns are silenced.

As the artillery called in by Alpha booms ahead of us, Colbert and his team remain halted in the canal area. It's about three in the afternoon. We've been stopped for an hour. No more fire has come from the hamlet on the left. Colbert has become obsessed with the little building that looks like a Spanish church 150 meters or so across the dry canal. Colbert spotted someone's head popping up behind the parapet on the roof. Now he's watching through the scope of his M-4 rifle, getting ready to shoot.

Person and Trombley crouch by his side with their weapons out, passing binoculars back and forth. Everyone thinks the guy up there is a sniper, and the team is going to take him out next time he shows his face.

"There," Person says.

"Don't shoot!" Colbert shouts. He throws the tip of his barrel up and lets out a sharp breath. "Jesus fucking Christ! It's a kid."

We get back into the Humvee. Trombley roots around in the ratfuck bag for a spaghetti. He sucks it out straight from the foil pouch. "I almost shot him," he says.

"Not yet," Colbert says. "Put your weapon on safety."

"Goddamn kid playing peekaboo." Colbert shakes his head. It's the first time I've seen him rattled.

"What are we doing?" Trombley asks, as more Marine artillery booms by the road ahead.

"The battalion is trying to find a way around that town up ahead, so we can link up with RCT-1 on the other side."

"Why don't we go through it?" Trombley asks.

"It's full of bad guys," Colbert says. "We'd get smoked." He gets out and pisses.

THIRTEEN

○

AL GHARRAF, the town lying just ahead of First Recon, is about two kilometers from end to end, a dense mass of two- and three-story houses and apartment blocks, like Nasiriyah, though with a much smaller population: around 20,000 inhabitants. By three-thirty in the afternoon, with First Recon's leading elements in Alpha perched on the eastern side of Al Gharraf, RCT-1 has reached the western side of the town. Col. Dowdy, the commander of RCT-1, halts his forces outside of Al Gharraf when one of his companies is ambushed on the outskirts. His Marines sustain several casualties and kill between twenty and thirty attackers. Originally, Dowdy had contemplated entering Al Gharraf with tanks and other armored vehicles. But as he did at Nasiriyah, Dowdy pulls his forces back—this time into an open desert at the northern fringes of the town—and hesitates. Because of the shamal now peaking with its impenetrable dust cloud, helicopters are unable to fly over the town to see what's inside. Just three days earlier, Task Force Tarawa had suffered approximately 100 casualties, with eighteen dead, when its commanders had sent a small force of Marines into Nasiriyah. Dowdy apparently doesn't want to make the same mistake.

First Recon's commander, Lt. Col. Ferrando, has no such compunctions. Initially, when his units came under intense fire on the eastern outskirts of the town, Ferrando contemplated circumventing it and finding another route to link up with RCT-1 on the other side. But by four in the afternoon, he decides to send the whole battalion straight through the town. While Ferrando might seem to his men like a martinet, obsessed with mustaches and the Grooming Standard, as a commander, he possesses a bold streak verging on recklessness. When I later ask him why he sent his lightly armed battalion through a hostile town—one that a better-equipped force dared not enter— he says, "I thought we'd cause some problems for those motherfuckers in that town."

When the Marines in Alpha are told to jump in their vehicles and get ready to drive through the town, they are incredulous. Capt. Patterson, who's found what looks to be a viable route around the town on his maps, attempts to debate the issue with Ferrando over the radio. Ferrando cuts him off: "Patterson, you have your orders. Do you understand?"

Burris, who several minutes ago had nearly been hit by friendly shrapnel, learns of the mission when Patterson approaches his vehicle commander with a map of the town. Burris's team will be in the lead Humvee. Patterson spreads out the map, puts his finger on the entrance to the town, slides it to the other side and tells Burris and the other men, "Get me from here to there as fast as you can."

Burris says, "That's insane, but okay." He and his fellow Marines climb into their Humvee. They are ordered to start driving immediately. Ferrando and others in charge figure the effects of their artillery strike might wear off, and enemy shooters might regroup if given too much time.

Burris's team, in the lead of Alpha and the entire battalion, race their Humvee up to about forty miles per hour as they make the final approach toward the town. Its dominant feature is the mosque, with its stunning, blue dome rising on the edge. To enter the town, Marines speed past high stucco walls on the left. Straight ahead there's a three-story building with a row of tall, thin windows on the upper floor. It almost looks like the road goes straight into this structure, but instead it turns abruptly left, forcing the driver in Burris's Humvee to hit the brakes as they cut into the town.

The street that had been a narrow lane on the outskirts becomes a broad, straight avenue, only now it's filled with rubble, burned vehicles and downed telephone poles from Marine artillery strikes. The main thoroughfare, like a lot of others in Iraqi towns, has a claustrophobic feel, since it's hemmed in on both sides with either high stucco walls or building fronts. The sky and the whole town before them are almost yellow from the dust storm. Wind blasts through the streets—and Burris's open Humvee—at fifty miles per hour.

Burris hears shots, but it's tough to see anything. The shamal winds sandpaper the lenses of the goggles the Marines wear. Some men remove the fogged goggles, but their eyes fill with tears from the dust. Burris glimpses three armed men in an alley and fires a 203 round in their direction. He has no idea if he hits them. Then Burris's team hits a river of "crap water" running through the middle of the town—the result of a blown sewer main or, just as likely, the natural state of things in this impoverished place. Sewage sprays all over his face. Then he hears his Humvee's driver and another

Marine shouting, "Left or right?"—repeating it urgently.

There's a T intersection ahead, and no one can figure out which way to go. They have the map out, ripping and flapping in the wind, and are trying to study it. "Left! Left!" one of them shouts, finally solving the puzzle.

They sideswipe a partially downed telephone pole, then, two to three minutes after entering Al Gharraf, they arrive on the western edge of the town, where Burris has his most terrifying moment of the invasion. Hundreds of Marines from RCT-1 are dug in, facing them with rifles, machine guns and Javelin, AT-4 and TOW missiles. Burris watches in horror as dozens of Marines drop their heads onto their sights, getting ready to open fire on his Humvee. He ducks, expecting a hail of bullets and missiles, but all he hears is the wind. Given the shaky communications between different Marine units, nobody in First Recon was completely confident the guys in RCT-1 waiting on the other side of the town would know they were coming. But the Marines in RCT-1—some of whom later say they were stunned when they saw First Recon's Humvees careening out of the town they considered impassable—hold their fire.

First Recon's headquarters and support units— many in lumbering, five- and seven-ton trucks—roll through Al Gharraf after Alpha Company. Enemy fire on the trucks remains intermittent, more on the level of pot shots, but one Marine officer riding in the convoy is amazed by the sheer chaos of it. Until several weeks earlier Major Michael Shoup, thirty-five, was working at the Pentagon as a budget analyst. Prior to that, Shoup was an F-18 "backseater"—weapons officer—and flew several combat missions over Kosovo. He volunteered to join First Recon as a forward air controller, responsible for calling in air strikes to assist the battalion. Today, with the Marine Air Wing grounded from the shamal, he has nothing to do but ride in a truck. What sticks out in his mind is not the intermittent enemy fire but something which is, in the scheme of things, almost trivial. Shoup sees an Arab standing in a doorway near where his vehicle is passing. The man is tall, well dressed in a brown suit, and has a close-cropped beard. He's smiling. Then Shoup sees a Marine officer he knows stick the barrel of his Benelli twelve-gauge automatic shotgun out the window of his vehicle and blast away at the man in the brown suit. Shoup can't be sure it wasn't a legitimate kill—perhaps he failed to notice a weapon on the Arab—but all he recalls seeing is the man's smile before he was gunned down.

ABOUT TWENTY MINUTES elapse from the time Alpha Company hits Al Gharraf until Bravo Company is ordered into the town. Bravo's Third Platoon is the first to enter. By now, the attackers have set up several ambush positions in the town. Kocher's team sees six different muzzle flashes as they make the first turn by the mosque. Most come from gaps in the walls or windows in the buildings on the right side. This is a good spot to start the ambush, since the Humvees have to slow down while rounding the initial corner.

At the wheel of Kocher's Humvee is a twenty-two-year-old corporal named Trevor Darnold. He grew up in Plummer, Idaho, and says the biggest influence on his joining the Marines was watching *G.I. Joe* on the Cartoon Network when he was a kid. He's a relatively small guy, quiet, and usually has a placid smile that gives him the face of a dreamer. He seems to spend most of his free time thinking about his wife, who gave birth to their first child, a daughter, shortly before he flew to Kuwait for the invasion. Now, while straightening the wheel after that first turn, Darnold's left arm suddenly feels like it has grown about ten sizes. It's numb and throbbing. "I'm hit!" he yells.

"Shut the fuck up!" Kocher shouts. "You haven't been hit." Kocher can see just by the way he's holding his arm that he is hit. But he wants him to believe he isn't so he'll focus on driving. For a moment, Kocher's power of suggestion works so well, Darnold not only keeps driving, he continues simultaneously firing his M-4 rifle out the side of the Humvee.

Then Darnold wavers. "I am hit!" he insists.

"Okay, you're hit, Darnold," Kocher concedes. "We're gonna fix it. Keep driving."

Enemy fire is now coming at the Humvee from both sides of the street, but the vehicle's primary gunner, Corporal Dan Redman, a twenty-year-old who stands on the .50-cal mount, decides he'll try to bandage Darnold. Redman rips out a dressing pack, and the white bandages immediately flutter away in the wind.

Kocher, who's pumping 203 grenades at muzzle flashes he sees in alleys and windows on both sides of the street, feels the Humvee weaving, then sees Redman's bandages flying from his hands.

"Get your weapon up!" Kocher shouts at Redman. Then Kocher climbs over the roll bar to get at Darnold's left arm. While hanging onto the roll bar, with the vehicle now careening half out of control and Redman's .50-cal blasting inches over his head, Kocher ties off Darnold's arm with a tourniquet (Recon Marines all carry tourniquets on their chest rigs).

Darnold still has his foot on the gas, but his head is turned down, watching the blood soak through the sleeve of his MOPP suit.

"You watch the fucking road!" Kocher shouts. "I'll watch your arm."

They bump out of the town, and twelve hours later Darnold is medevaced to a Kuwait hospital, with a small-caliber bullet lodged between the bones of his forearm. They let the bullet stay where it is, and a couple weeks later they give Darnold the option of going home or rejoining Kocher's team in Baghdad. He goes to Baghdad.

BY THE TIME Colbert's men start off toward Al Gharraf, reports fly over the radio telling us that we are about to drive into an ambush. "Make sure your weapons are red con one," Colbert says, instructing his team members to have their weapons loaded and safeties off. Everyone's guns rattle as they check and recheck them. It's a two-kilometer drive to the entrance of the town. The five Humvees in Bravo Second Platoon are the last to enter. Ours is in the lead. "Gentlemen," Colbert says, turning around and smiling. "You're now going to have to earn your stories."

It's the corniest line I've ever heard. But maybe the humor of it was intended to relax everyone. It works. The weirdest thing about a situation like this is that you actually want to turn the first corner—and not just to get it over with as fast as possible. You want to see what's going to happen next.

We come alongside the walls of the town. Just as Person makes the first turn, a machine gun clatters. It's coming from the high building with long, narrow windows ahead of us. Then, as we complete the turn into town, I see muzzle flashes spitting out from buildings, or gaps in the walls just two meters to our right. While the guns firing at us are set back from the road and we can't see the shooters, the barrels must be extremely close. Their muzzle flashes appear to be floating in front of us, like sparklers. We drive right into them.

Bullets striking the Humvee sound like whips cracking on the roof. Nearly two dozen rounds slam into it almost right away. As the lead vehicle of the platoon, Colbert's is the only one with doors, a roof and light armor. Even so, the windows are open and there are gaps in the shielding. A bullet flies past Colbert's head and smacks into the pillar behind Person. Several more slice through the edges of the door frames.

The shooting continues on both sides. Less than half an hour before, Colbert had been talking about stress reactions in combat. In addition to the embarrassing loss of bodily control that 25 percent of all soldiers experience, other symptoms include time dilation, a sense of time slowing down or speeding up; vividness, a starkly heightened awareness of detail; random thoughts, the mind fixating on unimportant sequences; memory loss; and, of course, your basic feelings of sheer terror.

In my case, hearing and sight become almost disconnected. I see more muzzle flashes next to the vehicle but don't hear them. In the seat beside me, Trombley fires 300 rounds from his machine gun. Ordinarily, if someone were firing a machine gun that close to you, it would be deafening. His gun seems to whisper.

The look on Colbert's face is almost serene. He's hunched over his weapon, leaning out the window, intently studying the walls of the buildings, firing bursts from his M-4 and grenades from the 203 tube underneath the main barrel. I watch him pump in a fresh grenade, and

I think, I bet Colbert's really happy to be finally shooting a 203 round in combat. I remember him kissing the grenade earlier. Random thoughts.

I study Person's face for signs of panic, fear or death. My worry is he'll get shot or freak out and we'll be stuck on this street. But Person seems fine. He's slouched over the wheel, looking through the windshield, an almost blank expression on his face. The only thing different about him is he's not babbling his opinions on Justin Timberlake or some other pussy faggot retard who bothers him.

Trombley turns, smiling gleefully, his red-infected eye shining brightly, and he shouts, "I got one, Sergeant!"

I can't believe that he is so eager to get approval from the team that he is choosing this moment to take credit for his kills.

Colbert ignores him. Trombley eagerly goes back to shooting at people out his window. A gray object zooms toward the windshield and smacks into the roof. My hearing comes back as the Humvee fills with a metal-on-metal scraping sound. Yesterday Colbert had traded out Garza for a Mark-19 gunner from a different team. The guy's name is Corporal Walt Hasser, twenty-three, from Taylorstown, Virginia. He bangs into the roof of the Humvee. Now his legs hang down from the turret, twisted sideways. He's been hit by a steel cable that attackers have stretched across the street to knock down turret gunners. Another cable swipes across the roof.

Colbert calls out, "Walt, are you okay?" Silence. Person turns around, taking his foot off the accelerator.

The vehicle slows and wanders to the left. "Walt?" Person calls.

I grab Hasser's leg by the calf and shake it hard.

"I'm okay!" he says, sounding almost cheerful. He was

temporarily knocked unconscious, but isn't hurt. Person has lost his focus on moving the vehicle forward. We slow to a crawl. Person later says that he was worried one of the cables dropped on the vehicle might still have been caught on Hasser. He didn't want to accelerate and somehow leave him hanging from a light pole by his neck in downtown Al Gharraf.

"Drive, Person!" Colbert shouts.

"Walt's okay?" he asks, apparently not having heard him.

"Yes!" Colbert shouts.

"Go, go, go!" Colbert and I both shout in tandem.

Person finally picks up the pace, and there is silence outside. We are still in the town, but no one seems to be shooting at us.

Colbert is beside himself, laughing and shaking his head. His whole face shines, almost like there's a halo around him. I've seldom seen a happier man.

"Before we start congratulating ourselves," Person says, in his unusual role as the voice of sanity, "we're not out of this yet."

ESPERA, IN HIS HUMVEE about thirty meters behind ours, sees the first wall on the way into the town light up with enemy muzzle flashes. He sees the smoke puffs of their rounds impacting along the roof and doors of Colbert's Humvee, and realizes he will be next. For him, it's all too much stimulus to process. Riding shotgun in a vehicle with no roof or door or armor of any kind, seeing the wall of fire he is about to drive into, his mind goes blank. Muscle memory takes over. He hunches over his M-4 in what he calls the "gangsta curl" and begins shooting. Like most others, he sees very few enemy fighters, just blank walls and muzzle flashes popping like strobe lights.

There are four other Marines in his Humvee. Garza, who had been on our Mark-19, now stands fully upright on the back of Espera's Humvee, manning a .50-cal, which immediately jams. Garza remains at the weapon, frantically trying to recharge it—repeatedly pulling on a lever, pounding it with his fist, squeezing the trigger. Enemy rounds shred through the rucksacks and gear piled on the Humvee and ping off the metal flooring.

Reyes, in the vehicle directly behind them, watches Espera's Humvee getting shot up. Reyes drives for Pappy's team, and beside him Pappy appears calm. As they turn into the fire, Pappy says, sounding almost cavalier, "Here we go, boys."

Because of the tightness of the turn into the town, everyone is going at lazy, parking-lot speeds, maybe ten, fifteen miles an hour. Reyes watches Espera's Humvee veer sharply as gunfire on the right pours into it. Fixating on Garza standing at the broken .50-cal, he marvels at what he later describes as "the expression of fear mixed with determination" on Garza's face as he remains standing, battling the jammed gun.

As soon as they see Hasser knocked down by a cable while on top of Colbert's vehicle, Pappy and Reyes realize they have the only Mark-19 operating to suppress enemy fire. The Mark-19 in their open Humvee is manned by Manimal. Due to the limited training everyone in First Recon has received on this equipment, Manimal has only fired a Mark-19 a few times. He's never done it from a moving Humvee, and it's not easy. Aiming a Mark-19 isn't like a rifle, where you just point it and shoot. The Mark-19 shoots 40mm grenades fed through it on a belt like a machine gun. Each round, about the size of a roll-on deodorant stick, can travel about 2,000 meters (though they're only considered accurate at less than half this range). They can penetrate up to two inches of armor, and when they burst, they spray shrapnel in all directions. Their shrapnel bursts have a "kill radius" of five meters and a "maiming radius" of fifteen. Mark-19 grenade rounds have an elliptical flight path, so after you point it in the proper direction, you then have to tilt the barrel up or down, depending on how far away the target is. This is done with a tiny wheel you have to spin, and doing it from the back of a bouncing Humvee, in a fifty-mile-per-hour dust storm, while people are shooting at you, is about as easy as changing a flat tire on a car parked on a hill during a blizzard. On top of all this, you're not supposed to shoot a Mark-19 (or a single-shot 203, which fires similar rounds) at anything less than seventy-five meters away. The problem is, rounds sometimes bounce back and blow up in your face. But while going into that first turn, Manimal ranges in on targets that are within five to twenty meters distant. He launches more than thirty grenades into the first set of buildings, where enemy forces are concentrated, and collapses the whole side of one of them.

Fick, driving behind Manimal, says later, "I saw all those muzzle flashes along that wall. Then Manimal brought a whole building down. Whatever had been shooting at everyone there wasn't shooting at us. It was just a pile of smoking rubble."

IN COLBERT'S VEHICLE, as soon as we make the T-turn near the end of the town, we hear gunfire ahead. Set back from the road are several squat cinder-block buildings, forming a small industrial district. White puffs of smoke streak out from the buildings: more enemy fire. Person floors the Humvee. Colbert and Trombley start shooting again.

As we swing under a blown-up telephone pole hanging sideways in the street, Trombley glimpses an Arab in black robes crouching by the road near some sandbags. He sprays him with a long burst. "I got another one!" he shouts. "I cut him in half!"

A white haze in the distance marks the end of the city. We fly out onto a sandy plain that looks almost like a beach. The Humvee lurches to a stop, sunk up to its doors in sabka. Sabka is a geological phenomenon peculiar to the Middle East. It looks like desert on top, with a hard crust of sand an inch or so thick that a man can walk on, but break through the crust and beneath it's the La Brea Tar Pits, quicksand made of tar.

We jump out, hunching low. The gunfire all around us sounds like trains banging down railroad tracks. There's a row of Humvees and trucks just south of us, pouring everything they have into the city.

Espera's vehicle halts about twenty meters behind ours. His driver can't figure out why we stopped. Gunshots ring out from the town. Then there's a massive explosion off the back tire of Espera's Humvee—an errant Marine Mark-19 round. Thinking it's enemy fire, a Marine in Espera's vehicle jumps out to take cover in a nearby berm. Espera, "scared as a motherfucker," ponders jumping out and abandoning the Humvee too, but he looks up and sees Garza relentlessly, almost insanely at this point, pulling the slide back and forth on his broken .50-cal, still trying to shoot it. Just before rolling through the town, Garza told Espera, "Whatever happens, just promise me you won't leave me alone."

Espera orders the Marine who jumped out to get back

in. They figure out Colbert's vehicle is stuck, and roll around to the right, avoiding the sabka.

Hunched down by Colbert's vehicle, I am so disoriented at this point that I actually think for a moment that the sandy field we are in is a beach. I turn around, looking for the ocean, then hear Colbert repeating, "We're in a goddamn sabka field."

I think he's saying "soccer field." I can't believe Iraqis would play on sand like this. I'm looking around for the goalposts when Trombley grabs my shoulder. "Get behind me and take cover," he says.

The battalion operations chief runs across the sand, shouting at Colbert, "Abandon your Humvee!" He orders him to set it on fire with an incendiary grenade, yelling, "Thermite the radios!"

Colbert pounds the roof of his Humvee, screaming, "I'm not abandoning this vehicle!"

One of Espera's Marines watching the spectacle from a distance glumly observes, "We're going to die because Colbert's in love with his Humvee."

Still taking sporadic fire from the town, Marines in Bravo run up with shovels and pickaxes to dig it out. Meanwhile, Colbert and Trombley dive under the wheel wells with bolt cutters, slicing away the steel cables—a gift of the defenders of Al Gharraf—wrapped around the axle. They try pulling it with a towing cable attached to another Humvee, but it snaps. Finally, a truck full of Marines from the battalion's maintenance unit rolls up. Support Marines—the POGs so often belittled by Colbert and others—jump out under fire, attach chains to the trapped Humvee and yank it out.

* * *

WE LIMP to a desert encampment a few kilometers away, the shot-up Humvee making grinding and flapping sounds. When the platoon stops at its resting point in the broad, open desert, Marines jump out and embrace one another. Even Colbert becomes emotional, running across the sand, lunging into Reyes and giving him a bear hug.

All the Humvees in Bravo Company are riddled with bullet holes, but Darnold is the only Marine who was hit. Counting the dozens of rounds that sliced through sheet metal, tires and rucksacks, the men can't believe they made it. In retrospect the whole engagement was like one of those cheesy action movies in which the bad guys fire thousands of rounds that all narrowly miss the hero. While everyone else stands around, slapping backs and laughing about all the buildings they shot up or knocked down, Colbert grows pensive. He confesses to me that he had absolutely no feelings going through the city. He almost seems disturbed by this. "It was just like training," he says. "I just loaded and fired my weapon from muscle memory. I wasn't even aware what my hands were doing."

The shamal grows into one of the worst storms anyone has experienced so far in the Middle East. The sky looks like someone picked up a desert and is now turning it upside down on us. Then it rains, which comes down in globs of mud. To top it off, it starts to hail. A junior officer walks a few meters out into this weather to take a dump and becomes hopelessly lost. A team of Recon Marines is organized to go look for him (and he is eventually found, dazed and sheepish, several hours later).

The nice thing about artillery is that, unlike aircraft, it still works in foul weather. Marine batteries begin bombing the town. Colbert and I sit in the vehicle, watching. Through the blackness of the night, orange puffs of artillery bursts are vaguely discernible over the town. Fick slips into the vehicle with a map, to tell us that the name of the town is Al Gharraf. "Good," Colbert says. "I hope they call it El Pancake when we're through with it." Marine artillery crews fire approximately 1,000 rounds into Al Gharraf and the vicinity during the next twelve hours.

Just before turning in to the hole I've dug outside the Humvee, I smell a sickly-sweet odor. During chemical-weapons training before the war, we were taught that some nerve agents emit unusual, fragrant odors. I put on my gas mask and sit in the dark Humvee for twenty minutes before Person tells me what I'm smelling is a cheap Swisher Sweets cigar that Espera is smoking underneath his Humvee.

FOURTEEN

○

MARINES AWAKEN in their holes in the desert outside of Al Gharraf at dawn, March 26, to find the shamal has worn itself out, leaving behind a cold, overcast morning. Fick gathers his team leaders for briefing by the hood of his Humvee. "The good news," he tells them, "is we will be rolling with a lot of ass today. RCT-1 will be in front of us for most of the day. The bad news is, we're going through four more towns like the one we hit yesterday."

Among the Marines this morning, the euphoria of having survived their run through the town has evaporated. Trombley gets into a dispute with another Marine after borrowing his grenade-box "shitter" and returning it with skid marks down the side.

The shitter belongs to Corporal Evan Stafford. A twenty-year-old from Tampa, Florida, Stafford is a white guy whose hair grows so blond fellow Marines call him "Q-tip." When not in uniform, he dresses like Eminem. He identifies so strongly with black culture, notably the music and philosophies of the late Tupac Shakur, that when other Marines use terms like "Nigger Juice" to describe black coffee, or refer to Arabs as "Dune Coons"— as a couple do—Stafford shakes his head and mutters,

"Racist ofay motherfuckers." While the one black guy in the platoon laughs off these slurs as Marine humor, Stafford is always ready to throw down and take on the "oppressors." The few heated arguments that ever take place in the platoon about racism are always between Stafford and another white guy who accuses him of being a "fucking wigger." (The arguments seldom last long, since Stafford and the wigger-hater are also best friends.) When Stafford isn't standing up for his chosen race, he seldom speaks, other than to say, "Screwby." No one's quite certain what "screwby" means, not even Stafford. "I guess it means, 'this sucks,' or 'kind of cool,' " he tells me.

This morning, as Trombley hands him back his fouled shitter, the usually unflappable Stafford seems on the verge of tears. "You shit on my shitter!" Stafford says, inspecting it at arm's length, being careful not to touch the offending marks.

"Wipe 'em off or something," Trombley says, trying to laugh it off.

"No." Stafford stares at the shit stains, struggling to come to grips with the enormity of this offense.

Trombley starts to look worried. Stafford is one of the Marines in the platoon guys like Trombley look up to. Not only is he a full-fledged Recon Marine, but Stafford is one of those people who simply project absolute cool, no matter what—except for now.

"This shitter is the only luxury I have out here." He looks at Trombley, deeply saddened.

"I could try to clean it," Trombley offers.

"Whatever, dog." Stafford cold-shoulders past him. "Screwby."

In the final hour before stepping off, other Marines fix up their Humvees, test-fire their weapons—nearly half of which jammed yesterday—and question their leadership.

"Why the fuck would Ferrando send us through that town?" one Marine in the platoon says, cleaning his M-4. "RCT-1 wouldn't go through there with armor. No doubt Ferrando is basking in the glory of us having made it through. But we only made it because we got lucky."

The lack of information provided to the Marines about their role in the grand scheme of things is beginning to erode morale. They simply don't know that brazenly driving into ambushes is part of the plan.

"I'll tell you why we're being used like this," a Marine in Second Platoon complains. "Our commander is a politician. He'll do anything to kiss the general's ass. The reason Dowdy didn't go through that town yesterday is he probably cares about his men. Ferrando is trying to get promoted on our backs."

On top of this mounting uncertainty, they have to deal with the men in the battalion they view as a waste of rations. This morning they are paid a visit by Casey Kasem. In addition to not having enough batteries for their thermal night optics, another serious omission became clear yesterday when the Mark-19s jammed in the ambush. To operate effectively in a dusty environment, the guns require a specialized lubricant called LSA. The men claim Casey Kasem forgot to bring it on the invasion. Without LSA, the guns jam constantly.

Casey Kasem traipses over and greets the Marines with hearty backslaps. "Outstanding job, gentlemen. The battalion commander thinks we did a stand-up job yesterday. I got some awesome footage outside the town, too," he says, referring to his effort to make a war documentary. Casey Kasem kneels down by Colbert and asks in low, confidential tones, "Are your men having any combat-stress reactions we need to talk about?"

"Nothing that a little LSA wouldn't help," Colbert says.

Casey Kasem frowns. "As you all know, that was out of my hands."

Casey Kasem has made reasonable-sounding arguments to me about why the shortages in the company are a result of matters beyond his control, but the men aren't buying them.

As he walks off, Colbert observes, "People that were just annoying in the rear, out here their behaviour can kill you. It's going to be awkward when we get home. I don't know how I'll be pleasant to these guys when we're all together again back at the office at Pendleton. I'm not going to forget any of this."

We climb into the Humvee. After Person starts the engine, Fick pokes his head in the window, grinning. "Present for you." He passes in a small water bottle, filled with about two inches of amber fluid. "LSA," he says. "I scammed it off some guys in RCT-1."

"Sir, not to get homoerotic about this," Colbert says. "But I could kiss you."

WE LEAVE THE OUTSKIRTS of Al Gharraf at about nine in the morning. Two men standing by the road outside the shattered town grin and give us the thumbs-up. "This place gives me the creeps," Colbert says.

The pattern that's emerged—being greeted with enthusiastic cheers and waves by the people you see beside the roads, then shot at by people you don't see behind walls and berms—is beginning to wear on the Marines. "These guys waving at us are probably the same ones who were trying to kill us yesterday," Person says.

We pick up Route 7 and head north on the two-lane blacktop. Other than Fick's vague instructions about passing through more towns like Al Gharraf, no one knows what the final goal is for this day, or even why they are in the Fertile Crescent. All they know is they must push north until Fick or somebody else tells them to stop.

The team's only concern is to observe the roughly 1,000 meters on either side of the Humvee to make sure there is nobody with a weapon trying to shoot them. The surrounding landscape is a mix of grasslands and dusty plains rippling with berms. The fields are dotted with shepherds and mud-brick dwellings. Every fifty meters or so on both sides of the road there are trenches and sand-bagged machine-gun bunkers—abandoned fortifications.

"RPG fire ahead," Colbert says at about nine-thirty in the morning, passing on the first of many similar reports from the radio.

Colbert's vehicle is the lead for the entire battalion, driving at an average speed of about fifteen miles per hour. Amtracs and other light armored vehicles from RCT-1 are rolling a few hundred meters ahead.

If you were to look at it from the air, you'd see a segmented column of American invasion vehicles—Marines in various units—stretching for several kilometers along the highway. Despite all its disparate elements, the column functions like a single machine, pulverizing anything in its path that appears to be a threat. The cogs that make up this machine are the individual teams in hundreds of vehicles, several thousand Marines scrutinizing every hut, civilian car and berm for weapons or muzzle flashes. The invasion all comes down to a bunch of extremely tense young men in their late teens and twenties, with their fingers on the triggers of rifles and machine guns.

We bump up against Amtracs 150 meters ahead pouring machine-gun fire into some huts. "They're schwacking some guys with RPGs," Colbert says.

Wild dogs run past.

"We ought to shoot some of these dogs," Trombley says, eyeing the surrounding fields over the top of his SAW.

"We don't shoot dogs," Colbert says.

"I'm afraid of dogs," Trombley mumbles.

I ask him if he was ever attacked by a dog when he was little.

"No," he answers. "My dad was once. The dog bit him, and my dad jammed his hand down the dog's throat and ripped up his stomach. I did have a dog lunge at me once on the sidewalk. I just threw it on its side, knocked the wind out of him. My aunt had a little dog. I was playing with it with one of those laser lights. The dog chased it into the street and got hit by a car. I didn't mean to kill it."

"Where did we find this guy?" Person asks.

We drive on.

"I like cats," Trombley offers. "I had a cat that lived to be sixteen. One time he ripped a dog's eye out with his claw."

We pass dead bodies in the road again, men with RPG tubes by their sides, then more than a dozen trucks and cars burned and smoking. You find most torched vehicles have charred corpses nearby, occupants who crawled out and made it a few meters before expiring, with their grasping hands still smoldering. We pass another car with a small, mangled body outside it. It's another child, face-down, and the clothes are too ripped to determine the gender. Seeing this is almost no longer a big deal. Since the shooting started in Nasiriyah forty-eight hours ago, firing weapons and seeing dead people has become almost routine.

"Whoa!" Trombley says. "That guy in that car was shot through the stomach. He just looked at me, then raised his arm, like he was asking for help. He looked at me right there," Trombley says, pointing to his inflamed eye.

I see the car Trombley's talking about, a bullet-riddled sedan by the road, doors hanging open, with at least one body in it.

"He was unarmed," Trombley says. "So I didn't shoot him."

I imagine that man in the car, an entire life lived, and the last thing in the world he sees is the face of an eager nineteen-year-old with a red, infected eye looking at him down the barrel of a SAW.

LATE IN THE MORNING Colbert's team reaches the outskirts of the first big town we are passing through: Ash Shatrah. We pull even with Marine artillery guns pounding away, their snouts blazing flames and smoke. One of the guns has the words BOB MARLEY stenciled along the barrel, a somewhat incongruous tribute to the bard of Jah Love and reefer.

"Thump 'em, boys," Colbert says darkly as he watches them fire. They're striking targets in and around Ash Shatrah, prepping it for our drive through. We wait for several minutes, then go.

The battalion's plan is to sprint past the town as fast as possible. With Colbert's vehicle in the lead, we speed up to about forty-five miles an hour. While driving, Person reaches around and hands me his M-4.

"Put it out the window," he says.

I look at him.

"What do you think? You're just gonna eat all our food, drink all our water for free?"

I place the rifle on my lap but find it distracting. All

I can think about are images of Geraldo Rivera waving his pistol around in reports he filed from Afghanistan, bragging about how he hoped to cap Osama. While rolling into Ash Shatrah, my biggest fear isn't enemy fire, it's that some reporter's going to see me holding an M-4 and I'll look like a jackass.

The town is set far back from the road. No fire comes from it. The most overwhelming impression Ash Shatrah makes is that it is one of the smelliest places I have ever encountered. From 200 meters away the town stinks like the inside of a garbage can. We drive four kilometers through it, and I pass the M-4 back to Person. I hand it to him barrel first, with a round in the chamber and the safety off, causing him to rethink his policy of arming the reporter.

OUTSIDE OF ASH SHATRAH we link up with a unit of Amtracs and other armored Marine vehicles parked near a rural hamlet. It's a cluster of three or four buildings 400 meters off the road, nestled in green pastures, with some palm trees behind them. Marines in the Amtracs stopped because they thought they took shots from one of the houses.

Now Marines are out on berms watching the house through binoculars and scopes. Several sniper teams in Bravo join them. Kocher in Third Platoon observes a "mom with two kids hiding in the back of the house, nervously peeping out."

The Marines study the house for forty minutes. Surrounded by verdant fields, with the rare quiet of all the Humvee engines having been shut off, the morning feels peaceful.

Then a 25mm Bushmaster on one of the armored

vehicles up the road begins pouring rounds into the house. The women and children Recon Marines had been observing through their optics disappear in a cloud of dust, as the Bushmaster rounds blast the adobe walls.

Colbert jumps out of the Humvee. "What are they shooting at?"

"There's civilians in there!" several Recon observers yell at once.

Colbert picks up his radio handset and shouts, "Tell those guys to cease fire! They're shooting civilians." But it's a fruitless effort. Even though the vehicle doing most of the firing is only 100 meters or so ahead, First Recon Battalion has no ability to reach it on the radio.

Now a dozen or more rifles and machine guns in the nearby armored units come alive, crackling and sending red streaks of tracer rounds into the entire hamlet.

Marines with mortars jump off a tracked vehicle in front of us, yelling and cursing. They're in such a rush to attack the village, one Marine falls off the vehicle, landing on his ass. They launch a volley of 60mm mortars, which fall short, exploding in the field immediately in front of us.

Colbert throws down his radio headset and stands outside his Humvee, screaming, "Cease fire!" The Marines shooting into the village 100 meters up from us continue unabated.

Then, behind us, Encino Man races up in his Humvee. He jumps out, so eager to get in the fight, it seems, he forgets to unplug his radio headset, which jerks his head back as the cord, still attached to the dash unit, tightens.

"Jesus Christ! There's fucking civilians in that house! Cease fire!" Colbert says.

Encino Man pops off a 203 grenade that falls wildly short of the house. Colbert, like other Marines in Bravo, is furious. Not only do they believe Encino Man is firing on civilians, but the guy hasn't even been able to range his 203.

Colbert gets back in the Humvee, trying to rationalize the events outside that have spiraled beyond his control: "Everyone's just tense. Some Marine took a shot, and everyone has just followed suit."

Outside, Marines' heavy 81mm mortars begin to land on the homes. They make a sort of crunching sound as they detonate, sending black plumes over the huts.

"They finally got good effects on target," Kocher says, watching them obliterate the hamlet.

THERE'S NO TIME to sit around contemplating the destruction of the little village. First Recon is ordered north again toward a town called Ar Rifa. We pass forty or fifty refugees streaming south, some on bicycles. A massive fire about a kilometer up the road sends flames and black smoke 100 meters or more into the sky. The day is chilly and gray. There's no wind, but the air is heavy with dust particles. They coat the windshield like frost. If you wipe your finger on it, a few minutes later the mark is covered over again with powder. Through this fog we hear AK rifles cracking off rounds ahead. The convoy bumps to a halt. We are several hundred meters south of Ar Rifa.

The two Marines who ride in the back of Fick's Humvee, which is configured sort of like a pickup truck with a canvas top over the back, stand by the tailgate singing Nelly's "Hot in Herre" over and over.

One of the combat-stress reactions not discussed in their training is singing. A lot of Marines, when waiting for minutes or hours in a position where they expect an ambush or other trouble, will get a song stuck in their heads. Often they'll sing it or chant the words almost as if they are saying Hail Marys.

The Marines' choice of a Nelly song in the back of Fick's vehicle shows the hip-hop influence of Q-tip Stafford. He rides there with nineteen-year-old Private First Class John Christeson, the newest guy in the platoon. The two of them spend twelve to twenty hours a day bouncing around in the back of the truck. Neither is sure when they both hit upon "Hot in Herre" as their combat song, but they were singing it yesterday while rolling into the ambush at Al Gharraf.

Now waiting on the ground by Fick's truck outside of Ar Rifa, Christeson observes a house 500 meters in the distance, barely discernible across the haze and scrub brush. He's chanting the lyrics, "Cuz I feel like bustin' loose and I feel like touchin you/And can't nobody stop the juice so baby . . . ," when he spots three to four men moving low. They're at least 300 meters away, moving closer to the Humvee, using the vegetation for cover. One seems to be carrying an RPG tube.

Other than a family cruise through the Caribbean, this is Christeson's first trip out of the United States. He grew up in Lebanon, Illinois, with parents still married—a dad who works for the state college and a mom who works at a title loan company. Even though he was shot at yesterday in Al Gharraf, the whole place seems unreal to him. It's the mud huts. He can't believe people in the twenty-first century actually live in huts with goats and sheep all around. Christeson grew up with computers, playing *Doom*, a game that to him is almost ancient history. After high school he received an appointment to go to the Naval Academy at Annapolis, but in the wake of 9/11 he decided to become a grunt Marine to do something for his country—and to get in on the action. Up until the invasion, his closest brush with history was the day Jared Fogle, the guy who lost 300 pounds on the Subway Diet, came to his town, and Christeson got to meet him in person. "I thought if I punched him in the face I would be on TV," he says, recalling the historic encounter. "But he wasn't as big as I thought he'd be, for someone you see all the time on TV."

Now, he's watching Fedayeen stalk his vehicle. "I think they've got an RPG," he says, trying to get a line on them through the sights of his SAW.

"Screwby," Stafford replies.

"Gunny!" Christeson shouts to Gunny Wynn. "Those men might have an RPG."

Gunny Wynn runs up, raises his binoculars and sees what looks to be a man setting up an RPG in some scrub. "Light 'em up!"

Christeson is so excited he's not sure he heard Gunny Wynn right. Even though he fired several dozen rounds into Al Gharraf, all he saw was buildings, dark spots and muzzle flashes. He's never before pulled the trigger on humans like this, cold.

Gunny Wynn repeats: "Light 'em the fuck up. They have RPGs."

Christeson hugs his SAW and squeezes off a fifteen- to twenty-round burst at the closest of the three men. They run south, one of them limping, heading toward a line of palm trees. Christeson rips out another burst.

Fick runs up to his side. "Keep shooting," he says.

Christeson blazes away.

"You're shooting too high," Fick says, calmly now, like he's teaching a kid how to cast a fishing rod. Christeson is still firing bursts toward the tree line where the men in the field took cover when the platoon is ordered forward.

He jumps in the truck, while Stafford provides covering fire with his 203 and M-4. As they bounce onto the road, Christeson fires the last of nearly 200 rounds toward the RPG team.

The war is suddenly real to him. "You know what?" he says to Stafford. "We were just fighting actual guerrillas."

"Screwby."

THE CONVOY HALTS just 200 meters up from where Fick's crew engaged the RPG team. That huge fire we saw earlier was an electrical substation. It's now a hundred meters in front of Colbert's vehicle. The flames have subsided; now it spews an acrid smoke that hangs over the area.

We are just fifty meters from the edge of a large, grim town. The outer buildings form a wall on the other side of the highway. There's a broad street into the city, but defenders have cut down palm trees, dragged the trunks across it and piled it with rubble, making barricades. Rifles and machine guns crackle intermittently from within.

But directly across from Colbert's vehicle, no one sees any muzzle flashes. All we see are hundreds of doors and windows, dark gaps in the stucco buildings, places for bad guys to hide.

"Get out of the vehicle," Colbert says.

Everyone takes cover on the ground, setting up their weapons. The whole platoon is out in the open here, high on the elevated road, with a hostile town on one side and fields on the other where there is believed to have been at least one RPG team operating. "I don't know what the fuck we're doing here," Colbert says.

Fick trots over, keeping his head low, staying behind Humvees as much as he can to avoid the intermittent sniper fire. Colbert asks him what the orders are.

"I don't fucking know either. He just told us to pull over," Fick says, referring to his commander, Encino Man.

In a combat zone, military convoys aren't supposed to just aimlessly pull over. When they stop, someone is supposed to issue orders—tell the men where to orient their vehicles, their weapons, whether to turn their engines off or keep them running. All of these details are supposed to flow down from command.

But right now command in Bravo Company is in a state of confusion. A few moments ago, Fick radioed Encino Man about contact with a possible RPG team. Encino Man immediately ordered everyone to pull over, without issuing any further directions.

Encino Man and Casey Kasem are now huddled by Doc Bryan's Humvee, trying to figure out what do about the RPG team. Even though Christeson is sure he wounded at least one of the guys, and his fire did push them back into a tree line, Encino Man and Casey Kasem seem to have become obsessed with the possibility of the RPG team reappearing and attacking the company.

Fick runs up to Encino Man and asks him, "What are we doing here?"

Fick's concern is that the company is spread out willy-nilly along the highway directly across from a town of about 75,000, some of whose occupants are now shooting at his Marines.

Encino Man ignores him. He and Casey Kasem are poring over a map, studying coordinates to call in an artillery strike on the suspected position of the suspected RPG team.

Doc Bryan is growing alarmed. "Sir, I don't like this," he says to Fick. Nodding toward Encino Man and Casey Kasem, he adds, "When those two put their heads together it's fucking dangerous."

Ever since Casey Kasem almost shot Doc Bryan a few nights earlier, he and the other Recon Marines have grown extremely wary of the man. And today the memory of seeing Encino Man trying to fire a grenade into a house with civilians in it is still fresh in the Marines' minds.

"Sir," Doc Bryan says to Fick, "we're fifty meters from a hostile city, and those two jackasses are worrying about a possible guy with an RPG three hundred meters from here."

Fick confronts Encino Man. "If you don't tell us what we're doing here, we should get the fuck out now."

"I'm calling in a fire mission," Encino Man says, still not explaining what he wants Fick's platoon to do on the highway.

Part of the reason Encino Man is so preoccupied with calling in the artillery fire mission is he's never done this before in combat. Now he tells the men the exact co-ordinates he's planning to bring the artillery down on.

Doc Bryan and Lovell use a laser designator to measure the distance from their Humvee to the spot where Encino Man intends to direct the artillery strike, and it's just over 200 meters distant.

Yesterday, when Capt. Patterson called in a danger-close artillery strike near his Marines, the distance was 300 meters, his men were behind berms and walls, and they were at the time under heavy enemy machine-gun fire.

Right now, Doc Bryan's team and the rest of the platoon are on an open road, with nothing between them and the place where the artillery, if called, will splash down. They see no enemy where Encino Man is trying to call in the fire mission, and on top of this, they are taking fire, but it's coming from the other side of the road. Doc

Bryan can't stand it any longer. He runs up to Encino Man and shouts, "You can't do this. That's a danger-close strike."

"What's 'danger close'?" Encino Man asks.

Lovell, a few meters away, cites from a military manual he keeps in his Humvee. "Danger close is an artillery strike within six hundred meters of friendly forces."

"You dumb motherfucker," one of the enlisted men shouts. "The most boot-fucking Marine knows danger close!"

Fick grabs the radio handset from Encino Man in an attempt to stop him from calling in the strike. Gunny Wynn now tries to intercede. "Sir, this is fucked up. Let's forget about the fire mission and get the platoons in a defensive perimeter. Then we can worry about the RPG team."

One thing about Encino Man is that he's stubborn. Having lost face in front of the men, he digs in deeper. He takes the handset back from Fick and attempts to call in the strike. But it never happens. There are protocols for calling in a Marine artillery strike, and Encino Man, it turns out, doesn't know them. When the officer on the end of the line receives Encino Man's confused request, he turns it down.

"For once," Doc Bryan observes, "we were saved by the man's incompetence."

AFTER THE ARTILLERY STRIKE is scratched, Encino Man finally issues orders. The Marines are to remain by the road—on the south end of Ar Rifa—and form defensive lines as best they can in this vulnerable place. Their job is to prevent enemy forces from advancing from the town and attacking RCT-1's convoys now rolling past on Route 7.

Enemy fighters in the town continue to take potshots. Person is manning the SAW set up outside the Humvee when he spots muzzle flashes coming from a window, fortified with barbed wire and sandbags, seventy-five meters away. He shoots into it, and Marines up the road join in. They saturate it with Mark-19 rounds, bringing down a wall of the building.

"Damn sucka!" Person says, watching dust rise from the partially destroyed structure.

Wild dogs run out from a gap in the town's walls. Women and children stand in an alley beside the building the Marines just hit. A rooster starts to cockledoodledo even though it's afternoon. There are several loud bangs behind us. Marine snipers set up facing the fields to the rear have no idea what caused the explosions.

Fick approaches, sprinting to the Humvee, low to the ground to avoid enemy snipers, and smiles when he reaches me behind Colbert's vehicle. Both he and Gunny Wynn are being threatened with disciplinary action because of the incident with Encino Man an hour ago. Fick has been told he might be relieved of his command for "disobeying orders." (The Marine who actually called the commander a "dumb motherfucker" never receives reprimand.)

Nevertheless, Fick has grown suddenly gabby. He crouches behind a Humvee tire beside me and says, "This truly illustrates how safety is entirely relative." Then, while machine guns rip and sniper rifles bang up and down the line, he launches into a discussion more appropriate for an all-night cram session at the Dartmouth library than for a low-intensity firefight.

"Most people in America right now probably think Iraq is a dangerous country." He gestures to a patch of dirt in the open, two meters from the Humvee. "Now, if I were to stand up there, I would probably get killed. But to us, behind this Humvee it's pretty safe. So relatively speaking, to us Iraq is a safe country right here behind this tire. I feel pretty safe here. Do you feel safe?"

"Pretty safe, I guess."

"See!" He laughs. "If you were to call somebody at home right now and say, 'Hey, I'm in Iraq right now. I'm with a handful of Marines. We're isolated on the south end of a hostile city, and there are people shooting at us on both sides, but I feel pretty safe right now because I'm on this patch of dirt behind a Humvee,' they'd think you were nuts." He laughs. "People don't understand how relative everything is on the battlefield." He laughs again. "Or it could be we invent this relativism in our minds to comfort ourselves." He taps the wheel well. "Because we both know this Humvee isn't going to stop an RPG or any number of other very bad things that could happen here at any moment."

Espera crawls up. "Sir, my men are all worried about the people in that ville organizing mass RPG volleys against us, like they did to those Amtracs we saw blown on the way up here."

"Just keep your men dispersed from the vehicles," Fick says.

"Roger that, sir," Espera says. "But we're still worried, sir."

"We're going to be here for a long time," Fick says. "I don't like it. But there's nothing you or I or anyone can do about it."

There are several loud cracks behind us—rounds from enemy snipers.

"Oh, sweet Jesus!" Colbert says, highly annoyed. He's lying on the ground, glassing the city through binoculars, listening to the company radio network on a portable unit. He turns to Fick. "Sir, our great commander," he says, referring to Encino Man, "just had the wherewithal to inform me there seem to be enemy snipers about. He suggests we ought to be on the lookout for them."

Person laughs. "Brad," he says, calling Colbert by his first name. "Check it out, over there." He points to a spot near the barricades into the city.

Colbert turns his binoculars in the direction Person is pointing.

"Person," he asks, "are those ducks . . . ?"

"Yeah, they're fucking." Person laughs.

TWO KILOMETERS up the road a group of townspeople waving white flags climb around the barricades carrying a five- or six-year-old girl with a sucking chest wound. Capt. Patterson's Marines in Alpha Company have been taking sporadic mortar hits all afternoon at their position on the northern end of Ar Rifa. But seeing the townspeople come out carrying the small body with limp, dangling legs, the Marines hold their fire.

Despite all the stories circulating among Marines of Iraqis posing as civilians and using false surrenders to lure them into ambushes, a corpsman and several enlisted Marines race up to the street to treat the wounded girl.

Patterson summons a translator, and the townspeople tell him that the girl was shot by Saddam loyalists. They say there are 1,500 to 2,000 of them in the city, with many of them concentrated around one building. Patterson checks the location of the building on his map. It corresponds with preexisting intelligence that had identified it as a Baath Party headquarters. He calls an artillery strike, with high-explosive (HE) rounds capable of destroying large structures. The first rounds scream in and fall 300 meters short of the target. Landing as they do in a dense urban area, Patterson is pretty certain they caused civilian casualties—and later this suspicion is corroborated when he hears ambulance sirens wailing in the city.

But Patterson's men adjust several more rounds onto the correct target, wiping it out. News that the Americans have destroyed the main Baath headquarters in Ar Rifa appears to spread quickly through the town.

Within several minutes of the final artillery blasts, people fill the streets and rooftops across the city. What appears to be happening is almost a textbook case of liberation. A show of American force, coupled with a somewhat pinpoint hit on a military headquarters, has caused a rout of hostile forces. Shooting on Marine positions ceases almost immediately.

Across from Colbert's position we see the outpouring of people. Initially, Marines who've been hunkered down receiving sniper fire and occasionally shooting up buildings across the street are wary. Old women in black robes rise up on rooftops where previously Marines had been trying to pick off enemy snipers.

"Don't shoot the old ladies," Colbert warns his team.

Then young men waving white flags walk onto the road. Bravo Company sends out its translator to greet them. The translator is a seriously overweight nineteen-year-old Kuwaiti who goes by the nickname "Meesh." I've gotten to know Meesh in the past few days. Beneath his MOPP suit he wears a tie-dyed Grateful Dead T-shirt and has a long ponytail he folds under his helmet. He speaks in colloquial American English and is a heavy dope smoker. The whole invasion he's been bumming because the night before we left Kuwait he got so stoned that, as he says, "Dude, I lost all my chronic in my tent. I'm hurtin'."

Despite his MTV American English, Meesh is Kuwaiti to the core. The first time I try speaking with him he refuses to talk until I bribe him with several packs of Marlboro Reds. The Marine utility vest he wears, designed to carry up to sixty pounds of ammunition, is instead loaded with baksheesh. Meesh hates Iraqis, who he claims killed one of his relatives during their invasion of Kuwait, and every time he interrogates civilians or soldiers on behalf of the Marines, he forces them to hand over any cigarettes, cash, valuable trinkets, liquor or beer they might be carrying. (Under Saddam's secular rule, Iraq operated numerous breweries and distilleries.) Given the fact that Meesh is invariably backed up by heavily armed Marines, Iraqis eagerly shower him with tribute. Meesh carries so many bottles of beer, liquor, cigarettes and other sundries in his vest, he looks like a walking kiosk.

The thing about Meesh that earns him the undying respect of Marines is his total obliviousness to danger. Outside Ar Rifa, he walks alone on the highway to greet the townspeople who've come out with surrender flags. Behind him, Marines tensely watch through their scopes and gun sights, half expecting Meesh to go down in a hail of ambush fire.

But after several minutes in which he stands there, chatting with townspeople, and no one shoots him, several officers join him, among them Fick.

"What did they say?" Fick asks.

Meesh belches. It takes him a long time to answer. Meesh does everything at a sclerotic pace. Even rolling his eyeballs to look at you seems to tax him. He builds up his strength, taking several drags from the Marlboro hanging from his lip, and says, "The people of Ar Rifa are grateful to be liberated and welcome the Americans as friends."

It's the stock answer Meesh always gives after speaking to Iraqis. Meesh claims he works for the CIA—"I got into some trouble in Kuwait, working for a 'party,' which is what we call drug gangs in my country, but I have some friends in the royal family, and they hooked me up with the CIA"—and his translations always seem to conform to a script provided by his handlers.

"That's all they said?" Fick asks. "You spoke to those guys for ten minutes!"

"They say they don't want us to leave the town," Meesh adds. "They're afraid as soon as we go the Baath dudes are going to come back and kill them."

Ar Rifa is another Shia city that rose up against Saddam after President George H. W. Bush's call to rebellion in 1991. As in Nasiriyah, the uprising was put down, and the citizens were treated to months of bloody reprisals.

Maj. Gen. Mattis's strategy of racing north as fast as possible precludes putting forces inside towns after they've been "liberated." The Marines or the CIA or who-ever is actually in charge of this operation at Ar Rifa have come up with a stopgap measure to protect the citizens. Right now, Meesh is the sole agent responsible for executing this plan.

He hands out infrared chemlites to the men who've come out of the town waving white flags. Their job tonight, after the Marines depart, is to put these chemlites on top of buildings and other locations inside the city occupied by Baath Party members or Fedayeen. American aircraft will then fly over the town and bomb any position they see illuminated by the infrared chemlites.

Fick is as intrigued by this plan as I am. After Meesh distributes the chemlites, we both accost him. I bribe him with several more packs of Marlboros, and Fick asks him, "How do you know those guys aren't just going to put those chemlites on the homes of people they owe money to, or have some other grudge against?"

"Believe me," Meesh says. "They're good dudes. We can trust 'em." He proffers a bottle to Fick. "Beer?"

"No thanks, Meesh," Fick says.

"Yeah," Meesh says. "It's not the good shit. It's local brewed."

As the sun drops, muezzins call the faithful to prayer from minarets and loudspeakers across Ar Rifa. Then the city erupts with celebratory AK fire. We sit inside Colbert's vehicle eating cold MREs in the darkness. In recent days, rations were cut from three to two meals per day. There is a silver lining to having your rations cut. When you eat MREs in abundance, they taste foul. Now, with everyone having a constant edge of hunger, meals that once tasted like dried kitchen sponges in chemical sauce are pretty tasty. Everyone plows through the ratfuck bag, eagerly retrieving meals like Chicken Jambalaya and Vegetarian Alfredo that a week ago no one would have touched.

We are happily eating when, from behind us on the highway, we hear the sound of rolling gunfire. All of us look out into the darkness and see dozens of orange tracer rounds spewing out from both sides of an approaching U.S. military convoy.

"Everybody get down!" Colbert shouts. We dive to the floor of the Humvee. The American trucks pass, mistakenly discharging a torrent of automatic weapons fire toward our Humvee and those in the rest of the company. Tracers skim over the hood. A high-caliber American round slices through the armor plates, penetrating the vehicle behind Trombley and me. The shooting lasts about twenty seconds. "It's fucking friendlies," Colbert says, uncurling himself from the floor.

After dark, the Marine Humvees put out infrared strobe lights invisible to the naked eye. Their rhythmic flashing is designed to be seen through NVGs, to help other drivers locate the position of your vehicle. The problem is, to nervous, inexperienced personnel the infrared strobes look like enemy muzzle flashes. Fick later finds out that we were shot at by Navy reservist surgeons on their way to set up a mobile shock-trauma unit on the road ahead. "Those were fucking doctors who a few weeks ago were doing nose and tit jobs in Santa Fe Springs," Fick tells his men, laughing. "The fucking POGest of the POGs. Luckily, they're not the best sharpshooters."

Several Humvees up the line are hit, but no Marines are injured. Within minutes of the latest near-death episode, Trombley is snoring, sound asleep.

FIFTEEN

○

AFTER THE FRIENDLY-FIRE incident outside Ar Rifa on the evening of March 26, Fick pokes his head into Colbert's vehicle to inform him that the Marines' night is just getting started. During the next six hours the battalion is going to race across open roads and desert trails, advancing twenty-five to thirty kilometers behind enemy lines, in order to set up observation on an Iraqi military airfield near a town called Qalat Sukhar. All of this has to be done as quickly as possible. A British parachute brigade is planning to seize the airfield at dawn. But reports have come in from U.S. spy planes that the airfield may be defended with AAA batteries and T-72 tanks. First Recon will go there to make sure the way is clear for the British.

The mission is plagued with snafus from the start. A battalion supply truck becomes stuck in the mud outside Ar Rifa. First Recon halts for forty-five minutes, while higher-ups debate whether or not to extract the truck. They decide to leave it and come back for it later. Shortly after we pull out, the truck is looted, hit by at least one RPG and burned to the ground. It had been carrying the battalion's main supply of food rations. As a result of this incident, everyone will be reduced to about one and a half meals per day until we reach Baghdad.

By midnight we have been driving for several hours. For the last forty-five minutes the Humvee has been rocking up and down like a boat. We are in the dark on a field covered in berms, each about a meter high, like waves. Despite Colbert's efforts to track the battalion's route using maps and frequent radio checks with Fick, he has no idea where we are.

"Dude, I am so lost right now," Colbert says. It's a rare admission of helplessness, a function of fatigue setting in after ninety-six hours of little or no sleep since the shooting started at Nasiriyah.

"I see where we're going, don't worry," Person says. His speech is clipped and breathless. He's tweaking on Ripped Fuel tablets, which he's been gobbling for the past several days. "Do you remember the gay dog episode on *South Park*, when Sparky runs away cause he's, like, humping other dogs and shit?"

"Fuck yeah," Colbert says. He and Person repeat the tagline from the episode: " 'Hello there, little pup. I'm Big Gay Al!' "

"They opened a gay club in the town where I'm from in Michigan," Trombley says. "People trashed it every night. They had to close it after a month."

"Yeah," Person says, a note of belligerence in his voice. "When I get back I'm gonna start a gay club. I'll call it the Men's Room. There will be, like, a big urinal with a two-way mirror everyone pisses against. It will be, like, facing the bar, so when everyone's drinking there will be, like, these big cocks pissing at them."

"Person," Colbert says. "Give it a rest, please."

* * *

AT THREE-THIRTY in the morning on March 27, the battalion reaches the edge of the enemy airfield, stopping about two kilometers from it. The Humvees set up a defensive perimeter. Colbert's team pulls down the cammie nets and we dig Ranger graves in the darkness. It's nearly freezing. Most of the Marines are kept up on watch. Two Recon teams are pushed out on foot to observe the airfield for what they have been told is the coming British paratrooper landing. But they are called back at dawn.

Sometime around six in the morning First Recon's commander, Lt. Col. Ferrando, receives a phone call from Maj. Gen. Mattis asking him what's on the airfield. The British are set to begin their air assault at seven-thirty. The latest reports from American observation planes say there are up to four T-72 tanks on the field and perhaps several batteries of AAA, enough to wreak havoc on the British. Ferrando is forced to tell Mattis he still doesn't know what's on the airfield. His Recon teams were unable to reach it within the allotted time.

Ferrando tells Mattis his battalion will seize the field. It's a bold decision, since Ferrando believes that if reports of armor on the field are true, the mission will result in "tens or hundreds of casualties among my men."

AT SIX-TWENTY in the morning, Colbert, who'd crawled into his Ranger grave ninety minutes earlier to catch some shut-eye, is awakened by Fick. "We are assaulting the airfield," he tells him. "We have ten minutes to get on the field."

The Marines race around the Humvee, pulling down the cammie nets, throwing gear inside. It's a clear, cold morning. Frost comes out of everyone's mouths as they jump in the vehicle, weapons clattering. Everyone's fumbling around, still trying to wake up and shake off that ache that comes from sleeplessness. In my case, just seeing the morning light hurts. "Well," Colbert tells his team. "We're assaulting an airfield. I know as much about this as any of you do." He laughs, shaking his head. "Person, do we have a map?"

By six twenty-eight the roughly forty vehicles from Alpha, Bravo and Charlie companies begin rolling out of the encampment to assault the airfield.

STILL EXTREMELY WORRIED about the prospect of his men encountering armor or AAA on the field, Ferrando changes the ROE. He radios his company commanders and tells them, "Everyone on the field is declared hostile."

In Vietnam the U.S. military sometimes designated certain areas "free-fire zones." Because of the large numbers of civilian casualties produced by these, the term fell out of vogue. Ferrando's order amounts to the same thing. Declaring everyone hostile means the Marines may or should shoot any human they encounter. When Capt. Patterson is issued the order, he says, "There's no fucking way I'm going to pass that to my men." In his mind, he later explains, turning the airfield into a free-fire zone does not help his men. Their problem is physics. AAA guns and tanks outrange and overpower everything they have on the Humvees. If his Marines race onto the field cutting people down, regardless of whether or not they're armed, it's not going to help them battle heavy guns. Besides this, in Patterson's opinion, Ferrando "doesn't have the right to change the Rules of Engagement." Patterson tells his top enlisted man, "Don't pass the word of the changed ROE over the radio. Our guys are smart enough to evaluate the situation within the existing ROE."

In Colbert's vehicle we are getting up to about forty miles per hour when word comes over the radio of the change in the ROE. "Everyone is declared hostile on the field," Colbert shouts. "You see anybody, shoot 'em!" he adds.

Colbert is multitasking like a madman. He's got his weapon out the window, looking for targets. He's on the radio, communicating with Fick and the other teams. They're trying to figure out how to contact the A-10 attack jets overhead. The Marines don't have the right comms to reach them. "I don't want to get schwacked by the A-10s," Colbert shouts. "They're goddamn Army. They shoot Marines." (As they did three days ago at Nasiriyah.) On top of this, Colbert has maps out, and is trying to figure out where the airfield actually is with respect to the road we are driving down. His maps indicate there are fences around the field. He and Person debate whether to smash through the fences or to stop and cut through them with bolt cutters.

"The bolt cutters are under the seat in the back," Person says. "We can't get at them."

"Smash through the fence, then."

Next to me in the rear seat, Trombley says, "I see men running two hundred meters. Ten o'clock!"

"Are they armed?" Colbert asks.

"There's something," Trombley says. "A white truck."

"Everyone's declared hostile," Colbert says. "Light them the fuck up."

Trombley fires two short bursts from the SAW. "Shooting motherfuckers like it's cool," he says, amused with himself.

A Marine machine gun behind us kicks in.

I look out Trombley's window and see a mud hut and a bunch of camels. The camels are running madly in all directions, some just a couple of meters from our Humvee. I can't figure out what the hell Trombley was shooting at.

Hasser standing in the turret, begins pounding the roof of the Humvee, screaming "Fuck!"

"What is it?" Colbert shouts.

"The Mark-19 is down!" Hasser yells. "Jammed!"

"My Mark-19 is down!" Colbert screams on the radio. Being the lead vehicle of the company, racing onto an airfield to fight tanks and AAA guns without a heavy weapon is a disaster in the making. "I repeat, my Mark-19 is down!"

It's the first time Fick has ever heard Iceman lose control on comms. "Calm the fuck down," Fick orders Colbert. "I'm putting Team Two in front."

THOUGH MARINES in Bravo Company have fired only three short machine-gun bursts so far, Captain America, rolling directly behind us, gets on the comms, screaming, "They're shooting everywhere! We are under fire!"

Seemingly caught up in the spirit of the free-fire zone, Captain America sticks his East German AK out the window and begins shooting. Riding in the back of Captain America's Humvee is twenty-one year-old Lance Corporal Andy Crosby. He sees a hut outside with people and animals. "What the fuck are you doing?" he yells at his commander. But Captain America continues blazing away. At one point, ricochets from his weapon ping off scrap metal by the road and zing back toward his men in the Humvee. "We're getting ricochets!" Crosby shouts.

*　*　*

THERE'S NO FENCE at the airfield. It's just long swaths of concrete tarmac concealed behind low berms. We don't even see the airfield until we've nearly driven on top of it. There are weeds growing out of cracks in the tarmac and bomb craters in the middle. There's nothing on it. The Humvees fan out and race into the bermed fields, searching for enemy positions.

"Oh, my God!" Person laughs. "He's got his bayonet out."

Captain America runs across the field ahead of his Humvee, bayonet fixed on his M-16, ready to savage enemy forces. He turns every few paces and dramatically waves his men forward, like an action hero.

"He thinks he's Rambo," Person guffaws. "That retard is in charge of people?"

We stop. Marines observe low huts far in the distance that could be either primitive barracks or homes. Captain America runs up to Kocher's team and shouts, "Engage the buildings!"

Redman, the .50-cal gunner, looks at him, deadpanning to hide his contempt. A veteran of Afghanistan, he's a big, placid guy and talks like a surfer even though he's originally from Phoenix, Arizona. "Dude," Redman says, "that building is four thousand meters away." He adds a remark that pretty much anyone in boot camp knows. "The range on my .50-cal is two thousand meters."

"Well, move into position, then. Engage it." He stalks off.

They roll forward. Kocher observes the building through binoculars. "No, Redman. We're not engaging. There's women and children inside."

We roll back from the field. A-10s cut down low

directly overhead. The British never come. The Marines beat them to the field. It's a beautiful, clear day. In the sunlight—the first we've seen in days—dust, impregnated in everyone's MOPP suits, curls off like cigarette smoke. Everyone looks like they're smoldering. "Gentlemen, we just seized an airfield," Colbert says. "That was pretty ninja."

SIXTEEN

○

AN HOUR LATER, the Marines have set up a camp off the edge of the airfield. They are told they will stay here for a day or longer. For the first time in a week, many of the Marines take their boots and socks off. They unfurl cammie nets for shade and lounge beside their Humvees. The dirt here, augmented by a luxuriously thick piling of dung from camels who graze on the local scrubweed, is pillow-soft. Distant artillery thunders with a steady, calming rhythm. Half the platoon is on watch, and everybody else is snoozing.

A couple of Recon Marines walk over to Trombley and tease him about shooting camels while seizing the airfield.

"I think I got one of those Iraqis, too. I saw him go down."

"Yeah, but you killed a camel, too, and wounded another one."

The Marines seem to have touched a nerve.

"I didn't mean to," Trombley says, upset. "They're innocent."

Then two Bedouin women appear at the edge of the perimeter, thirty meters from Colbert's Humvee. One of the women is dressed in a purple shawl with a black scarf on her head. She seems to be in her early thirties. The other is an old woman in black. The two of them are pulling a heavy object wrapped in a blanket. They stop on top of a high berm about twenty meters away and start waving. Doc Bryan walks over to them.

The women are highly agitated. When Doc Bryan approaches, they unfurl the bundle they've been dragging across the berms, and what looks to be a bloody corpse rolls out. Doc Bryan thinks it's a dead twelve-year-old boy, but when he kneels down, the "corpse" opens his eyes. Doc Bryan immediately begins to examine him. There are four small holes in his torso, two on each side of his stomach.

I walk up behind Doc Bryan. After looking at the boy, with Doc Bryan kneeling over him, the next thing I notice is the younger woman, the mother of the boy. She has a striking, beautiful face. She is half naked. Somehow, in her effort to drag her son across the fields, her shawl has come undone in front. Her breasts are exposed. She is on her knees, praying with her head tilted up, talking non-stop, though no words come out. She turns to me and continues talking, still making no sound. She looks me in the eye. I expect her to appear angry, but instead she keeps talking silently, rolling her eyes up to heaven, then back to me. She seems to be pleading.

"This kid's been zipped with five-five-six rounds!" Doc Bryan shouts, referring to a caliber of bullet commonly used in American weapons. "Marines shot this boy!" He has his medical kit out, rubber gloves on, and is frantically cutting off the kid's filthy clothes, checking his vital signs and railing at the top of his lungs. "These fucking jack-asses," he says. "Trigger-happy motherfuckers."

The older Bedouin woman and I kneel down close to

Aftermath: Cpl. Michael Saucier, Sgt. Charles Graves and Cpl. Aaron Bousley following their bloody three-week slog to Baghdad. *(All photos taken by the author unless otherwise noted)*

Cheering the destruction: Sgt. Brad Colbert greets a Cobra attack helicopter making its final turn before a strafing run on enemy positions outside Al Hayy.

They call him 'Manimal': Cpl. Anthony Jacks before his heroics, at Camp Mathilda, Kuwait, with Cpl. James Chaffin.

Lt. Nathaniel Fick, who would challenge his commander but never break faith with his men, loads his rifle magazine in preparation for the invasion south of the Iraqi border.

Second Platoon's outspoken medical corpsman, Navy HM2 Robert Timothy 'Doc' Bryan, outside Qalat Sukhar just after treating civilians shot by his platoon.

Sgt. Brad Colbert, the 'Iceman,' whose team would often lead the assaults north of Nasiriyah, briefs his men at Camp Mathilda, Kuwait.

Attitude: Marines in Bravo Company suited up for a series of gas attacks that never came on the first day of the war. *(Courtesy Sgt. Eric Kocher, USMC)*

The northernmost Marine unit in Iraq: First Recon punches up the flat and unforgiving desert trail on the second day of the war.

The men who stood up to Captain America: Sgt. Eric Kocher's Team Two. Seated, from left: Cpl. Trevor Darnold and Cpl. Jason Simon; standing, from left: Lance Cpl. Makala St. James, Sgt. Eric Kocher and Cpl. Dan Redman. *(Courtesy Sgt. Eric Kocher, USMC)*

Race on the highway of destruction outside Nasiriyah: Cpl. Jason Lilley at the wheel of Team One–Bravo's Humvee.

Weary Marines in Second Platoon moments after their first ambush in the Fertile Crescent outside Al Gharraf.

Sgt. Eric Kocher outside Baghdad, holding a 203 40mm grenade round customized with a smiley face.

Cpl. Gabriel Garza firing the .50-caliber machine gun outside Al Gharraf.

The first of many civilian casualties: Navy HM2 Robert Timothy 'Doc' Bryan tends a shepherd accidentally machine-gunned by Second Platoon, with the boy's mother watching.

The deadly bridge into Muwaffaqiya, the site of one of the most vicious ambushes Second Platoon faced. The group of trees on the right hid foreign jihad warriors until the Marines drove straight into their 'kill zone.'

The bullet that hit Sgt. Larry Shawn 'Pappy' Patrick – Second Platoon's most popular team leader – displayed by Sgt. Rudy Reyes.

Caught on the cross fire of a guerrilla war: The town of Muwaffaqiya following the Marine artillery bombardment in the wake of First Recon's firefight with Syrian militants.

Cpl. Walt Hasser manning the Mark-19 grenade launcher on Sgt. Brad Colbert's Humvee during a Cobra strike outside Al Hayy.

Cpl. Michael Saucier flaunts his Jesus tattoo; Cpl. Anthony 'Manimal' Jacks is in background.

Sgt. Rudy Reyes in his bullet-riddled Humvee after an enemy attack.

First Recon's convoy en route to a firefight south of Al Gharraf.

A Bravo Company Recon Team rolling atop one of the endless berms beside a dry canal bed.

The team's youngest and most lethal machine gunner, nineteen-year-old Cpl. Harold James Trombley, kicks back in his Ranger grave on the outskirts of Baghdad.
(Author's collection)

One of First Recon's deadliest sniper teams: Sgt. Ken Sutherby (front) with his spotter, Cpl. David Raby.

The bonds of brotherhood: Cpl. Jason Lilley and Sgt. Antonio Espera at Camp Mathilda before the war.

Ripped-Fueled Warrior: Cpl. Josh Ray Person seldom slept.

Cpl. Anthony 'Manimal' Jacks relaxing with a comic book in a Baghdad soccer stadium, while Sgt. Rudy Reyes pumps muscles.

Mired in quicksand, under enemy fire during a dust storm, Sgt. Brad Colbert's team digs out their Humvee on a typical day early in the invasion.

More than thirty days without a shower: Sgt. Eric Kocher and Cpl. Jeffrey Carazales sleep in the dust at Bravo Company's final camp, south of Baghdad.

Sgt. Brad Colbert tends to a shrapnel-wounded girl near a park in Baghdad.

Cpl. Gabriel Garza mans his SAW machine gun and prepares to duel with enemy snipers outside Ar Rifa, a hostile town in central Iraq.

Sgt. Larry Shawn 'Pappy' Patrick (left) and Sgt. Rudy Reyes enjoying a break from combat before Pappy's shooting at Muwaffaqiya.

Bravo Company Second Platoon by a statue of Saddam Hussein at a Baghdad power plant. *(Courtesy of HM1 George 'Doc' Graham, U.S. Navy)*

1 ROBERT TIMOTHY 'DOC' BRYAN
2 CPL. HECTOR LEON
3 CPL. EVAN STAFFORD
4 CPL. ANTHONY 'MANIMAL' JACKS
5 GUNNERY SGT. MIKE WYNN
6 CPL. WALT HASSER
7 CPL. NATHAN CHRISTOPHER
8 CPL. JAMES CHAFFIN

9 CPL. HAROLD TROMBLEY
10 CPL. TEREN HOLSEY
11 PFC. JOHN CHRISTESON
12 SGT. MICHAEL BRUNMEIER
13 SGT. RUDY REYES
14 CPL. JASON LILLEY
15 CPL. MICHAEL STINETORF
16 LT. NATHANIEL FICK

17 SGT. BRAD COLBERT
18 SGT. ANTONIO ESPERA
19 CPL. JOSH RAY PERSON
20 SGT. LEANDRO BAPTISTA
21 EVAN WRIGHT
22 CPL. GABRIEL GARZA
23 SGT. STEVEN LOVELL

Doc Bryan and watch him work. The old lady's fingers are covered in silver rings filled with jade. Her face is completely wrinkled and inked with elaborate tribal tattoos from chin to forehead. She nudges me. When I turn, she offers me a cigarette. She says something in Arabic. When I respond in English she laughs at me almost playfully. Like the mother of the boy, she displays no anger.

Meesh, the translator, shows up, groggy, not having had his first beer of the morning yet. He asks the old lady what happened. She's the grandmother. Her two grandsons were by the road to the airfield when the Marines' Humvees scared the camels. The boys ran out after them and were shot by the Marines. (A second, older boy is later carried into the camp with a wounded leg, a victim of the same shooting.) Bedouins don't keep track of things like birthdays, but the grandmother thinks the youngest boy might be twelve or fourteen.

I ask Meesh why the family doesn't appear to be angry.

He thinks a long time and says, "They are grateful to be liberated and welcome the Americans as friends."

"We fucking shot their kids," Doc Bryan says.

"Dude, mistakes like this are unavoidable in war," Meesh responds.

"Bullshit," Doc Bryan says. "We're Recon Marines. Our whole job is to observe. We don't shoot unarmed children."

Doc Bryan's examination of the boy has revealed that each of the four holes in the boy's body is an entry wound, meaning four bullets zoomed around inside his slender stomach and chest cavity, ripping apart his organs. Now the bullets are lodged somewhere inside. If the kid doesn't get medevaced, he's going to die in a few hours.

Fick and the battalion surgeon, Navy Lieutenant Alex Aubin, a twenty-nine-year-old fresh out of Annapolis and the Naval medical school in Bethesda, Maryland, arrive with bad news. Ferrando has denied their request to medevac the boy.

Just then, a Predator unmanned spy plane flies low overhead. Predators, powered by gasoline engines, make a loud, annoying buzzing sound like a lawn mower with a broken muffler. Doc Bryan looks up, angrily. "We can afford to fly fucking Predators," he says, "but we can't take care of this kid?"

"I'm going to go ask the battalion commander again," Aubin says.

Colbert appears, climbing over the berm. He sees the mother, the kid, the brother with the bloody leg, other members of the family who have now gathered nearby. He seems to reel back for an instant, then rights himself and approaches.

"This is what Trombley did," Doc Bryan says. "This kid was shot with five-five-six rounds from Trombley's SAW." Doc Bryan has concluded that Trombley was the only one to fire a weapon using this type of bullet. "Twenty other Marines drove past those kids and didn't shoot. Bring Trombley up here and show him what he did."

"Don't say that," Colbert says. "Don't put this on Trombley. I'm responsible for this. It was my orders."

Colbert kneels down over the kid, right next to his mother, and starts crying. He struggles to compose himself. "What can I do here?" he asks.

"Apparently fucking nothing," Doc Bryan says.

Aubin returns, shaking his head. "No. We can't medevac him."

Even though Aubin is simply the bearer of bad news, Doc Bryan glares at him accusatorily. "Well, that just sucks, don't it?"

Aubin grew up on St. Thomas, Virgin Islands, and he gives the impression of being sort of preppy. Even in a filthy MOPP suit, he's the type of guy you picture with a nice tan, in loafers with no socks. He's about the last guy you would expect to come up with a plan for an insurrection. But after no one says anything for a few moments, Aubin looks up at Doc Bryan, formulating an idea. He says, "Under the rules, we have to provide him with care until he dies."

"Yeah, so?" Doc Bryan asks.

"Put him in my care. I stay next to the battalion commander. If he's in my care, the boy will stay with me at the headquarters. Colonel Ferrando might change his order if he has to watch him die."

Fick approves of the plan, even though it represents an affront to his commanders and a risk to his own career, already under threat from his confrontation with Encino Man at Ar Rifa. But he endorses this effort, he later says, "because if we didn't do something, I was going to lose Colbert and Doc Bryan. The platoon would have fallen apart. I believed we had at least ninety days of combat ahead of us, and my best men had become ineffective— angry at the command and personally devastated. We had to get this blood off the platoon's hands. I didn't care if we threw those kids onto a helicopter and they died thirty seconds later. My men had to do something."

With Colbert and Doc Bryan at the front of the stretcher, the Marines carry the wounded boy nearly a kilometer to the battalion headquarters. The whole Bedouin family follows. They reach the antenna farm and the cammie nets covering a communications truck and the commander's small, black command tent. They enter the inner sanctum beneath the nets. The Marines lower the stretcher. Several officers, sitting in their skivvies at laptop computers on MRE crates, look up, aghast. With Bedouin tribespeople now pouring in, it looks like the perimeter has been overrun.

The Coward of Khafji runs up, veins pulsing on his forehead. He comes head-to-head with the grandmother, who blows a cloud of cigarette smoke in his face.

"What the hell is going on here?" he shouts, confronting this near-mutinous breakdown of military order inside the battalion headquarters.

"We brought him here to die," Doc Bryan says defiantly.

The Coward of Khafji looks down at the kid on the stretcher.

"Get him the fuck out of here," he bellows.

The Marines carry the kid out in silence and place him under a nearby cammie net. Five minutes later, word is sent back that Ferrando has had a change of heart. He orders a platoon from Alpha to bring the Bedouins to RCT-1's shock-trauma unit, twenty kilometers south.

I catch up to Colbert walking alone through the center of the encampment. "I'm going to have to bring this home with me and live with it," he says. "A pilot doesn't go down and look at the civilians his bombs have hit. Artillerymen don't see the effects of what they do. But guys on the ground do. This is killing me inside." He walks off, privately inconsolable.

LATER, I'm passing by the battalion headquarters when Ferrando calls out to me from beneath the netting in his rasping voice. I veer under the nets and find him sitting up in his hole, wrapped in a poncho. He wants to talk about the incident with the Bedouins. Like his men, he hasn't slept much—"an hour in the past thirty-six hours," he tells me. He looks haggard. His face is gaunt and filthy.

"In my mind this situation is the result of the enemy's law of war violations," he says. "When the enemy purposely position themselves within civilians, it makes the complexity of my decision-making or that of my Marines ten times more difficult. They hope to draw more casualties on our side because of the restraint that we show. It's a deadly situation, and we have to make twenty to thirty life-or-death decisions every hour, and often we do this without sleep. I'm amazed it's going as well as it has."

He brings up the moral dilemma posed by the situation the battalion was in yesterday. "At Ar Rifa," he says, "we were lying out in front of God and everybody as an easy target. Hostile forces were on the rooftops. Based on intelligence gathered by the interpreter from townspeople, I believed we'd located a military headquarters in that town. I ordered artillery rounds dropped on that building to prevent them from organizing an attack on us. Was I right?" he asks.

"I can't say I know for sure they were organizing for an attack, or even that the building we hit was a headquarters. What I do know is, we dropped artillery. I'm certain civilians did die as a result of my order to do so. I don't like making this kind of choice, but I will err to protect these Marines when I can.

"Now, this morning, they requested I send those wounded civilians to the RCT for aid. Problem: Our tactical situation is extremely precarious here. I could not send a platoon to accompany them until the situation had stabilized." He concludes, "It's a shitty situation for these Marines. But no one put a gun to their heads and forced them to come here."

THE TALK COLBERT DELIVERS to Trombley is considerably more concise. After returning from the battalion headquarters, he sits him down beside the Humvee and says, "Trombley, no matter what you might think, or what anybody else might say, you did your job. You were following my orders."

Colbert then strips down to his T-shirt—the first time he's removed his MOPP in more than a week. He crawls under the Humvee and spends several hours chipping away at the three-inch layer of tar and sand clinging to it from the sabka field.

Late in the afternoon, Fick comes by, gathers the team for a morale talk and tells them, "We made a mistake today, collectively and individually. We must get past this. We can't sit around and call it quits now."

Gunny Wynn is harsher. "We're Americans," he lectures the men. "We must be sure when we take a shot that we are threatened. You have got to see that these people are just like you. You've got to see past the huts, the camels, the different clothes they wear. They're just people. This family here might lose a son. We shot their camels, too. If you kill one camel, that could be a year's income. We're not here to destroy their way of life."

But then Gunny Wynn seems to almost reverse himself. "I'm not saying don't protect yourselves. If it's a case of losing one Marine versus one hundred civilians, I will save the Marine. You've just got to be goddamn careful."

However admirable the military's attempts are to create ROE, they basically create an illusion of moral order where there is none. The Marines operate in chaos. It doesn't matter if a Marine is following orders and ROE, or disregarding them. The fact is, as soon as a Marine pulls the trigger on his rifle, he's on his own. He's entered a game of moral chance. When it's over, he's as likely to go down as a hero or as a baby killer. The only difference between Trombley and any number of other Marines who've shot or killed people they shouldn't have is that he got caught. And this only happened because the battalion stopped moving long enough for the innocent victims to catch up with it.

Before leaving, Fick and Gunny Wynn raise the possibility of there being a formal inquiry into the shooting. After they walk off, Trombley turns to Colbert and asks, "Is this going to be okay, I mean with the investigation?"

"You'll be fine, Trombley."

"No. I mean for you, Sergeant." Trombley grins. "I don't care what happens, really. I'm out in a couple of years. I mean for you. This is your career."

"I'll be fine." Colbert stares at him. "No worries."

Something's been bothering me about Trombley for a day or two, and I can't help thinking about it now. I was never quite sure if I should believe his claim that he cut up those Iraqis in Al Gharraf. But he hit those two shepherds, one of whom was extremely small, at more than 200 meters, from a Humvee bouncing down a rough road at forty miles per hour. However horrible the results, his work was textbook machine-gun shooting, and the fact is, from now on, every time I ride with Colbert's team, I feel a lot better when Trombley is by my side with the SAW.

SEVENTEEN

○

SUNSET ON THE NIGHT of March 27 turns the surrounding fields red. First Recon's camp by the airfield is spread across three kilometers, with the Humvees on the outer perimeter spaced about seventy-five meters apart, hidden under cammie nets. Looking out, all you see are dried mudflats, rippled with berms and sliced with dry canals. It looks like a 1950s sci-fi fantasy Martian landscape.

They tell us to dig our holes extra deep tonight. The battalion remains cut off, deep in "bad-guy country," as Fick says. To prevent hordes of RPG teams or enemy tanks from overrunning the perimeter, the Marine Division, about twenty kilometers southwest of here, has pretargeted its artillery to land within "danger-close" range of the camp should it be requested. If the enemy appears in the nearby fields, a quick SOS to division headquarters will bring dozens or hundreds of artillery rounds splashing down near where we are sleeping.

For the first time in several days, the night sky is clear. I watch shooting stars from my hole. There are more stars than you would typically see in North America because there are no streetlights. Clear skies also mean U.S. military aircraft, hampered by dust storms the past several days, now have free rein. It's a busy night in the sky. Past sunset we hear unmanned drones crisscrossing overhead, then the buzzing of propeller-driven P-3 observation planes. Antimissile flares, thrown out by unseen jets, make the whole sky blink. Bombs flash on the horizon. Iraqi AAA guns send up tracer rounds, which look like strings of pearls. I see the enemy AAA batteries firing north, east and west of us, a graphic reminder that there are hostile forces all around.

Near midnight, a team on Alpha Company's sector of the perimeter observes lights that appear to be moving about six kilometers away. The Marines count somewhere between 120 and 140 different lights. Lights could be produced by all sorts of things—a small town with electricity (south of here a few days ago we did see some towns that still had power), a bunch of civilian vehicles or an Iraqi military convoy. Since these lights seem to be moving, the Marines rule out the town option. The men on the team aren't sure what's producing the lights, but their nervous platoon commander believes they represent a possible threat. He radios the battalion that a convoy of "one hundred forty vehicles" is on the move about six kilometers from First Recon's position.

The battalion contacts First Marine Division and reports a possible enemy column moving nearby. One hundred forty Iraqi military vehicles—be they tanks or even trucks filled with men—would be enough to hammer First Recon in its remote position. The division takes this threat extremely seriously. Earlier, the crew of a P-3 observation plane had spotted what they thought might be a column of twenty-five vehicles in the same area. With two independent reports, the division immediately sends all available aircraft toward the "convoy."

When the alarm reaches Colbert's team, everyone not

on watch is woken up and told to load the Humvee and get ready to move or to fight. I made the mistake tonight of stripping out of my MOPP suit and trying to sleep in my underpants. I hadn't removed the MOPP in ten days. It's a near-freezing night, and sliding back into the cold, plastic-lined MOPP is a torture all its own. But just as continual hunger makes MRE food rations taste better, your own petty physical discomforts obliterate grander fears. Sitting in the darkened Humvee, shivering in my icy MOPP, I'm much more concerned about the cold than reports now popping over battalion radios of enemy tanks, or RPG teams moving in to attack. Adding to my misery is the prevailing mood of cheerfulness in the Humvee.

Colbert and his Marines are wide awake, eagerly passing around optics, peering into them, debating about what they see. The prospect of an enemy column moving their way excites them. Besides, Recon Marines like Colbert are in their hearts almost like bird-watchers. They have a passion for observing things that exists all by itself, separate from whatever thrills they get out of guns and blowing things up. They seem truly happy whenever a chance comes to puzzle out the nature of small (but potentially lethal) mysteries on the horizon. This time, in the case of these enigmatic lights, Colbert concludes, "Those are the lights of a village." He sounds almost disappointed.

Waves of F-18s and A-10s fly over the location of the suspected enemy column. Initially there's confusion. When Alpha's platoon commander called in the location of the "convoy," he used incorrect protocols in giving its location (making the same error Encino Man had committed when he'd tried to call in artillery on top of his company outside Ar Rifa). "This mistake created an entire chain of error up to the division," Capt. Patterson later says. After the aircraft finally figure out what their pilots think are the correct coordinates of the suspected convoy, they attack the area by dropping bombs and firing Maverick air-to-ground missiles.

U.S. military doctrine is pretty straightforward in situations like this: If there even appears to be an imminent threat, bomb the shit out of it. One of First Recon's officers, Captain Stephen Kintzley, puts it this way: "We get a few random shots, and we fire back with such overwhelming force that we stomp them. I call it disciplining the Hajjis."

During the next few hours, attack jets drop nearly 10,000 pounds of bombs on the suspected position of the alleged enemy convoy. It's a spectacular show. From Colbert's vehicle we watch numerous smaller bombs flash and count two huge mushroom clouds roiling up in the night sky.

Planes flying over the target areas in daylight give conflicting reports of what they hit. Some report seeing wrecked armored vehicles; others see nothing. First Recon punches out foot patrols. They observe craters outside one village, but no sign of any bombed armor. Some villagers venture out and offer to roast the Marines a goat, apparently with the hope that an offering will propitiate them into calling off further bombing.

Maj. Shoup, who was in communication with some of the pilots during the bombing, later tells me, "I don't think there was any armor there in the first place. Maybe the first P-3 picked up an abandoned piece of armor or some poor farmer's tractor, and it spiraled from there." As the bombing continued, some of the pilots reported that their optics were picking up heat signatures on the ground, indicating there was armor or vehicles of some sort down there. But Shoup believes their thermal optics were actually picking up hot shrapnel from previously dropped bombs. "As soon as you drop a bomb it creates its own heat signature on the ground, which later pilots were reading as armor."

As for the lights that the Marines saw six kilometers away, Shoup believes they were actually seeing lights from a town seventeen kilometers distant. They had misread the lights of a distant city as headlamps from a much closer convoy. Shoup attributes the perception that these headlamps appeared to be moving to a phenomenon called "autokinesis." He explains, "When you stare at lights long enough in the dark, it looks like they are moving. That's autokinesis."

What it boils down to is that under clear skies, in open terrain with almost no vegetation, the Marines don't have a clue what's out there beyond the perimeter. Even with the best optics and surveillance assets in the world, no one knows what happened to nearly 10,000 pounds of bombs and missiles dropped a few kilometers outside the encampment. They may as well have been dropping them in the Bermuda Triangle. It's not that the technology is bad or its operators incompetent, but the fog of war persists on even the clearest of nights.

EIGHTEEN

○

MARCH 28, the day after the bombing, First Recon Battalion remains at its encampment outside the airfield, with no orders for its next mission. A little more than a week into the invasion, the U.S. military has called an "operational pause." The Army, moving up a western highway, met fierce resistance outside Al Najaf, where nearly twenty of its most technologically advanced Apache helicopters were shot down or severely damaged, with two American pilots captured by the Iraqis. According to Marine commanders, the unexpected stiffening of opposition caught the Army off guard, and it has now gone into resupply mode, steeling itself for tougher engagements ahead. For their part, the Marines are continuing to encounter guerrilla tactics—snipers and RPG ambushes—along Route 7. According to Lt. Col. Ferrando, 90 percent of RCT-1's supply chain is being used to haul artillery rounds to feed the big guns as they pummel towns and suspected Fedayeen hideouts around the clock.

The Marines in First Recon, the northernmost unit in central Iraq, have had their rations reduced, a result of both supply problems across the First Marine Division and the fact that the battalion truck with MREs on it was destroyed outside of Ar Rifa. The Marines' water, also in short supply, smells, in the opinion of Colbert, like "dirty ass." The camp is infested with flies from all the camel dung.

Many Marines who have taken their boots off for the first time in a week discover the skin on their feet is rotting off in pale white strips like tapeworms, as a result of fungal infections. The green T-shirts they've worn for eleven days straight underneath their MOPPs are so impregnated with salt from their sweat that they've turned white. Some Marines attempt to wash their crusty T-shirts and socks, but there's not enough water to adequately clean them.

Everyone is coughing and has runny noses and weeping, swollen eyes caused by the dust storms. About a quarter of the Marines in Colbert's platoon have come down with vomiting and diarrhea. Now, with the time to dig through packs and retrieve mirrors, many are amazed by the gaunt reflections staring back at them. In just a short time in the field, most have already shed five to ten pounds. Colbert finds what he thinks is an enormous blackhead on his ear. When he digs it out, he discovers it's a bullet fragment.

It's not a good day for God in Iraq. The battalion chaplain, Navy Lieutenant Commander Bodley, takes advantage of the downtime by circulating among his flock. He finds ministering to Recon Marines a daunting task. "I've been around other Marines and sailors before," he says. "But I'd never heard such profanity—the offensive put-downs—so commonly used until I came to First Recon."

The chaplain was attached to the unit shortly before the invasion. He never swears, seldom drinks. He grew up on Chicago's South Side, and from a young age he felt called to do the work of the Lord. He was ordained a Lutheran minister after attending Concordia Theological Seminary in Ft. Wayne, Indiana, and shortly after became a chaplain in the Navy Reserves. (The Navy provides the Marines with chaplains.) Married with three children, and a minister in a church in Orlando, Florida, his first immersion in Marine culture didn't occur until he was called up before the war and attached to First Recon at Camp Mathilda. He has labored to open his heart to the profane young men in First Recon. "I've come to understand that they use the language to harden themselves," he says. "But my question is, once they've turned it on, can they turn it off?"

Today, circulating among the Marines, he has only grown more disturbed. "Many of them have sought my counsel because they feel guilty," he tells me. "But when I ask them why, they say they feel bad because they haven't had a chance to fire their weapons. They worry that they haven't done their jobs as Marines. I've had to counsel them that if you don't have to shoot somebody, that's a good thing. The zeal these young men have for killing surprises me," Bodley admits. "It instills in me a sense of disbelief and rage. People here think Jesus is a doormat."

THE CHAPLAIN has no takers in Colbert's team when he approaches to offer his counselling. After being up all night dealing with the phantom enemy convoy, Colbert's Marines loll under the cammie nets, attempting to nap. Person lounges outside on a poncho, naked but for skivvies and a pair of golden Elvis-impersonator sunglasses. He's trying to roast the "chacne"—chest zits—off in the harsh Iraqi sun, while busting bass beats with his lips, chanting Ice Cube's lyrics, "Today I didn't even have to use my AK/I gotta say it was a good day."

Gunny Wynn stops by to pass on the latest gossip. "Word is we might go to the Iranian border to interdict smugglers."

"Fuck, no!" Person shouts from beneath his Elvis glasses. "I want to go to Baghdad and kill people."

A couple of Marines nearby pass the time naming illustrious former jarheads—Oliver North, Captain Kangaroo, Lee Harvey Oswald and John Wayne Bobbit. "After they sewed his dick back on, didn't he make porn movies where he fucked a midget?" one of them asks.

Gunny Wynn chuckles, beaming with a sort of fatherly pride. "Yeah, he probably did. A Marine will fuck anything."

Gunny Wynn, along with Fick, is still facing threat of disciplinary action for his role in trying to stop Encino Man from dropping danger-close artillery by the platoon's position the other day outside Ar Rifa. Casey Kasem has told me he is attempting to have Gunny Wynn removed from his job. "It's wrong to question the commander," Casey Kasem says. "Lieutenant Fick and Gunny Wynn don't understand that. Their job is to execute whatever the commander tells them to do. By questioning his orders or his actions, they risk their men's lives by slowing down the commander. Discipline is instinct, a willingness and obedience to orders. What Fick and Gunny Wynn have is the opposite of discipline."

When I ask Gunny Wynn if he's worried about the action brewing against him—Casey Kasem and Encino Man are drafting a memo detailing his "disobedience to orders"—he laughs. "Some guys care about advancing in the Marine Corps. Me, I don't give a fuck. I care about my men being happy, shielding them from the bullshit, and keeping them alive." He adds, "Guys that believe no orders ever should be questioned are usually the same ones who are too dumb to explain them. They just don't want to look stupid in front of their men. I encourage my men to question orders."

This morning, looking out at the expanse beyond the perimeter, Gunny Wynn says he has only one fear in his mind. "Man, I hope this doesn't turn into another Somalia."

DESPITE THE CHAPLAIN'S DESPAIR over the Marines' seeming insensitivity to the suffering brought on by war, discussing it among themselves, Marines express deep misgivings. I join Espera's team, dug in by his Humvee several meters down from Colbert's. He's enjoying his first cup of hot coffee in more than a week, brewed on a fire made from dried camel dung mixed with C-4 plastic explosive (which, when ignited, blazes intensely).

"This is all the tough-guy shit I need," he says. "I don't like nothing about combat. I don't like the shooting. I don't like the action."

Espera believes the whole war is being fought for the same reason all others have for the past several hundred years. "White man's gotta rule the world," he says.

Though Espera is one quarter Caucasian, he grew up mistrusting "the white man." A few years ago, he deliberately avoided earning his community-college degree, though he was just a couple of credits short of receiving it, because, he says, "I didn't want some piece of paper from the white master saying I was qualified to function in his world."

Before joining the Marines, Espera worked as a car repo man in South Central Los Angeles. While in a job he hated, he watched his friends and one close family member go to prison for violent crimes, which were fairly routine in his world. Then one day, after four years of repo-ing cars in L.A.'s poorest neighborhoods, Espera had an epiphany: "I was getting shot at, making chump change, so I could protect the assets of a bunch of rich white bankers. The whole time I'm hating on these motherfuckers, and I realized I'm their slave, doing their bidding. I thought, if you can't beat 'em, join 'em."

So he enlisted in the Marines. Espera reasoned that as a Marine he might still be serving the white man, but he'd be doing so with "purity and honor."

As he's gotten older, Espera's begun to accept that maybe the white man's system isn't all that bad. Travelling the world as a Marine has opened his eyes to stark differences between the way Americans and those in less fortunate parts of the planet live. "All these countries around the world, nobody's fat," he says. "Back home, fat motherfuckers are everywhere. Seventy-five percent of all Americans are fat. Do you know how hard it is to put on thirty pounds? A motherfucker has to sit on the couch and do nothing but eat all day. In America, white trash and poor Mexicans are all fat as motherfuckers. The white man created a system with so much excess, even the poor motherfuckers are fat."

Those who know Espera understand he's not a racist. He's a humorist whose vitriol is tongue-in-cheek. Even so, Espera questions the white man's wisdom in sending him tearing through a hostile country in an open Humvee. "Every time we roll through one of these cities, I think we're going to die. Even now, dog, sitting here in the shade, my heart's beating one hundred forty times per minute. For what? So some colonel can make general by throwing us into another firefight?"

In their most paranoid moments, some Marines believe Ferrando is trying to get them killed. Sergeant Christopher Wasik, a thirty-one-year-old Marine who sometimes serves as Ferrando's driver, comes over this day to share some coffee and gripe with his friends in Second Platoon. Before the invasion, Wasik openly rebelled against Ferrando's Grooming Standard after having been severely upbraided for allowing his mustache to grow too far beyond the corners of his mouth. He shaved it into a perfect Hitler mustache, which he wore for weeks at Camp Mathilda. Nevertheless, his rebellion was a failure. His superiors commended his Hitler mustache for complying with the Grooming Standard. Now, he and the other Marines speculate on Ferrando's motives in Iraq. "In some morbid realm," Wasik says, "it may be a possibility that the commander wants some of us to die, so when he sits around with other high leaders, they don't snicker at him and ask what kind of shit he got into."

WHATEVER FEELINGS Colbert has over his involvement in the shooting of the shepherds, he seems to have filed them away. His mood has been chipper since the all-night watch for the enemy column. Late in the morning, however, he receives another reminder of the incident. The tattooed grandmother and a man from the family who appears to be in his late forties walk through the perimeter toward his Humvee. Person, now on his stomach, tanning his bacne, is the first to notice their approach. "Hey," he says, lifting his head up. "We got Hajjis. Anyone know how to say, 'Get the fuck away from my Humvee' in Habudabi?" he says, using Marine slang—"Habudabi"—for Arabic.

"I'll take care of this," Colbert says. He scrounges in the Humvee for an English-to-Arabic cheat sheet, then walks up to the man and the old lady.

"Al salam al'icum," he says haltingly, reading the customary Arabic salutation from his cheat sheet.

His greeting provokes a torrent of words and frantic gestures from the couple. Colbert queries them in Arabic, then repeats in English, "I have pain?" "I am hungry?"

They shake their heads no. Then he asks, "Bad people?"

They nod, point across the field and speak more urgently. Colbert tries to radio for the translator, but he can't be found. The grandmother keeps repeating something. He can't figure out what it is. He shakes his head. "I don't understand. I'm sorry."

She shrugs. Colbert hands her several humrat packs. "I'm sorry," he says in Arabic and English. "You have to go."

They walk off. He watches them, exasperated. "We can't have civilians hanging out here. There's nothing I can do about this."

DOC BRYAN RETURNS from the RCT-1's medical unit with good news. "We got the kid stabilized and medevaced out on a bird." Even so, Doc Bryan takes little satisfaction from the effort. "The whole drive down I was staring in the kid's eyes," Doc Bryan says. "He was staring at me like, 'You just shot me, motherfucker, and now you think you're great because you're trying to save my life?' "

Later that day, Encino Man walks the perimeter, talking informally with his men in an attempt to ease the tensions. Meeting with Doc Bryan and the other Marines in Team Three, he apologizes for the incident a few days earlier when he tried to fire a 203 grenade into a house where the men had observed civilians.

His candor earns high marks from the Marines. Then he asks them to speak up about anything that's bothering them. The funny thing is, the Marines have been laughing off hardships caused by the lack of food, the filth, the flies, the dysentery, even the uncertainty of not knowing what their next mission is. The one thing that no one laughs about is the loss of First Recon's "colors"—a Marine Corps flag affixed with battle streamers. The colors are reputed to have been carried by Marines into combat since at least the Vietnam War. A few nights ago, they were lost on the supply truck blown up outside of Ar Rifa. One of the Marines tells Encino Man, "The colors should never leave the commander's side. Losing them is a reflection on his leadership and on all of us."

The only other serious complaints the Marines air are the usual ones about the battalion commander's continued obsession with the Grooming Standard. Ferrando recently sent the Coward of Khafji around to lecture the men about committing petty violations—from allowing their hair to grow a quarter inch too long to lying in the sun by their vehicles with their helmets off.

One of the Marines complains to Encino Man, "They're treating men who've shown discipline in combat like a bunch of six-year-olds."

Encino Man listens, staring cryptically from blue eyes beneath the shelf of his Cro-Magnon brow. Then he turns to Doc Bryan, who's been lying quietly on the ground the whole time. "Doc, is there anything you want to talk about?"

"I'm fine, sir," Doc Bryan answers.

"If there's anything on your mind, now's the time to bring it up," Encino Man says.

"If you insist, sir," Doc Bryan says.

"It's okay, whatever it is," Encino Man encourages him.

"Frankly, sir, I think you're incompetent to lead this company."

"I'm doing the best I can," Encino Man says.

"Sir, it's just not good enough."

CAPTAIN AMERICA'S PLATOON is also experiencing a deepening rift, exacerbated by the shepherd-shooting incident. Marines in his platoon speculate that Trombley might have been provoked into shooting the shepherds after hearing gunfire from Captain America's vehicle. The fact is, Trombley denies Captain America's AK fire had anything to do with his actions. Nevertheless, the morning after the incident, Marines in Third Platoon witnessed a remarkable confrontation between Kocher and Captain America. In the belief that his commander's antics were beginning to jeopardize the safety of the men, Kocher took it upon himself to lay down the law. He backed Captain America against the side of his Humvee and told him: "If you ever fire an AK from this truck again, I will fuck you up." Captain America denied shooting his AK. He blamed the reckless gunfire on Crosby, riding in the back of his truck.

Now a day later at the encampment, Crosby accosts Captain America in front of several other Marines. Crosby, not the biggest Marine in the platoon, steps up to Captain America and tells him he is asking for a "request mast." Request mast is a formal process in which Marines, when accused of committing a serious infraction, may ask permission to appear before the commanding general and defend themselves.

Captain America shoots Crosby an amiable smile.

"On what grounds are you requesting mast?" he asks.

"Sir, you're telling other people I was firing an AK out of the back of the truck," Crosby says.

Captain America tries to calm him. "We're under a lot of stress right now. No one's getting any sleep."

"I'm not getting sleep," Crosby says. "You're the one who's sleeping. You're going around saying I'm a shitbag. I've never fired an AK."

Captain America stares at him, apparently speechless.

"I'm not the one shooting AKs out of the vehicle," Crosby persists. "You are."

Captain America walks off, having just, in his men's opinion, "bowed down" to a lance corporal. In this moment he loses whatever remaining authority he had. As Crosby says later, "I'm only a lance corporal. In the Marine Corps, the captain is God. But in this platoon, we've taken over. Now, when the captain tells me to do something, I ask Kocher if I should do it, and he says, 'Fuck no.' Because out here, the captain hasn't given one order that's made sense."

SENSING THE GROWING RANCOR within the battalion, Ferrando calls his officers in for a meeting early in the afternoon on their second day by the airfield. About thirty of them gather by a blown-up mud hut. "The men are bitching too much," he tells his officers. In Ferrando's opinion, his Marines' bitching about the Grooming Standard, the loss of the battalion colors and questionable decisions he and others have made is the fault of his officers, who, he says, have poor attitudes. "I'm starting to hear some of you questioning and bitching just like the troops," Ferrando lectures. "That is a fucking no-go. Attitude is contagious. It breeds like a fucking yeast infection."

Ferrando's assessment of how the invasion is going is grim. "Saddam is winning the strategic battle," he tells his men, citing negative publicity American forces have received for killing civilians. "Major General Mattis has expressed a concern to me that division-wide, we're shooting more civilians than we should."

Later, when I talk to Mattis about the invasion, he insists that the resistance the Marines met in cities and villages in central Iraq "was not much of a surprise." Ferrando's comments to his men on this day are at variance with Mattis's assertions. He tells them, "The resistance in the urban areas has been stiffer than we expected. It's caught us by surprise. We expected the resistance to be regular military, but it's paramilitary. We've got to make sure we don't let this get the best of us."

After dismissing his officers, Ferrando calls in Colbert and other senior enlisted men for a briefing intended to quell discontent. "The civilian engagement," he says, referring to the shooting of the two shepherds, "was largely reflective of the ROE guidance I gave as we pushed to the airstrip—the order that everyone is declared hostile."

He explains, "I pushed the ROE because we had reports of enemy tanks and armored personnel carriers on the airstrip. It was a military target. I had seen no civilians. It was five in the fucking morning. The general told me to get on the field. I knew that slapping everyone together and moving onto the airfield in twenty minutes was reckless, but that was my order. It was the most rash fucking thing I've done. Borderline foolish. But I can't tell the general we don't do windows."

He then tries to dispel the resentment some men feel for his initial order to not medevac the wounded boy. "If that casualty had been you, I would not have medevaced you because I still thought we had armor to the south." He expounds his interpretation of the rules of war. "Some of you seem to think we have to give wounded civilians every consideration we give ourselves. That is not true. The ROE say we have to give them the same medical care they would get by themselves. That is zero."

Ferrando makes a play for his men's support. "We are going to get tasked to do things that suck," he says. "You have to have faith in me. You may not like me. That's okay. But you have to understand that my number-one priority is protection of our forces." He concedes, "We've done a few things that could have been catastrophic, but we made it through. The bottom line is, we volunteered to fight."

As they walk back to their positions on the perimeter, one of the men says, "Yeah, we volunteered to be here, but we didn't volunteer to be treated like idiots. His story always changes. 'Protection of forces' my fucking ass. He sent us onto an airfield where he thought there were fucking tanks. Why did we make that pell-mell fucking rush? So a colonel could score a few extra brownie points with his general."

NINETEEN

○

IT'S ANOTHER BITTERLY COLD MORNING on March 30, and the men have again been up all night. The Marines in Bravo Company spent their final hours at the airfield camp in their Humvees, crashing around in the darkness, trying to execute orders that changed every forty-five minutes or so until dawn. At around midnight, they were told enemy forces had gotten a fix on their positions and they needed to move to new ones in order to avoid mortar or artillery strikes. They kept moving a few hundred meters this way and that until four in the morning, when Fick announced, "For First Recon, the operational pause is over. We have warning orders for a new mission."

But even with Fick's promise that clarity of purpose was on its way, the company kept up its hectic maneuvers until dawn. Now everyone is sitting out by some berms, watching a beautiful rose-tinted sunrise. Lovell is freezing after having fallen into a canal while retrieving a claymore mine during the frantic night moves. Reyes, who has just spent half an hour cutting concertina wire out of his Humvee's undercarriage—after having driven through it while circling the camp in the darkness—says,

"We're Pavlov's dogs. They condition us through rules, through repeatedly doing things that have no purpose." He laughs. "They probably knew at midnight we would just spend the next five hours driving around aimlessly. They know it just makes us mad and gets us keyed up to do something."

He has a point. Despite another night of sleeplessness, spirits are soaring. Most men are elated at the prospect of another mission. It's like they've forgotten the horrors of Nasiriyah and Al Gharraf, twisted Amtracs with dead Marines in them, mangled civilians on the highway. Three days of stewing in the camp, being shouted at by the Coward of Khafji for not having proper haircuts, has made them eager to get back on the road. In their minds, at least when they're in the field, getting shot at and bombed, they don't have to deal with irritants in the rear.

Fick now adds to their élan with good news. He tells his team leaders, "It looks like we are going to be doing interdiction and ambushes along Route 17, west of 7."

Instead of driving blind into enemy positions, the Recon Marines will be turning the tables. They will be setting up their own ambushes on enemy fighters. Even Pappy, among the most reserved of the men, is guardedly optimistic. "Finally, it looks like we're going to be doing to them as they do to us."

"I feel like it's Christmas morning and I'm about to open my presents," Trombley says.

Fick treats the Marines to a special breakfast. He distributes two meal packs of humrats to each team, for the men to divide among themselves.

While eating hot lentil stew and rice, Espera ponders American culture. "Dog, before we came over here I watched *Pocahontas* with my eight-year-old daughter. Disney has taken my heritage as an American Indian and fucked it up with this typical American white-boy formula."

"*Pocahontas*. Wonderful children's cartoon," Colbert says. "I like the music."

"Dog, *Pocahontas* is another case of your people shitting on mine. What's the true story of Pocahontas? White boys come to the new land, deceive a corrupt Indian chief, kill ninety percent of the men and rape all the women. What does Disney do? They make this tragedy, the genocide of my people, into a love story with a singing raccoon. I ask you, would the white man make a love story about Auschwitz where a skinny-ass inmate falls in love with a guard, with a singing raccoon and dancing swastikas? Dog, I was ashamed for my daughter to see this."

Trombley slides in next to Espera. "You know, my great-great-great-grandfather was a mercenary up in Michigan who had a militia where they'd kill Indians for hire. He was really good at it."

"You know, Trombley," Espera says, "in the fishing village I'm from, Los Angeles, if I mention that I'm part Indian, most white motherfuckers will bring up some great-great-great-grandparent who was part Indian because they want to let me know that even though they look like white motherfuckers, they're actually down with my people. You are the first white motherfucker I've ever met who's said that."

"Just what race are you, Poke?" Colbert asks, referring to Espera by the nickname only his friends use. "I mean, are you Latino, Indian or white? Or are you just whatever race happens to be cool at the time?"

"Shut up, white boy, and go eat a baloney sandwich," Espera says.

"No, I mean it," Colbert continues. "Your wife is half

white. I've met your friends from L.A. They're all white."

"Bro, you've got a point," Espera says. "I'm afraid to hang out with my Mexican friends at home. I'm afraid if we go to the liquor store together they'll stick it up. My Mexican friends are shady motherfuckers. No job, twenty-thousand-dollar entertainment system at home, more guns than a fucking armory. The only Mexicans I hang out with are in the Marine Corps."

Breakfast ends with Fick's order to get in the Humvees and link up with RCT-1 in preparation for the new mission. "Finally, we get to fuck shit up again," Person exults as we leave the road by the airfield. Colbert, however, gazes morosely out the window at Marines rolling up the road in Amtracs. They will be stationed here as guards. "That would be sweet," Colbert says. "Guarding an airfield for three weeks."

FICK HAS SOME BAD NEWS when the Marines reach RCT-1 at a muddy, bomb-cratered camp at the junction of Routes 7 and 17. "Our original warning order seems to be changing," he tells his team leaders. "Instead of staging ambushes on enemy positions along Route 17, we will bust north adjacent to Route 7 and do a movement to contact."

"Movement to contact" is another way of saying they will again be driving into suspected enemy positions in order to see if anybody will shoot at them. Once again they will be following the Gharraf canal on a backcountry trail. "One thing I've learned," Fick tells me. "Is if we do anything involving something named 'Gharraf,' it's not good."

Encino Man holds a company formation in an attempt to bring out the moto in his men. They stand in a sloping field at parade rest, hands clasped behind their backs, each young man looking ahead with a hard, Marine-Corps-correct thousand-yard stare. "We all know what happened to the chow," Encino Man says, bringing up the supply truck destroyed by Iraqis. "This wasn't our bad planning." He tries to muster a fierce expression, but despite his ape-like features, Encino Man's face doesn't project anger well. It remains about as placid as an oatmeal cookie as he mumbles through his attempt at a rousing speech. "They did this. The Iraqis took your food. I hope this makes you mad at the enemy. You should be really mad at them. Okay?"

FOLLOWING ENCINO MAN'S pep talk, Fick now piles on more depressing news. "Yesterday, Marines in a supply convoy south of here were caught in an RPG ambush. They were cut off and surrounded by bad guys. They called in for help, but by the time it arrived one was dead and one was missing."

No one knows for sure what happened to the missing Marine, but according to Fick (and to media reports), it's believed that the Marine was killed, that his corpse was mutilated, dragged through a town and strung up for public display. Hearing this account, Lovell turns to his men and vows, "I am not going to be a POW, and I'm not going to die here."

The Marines aren't just grim now. They're slightly freaked out by the specter of mobs attacking them. They can't help but think of the Army Rangers who were attacked and mutilated in Somalia. By coincidence, the last movie shown to their unit at Camp Mathilda before they embarked on the invasion was *Black Hawk Down*, the slow-motion retelling of disaster befalling a small band of

Americans trapped in a hostile third-world city they'd entered to liberate. The parallels now seem clear.

Doc Bryan leans against the wheel of a Humvee, telling his fellow Marines, in all seriousness, "What we should do is paint skulls on our faces. Come into these towns like demons. These are primitive people. We would scare the shit out of them. We need to use fear, not give in to it."

Carazales, the twenty-one-year-old who now serves as the driver on Kocher's team, says, "What we ought to do is send everyone off to Ace Hardware, get some chain saws, capture some Fedayeen, cut their limbs off, tie them to wheelchairs, load them in a C-130, and drop them on Baghdad. We'll just sit back in our Humvees reading *Playboys*."

Carazales is not much taller than an M-16 rifle. He has a Marine Corps eagle-globe-and-anchor tattoo on one leg and a BORN LOSER tattoo on the other. He wound up in the Corps, he says, "Because I got tricked into this mother-fucker. I was eighteen, in jail, facing probation, and the DA and a Marine recruiter made a deal I couldn't refuse." He complains, "If I weren't in the Marines, by now I'd be making real money. I'd've worked my way up to fourteen dollars an hour, working on rigs or as a welder's assistant."

Carazales is from Cuero, Texas, hates the Marine Corps, hates officers, hates rich people. "They should make a holiday every year where if you make less than thirty thousand dollars a year you get to drive into rich neighborhoods and fuck up rich people's houses. Go inside and break their shit. Every blue-collar man gets to sleep in a white-collar man's house." Sometimes he asks fellow Marines, "Have you ever read the *Communist Manifesto*? That sounds ideal. How the upper classes are oppressing the lower classes. That's how it happens back home. Rich people, corporations, get all sorts of secret government handouts they don't tell us about."

Not only is Carazales apparently the battalion's leading Communist, he's also among the most popular men in Bravo Company. He's a POG mechanic, but he volunteered to drive for Kocher, one of his closest friends, after Kocher's original driver, Darnold, was shot in Al Gharraf. Now, not only does he drive for Kocher's team, he's still responsible for maintaining the battalion's vehicles. He seldom sleeps, and his face and hands are invariably black with axle grease, hence his nickname: "Dirty Earl."

Volunteering to be on Kocher's team has also spared him from one of the least popular burdens in the company. Carazales previously had to drive for Captain America. Now, sitting around waiting to begin their hunt for ambushes on the route north, Carazales brings up the subject of Captain America. "Driving for that mother-fucker was jacked. Every time we'd come across more of them fucked-up civilians—he had to jump around getting pictures, worried my driving was too fast for his Canon stabilization system to work right."

"Man, I'm glad I didn't see any dead little children," Garza says.

"How do you think we would feel if someone came into our country and lit us up like this?" Carazales says. "South of Al Gharraf I know I shot a building with a bunch of civilians in it. Everyone else was lighting it up. Then we found out there were civilians in there. It's fucked up." Carazales works himself into a rage. "I think it's bullshit how these fucking civilians are dying! They're worse off than the guys that are shooting at us. They don't even have a chance. Do you think people at home are going to see this—all these women and children we're killing? Fuck no. Back home they're glorifying this motherfucker, I guarantee you. Saying our president is a fucking hero for getting us into this bitch. He ain't even a real Texan."

Carazales slumps back in the dirt. No one says anything. Then he brightens. "I just thought of a tight angle. All the pictures Captain America's taking of shot-up, dead Iraqi kids? I'll get my hands on those. I'm going to go back home and put them in Seven-Elevens and collect money for my own adopt-an-Iraqi-kid program. Shit, I'll be rolling in it. A war veteran helping out the kids. I ought to run for office."

For whatever reason this night, Ferrando allows his men to sleep in the open beside their Humvees. It's the first time in two weeks we haven't dug Ranger graves. At about midnight, I awaken to see the fields and palm trees across from our Humvee lit up by illumination flares. Suspended from parachutes, the chemical flames drift slowly down into the field.

I wake Person, who is sleeping next to me, and ask him what's going on.

"It's illume," he mumbles. "Ours."

"Why are we lighting up our own position?" I ask.

Person snores.

I fall back asleep. Then I awaken again a few minutes later to the sound of artillery or rockets shrieking through the sky, exploding a few hundred meters directly in front of us. The blasts turn the field into a sea of molten orange and blue liquid, with waves splashing up against the palms in the background. In my effort to roll underneath the Humvee for cover, I bang into Person.

"Shit!" I yell, panicking about the explosions.

"Don't worry about that," Person says over the continuing roar. "That's our artillery." He lifts his head up and observes the firestorm. "It's just danger close." He falls back asleep.

The next morning, we are informed that we are lucky to be alive. "That was an enemy artillery strike from a BM-21 multiple-launch rocket system," Fick says, delivering the news with a grimly amused smile. "That system kills everything in an entire grid square"—a square kilometer. "They knew our coordinates and came within a few hundred meters of us. We got lucky, again."

TWENTY

○

On the morning of March 31, at about nine, Colbert's team and the rest of First Recon leave their encampment at the intersection of Routes 7 and 17 in central Mesopotamia to begin the next mission. Today's objective is a town of about 50,000 called Al Hayy. It's a Baath Party headquarters and home to a Republican Guard unit of several thousand about thirty kilometers to the north.

RCT-1's force of 6,000 Marines is planning to assault through the center of Al Hayy sometime in the next twenty-four hours. But the Recon Marines will go there first. As it did on its movement to the town of Al Gharraf, the battalion will leave Route 7 and use a dirt trail hugging the edge of a canal. Initially, RCT-1 will parallel First Recon's movement on the other side of the canal. Then First Recon will race ahead, cross a series of canal bridges into Al Hayy, speed north and seize the main highway bridge out of the city in order to block the retreat of enemy forces during RCT-1's attack.

On this mission, First Recon will be an even smaller force than it usually is. Alpha Company has been temporarily detached from the battalion to go on a separate mission in search of the lost Marine believed to have been lynched in an Iraqi town.

We drive across a low, narrow bridge over the canal, and First Recon's reduced force of 290-odd Marines in fifty vehicles again becomes the northernmost unit in central Iraq. It's the first warm morning in several days. Rain clouds blow across the sky, but the sun pokes out and the air is dust-free. The canal flows past us on the right, about thirty meters wide in some places.

The battalion rolls single-file on a one-lane, unpaved road that passes through the now familiar patchwork of grassy fields, mudflats crisscrossed with trenches and berms, palm groves and small hamlets. Some have walls that come right up to the edge of the road, channeling the Humvees between the villages on the left and the canal on the right. Perfect terrain for ambushes.

We pass farmers in a field to our left. Colbert regards them warily and says, "These are a simple people. These are the people I'm here to liberate."

"Small-arms fire ahead," Person says, passing word from the radio.

We hit a hard bump at about twenty miles per hour. A wild dog appears out of nowhere, lunging and snarling against the windows on the right side of the vehicle. "Jesus Christ!" Colbert jumps, more startled than I have ever seen him.

Despite the fear and stress, Colbert remains an extremely polite invader. When we pass more farmers on the road, he pulls the barrel of his M-4 up, so as not to point it directly at them.

A pair of Cobras drops low to our left. The armored helicopters, which we haven't seen in a few days, soar overhead with the grace of flying sledgehammers. They make a distinctive clattering sound—as ugly and mean as they look. "Cobras spotted a blue Zil"—Russian military truck—"ahead, carrying uniformed Iraqis," Colbert says, passing along a report from the radio. We stop.

A machine gun buzzes somewhere up the road. "Shots fired on our lead vehicle," he says. We remain halted. Colbert gazes longingly at some weeds beside his window. "This would have been the perfect shitting opportunity," he says. "I should have done it when we first stopped." Colbert's initial attempt to clear his bowels this morning was interrupted when the team's mission was unexpectedly moved up by two hours. Now, at ten in the morning, with the gunfire starting, this problem is foremost on his mind.

I've learned a few things about the Marines by now. There are certainties in their world, even in the chaos of war. As soon as a unit sets in for the night and finishes digging its Ranger graves, everyone will be moved to a slightly different position and forced to start all over again. When a team is told to be ready to move out in five minutes, they will sit for several hours. When the order is to remain in position for three hours, their next order will be to roll out in two minutes. Above all, it is a certainty that Colbert will never be able to take a crap in peace.

Fick walks up. "They found RPGs two hundred meters up the road in a ditch. There is a dismounted Iraqi platoon ahead that we know about."

A ripping sound fills the air. Cobras skim low over palm trees about a kilometer ahead, firing machine guns and rockets into a hamlet on the other side of the canal.

"They're smoking some technicals"—civilian trucks with weapons on them—"in a cluster of buildings up ahead," Colbert says.

Directly across the canal from us—on our right about seventy-five meters away—Amtracs from RCT-1 rumble through some scrub brush outside some mud-hut homes. When moving, Amtracs produce an unmistakable sound—sort of like what you'd hear if you went to a Laundromat and filled all the dryers with nuts and bolts and pieces of junk and turned them on high. Driving next to one is deafening. Even creeping at low speed through the weeds across the canal from us, they make a ferocious racket. Then their machine guns start spitting at targets by some huts. Mark-19s boom. We have no idea what they're shooting at. All we see are the gray vehicles rising from the brush, bumping forward a few meters, stopping, then little orange flashes.

Listening to this mini-firefight taking place outside the doors of our Humvee, Colbert leans out his window and peers at the action through his rifle scope. He leans back in his seat and says, annoyed, "I just hope they don't orient their fire onto us."

We wait.

"Fuck it," Colbert says amidst the sporadic machine-gun fire. "I'm gonna do it."

He jumps out into the scrub vegetation beside the vehicle, squats and takes care of business.

Person starts singing Country Joe McDonald's antiwar song, "I-Feel-Like-I'm-Fixin'-to-Die," with the lyrics, "And it's one, two, three/What are we fighting for?" He's interrupted by an order sent over the radio to move out. He shouts at Colbert, squatting in the field. "Hey! We're moving again!"

Colbert hops in, suspenders from his partially dis-assembled MOPP flapping. "I made it." He sighs.

As Person drives forward, Colbert says, "I think we're gonna take some fire when we come around the next bend."

Colbert's instincts are money. The first mortar of the day explodes somewhere outside the vehicle as soon as we make the turn. No one can see where it hit, and judging by its muffled sound, it was probably several hundred meters away. We stop. To the left, there's a hamlet: four to six earthen-walled homes. They're clustered together about fifteen meters from the road, nestled beneath low-hanging fig trees. In front there are crude fences made of dried reeds, used as paddocks for sheep and goats. It has the primitive feel of one of those Nativity sets they build in town squares at Christmas. Chickens run about, and a half dozen villagers—older women in black robes, older men in dingy white ones, all of them barefoot—stand gawking at us. Despite the almost biblical look of the place, there are power lines overhead with electric wires feeding into the huts. The Marines get out, take cover behind the hoods and open doors of the Humvees, and scan the rooftops, walls and bermed fields behind the hamlet for enemy shooters.

But after about five minutes of this standoff, the villagers approach. The Marines step out from around their vehicles. A translator is brought up. The villagers say there are no enemy forces in their hamlet. Even as they speak, there are more explosions in the distance. Person, still sitting in the Humvee, hears a report from the radio that other units in First Recon, now spread out along two kilometers or so of this narrow lane, are receiving enemy mortar fire.

A shoeless farmer approaches. His face is narrow and bony from what looks to be a lifetime of starvation. Shaking his fist, speaking in a raspy voice, he says through a translator that he's been waiting for the Americans to come since the first Gulf War. He explains that he used to live in a Shia marshland south of here. Saddam drained the marshes and ruined the farmland to punish the people there for supporting the 1991 rebellion. "Saddam believes if he starves the people we will follow him like slaves. It's terrorism by the system itself."

I ask the farmer why he welcomes Americans invading his country. "We are already living in hell," he says. "If you let us pray and don't interfere with our women, we accept you."

The farmer, with gray hair and his narrow face wrapped in wrinkles, looks to be about sixty, with a lot of those being hard years. I ask him when he was born. 1964. I tell him we're the same age. He leans toward me, smiling and pointing to his face. "Compared to you, I look like an old man" he says. "This is because of my life under Saddam."

I find his self-awareness unsettling. One of the few comforts I have when looking at images of distant suffering is the hope that the starving child with flies on his face doesn't know how pathetic he is. If all he knows is misery, maybe his suffering isn't as bad. But this farmer has shattered that comforting illusion. He's wretched, and he knows it. Before going off, he warns the translator that we are entering an area where the Baath Party is strong. Then he asks if he can join the Marines and go to Baghdad with them. "I will kill Saddam with my own hands," he says.

ABOUT 500 METERS AHEAD of Second Platoon's position by the hamlet, Marines in Third Platoon spot a Zil bouncing through the field. There are about twenty young Iraqi men packed into the rear bed. They're armed but wearing civilian clothes. The truck stops, and the Iraqis attempt to flee by the canal. Marines train their guns on them and they throw their arms up in surrender. The Iraqis insist they are farm laborers who have weapons because they are afraid of bandits. But before being stopped, they tossed bags into the field. The Marines retrieve them. Inside, they find Republican Guard military documents, and uniforms still drenched in sweat. Obviously, these guys just changed out of them. The men in Third Platoon take the Iraqis prisoner, bind their wrists with zip cuffs (sort of a heavy-duty version of the plastic bands used to tie trash bags) and load them into one of the battalion's transport trucks.

THE BATTALION PUSHES FORWARD a few more kilometers. Cobra machine guns buzz in the distance. Mortars explode every few minutes now, but they're still far off—hundreds of meters away, we guess.

In places the trail is almost like a tunnel bounded by reed fences and overhanging trees. It's the most dangerous terrain to operate in, short of being inside a city. But the weird thing is, it's awfully pretty, and everyone in the vehicle seems to be feeling it. A few days earlier, when the battalion raced into Al Gharraf under fire, there were Marines I talked to afterward who said that when they saw the dazzling blue dome of the mosque by the entrance, they felt peaceful, despite the heavy-weapons fire all around.

Basically, there are things you react to almost automatically, even in times of stress. A tree-lined trail bending past a canal is still pretty, even with hostile forces about. During one halt, Colbert's team is completely distracted by several water buffalo bathing on the banks of the canal. Trombley gets out of the vehicle and walks over to them—even as several mortars boom nearby—and has to be ordered back by Colbert.

Second Platoon reaches another hamlet, a walled cluster of about seven homes. Colbert's team and the others are ordered to dismount and clear this and the next several hamlets, going house-to-house. Higher-ups in the battalion have grown increasingly concerned about the mortar fire. The Cobras overhead haven't been able to find the positions of those launching them. The hope is that by making the Marines more aggressive on the ground, they can scare up better information from the villagers.

Colbert leads his team into the hamlet by bounding toward it in stages, their rifles ready to fire. Several men emerge. Colbert shouts, "Down!" gesturing with his M-4. They drop to their stomachs in the dirt. Marines step toward them, rifles drawn, and force them to interlock their fingers behind their heads. Then about twenty women and children stream out. Espera is tasked with herding them toward the road.

A salvo of three mortars hits a couple hundred meters northwest, sending geysers of dirt and smoke up behind the village. The Marines pay them no heed. A much closer mortar, impacting maybe seventy-five meters to the west, seems to come out of nowhere. When they're this close, you hear a sound—*fffft!*—just before the boom. Then, as a result of the sharp increase in air pressure, your body feels like it's been zapped with a mild electric charge. But we're stopped here, and there's nothing to do about it. Mortars fall in a totally random pattern. It's not like there's a guy crouched somewhere in a field with a rifle, trying to pick you up in his scope. You're not being individually targeted. You have to take comfort in the randomness of it all.

I walk up to Espera, guarding the hamlet's women and children on the road. An old lady in black screams and shakes her fists at him. "This brings me back to my repo days," Espera says. "Women are always the fiercest. You always have to look out for them. Doesn't matter if it's a black bitch in South Central or some rich white bitch in

Beverly Hills. They always come after you screaming. Don't matter if you've got a gun. It's like women think they're protected."

Colbert's team enters the first group of homes. Earthen walls are adorned with bright pictures of flowers and sunsets, artwork clipped from magazines. The day has grown hot—hitting the mid-nineties outside—but the homes are naturally cool. Trombley is impressed. "It'd be pretty neat to live in one of these," he says.

A bedroom in one hut stuns the Marines. Against the bare walls, there's a CD player, a TV with DVD, mirrors, a painting of a horse on velvet, electric lamps and what looks to be a California King bed—chrome and black-lacquered frame with leopard-print covers. It looks like they've stumbled into the crib of an East L.A. drug lord.

Nearby, there's a locked windowless hut. Marines try to kick the door in, but it's padlocked with a chain. They chop it off with bolt cutters and find the village stash: two AK rifles, piles of weed and some bags with white powder that looks like either cocaine or heroin. Colbert confiscates the rifles but leaves the drugs. "We're not here to fuck with their livelihoods," he says.

Mortars continue to fall for the next hour while we slowly bump up the trail. With the rising heat, and Marines in their MOPP suits bounding across fields, scrambling up walls and kicking in doors, everyone is pouring sweat. Tiny gnats swarm everywhere. They seem to have miniature teeth. Black clouds of them descend, then you feel your neck and eyelids and ears being chewed on.

Colbert slumps against the Humvee, taking a rest, his face throbbing red. "I almost went down in that last village. I'm at my limit." He sucks water from a drinking tube attached to a CamelBak pouch and starts to sing,

"I'm Sailing Away!" He stops. "This is dangerous as hell," he says.

There's a shot ahead. Person picks up a report from the radio. "A dog tried to attack a friendly, so he shot him."

"That was needless," Colbert says.

Two mortars explode somewhere.

Captain America struts past with his bayonet out. "Charlie's in the trees!" Colbert calls after him, quoting a line from *Platoon*.

BY THREE-THIRTY in the afternoon we have reached a bend in the canal, approximately ten kilometers south of the Marines' objective, Al Hayy. There is a mosque ahead. A few moments earlier, Cobras shot up the fields beside it, pulverizing suspected ambush points, but all is quiet now. The battalion halts while officers plan the final push to Al Hayy.

Everyone remains sitting inside Colbert's Humvee, waiting. After six hours of searching for an elusive enemy on this back trail, the men on Colbert's team are worn down, their nerves frayed. The chatter and happy profanities and inside jokes have ceased. Even Person just stares vacantly out the window.

The silence is broken by an unusual new sound, a series of high-pitched zings. Orange-red tracers streak through the air and slam into the berms in front of and behind the Humvee. Large-caliber rounds are being fired at us from across the canal. You can actually see some bounce and tumble after they strike the ground just a few meters from us. For a moment, we simply watch, mesmerized.

"Person, get out of the vehicle," Colbert orders.

All of us dive out of the left side of the Humvee to avoid the incoming fire on the right. We scramble up and then down a meter-high berm, which shields us from the attack.

Rounds rake across the row of Humvees, making that weird noise—*zip zip zing*. They sound like the screaming cartoon bullets fired by Yosemite Sam. Up and down the line, Marines jump out of their vehicles and take cover.

Behind our berm, Colbert says, "That's a goddamn Zeus!" Zeus, the nickname for a ZSU, is a powerful, multi-barreled Russian anti-aircraft gun. (Other Marines later posit that the Iraqis were using a slightly different weapon, a ZPU.)

Several Marines in the battalion fire rifles and .50-cal machine guns wildly and ineffectually across the river. But as more Zeus rounds streak in, they dive for cover, too. No one can figure out where the enemy position is located. Marines, who often laugh off other forms of gunfire, now burrow facedown in the nearest comforting patch of mother earth. The entire battalion is pinned down.

The only guy I see poking his head up is Trombley. He had the presence of mind to grab the binoculars when he dove out of the Humvee. Now he scampers to the top of the berm, sits up like a gopher and scans the horizon. He looks around excitedly, eagerly taking in this terrifying new experience. I see him smile.

"That's cool," he says in a low voice as another salvo of Zeus rounds zings past. Then he adds, "I think I see where it is, Sergeant."

Colbert and Person now rise over the berm, somewhat more cautiously than Trombley. Following his initial directions, they spot what they think is the enemy-gun position about a kilometer away. Colbert orders Hasser onto the vehicle's Mark-19 grenade launcher, and with Zeus rounds still screaming in, the team methodically directs fire toward the enemy position.

A Cobra noses down over the field across the canal to join in the hunt. It rears up as AAA fire comes at it from the ground. The enemy rounds miss the helicopter, and it doubles back to renew its attack.

The Cobra strikes a white truck parked in the field with its 20mm Gatling gun, causing the truck to burst into flames. Then it fires a Hellfire missile at what the pilot thinks is one of several Zeus AAA guns. Low on fuel, the Cobra is forced to break off its attack.

Different perspectives on the ground produce radically different versions of events. Kocher, just 150 meters up from Colbert's position, watches the white truck set on fire by the Cobra and believes this is one of the worst things he's seen so far in the war. He later says, "I saw civilians in that truck, and I watched them burn up alive."

Captain Daniel O'Connor, a First Recon officer also involved with controlling the air strikes that afternoon, later says, "I couldn't prove the white vehicle the Cobra lit up was enemy, but every time it showed up, bad stuff happened. So we were okayed to take it out."

Two columns of inky black smoke rise on the opposite side of the river. We take no more Zeus fire. I ask Trombley why he showed no signs of fear, seemed quite calm in fact, when he sat up on the berm and located the position of the gun that seemed to be terrorizing just about every other Marine in the battalion. "I know this might sound weird," Trombley says, "but deep down inside, I want to know what it feels like to get shot. Not that I want to get shot, but the reality is, I feel more nervous watching a game show on TV at home than I do here in all this."

He tears into his plastic meal-ration bag. "All this gun-fighting is making me hungry," he says with a cheerful smile.

"All this stupidity is making me want to kill myself," Person counters grimly, one of his first displays of low spirits in Iraq.

Despite having wiped out several AAA guns with the help of the Cobras, the battalion is again starting to take incoming mortars by the bend in the canal. The Marines are ordered to break contact and roll back two kilometers.

The battalion pulls off the trail into a muddy depression surrounded by berms. The vehicles pull in close together. We wait for the Cobras to refuel in order to accompany the battalion on its final dash into Al Hayy.

Mortar fire grows more steady. With each wave of incoming bombs, the explosions get a little louder, a little closer. The initial volleys land more than a kilometer away, then move to within about five hundred meters of First Recon's position. The orderly progression of the mortars suggests that an enemy observer is on the ground nearby, directing them. Marine snipers push out to the perimeter and try to spot a man or woman with a radio amidst the shepherds, farmers and other civilians in the surrounding fields.

Colbert's vehicle is parked beside one of the battalion's fuel trucks. I decide I don't like sitting next to 1,000 gallons of diesel fuel during a mortar attack. I walk over to the truck holding the roughly twenty enemy prisoners of war (EPWs) Third Platoon picked up earlier in the day.

They're packed into the rear of the flatbed, sitting on benches along either side. During the Zeus attack, the prisoners, who were left in the truck while their Marine captors dove out and took cover, gnawed through their plastic wrist cuffs.

Marines are retying the Iraqis' hands behind their backs with parachute cord. The EPWs are men in their twenties, wearing jeans or black trousers, striped soccer jerseys, one guy with an Opel car logo on his shirt. But these aren't the docile, defeated EPWs First Recon encountered earlier in the war.

Several of these guys are defiant. They mad-dog the Marines with angry stares and wiggle in their seats, trying to cut the cords binding their wrists. Others turn their backs and squirm away from Marines attempting to retie them. They make exaggerated grimaces and complain loudly in Arabic. Binding EPWs' wrists tightly enough to cut off their circulation and make their skin bleed is a passive way of punishing them. A few Marines I talk to later on will brag of doing this, or of slamming a guy in the face or nuts when no one is looking.

But it's also extremely hard to deal with twenty guys who are resisting being tied up. Americans, of course, are also trained to evade and resist capture, but this doesn't make it any less enraging when the enemy is doing it to them.

"What would these guys be doing to us if they were holding us prisoner?" a Marine shouts nearby. "How do you think we'd be treated?"

"We ought to tie these motherfuckers to the hoods of our Humvees before we drive into the next ambush," another Marine says.

An officer with a shaky knowledge of Arabic steps forward to calm the rising tensions. In halting, polite Arabic, he tells the EPWs they will not be harmed or executed, then asks them to please stop trying to escape, or the Marines will be forced to wrap burlap sacks over their heads. The EPWs immediately calm down. Two guys in the rear of the truck, both of whom have matching Saddam mustaches, start making buffoonish faces, trying to ingratiate themselves to the Americans. One of them repeats in English, "Fuck Saddam!" Each time he says it, his buddy squeals with laughter. Soon, several others join in—howling and making funny faces—and the truck suddenly takes on the character of a small, clown-only travelling circus.

Then a salvo of incoming mortars puts a stop to their antics. They explode about 200 meters away, with columns of smoke rising up from the nearby field. Several of the EPWs try ducking down, but their wrists are bound to the sides of the truck. One EPW squirms ashamedly on the bench. A powerful odor comes from the truck. Apparently, he's just had a classic combat-stress reaction and defecated in his pants.

PAPPY AND REYES have pushed out together onto the perimeter as a sniper team, hunkering down behind a berm and setting up their M-40 rifle. They spot a man whom they believe to be a forward observer for the mortars. He's in a white pickup parked nearly 600 yards away across the field. With the rules of evidence being somewhat looser in a combat zone than they are back home, the man in the truck earns himself a death sentence for the crime of holding what appear to be binoculars and a radio. Pappy fires three shots, aiming at the man's center mass through the door. After his rifle steadies, Pappy observes his target for a few moments. The man is slumped forward in the truck, apparently dead.

This is Pappy's second sniper kill in Iraq. Returning to his Humvee, he seems to take no satisfaction from it. When some fellow Marines excitedly press him for details of the kill, he doesn't want to talk about it. All he says is, "The man went down." The mortar fire ceases. Evidently, Pappy killed the right man.

Fick gathers his team leaders to explain the final phase

of the mission. In about five minutes the battalion is going to head back up to the bend in the canal, push beyond the mosque, drive through a few kilometers of densely concentrated hamlets, then approach the western edge of Al Hayy. The trickiest part will be entering the town. The convoy will be forced into a series of S-turns while crossing two separate bridges over canals. Then the Marines will race past about two kilometers of built-up urban terrain, reaching an elevated roadway. There, the Marines will drive up an earthen ramp onto the main highway out of the town and seize a key bridge. The goal is to seal off the primary escape route out of Al Hayy, in preparation for RCT-1's assault through the city's center, which is now expected to come in about ten hours, at four in the morning.

After briefing his men, Fick says privately to me, "This is *Black Hawk Down* shit we are doing." He adds, "The fact that we never initiate contact with the enemy—it's always them on us—is wearing on these guys. In their training as Recon Marines, it's a failure every time they get shot at first. It doesn't matter that we've done well shooting our way out of these engagements. They're supposed to be the ones initiating the contact, not the enemy."

AS THE CONVOY MOVES OUT from its position in the mudflats and starts rolling, single-file, on the trail toward Al Hayy, Cobra escorts pour rockets and machine-gun fire into a nearby palm grove. Watching the attack, Colbert says, "This country is dirty and nasty, and the sooner we are out of here the better."

Though almost no one ever talks about religion, some Marines silently say their prayers. At a wide spot in the trail just before the mosque, Espera's vehicle pulls up beside Colbert's. Both vehicles are going about twenty-five miles per hour. I glimpse Corporal Jason Lilley, the twenty-three-year-old driver of Espera's vehicle, clenching the wheel, staring ahead unblinking. His lips are moving. He later tells me that although he's not a big Christian, he was saying, "Lord see us through," over and over.

After we pass the mosque, machine guns and small rockets, called "zunis," being fired by the Cobras kick up a massive dust cloud that envelops the convoy. The road sinks down and snakes between tree-lined hamlets. Some of Recon's transport trucks rolling in the middle of the convoy take fire. At least one has its tires shot out but rides on the rims.

We reach the edge of the city and cross the first bridge into an industrial area of low-slung cinder-block buildings, with a dense cluster of apartment blocks to our right. In all the dust kicked up, several of Recon's supply trucks take a wrong turn.

Colbert's team and the rest of his platoon hang back to provide cover while the drivers of the lost team unfuck themselves and turn around. We stop for several minutes, surrounded by walls and windows in the hostile city. We hear AKs and machine guns clattering, but don't see any muzzle flashes.

Charlie Company, which is now crossing the second bridge in the S-turn, is coming under fire from a building seventy-five meters away. Charlie's lead vehicle is commanded by Sergeant Charles Graves, a twenty-six-year-old sniper. An RPG round blows up beside his open-top Humvee. Shrapnel superficially wounds one of his Marines in the leg. Their vehicle is raked with machine-gun fire. One round cuts through a piece of metal inches from Graves's head. His Mark-19 gunner opens up on the building where the enemy shooters are concealed. The building is kind of pretty—a long, pale-blue stucco structure with arches along its second story. Graves's Mark-19 gunner saturates it with thirty-two rounds, blowing giant holes in the front of it, collapsing part of the roof. Watching the destruction as his team speeds past, Graves thinks, he later tells me, "It's fucking beautiful."

No more fire comes from the building. By now, Colbert's team has picked up the lost supply trucks. We turn toward the building hit by Charlie Company. As we roll by the smoking ruins, Person shouts, "Damn, sucka!"

Across from the building, a live Arab lies in the road. He's in a dingy white robe, squeezed between piles of rubble. The man is only about two meters from where our wheels pass, on his back with both hands covering his eyes. After being subjected to hostile fire all day, there's a kind of sick, triumphant rush in seeing another human being, perhaps an enemy fighter, now on his back, helplessly cowering. It's empowering in a way that is also depressing. All the Marines who drive past the man train their guns on him but don't shoot. He's not a threat—childishly trying to protect his face with his hands. To the Marines, the man doesn't even merit being shot.

After clearing the second bridge, the convoy races up to about forty miles an hour, speeding past the urban mass of Al Hayy to our right. Ahead of us Charlie Company comes under sporadic AK fire from the town. Marines shoot back. Corporal Caleb Holman, a nineteen-year-old .50-cal gunner, sees a man perking up in some scrub grass fifty meters from his Humvee near the middle of the convoy. Firing armor-penetrating SLAP rounds from his .50-cal, Holman blows the top of the man's head off.

TWENTY-ONE

○

A FEW MINUTES BEFORE SUNSET on March 31, First Recon reaches its objective: the bridge that serves as the main road out of Al Hayy. It presents another strange juxtaposition typical of Iraq. After moving all day through primitive hamlets, the Marines now stand at the foot of a span that, with its long, graceful concrete lines, wouldn't be out of place on the German autobahn. Bravo Company is tasked with setting up the blockade on the highway at the north end of the bridge. The rest of the battalion pushes a kilometer farther north up Route 7.

Colbert's team and the others in the platoon pull their Humvees up to where the guardrails start at the foot of the bridge. They point their main guns toward the bridge, which rises in a slight crest about 200 meters from their position, where it stretches over a canal. Beyond that, the highway drops out of view, as it descends toward Al Hayy about two kilometers to the south.

Three Marines sprint onto the bridge with a bale of concertina wire, which they stretch across the roadway. They run back to the Humvees in the last minutes of daylight. The area around the highway where the Marines have their blockade is a barren no-man's-land. The ground is saturated with salts that push up to the surface, forming a white crust on the mud. In the twilight gloom, all you see is the pale whiteness of the salty flats. Fick walks up, grinning. Even loaded down with his vest, flak jacket and bulky chemical-protection suit, he displays his characteristic bouncing stride. Right now it's more buoyant than usual. "I feel like for the first time we seized the initiative," he says, surveying the roadblock. Everyone seems to be swaggering.

After nearly two weeks of feeling hunted, the Marines have done what they were supposed to do: They assaulted through resistance and took an objective. Psychologically it's like a game of king of the hill, and they now occupy the high ground. This small band of young men controls the key exit from a town of 50,000.

First Recon Battalion is completely alone. The Marines are twenty kilometers north of the nearest American unit, RCT-1. They are thirty kilometers south of Al Kut, home to approximately 15,000 Iraqis in a mechanized division. There is nothing between them and those thousands of Iraqis but a straight, narrow highway. Only later will it become clear that most regular Iraqi forces won't fight; on the night of March 31, that fact is unknown. Adding to their sense of isolation, First Recon has lost communication with its air cover this evening, as the result of a technical glitch. If the battalion is attacked, it will have to fight on its own.

ONE THING THE MARINES haven't trained for, or really even thought through, is the operation of roadblocks at night. The basic idea is simple enough: Put an obstacle like concertina wire in the road and point guns at it. If a car approaches, fire warning shots. If it keeps coming, shoot it. The question is: Do the Iraqis understand what's going on? When it gets dark, can Iraqi drivers actually see the concertina wire? Even Marines have been known to drive through concertina wire at night.

The other problem is warning shots. In the dark, warning shots are simply a series of loud bangs and flashes. It's not like this is the international code for "Stop your vehicle and turn around." As it turns out, many Iraqis react to warning shots by speeding up. Maybe they just panic. Consequently, a lot of Iraqis die at roadblocks.

The initial killings at First Recon's roadblock come just after dark. Several cars approach the bridge with their headlights on, coming from the direction of Al Hayy. Bravo's .50-caliber gunners fire warning bursts. The cars turn around and leave. Then a tractor-trailer appears, its diesel engine growling. The Marines fire warning shots, but the truck keeps coming.

A few seconds after the truck fails to heed the second warning burst, its headlights dip onto Bravo's position, blinding the Marines. The truck sounds like it must be doing thirty or forty.

"Light it the fuck up!" someone shouts.

Under the ROE, a vehicle that fails to stop at a roadblock is declared hostile, and everyone in it may justifiably be shot. Almost the entire platoon opens fire. But for some reason, these Marines who have previously put down enemy shooters with almost surgical precision are unable to take out even the truck's headlights after several seconds of heavy fire. Red tracers and white muzzle flashes streak across the bridge. Mark-19 grenades burst all around the truck, but it keeps coming, horn blaring.

Just before reaching the concertina wire, the vehicle jackknifes and screeches. Someone has finally managed to hit the driver, whose head, they later discover, is blown clean off. Meanwhile, three men jump from the cab. Espera, who is wearing night-vision goggles, sees them and fires his M-4 from a crouching position, methodically pumping three-round bursts into the chest of each, as he was trained. Almost as an afterthought, the Marines shoot out the last headlight of the truck.

THERE'S NO TIME to examine the scene of the shooting. The entire battalion pulls back from the bridge, moving a couple of kilometers north to a more defensible position. The triumphant feelings that soared a half hour ago have vanished. It's suddenly cold, a Humvee becomes stuck in the mud and in Bravo's Second Platoon, Marines are again dealing with weapons that jammed catastrophically in the engagement with the truck. Next to Colbert's vehicle, the .50-cal on Lovell's Humvee had a round explode in the chamber, puffing out the gun's chassis—a fifty-pound block of forged steel—like a balloon. In the darkness Lovell marvels, "Fellas, we just destroyed a ten-thousand-dollar piece of U.S. government property." They are lucky the gun didn't blow up.

In Colbert's vehicle, the Mark-19 jammed again—as it has in two previous engagements. Hasser, who's manning the weapon, screams, "Shit! Shit! Shit!" and pounds the roof of the Humvee, trying to unjam it. He lets out a half-crazed scream. *"Raaah!"*

Colbert shouts up to him, "Walt! You're losing control of yourself. Shut the fuck up and take a deep breath."

"This goddamn gun!" Hasser shouts. His voice cracks. "It's a piece of shit!"

"Walt, you know I like you a lot," Colbert says, trying to calm him. "But it's not going to help if you lose control of your emotions. We just don't have enough LSA to keep it lubed properly. There's nothing we can do about it." He adds, "I'm sorry I had to yell at you."

Colbert's platoon falls back from the bridge to defend the battalion's eastern flank along the highway. Everyone digs holes in the darkness. The soil here is a waterlogged mixture of clay and rocks. It's like chopping through partially hardened concrete. After we finish our Ranger graves, the platoon is ordered to move up the road 300 meters, where we dig a new set.

A string of headlights appears a kilometer or so to the west. It is a stream of vehicles escaping the city on a back road. It could be civilians fleeing. But using night-vision equipment, Marines observe what appear to be trucks with weapons on them.

"They're fucking flanking us!" Fick says, worried that the enemy fighters are trying to come up and attack the battalion from the side. Marines then observe one truck with its lights off, stopping directly across from their position and unloading men and equipment, possibly guns. Fick requests an artillery strike to take out the vehicles.

Marines in Bravo who are not on watch gather around to eat their meager food rations before crawling into their wet holes to take quick "combat naps."

"I felt cold-blooded as a motherfucker shooting those guys that popped out of the truck," Espera says, glumly describing the details of each killing he participated in at the roadblock an hour earlier. Perhaps keeping in mind his priest's admonishments to not enjoy killing, Espera seems to deliberately wallow in a black, self-flagellating mood. "Dog, whatever last shred of humanity I had before I came here, it's gone," he says.

Warning shots erupt at the roadblock manned by

Charlie Company a few hundred meters to our north. Tracers light up the sky. We hear a car gunning its engine, apparently still driving toward the blockade. Marines shout. Weapons crackle. We hear the engine still whining, drawing closer, then the screeching of tires. In the silence that immediately follows, someone in our group says, "Well, that stopped him." For some reason, everyone bursts into laughter.

UP THE ROAD FROM where we are laughing, the men in Charlie Company watch as two men run from a car the Marines have just riddled with dozens of rounds. It's a four-door sedan. Doors are open, lights are on despite the heavy-weapons fire it took from a platoon of Marines. It's a miracle that these two men, including the driver, have stepped out alive.

The Marines hold their fire as the men, dressed in robes, throw their hands up. They are unarmed. As Marines shout at them, they drop obediently to the side of the road.

Graves, whose team beautifully destroyed the building that shielded the enemy gunmen during the assault through Al Hayy, approaches the car with another Marine. Graves sees a little girl curled up in the backseat. She looks to be about three, the same age as his daughter at home in California. There's a small amount of blood on the upholstery, but the girl's eyes are open. She seems to be cowering. Graves reaches in to pick her up—thinking about what medical supplies he might need to treat her, he later says—when the top of her head slides off and her brains fall out. When Graves steps back, he nearly falls over when his boot slips in the girl's brains. It takes a full minute before Graves can actually talk. The situation is one he can only describe in elemental terms. "I could see her throat from the top of her skull," he says.

No weapons are found in the car. Meesh asks the father, sitting by the side of the road, why he didn't heed the warning shots and stop. The father simply repeats, "I'm sorry," then meekly asks permission to pick up his daughter's body. The last the Marines see of him, he is walking down the road, carrying her corpse in his arms.

WHEN THEY TALK about this shooting later, the Marines have mixed reactions. Graves is devastated. "This is the event that is going to get to me when I go home," he says. Prior to this shooting, when his team had passed by all those shot-up corpses on the roads, Graves says, "I felt good about it, like, 'Yeah! Marines have been fucking shit up!' " He adds, "I cruised into this war thinking my buddy's going to take a bullet, and I'm going to be the fucking hero pulling him out of harm's way. Instead, I end up pulling out this little girl we shot, hiding in the back-seat of her dad's car."

Graves's buddy, twenty-two-year-old Corporal Ryan Jeschke, who was with him at the car, says, "War is either glamorized—like we kick their ass—or the opposite— look how horrible, we kill all these civilians. None of these people know what it's like to be there holding that weapon. After Graves and I went up to that dead girl, I was surprised, because honestly, I was indifferent. It's kind of disturbed me. Now, sometimes, I think, 'Am I a bad person for feeling nothing?' "

Despite his professed indifference, Jeschke is haunted by the memory of seeing the girl's father walk down the road, cradling his dead daughter. Jeschke says, "I asked Meesh what he thought the father was going through, and Meesh said Arabs don't grieve as hard as we do. I don't really believe him. I can't see how it would be any different for them."

After this shooting and the others like it, Marines deal with the stress through black humor. Even guys privately broken up by the shootings circulate jokes, one of them: "What's the first thing you feel when you shoot a civilian? The recoil of your rifle."

THE ARTILLERY STRIKE Bravo Company called previously on vehicles fleeing the city finally starts to arrive. Since First Recon is so far north, the artillery gunners can only reach them by using rocket-assisted projectile (RAP) rounds, which give their guns a range of thirty kilometers. After RAP rounds are fired, they flash in the sky and then make a sort of fizzing sound, as a rocket motor mounted on each projectile kicks in and drives it to its target. They make for an even more spectacular show than normal artillery. We lie back in our holes and watch 164 RAP rounds shriek across the sky. Seen from a distance, the fiery explosions are beautiful and hypnotizing, just like any decent Fourth of July display. Any carnage visited on the vehicles, hamlets, farms or people is shrouded from us by the darkness. All we see are the pretty lights of the rockets' red glare.

TWENTY-TWO

○

On March 30, Capt. Patterson's Alpha Company was ordered to temporarily detach from First Recon and go on a mission to find the body of the Marine who went missing when his supply convoy was ambushed on Route 7 outside Ash Shatrah. No one knows if rumors of his body's public mutilation are true, but many Marines inevitably see Alpha's task to recover it as a revenge mission. When Alpha Company had pulled out of First Recon's camp for Ash Shatrah, men in Bravo had shouted after them, "Fuck the shit out of that town!"

Now, on the morning of March 31, with the rest of the battalion making its way north toward Al Hayy, the eighty Marines in Alpha Company are heading south on Route 7 toward Ash Shatrah. To Sergeant Damon Russell Fawcett, a twenty-six-year-old team leader in Alpha's Second Platoon, the mission fills him, he later admits, with conflicting emotions. Fair-haired and blue-eyed, Fawcett grew up in Southern California, a "water baby," surfing and playing water polo. After several semesters in college, he joined the Marines not just for adventure but because he was so "disenchanted with the human factor in society, the emphasis on technology. I came in to see if the better man will dominate."

For the past eighteen hours since departing on the mission, Fawcett has listened to fellow Marines rage about the motherfuckers in Ash Shatrah, and their plans to get payback once their commanders clear them hot to assault the town. A lot of guys are talking not just about the lost Marine but about rumors now circulating of Iraqis abusing American female POWs. (Within the next twenty-four hours, when the tale of Jessica Lynch's captivity and rape reaches the men, she becomes the campaign's unofficial Helen of Troy, a rallying point for generalized anger against Arabs.) Fawcett is particularly disturbed by an acquaintance of his, a sniper, who recently bragged that after being cleared to shoot an armed Iraqi who was taking cover behind a child, the sniper fired at the man through the kid, telling Fawcett, "I just killed a future terrorist."

Fawcett has a desire for revenge like everyone else, but at the same time he keeps thinking, as he later tells me, "When I get home people will probably ask me to speak at high schools about this. I don't know how I'm going to explain all the dead women and children I've seen, the things we've done here." Now he tells some of the guys he's with, "If you're mad about them mutilating a Marine, it's not like this is the only country on earth with sociopaths. We've got people at home in American cities who hurt and degrade people all the time."

Not only are the men in Alpha thirsting for payback, they're so hungry that when their convoy pauses on its journey to Ash Shatrah, they jump out and ratfuck trash piles along Route 7. POG supply units passing by in recent days have left mountains of MRE litter beside the road. Marines in Alpha, having endured reduced rations for several days, dig through them, hunting for uneaten Tootsie Roll or peanut butter packets.

Alpha Company's commander is dealing with a whole different set of problems. The mission has gone through so many permutations in the last several hours that it's now clear to Capt. Patterson that finding the body of the lost Marine is a distant secondary objective. In fact, Patterson's orders now verge on the fantastic. His Marines in Alpha, along with a much larger force from RCT-1, will link up outside the city and join a CIA-controlled operation to liberate Ash Shatrah, assisted by an indigenous army of "freedom fighters."

According to the portions of the plan Patterson has been let in on, the CIA has spent months training and equipping a small army of Iraqi "freedom fighters" in an unnamed foreign country. Now these freedom-loving patriots have been flown into Iraq, where they will face their first test, liberating Ash Shatrah.

The Marines will not be leading this mission. Their role is simply to be there to help out the Iraqi freedom fighters in case they get into a jam. Once the CIA-controlled exiles have liberated the city in the name of Free Iraq, the Marines will enter, brave the crowds who some are now predicting will be dancing in the streets, and search for the lost Marine.

Patterson has been careful in the past several hours to try to tone down the mood of his men. He later says, "I didn't want some dramatic idea of revenge to be motivating everybody." Even so, as his company rolls up to Ash Shatrah, Patterson experiences what he later describes as a "feeling that there is a heroic aspect to what we're doing, that we are going to go into this town, getting one of our fallen brothers, and we're going to be the saviors of everyone."

* * *

IT'S OVERCAST when Alpha Company arrives on the northern outskirts of Ash Shatrah at about six in the morning on March 31. The ground is wet from recent rains, and the place smells like decay. First Recon had passed through Ash Shatrah on March 26 on its thrust up from Nasiriyah, and the town had been exceptionally foul smelling then. This morning, Patterson realizes the odor comes from the corpses of shot-up Iraqi fighters rotting in nearby ditches. Ash Shatrah runs for about two kilometers north down the eastern side of the road. Alpha Company sets up along the north end of the town. Several hundred infantry Marines from RCT-1's Third Battalion are deployed farther down the road, bolstered with tanks and armored vehicles.

Patterson realizes just how big a deal this mission is when he sees General Kelly, Maj. Gen. Mattis's personal emissary, arrive by helicopter to consult with high-level Marine officers and the CIA officials running the show. The CIA guys, three young men who look to be in their late twenties, arrive in an armored vehicle, and emerge wearing jumpsuits, flak vests and black caps. The CIA men ratchet up the anticipation level of the mission with exciting new intelligence: One of Saddam's top henchmen, General Ali Hassan al-Majid, known as "Chemical Ali," is believed to be holed up in the town.

AFTER FAWCETT'S TEAM gets into position by the highway at the north end of Ash Shatrah—using the road's elevation to provide cover—they notice the town is filled with military installations. Just a couple hundred meters away, they spot barracks, artillery pieces, stockpiles of munitions, an obstacle course for training soldiers and, most amazingly, Iraqis in uniform walking around outdoors in broad daylight. Fawcett can't believe that Marine convoys have been driving up and down this road for nearly a week next to a sizable, heavily armed force of Iraqis. Watching this, he later tells me, makes him wonder "what's going through the minds of the guys we have planning stuff for us."

It's not like the Iraqis don't have a clue the Americans are coming. The night before, U.S. ships launched several Tomahawk cruise missiles into the town (at a cost to U.S. taxpayers of approximately 1.5 million dollars per Tomahawk). Patterson, who's told about the cruise missiles when he arrives, is impressed. Comparable Marine operations against small, run-of-the-mill hostile towns like Ash Shatrah haven't rated the use of such high-tech weaponry. Clearly, this shows the hand of the CIA, sparing no expense in its effort to make the liberation of Ash Shatrah go as smoothly as possible and become a showcase for its handpicked army of Iraqi freedom fighters.

Patterson and his counterpart in the infantry battalion sit down outside the town and coordinate "control measures." They make sure they know each other's radio frequencies so they can communicate. They study maps of the town so their men don't run into each other later on. They rename all the main routes in the city, replacing confusing Arabic names with ones that are easier to remember, like "Sally," "Jane" and "Mary." Marines tend to be methodical about things like this, few more so than Patterson. Within forty minutes of these consultations, Patterson is all set to participate in this small, history-making event: the first liberation of a town in central Iraq by Iraqi forces.

There's just one problem: The freedom fighters have gone missing. Several of them had infiltrated the town the night before, under cover of the Tomahawk strike, in order to find sympathizers among the ranks of the Iraqi soldiers garrisoned there, but they were captured. Apparently, the Baathists who apprehended them had not been impressed by the missile strike, and they were summarily executed. Their comrades waiting outside the town lost heart. Early in the afternoon Patterson's men are told, "The freedom fighters have fled." After all their elaborate preparations, the CIA's army has vanished into the countryside.

BY NOW PATTERSON'S MARINES have started to come under sporadic small-arms fire from the town. They call in a mortar strike on suspected enemy positions. The Marines, who've driven all night to carry out what they thought would be a sweet, revenge-fueled version of *Saving Private Ryan*, grow frustrated.

Very quickly their mission outside Ash Shatrah becomes as confusing as all the others they have participated in. Commanders begin to change the ROE. Initially, Marine snipers are cleared to kill anyone in uniform. They get in a few shots, then word is passed down that soldiers are surrendering and they shouldn't automatically be shot.

Following this, Marines see a truck filled with soldiers zoom onto a street directly across from their position. The Marines hold their fire. The Iraqi soldiers drive past, waving white flags, then speed off, throwing the flags from the back of the truck. "We're letting all these soldiers escape," one of Fawcett's men complains.

Fawcett requests an artillery strike on a headquarters building 600 meters across from his position. His team has observed Iraqis in green military uniforms coming and going from the front door of this building all morning. Fawcett regrets passing his request up almost immediately.

In Fawcett's opinion, his platoon commander doesn't know how to properly call in a strike (a similar complaint men in Bravo Company have about their commander, Encino Man). Fawcett believes the best way to take out the building is to order one or two rounds of artillery, see where they land, and if they don't hit the building, have the artillerymen adjust their fire. Instead, his commanding officer requests a "fire for effect" strike—four to six rounds of artillery shot all at once, then repeated without any adjustment. "It's an officer thing," Fawcett tells his men. "He just wants the glory of calling in a big strike. I can't go over his head."

Fawcett and his men watch at least sixteen HE rounds slam into the city and explode pretty much randomly in the streets. When the smoke clears, the only damage to the intended target is that a corner of the building has been clipped off. Fawcett turns to several of his buddies and asks, "Don't you think if some foreign army came into a small American town and did what we're doing here, you wouldn't find some American good old boys eager to string one of them up if they fell into their hands?"

A FEW HOURS BEFORE SUNSET, the Marines are ordered to assault the town. The infantrymen from Third Battalion lead the way in, advancing under heavy machine-gun fire, blowing up buildings in their path with shoulder-fired missiles. They seize several military structures and clear the surrounding houses. Nearly all of the Iraqi soldiers have fled or changed out of their uniforms in order to blend in with the populace. They fire few shots. There's no sign of Chemical Ali or the body of the missing Marine.

Fawcett's platoon and another from Alpha drive their Humvees about 500 meters into the town, with Cobras launching Hellfire missiles ahead of them. They move into a water-purification plant, a complex of industrial structures filled with trucks and machinery. The men are ordered to stay here for the night.

By sundown, any thought that this could be a revenge mission completely disappears. Dozens of Iraqi citizens approach Alpha's hungry Marines on the perimeter, bearing gifts of tea, bowls of rice and flat bread, which Marines refer to as "Hajji tortillas." Some townspeople, speaking broken English, are eager to point out enemy positions. A few invite the Marines to come into their homes for a proper meal. Patterson is now forced to order his Marines, who hours before had been fantasizing about killing everyone in the town, to stop eating food brought to them by the locals.

After dark Patterson gets the clearest confirmation yet that the Baath Party and Iraqi military forces have abandoned the town. Through his NVGs he observes hundreds of people streaming in and out of government buildings "like ants, carting off everything they can carry—desks, chairs, mattresses."

Iraqis aren't the only ones looting. Inside the water-purification plant Fawcett watches fellow Marines "rape the buildings—smashing things up, pissing everywhere, hunting for souvenirs." The water-purification plant must have been some sort of exemplary public-works project. Much of the equipment is new. Many of the trucks parked inside the buildings haven't even been driven; they still have plastic on the seats. Marines use Ka-Bar knives to rip apart their interiors for material to reupholster their Humvees and trucks.

After their exciting night at the water plant, the Marines leave Ash Shatrah early in the morning. Locals cheer. To one of Patterson's officers, "the change in the town was dramatic, like someone pulled a thumb off their backs. We liberated them."

While the CIA mission failed, the liberation of Ash Shatrah proves to be precedent-setting in another sense. The Marines pull out of the town, leaving behind little or no civil authority, hordes of looters roaming through blown-up, trashed buildings and a scattered army of Baathists, soldiers and other loyalists, many of them still armed and all of them completely unaccounted for. The type of liberation seen at Ash Shatrah will play itself out again and again in other towns across Iraq until the U.S. military reaches Baghdad, where it will do pretty much the same, resulting in a much grander scale of anarchy.

Fawcett's men don't hear any word about the missing Marine until they've pulled out of the town. They are told that an old man in Ash Shatrah met with officers in the infantry battalion and informed them that the body of the lost Marine had been dragged through the streets and strung up, but was cut down and buried by "good Samaritans." According to the story passed among Marines, the old man claimed that the good Samaritans did their best to give the Marine a Christian burial, then fled the city, fearing reprisals. After hearing this, Fawcett says, "All we've been looking for is a corpse. The Marine was gone before we got here."

The body of this Marine is discovered a week later by other American forces. They find it buried in Ash Shatrah's trash dump.

TWENTY-THREE

○

ON THE MORNING OF APRIL 1, the Marines of First Recon—less Alpha Company, not yet returned from its mission—greet the new day from their wet, muddy holes dug alongside the highway, north of Al Hayy. Few of the troops slept much the night before. After the fatal shooting of the little girl at Charlie Company's roadblock, the Marines fired warning shots at several more vehicles, and also killed the occupant of one car, a heavyset man in a twenty-year-old Buick, which had failed to stop. Later the Marines came under attack from a BM-21, which saturated a nearby field with bombs, though no one was hit. The destruction continues after sunrise.

Below our position on the highway, slow-moving A-10 jets circle the fringes of Al Hayy, belching out machine-gun fire. The airframe of the A-10 is essentially built around a twenty-one-foot-long, seven-barreled Gattling gun—the largest such weapon in the U.S. arsenal. When it fires, it makes a ripping sound like someone is tearing the sky in half. The A-10s wrap up their performance by dropping four phosphorous bombs on the city. These are chemical-incendiary bombs that burst in the sky, sending long tendrils of white, sparkling flames onto targets below.

The air attacks are part of RCT-1's advance into Al Hayy from the south. Now, in coordination with that effort, First Recon is ordered to move to a canal on the western side of the town and seal off another escape route.

Civilians line up by the side of the road when First Recon's convoy assembles for its departure. The morning's show of American airpower has whipped them into a frenzy. They greet the Marines like visiting celebrities. "Hello, my friend!" some of them shout. "I love you!" It doesn't seem to matter that these young men have just witnessed portions of their city being destroyed. Or maybe this is the very appeal of the Marines. One of the promises made by the Bush administration before the war started was that the Iraqi populace would be pacified by a "shock and awe" air-bombing campaign. The strange thing is, these people appear to be entertained by it. "They think we're cool," says Person, "because we're so good at blowing shit up."

First Recon's convoy pauses on the road by the bridge. Waving and jumping up and down, kids gathered by the tractor-trailer shot up the night before pay no heed to the corpses scattered not far from their feet. Farther on, there's another shot-up car, with a male corpse next to it in the dirt. More kids dance around the carnage, giving thumbs-up to the Americans, shouting, "Bush! Bush! Bush!"

I walk up to Espera's vehicle. He gazes out at the grinning, impoverished children with dirty feet and says, "How these people live makes me want to puke."

Garza, standing at his vehicle's .50-cal, says, "They live just like Mexicans in Mexico." He smiles at the children and throws them some candy. His grandmother is from Mexico, and by the way he is grinning, you get the idea that to him living like Mexicans is not all bad.

Espera turns away in disgust. "That's why I fucking can't stand Mexico. I hate third-world countries."

Despite Espera's harsh critique of the white man—he derides English as the "master's language"—his worldview reflects his self-avowed role as servant in the white man's empire, a job he seems to relish with equal parts pride, cynicism and self-loathing. He says, "The U.S. should just go into all these countries, here and in Africa, and set up an American government and infrastructure—with McDonald's, Starbucks, MTV—then just hand it over. If we have to kill a hundred thousand to save twenty million, it's worth it." He lights a cigar. "Hell, the U.S. did it at home for two hundred years—killed Indians, used slaves, exploited immigrant labor to build a system that's good for everybody today. What does the white man call it? 'Manifest Destiny.' "

Within a half hour, First Recon's convoy is again creeping north on an agricultural back road. Colbert's Humvee passes a tree-shaded hamlet on the left as a series of explosions issues from it. The blasts sounds like mortars being launched, perhaps from inside the village. Ten days ago, being within a couple hundred meters of an enemy position would have sent the entire team into a high state of alert, but this morning nobody says a word. Colbert wearily picks up his radio handset and passes on the location of the suspected enemy position.

Once the initial excitement wears off, invading a country becomes repetitive and stressful, like working on an old industrial assembly line: The task seldom varies, but if your attention wanders, you are liable to get injured or killed. Colbert's team stops in a grassy field a few hundred meters down from the village. There's a canal directly across from his Humvee, with a paved road running along it on the other side.

That canal road, another route out of Al Hayy, is the one the battalion is tasked with observing. Marines are to shoot any armed Iraqis fleeing the road.

Despite the lethal mission, the grassy field we stop in is idyllic. Half of Colbert's team—those who were up all night on watch—take advantage of the tall grass to stretch out and doze. It's a beautiful day, warm and clear, a bit humid. There's a stand of palm trees nearby. Birds fill the air with a loud, musical chattering. Trombley counts off ducks and turtles he observes in the canal with his binoculars. "We're in safari land," Colbert says.

The spell is broken when a Recon unit 500 meters down the line opens up on a truck leaving the city, putting an end to the birdsong in the trees. In the distance, a man jumps out holding an AK. He jogs through a field on the other side of the canal. We watch lazily from the grass as he's gunned down by other Marines.

The birds have resumed their singing when the man shot by the Marines reappears across the canal, limping and weaving like a drunk. Nobody shoots him. He's not holding a gun anymore. The ROE are scrupulously observed. Even so, they cannot mask the sheer brutality of the situation.

A few vehicles down from Colbert's, Team Three monitors the hamlet from where mortars seemed to have been launched when we rolled in. Doc Bryan and the others on the team have been watching the village through binoculars and sniper scopes for about an hour now. They have seen no signs of enemy activity, just a group of civilians—men, women and children—going about their business outside a small cluster of huts. But it's possible that rounds were fired from there. The Fedayeen often drive into a town, launch a few mortars and leave.

In any case, the place is quiet when, at about eleven o'clock in the morning, a lone 1,000-pound bomb dropped from an F-18 blows the hamlet to smithereens. The blast is so powerful that Fick jumps over a berm to avoid flying debris and lands on Encino Man. As the shock wave rolls through Colbert's position, I feel the concussion in my chest as if my internal organs are being picked up and slammed against my rib cage. A perfectly shaped black mushroom cloud rises up where the huts had been.

The only survivor observed by the Marines is a singed dog that runs out of the smoke, making crazy circles—indicative of blown eardrums and a subsequent loss of balance. Team Three's Corporal Michael Stinetorf, twenty-one, who was watching when the bomb hit, is livid: "I just saw seven people vaporized right before my very eyes!" Behind Team Three's position, the men observe the commanders who called in the strike smoking cigars and laughing. One of them gripes, "Those fuck-heads are celebrating. They're laughing like it's a game."

But as in other bombing and shooting incidents, Marines don't all agree on what happened. Maj. Shoup, the air officer who helped coordinate the strike, sees it as a good hit. Prior to the bombing, Shoup was communicating with the F-18's backseater, a friend of his whose call sign is "Curly." Before releasing the bomb, Shoup says, "Curly reported seeing puffs of smoke coming from the courtyard of the village. These looked like mortars being launched." Shoup adds, "You want to improve the morale of Marines? They see that thousand-pound bomb go off, it really improves their morale."

By noon RCT-1 has completed its thrust through Al Hayy, and several thousand of its Marines now occupy positions north of the highway bridge seized by First Recon. RCT-1 met with only light resistance through the city, and its signal teams tasked with picking up enemy radio transmissions overhear Iraqi commanders telling their men, "Retreat north."

First Recon is moving north as well. The plan is for the battalion to continue pushing ahead of RCT-1 and move into Al Muwaffaqiyah, a town of 5,000 people, about five kilometers north of the field where we spent the morning.

The battalion convoy pulls onto a dirt lane and enters a series of shaded agricultural hamlets. We stop, and the residents pour out from their homes, waving and smiling. To the Marines, the villagers' warm welcome is confusing, given the fact that less than two kilometers down the road their neighbors were just wiped out by a 1,000-pound bomb dropped by an American F-18.

"They're probably just glad we're not blowing up their houses," Person observes.

We see the tiny heads of children poking around the corner of a small adobe hut. Several girls, maybe eight or nine, run toward us.

Ever since the shepherd-shooting incident, Colbert's demeanor has changed toward civilians, especially children. When he sees them now, he's prone to un-inhibited displays of sentimentality.

"How adorable," Colbert gushes as the girls laugh play-fully a few meters outside his window. "They're so cute."

He orders Trombley to dig out the last remaining humanitarian rations, hoarded by the Marines to supple-ment their one-MRE-a-day diet. Colbert steps out of the vehicle, holding the fluorescent-yellow humrat packs. Espera walks up, hunched over his weapon, scowling from his deep-set eyes, perspiring heavily. "Dog, I don't like being stopped here."

"Poke," Colbert says, calling him by his nickname. "Give these to the kids. I've got your back."

It's not that Colbert is afraid to walk across the yard. For some reason, he wants Espera to participate in this act of generosity. "Go on. You'll feel good," Colbert urges him.

Espera stalks up to the girls and hands them the packs. They run, squealing, back to the hut to show off their prizes to a woman in black standing outside.

"See, Poke," Colbert says. "They're happy."

In Iraq Espera spends his free moments reminiscing about his wife and eight-year-old daughter back home in Los Angeles. Outside of the Marine Corps, his family is the center of his life. He spent his final night before deploying to the Middle East camping with his daughter in a tree fort he'd built for her in his backyard. But out here, Espera doesn't seem to want to connect with civilians in any way. Most of all, he doesn't even want to look at the children. While Colbert continues to wave at the kids now opening the humrats by the hut, Espera breaks the Kodak moment. "Fuck it, dog. You think handing out some rice and candy bars is gonna change anything? It don't change nothing."

A FEW HUNDRED METERS up from Colbert's team, Meesh meets with villagers, who warn the Marines against trying to enter Al Muwaffaqiyah. They give Meesh detailed information about paramilitary forces that are setting up an ambush on the main bridge leading into the town.

When this report is passed over the radio to Colbert's team, Person speculates that the villagers might be helping because they are genuinely on our side.

"They're not on anybody's side," Colbert says. "These

are simple people. They don't care about war. They'd probably tell the Iraqis where we were if they rolled through here. They just want to farm and raise sheep."

Because of the villagers' warnings, First Recon's commander orders the battalion to leave the trail and set up in a wadi—a dry riverbed—four kilometers back from the bridge, where the ambush is supposedly being planned for them.

The Marines dig Ranger graves and set up a defensive perimeter. The battalion orders an artillery strike on the area around the bridge, then a couple of hours before sunset, RCT-1 sends Marines in several light armored vehicles (LAVs) to try to cross the bridge. They are turned back by heavy enemy gunfire. When the LAVs return down the road past the wadi we're in, Gunny Wynn spots one moving slowly with its rear hatch open and a wounded Marine in the back. "Guess the locals were right about that bridge," he says.

The Marines are told to prepare to stay here for the night. Despite the civilian deaths they've witnessed or caused in the past twenty-four hours, most Marines are still on a high from seizing the bridge the night before. Being told they're going to stay in one place for the next twelve hours or so adds to the morale boost.

The men spend the remaining hours of daylight partially stripping out of their MOPPs and washing up. Reyes breaks out an espresso pot, which he fills with Starbucks coffee, luxury items packed in his gear for special occasions. While brewing it, he accosts Pappy, his team leader, who's just finished shaving. "Pappy, you missed a spot."

Reyes takes his razor and cleans up around the edge of Pappy's sideburns. "Sometimes before a big meeting with the boss, I have to clean him up a little," Reyes explains.

"The battalion commander thinks I'm a bum," Pappy says, tilting his head slightly.

"Brother, that's 'cause he don't know what a true warrior be," Reyes says, clowning.

The close relationship shared by Reyes and Pappy is between two men who are complete opposites. While Reyes has so much bubbly effervescence that he manages to be flamboyant even in his MOPP suit, Pappy is a rangy, quintessentially laconic Southern man raised in a churchgoing, Baptist family in Lincolntown, North Carolina, a mountain town of a few thousand souls. Pappy jokingly describes himself as "your normal North Carolina loser," and says he'd barely ever met a Mexican before joining the Corps. Now Reyes is not just one of his best friends but his assistant team leader, his spotter when sniping, his second in battle. Reyes quips that their relationship is like that of "husband and wife." After Reyes finishes shaving him, he nudges Pappy's head to the side for a close inspection and pronounces, "Looking like a warrior, Pappy."

Everyone sits around enjoying the waning moments of daylight, as artillery booms into Al Muwaffaqiyah. One of the senior men in the platoon walks up and announces, "Looks like there's a big meeting going on with the battalion commander. I just hope he isn't coming up with some stupid-ass plan."

TWENTY-FOUR

○

At about eight o'clock that night, Fick returns from his meeting with his superiors and gathers his team leaders for a briefing. "The bad news is, we won't get much sleep tonight," he says. "The good news is, we get to kill people."

It's rare for Fick to sound so "moto," regaling his men with enthusiastic talk of killing. He goes on to present Lt. Col. Ferrando's ambitious last-minute plan to cross the bridge into Al Muwaffaqiyah, push north of the town and set up ambushes on a road believed to be heavily travelled by Fedayeen. "The goal is to terrorize the Fedayeen," he says, looking around, smiling expectantly.

His men are skeptical. They're all aware that when Marines approached the bridge a few hours ago in LAVs, they were hammered by enemy ambushers. Pappy repeatedly questions Fick about the enemy situation on the bridge. "It's been pounded all day by artillery," Fick answers, waving off his objections, sounding almost glib, like a salesman—all of this unusual for him. "I think the chances of a serious threat are low."

Fick walks a delicate line with his men. A good officer should be eager to take calculated risks. Despite the men's complaints against Ferrando for ordering them into an ambush at Al Gharraf, the fact is, only one Marine was injured, and the enemy's plans to halt the Marines' advance were thwarted. Fick privately admits that there have been times when he's actually resisted sending his troops on missions because, as he says, "I care a lot about these guys, and I don't like the idea of sending them into something where somebody isn't going to come back." While acting on these sentiments might make him a good person, they perhaps make him a less good officer. Tonight he seems uncharacteristically on edge, as if he's fighting his tendencies to be overly protective. He admonishes his team leaders, saying, "I'm not hearing the aggressiveness I'd like to." His voice sounds hollow, like he's not convinced himself.

The men, who ultimately have no choice in the matter, reluctantly voice their support of Fick's orders—ones that he has no choice but to follow, either. After he goes off, Pappy says, "The people running this can fuck things up all they want. But as long as we keep getting lucky and making it through alive, they'll just keep repeating the same mistakes."

What galls the men is the fact that they are situated just a few kilometers from the bridge. To them, it seems like a no-brainer to send a foot patrol out and observe the bridge before driving onto it. "Reconnaissance," Doc Bryan points out, "is what Recon Marines do."

Confidence is not bolstered when an Iraqi artillery unit—thought to have been wiped out by this point—sends numerous rounds kabooming into the surrounding mudflats. The men break up their discussion. However beautiful artillery might look when it's arcing across the sky onto enemy positions, when it's aimed at you, it sounds like somebody's hurling freight trains at your head. Everyone runs for the nearest hole and takes cover.

Following the Iraqi strike, we watch Marine batteries pour about 100 DPICM rounds onto the town side of the bridge four kilometers distant. Each DPICM round, loaded with either 66 or 89 submunitions, produces spectacular starbursts as it explodes over the city.

For tonight's mission, Colbert's team wins the honor of driving the lead vehicle onto the bridge. The team climbs into the Humvee just before eleven o'clock, some gobbling ephedra for what's expected to be an all-night mission. Colbert is not especially sanguine about the condition of the team's equipment. Due to the shortage of LSA lubricant, his vehicle's Mark-19 keeps going down. On top of this, on a night when they are going to be rolling through a hostile town, then setting up ambushes on back roads, there's almost no moon, which makes the operation of NVGs less than ideal. Ordinarily, the team would turn on its PAS-13 thermal-imaging scope, but tonight they have no batteries for it. (Fick does not hide his anger toward Casey Kasem for failing to keep the teams supplied with these items. "That guy's either running around with his video camera shooting his war documentary or sitting in his hole reading *Maxim*, while my men don't get what they need," he complained earlier.) Even though the team will be moving with impaired night-vision and a faulty main gun, Colbert tries to put a good spin on things. "We'll be okay," he says as they start the engine. "Just make sure you look sharp through those NVGs, Person."

We roll onto the darkened road, heading toward the bridge at about twenty-five miles per hour. Far up ahead, we see headlights from a lone vehicle moving down

perpendicular to the road we're on. It reaches the approx-
imate location of the bridge and the lights go off. Colbert
is watching this, debating its meaning: Some farmer
driving at night toward a bridge that's been pounded with
artillery for several hours? Fedayeen sending up re-
inforcements or using the headlights to signal someone?

The team ceases its speculation when Cobras thump
overhead. They fire multiple volleys of zuni rockets,
striping the sky in front of us with white burn trails that
culminate in multiple explosions near the bridge. We
make out trees—not palms but spiky eucalyptus trees—
silhouetted in the light of the bursting rockets.

Cobra pilots radio down to Maj. Shoup that their
thermal-imagining devices are picking up "blobs"—
possible heat signatures of people—hiding amidst the
eucalyptus trees by the foot of the bridge. The pilots tried
hitting them with their zunis, but the rockets overshot the
trees. Now they're concerned about firing any more for
fear of hitting the Marines approaching on the ground.
Due to a comms error in the battalion, none of this information is passed to Colbert, Fick or anyone else in the
platoon.

Colbert orders Person to continue driving into the
direction of the explosions. Everyone's life depends on
Person. He's the only one inside the Humvee with NVGs
on, allowing him to see the road ahead. He hunches forward over the steering wheel, his face obscured by the
apparatus. The NVGs give their wearer a bright gray-
green view of the night and offer a limited, tunnel-vision
perspective but no depth perception. Person is having
trouble finding the bridge. It's not quite where the map
indicated it would be. Colbert radios this news to Fick.

He radios back, "Not good. Not good."

Then Person figures out that reaching the bridge

requires a sharper right turn than he'd thought. He makes it. "There's an obstacle on the bridge," Person says in a dull monotone that nevertheless manages to sound urgent.

"What?" asks Colbert. He has night-vision capabilities on his rifle scope but in the cramped Humvee can't turn it forward to see what Person is looking at.

"It's like a shipping container," Person says. "In the middle of the road."

It's actually a blown-up truck turned sideways on the road several meters before the entrance to the bridge. We stop about twenty meters in front of it. To the left is that stand of tall eucalyptus trees. They're about five meters from the edge of the road. Behind us, there's a large segment of drainpipe that's been dragged across part of the road.

Person drove around the pipe a moment ago. Through his NVGs it had appeared to be a small trench in the road—what he'd thought was the result of natural erosion. Now the team behind us is radioing, "You guys just drove around a pipe."

It's becoming clear to the team that this is not random debris. The pipe and the ruined truck in front of us were deliberately placed where they are in order to channel the vehicle into what is known in military terms as a "kill zone." We are sitting in the middle of it.

Everyone in the Humvee (except me) has figured this out. The men remain extremely calm. "Turn the vehicle around," Colbert says softly. The problem is, the rest of the convoy has continued pushing into the kill zone behind us. All five Humvees in the platoon are bunched together, with twenty more pressing from behind. Person gets the Humvee partially turned around; the eucalyptus trees are now on our immediate right. But the pipe, which was behind us, now prevents the Humvee from moving forward.

Person guns the engine, starting into a sharp turn, intending to cut around the pipe by going off the road.

"Halt! Stop it," Colbert says. "Don't go off the road. It could be mined. We've got to go out the way we came in."

Colbert radios the rest of the platoon, telling them to back the fuck up, while simultaneously peering out his window through his night-vision rifle scope.

"There are people in the trees," he says, no trace of alarm in his voice. He repeats the message over his radio, hunches more tightly over his rifle and begins shooting.

His first shot kicks off an explosion of gunfire. There are between five and ten enemy fighters crouched beneath the trees—just five meters from the edge of our Humvee. There are several more across the bridge in bunkers, manning a belt-fed machine gun and other weapons, and still more ambushers on the other side of the road with RPGs. They have the Marines surrounded on three sides, raking the kill zone with rifle and machine-gun fire and RPGs.

Why they did not start shooting first is a mystery. Colbert believes, he later tells me, that they simply didn't understand the capabilities of American night-vision optics. The Marine rifles have night-vision scopes wedded to laser target designators—a little infrared beam that goes out and lights up the spot where the bullet will hit. Since it's infrared, the dot can only be seen through a night-vision scope or NVGs. What each Marine sees is not only his own laser dot lighting up a target, but those emitted by his buddies' weapons as well. The effect is sort of like a one-sided game of laser tag.

Now, in the kill zone, Marines looking through their scopes are seeing the heads and torsos of enemy fighters lit up by two or three laser dots at once, as they pick them off tag-team style, carefully transitioning from target to target. The Marines have to be careful. Their advantage in night optics is precarious. Bunched up as they are together, if they start shooting wildly, they risk killing one another. The other problem is, while the Marines are getting in good shots, their vehicles are so jammed up, no one's able to move out.

Fick can feel his truck jolting as enemy rounds rip through the sheet-metal sides. Through his window, he sees muzzles spitting flames in the darkness like a bunch of camera flashes going off at once. Then he sees an RPG streak right over the rear hatch of Colbert's Humvee and explode. He decides to jump out of his vehicle and try to direct the Humvees out of the kill zone. Fick's own coping mechanism for combat is what he calls the "Dead Man Walking Method." Instead of reassuring himself, as some do, that he's invincible or that his fate is in God's hands (which wouldn't work for him since he leans toward agnosticism), he operates on the assumption that he's already a dead man, so getting shot makes no difference. This is the mode he's in when he hops out of his Humvee, armed only with his 9mm pistol, and strides into the melee. Marines on Humvees shoot past his head while low-enfilade rounds from the enemy machine gun across the bridge skip past his feet. To the Marines seeing him approach, their lieutenant almost appears to be dancing. Fick later says he felt like he was in a shoot-out from *The Matrix*.

In our vehicle, Colbert seems to have entered a private realm. He fires bursts and, for some inexplicable reason, hums "Sundown," the depressing 1970s Gordon Lightfoot anthem. His M-4 jams repeatedly, but each time he calmly clears the chamber and resumes firing, while mumbling the chorus: "Sometimes I think it's a sin/When I feel like I'm winnin' when I'm losin' again."

Meanwhile, Person, frustrated by the traffic jam, opens his door and, with shots crackling all around, shouts, "Would you back the fuck up!" In the heat of battle, his Missouri accent comes out extra hick. He repeats himself and climbs back in, his movements almost lackadaisical.

Two Marines are hit in the first couple of minutes of shooting. Q-tip Stafford is knocked down in the back of Fick's truck by a piece of shrapnel to his leg. He ties his leg off with a tourniquet, gets back up and continues firing.

Pappy has a bullet rip through his foot and come out the other side, his torn boot gushing blood from both holes. He tourniquets the wound, resumes firing, gets on the radio and says, "Team Two has a man hit." He speaks of himself in the third person, he says, because he doesn't want to panic the rest of the platoon. Beside him in the driver's seat, Reyes, often teased for being the platoon's pretty boy, narrowly escapes a bullet that shatters the windshield and passes within an inch of his beautiful head. But Reyes feels oddly calm. He later says, "Wearing NVGs blocks your peripheral vision. You feel cocooned in this tunnel. It gives a false feeling of safety." He concentrates on executing a three-point turn, surrounded by four other Humvees all trying to do the same, each with Marines on top blazing away. But one of Reyes's tires is shot out. Driving on rims makes the Humvee wobble like a circus clown car. Pappy, riding beside him and shooting out his door, with his wounded foot elevated over the dashboard, repeatedly shouts, "You're going off the damn road!"

When Team Three's .50-caliber machine gun opens up over Doc Bryan's head where he's perched on the back of the Humvee, the concussive blasting is so intense that his nose starts bleeding. With his weapon growing sticky with blood and snot, he squeezes off two separate, very effective bursts, getting head shots on a pair of enemy ambushers.

Through it all, Espera fights from his Humvee beside ours while saying Hail Marys. In his NVGs he sees a man cut down in the extremities by a blast from Garza's .50-cal. When he sees the guy attempt to crawl off, Espera fires a burst, clipping the top of his head, and resumes his Hail Marys.

It takes five to ten minutes for the platoon to extricate itself from the kill zone, leaving most of the would-be ambushers either dead or in flight. Doc Bryan counts nine bodies scattered on both sides of the road. Corporal Teren Holsey, a twenty-year-old on Team Three, gets in the platoon's final kill. He rides hanging off the back of the last Humvee to leave the zone. After his vehicle makes it about fifty meters away from the pipe in the road, he looks back to see if anyone is following. He observes a man limping by the road and cuts him down with a burst from his M-4.

TWENTY-FIVE

○

JUST BEFORE MIDNIGHT on April 1, the platoon falls back a couple of kilometers from the ambush zone, then turns around on the road, orienting its Humvees toward the bridge. Unlike after the ambush at Al Gharraf, when the team became giddy at the cessation of fire, everyone is now subdued. Colbert is concerned about a loud scraping sound the Humvee had made while pulling back from the bridge. He and Person climb out and find cables tangled around the axles—debris from the road. The team spends several minutes cutting them away, then clambers back in. No one says anything in the darkness. They are ordered to prepare for another attempt on the bridge. Trombley falls asleep, snoring loudly in the seat next to me.

Pappy, now in a lot of pain from his wounded foot, is unloaded and sent back to the battalion's rear for medical aid. Reyes is promoted to team leader, and takes Pappy's seat in the Humvee. Q-tip Stafford, wounded in the leg, decides to stick around for the second assault.

At about twelve-thirty, we witness a monster artillery barrage. Marine batteries lob numerous HE rounds into the city on the far side of the bridge, trying to break apart the machine-gun bunkers. Helicopters fire their chain guns, rockets, then a TOW missile into the obstacle blocking the entrance to the bridge. All the missile blast does is lift the obstacle up, then drop it in the same place.

RCT-1 sends up two M1A1 tanks and eight LAVs. When we hear them rumble past, everyone's spirits lift, then soar when the LAVs maneuver up to the bridge and rip into the city with their Bushmasters. The cannons thunder, spouting red fireballs. The sky sounds like it's cracking. With their heavy weapons flashing in the darkness, the armored vehicles resemble fire-breathing dragons. "Look at them, dog," Espera says, poking his head into Colbert's vehicle. "Pouring down hate and discontent like a motherfucker."

The tanks roll forward and push the obstacle out of the way, but their commanders decide the bridge is too unstable to cross. The armor pulls back.

Bravo Company is sent back to the bridge. This time, due to the two wounded in Second Platoon, Third Platoon is ordered into the lead. I experience a sinking feeling as we approach the bridge behind them. I keep myself wrapped tightly in a poncho. I've been freezing all night. Earlier, when we pulled back from the ambush, I was shivering so badly that my feet were bouncing off the floor. Doc Bryan later tells me this was likely a physical reaction to excessive adrenaline, which cuts the flow of blood to the extremities, resulting in a sensation of extreme cold. It starts again when we pass the last tank on our way to the bridge. I can't keep my feet flat on the floor. My heels keep bouncing up like they're spring-loaded.

Next to me, I hear Trombley snoring again, slumped over his SAW, asleep. I nudge him and whisper, "We're at the bridge."

The bridge appears directly in front of us in a blinding flash. Cobras fire zuni rockets, skimming them low over the roadway a few meters in front of our hood. This close, the rockets make a shrill, ear-stabbing sound. They smash into bunkers across the water. In the light of their explosions, I see the outlines of the Humvees in Third Platoon ahead of us.

"There's a hole in the bridge," Colbert says. "Bravo Three is stuck. We're turning around."

KOCHER'S TEAM makes it across the bridge with Carazales flooring the vehicle, bitching the entire way. "This is fucking bullshit, man. We've got no armor." Somehow, he manages to swerve around the meter-wide hole blown through the middle of the bridge by a Marine artillery round.

Just after clearing the hole, Redman, standing at the vehicle's .50-cal, is thrown down by a low-hanging wire from a blown-up utility pole. He slams his head on an ammo box at the rear of the Humvee and is knocked out. Redman comes to moments later and sees smashed buildings on either side of him. A Cobra, flying so low it looks like he could reach up and touch it, is dumping machine-gun fire into one of the structures. Redman smells a powerful odor of burning flesh. They have arrived in Al Muwaffaqiyah.

Two other teams make it across the bridge before a Humvee towing a trailer becomes hung up in the hole, blocking it off. The fourteen Marines who made it across are now cut off, alone in the town. Kocher's team pushes forward about seventy-five meters, then is forced to halt. Buildings on both sides of the road are collapsed into it. Rubble in some places is piled higher than the hood of their vehicle. "There's nowhere to go, dude," Redman observes.

Another Cobra strafing run sends Carazales diving down to the floor. The rounds impact so close that he thinks it's enemy fire. When he gets back up, he sees Kocher on the ground, walking alone into the demolished city. Carazales says, "Kocher's happy now because he's got his own little suicide mission."

Kocher is determined to find a route through the town. Much as he dislikes his immediate superior, Captain America, Kocher loves his job. He grew up outside of Allentown, Pennsylvania, and spent his youth "running around in the backwoods." He hunted deer, wrestled and listened to tales of war adventure from relatives who had served in World War II and in the Korean conflict. He knew from the time he was very little he would be a Navy SEAL or a Recon Marine. He likes being out on his own in a dark, alien town. After the Cobras fire a final Hellfire into a building in front of him, the place grows silent. All he can think of, Kocher later tells me, is a basic rule of combat reconnaissance: "The lead element's expendable. Guess I'm it."

He picks his way through the rubble and tries to clear a path for the Humvees by pulling twisted rebars from fallen buildings out of the street. Then he sees movement in an alley and fires several shots at it. He and the other men on his team take cover, but no fire is returned. The town is about a kilometer long. Kocher soon figures that the Marine artillery leveled only about a quarter of the town. One strip of buildings close to the bridge was left standing, and near them there's a clear alley that the Humvees could pass through. He returns to the Humvee with the news.

When Carazales hears it, he tells the radio operator, "Don't pass that word up to the battalion. They'll probably want to send us through this bitch."

But the radio operator sends the news. They're ordered to remain in position.

SEVERAL VEHICLES FROM BRAVO COMPANY remain stuck on the bridge behind a Humvee trailer with one wheel hanging through the hole in the roadway. Encino Man originally took charge of the effort to free the trailer, but repeated attempts to rock it out have only succeeded in making the hole larger.

When Maj. Shoup comes up to the bridge to help out, he sees that nothing is happening. Several Marines stand around doing nothing, while Encino Man and Captain America shout excitedly into their radios. To Shoup it looks like they've lost focus of the situation and are "stuck on their radios, not commanding."

As an air officer, Shoup has no authority within Bravo Company. But in his mind, having three teams of Marines stuck in the town, with daylight rapidly approaching, is an urgent matter, and Encino Man's paralysis is threatening everyone. He takes a somewhat radical measure. He steps up to Encino Man and tells him, "Give me all your radios."

Encino Man is baffled, but he hands his radio handsets over. Shoup later says, "I think taking the handsets from him was the most useful thing I did that night."

Encino Man admits, "It turned out good. I went out to help manually pick up the trailer."

With Shoup effectively in command, Encino Man's brawn as a former college football star is put to good use. He and other Marines heave the stuck trailer wheel onto metal slats and pull it out of the hole, clearing the bridge at sunrise.

* * *

By the time Bravo pulls its teams out of Al Muwaffaqiyah and regroups on the other side of the bridge, a small mob of officers and senior enlisted men are gathered by the eucalyptus trees where we were ambushed. There are five bodies of enemy fighters scattered under them, along with piles of munitions, RPGs, AKs and hand grenades. One corpse still holds a weapon in its hand, a Russian stick grenade, with the end shot off.

Several officers mill about, talking excitedly and snapping souvenir pictures of the dead. No one has bothered to search the area or examine the corpses in any methodical manner. Captain America is yelling at the top of his lungs, picking up AKs and hurling them into the canal.

Fick walks up, sees the pandemonium and says to Encino Man, "What the fuck are these people doing taking pictures when there're guns on these guys, and none of them have been searched?"

No one pays him any heed. They're distracted when Maj. Eckloff, the battalion XO, makes a curious discovery. He leans down and picks up the hand of one of the dead fighters. Between his thumb and index finger there are words tattooed in English: I LOVE YOU. Eckloff reads it aloud for the benefit of the other Marines nearby. The tattoo is in keeping with the anomalous attire of the fallen fighters. They're dressed in pleated slacks, loafers and leather jackets, and wear cheap but stylish watches. Eckloff says, "These guys look like foreign university students in New York."

Kocher arrives by the trees and notices one of the "dead" men peeling his head off the ground, looking around at the Americans.

"This guy's still alive," Kocher says. Like Fick, he can't

believe that the area still hasn't been searched. The wounded fighter is lying within arm's reach of seven RPG rounds. Kocher trains his rifle on him.

Captain America runs up shouting, "Shoot him!"

Kocher ignores him as usual.

Someone else calls for a corpsman. One arrives, along with Lt. Col. Ferrando.

"Can you help this man?" Ferrando asks.

Initially, the corpsman says no. He's worried about booby traps.

Kocher volunteers to search him. As he pats him down for hidden weapons, the man shrieks. He's shot in the right arm and has a two-inch chunk of his right leg missing, the bone blown out by a .50-cal round. He carries a Syrian passport that bears the name Ahmed Shahada. He's twenty-six years old, and his address in Iraq is listed as the Palestine Hotel in Baghdad, which is by local standards one of the better hotels, catering to foreign journalists and European aid workers. He's carrying 500 Syrian pounds, a packet of prescription painkillers in his shirt pocket and an entry visa to Iraq dated March 23. He arrived barely more than a week ago. Handwritten in the section of his visa that asks the purpose of his visit to Iraq is one word: "Jihad."

When the corpsman begins treating the wounded Syrian, Captain America stalks over, enraged. "The guy's a terrorist!" he shouts. He leans down, rips the wristwatch from him and stomps it under his boot. "Goddamn terrorist," he shouts. Then he notices the 500 pounds in Syrian notes sticking out of the wounded man's pocket. Earlier, Kocher had found the bills when searching him and had returned them to his pocket. Captain America grabs the money—worth about $9.55 U.S.—offers a few notes to the corpsman, who declines them, then stalks off.

When they finally get around to searching the rest of the fighters, every one of them has a Syrian passport. After news spreads of the foreign identities of the enemy combatants, the Marines are excited. "We just fought actual terrorists," Doc Bryan says. After nearly two weeks of never knowing who was shooting at them, the Marines can finally put a face to the enemy.

Later, intelligence officers in First Marine Division will estimate that as many as 50 percent of all combatants in central Iraq were foreigners. "Saddam offered these men land, money and wives to come and fight for him," one officer tells me. He adds that foreign fighters were simply dropped off at intersections by Iraqi Fedayeen, given weapons and told to attack the Americans when they came up the road. At times, the foreign jihadis were simply used to buy time for Iraqi soldiers to change out of their uniforms and flee.

Given the Syrians' poor performance at the bridge— trying to use skinny eucalyptus trees for cover, being wholly unaware that they could be observed through American night optics—Eckloff concludes, "The concept of being a guerrilla fighter was like something they'd gotten out of the movies."

Encino Man walks up, gazing at the dead Syrians. "I wonder if President Bush will ever find out about this," he says, his voice full of awe. "This is what the president's been talking about with the war on terrorists. This is why we're here."

FICK AND I DRIVE TOGETHER to the platoon's position down the road from the bridge (actually the same wadi they'd encamped in before attempting to take the bridge the night before). Sunlight streaks through his filthy windshield. "It's a beautiful morning," he says, gazing at the surrounding fields, where shepherds are now walking among sheep and cows.

It's among the most beautiful mornings I've ever seen. It's exciting to see daylight after getting shot at.

Nevertheless, Fick is grim. Unlike the others who'd been cheered by capturing a foreign jihadi, Fick thinks it's an ominous development. While Fick had never been avidly pro-war, he'd always radiated quiet confidence about the Americans—at least the Marines—reaching their basic objective: regime change. The arrival of Syrians has shaken him. "Isn't this the absolute opposite of what we wanted to have happen here?" he asks. "I can see this effort"—as he refers to the war—"becoming seriously complicated."

We drive in silence. Fick sinks deeper into his state of morbid reflection, turning over the events of the previous night. "We should never be in that position again. We rolled into a three-sided ambush. That was bad tactics."

When he stops the Humvee near Bravo's position, Fick drops his head toward his chest and shuts his eyes. A moment later, he looks up, smiling with a profound realization. "I know what we did last night," he says.

To explain his epiphany, Fick brings up an incident that occurred several weeks earlier at Camp Mathilda between Pappy and some other Marines. Part of the reason Marines nicknamed Sgt. Patrick "Pappy" was his style of dressing. In Camp Mathilda, he invariably wore his physical-training shorts with combat boots and socks pulled up to his knees. His fellow Marines thought the look was "old-mannish." As he was walking past a group of them one day in his customary attire, a Marine stopped him and said, "Pappy, give us some old-man wisdom." Pappy turned, waved his finger and said, "Don't pet a burning dog." It was the sort of nonsense wisdom for which Pappy is famous. In Afghanistan, he and Kocher were sitting in a Marine camp outside Kandahar when a female Marine walked past. Gazing at her, Pappy said, "If she sees something without a purpose she could chuck a stone at it." Generally, no one knows what Pappy means when he comes up with these odd pronouncements, but this morning after the ambush on the bridge, Fick believes he's deciphered the meaning of Pappy's warning against petting a burning dog.

Fick turns to me and says, "Last night on the bridge we petted a burning dog."

At around eight in the morning on April 2—following their all-night action in the ambush—the Marines in First Recon are told they will be moving into Al Muwaffaqiyah in an hour, via a southern route that avoids the damaged bridge. Given Kocher's experience of moving freely through town early that morning, it's believed that the attackers have all fled or been killed.

Pappy is loaded onto a supply truck with the wounded Syrian and driven to RCT-1's camp, where they are medevaced to a hospital in Kuwait.

The Marines in the wadi camp are in a near-hypnotic state. No one's slept in two nights. Reyes sits by his Humvee beside the spot where Pappy's blood has spilled over the edge of the passenger-seat compartment. "I should be thankful Pappy wasn't hit worse," he says. "Instead I'm feeling sorry for myself because I already miss him so badly. I don't like being here without him at my side. It's like I'm missing a piece of my body."

Several Marines gather around Colbert's vehicle, drinking water, tearing into food rations and cleaning and reloading the weapons they will likely be using again later in the day. They recount events of the previous night.

Redman, who witnessed the sunrise in Al Muwaffaqiyah, walks over in a daze. "Dude, we destroyed that place," he says, sounding morose about it. "We had one guy shot in the foot, and we blew up their whole town."

They talk about different reactions they have to combat. Person says he felt no fear whatsoever last night at the bridge. "When I am in these situations," he asserts confidently, "I don't feel like I'm going to die."

Trombley, who repeatedly fell asleep last night during breaks in the fire, seems interested in combat only during its intense moments—when the bullets are coming directly at us. This morning he says, "I had a funny combat-stress reaction. When we rolled back from the bridge the first time, I had a chubb. It wouldn't go away. Maybe it was 'cause I didn't get to shoot my SAW."

Colbert is excessively cheerful this morning. It's not like he's maniacally energized from having escaped death. His satisfaction seems deeper and quieter, as if he's elated to have been involved in something highly rewarding. It's as though he's just finished a difficult crossword puzzle or won at chess.

When Espera comes by to share one of his stinky cigars, he looks as he always does after combat, as though his eyes have sunk deeper into their sockets and the skin on his shaved skull has just tightened an extra notch. He jams the chewed, mashed tip of his cigar in my mouth without asking if I want it, and points to Colbert. "Look at that skinny-ass dude," he says. "You'd never guess what a bad motherfucker he is."

Espera felt sorry for Colbert when they met a few years ago. They were in different units but happened to find themselves on leave together in Australia. While other Marines were out drinking and chasing whores, Colbert went off alone to prowl electronics stores. "I thought he had no friends—he was such a loner," Espera says. "But now that I know him better I figured out he just can't stand people, even me. I'm only his friend to piss him off. I look up to him because the dude is a straight-up warrior. Getting bombed, shot at don't phase him a bit. Shit, in the middle of all that madness by the bridge he observes those dudes in the trees waiting to kill us. That's the Iceman."

He kneels down and punches Colbert on the shoulder. "You've got superhuman powers, Iceman, but it comes with that freakish taint I wouldn't want to have."

Colbert ignores the backhanded praise. He's just opened his one MRE of the day and discovered a horrible mistake. His burrito MRE meal contains a condiment packet of peanut butter instead of jalapeño cheese. "What kind of sadist would put peanut butter in my burrito MRE?" he fumes.

Doc Bryan walks over to make sure everyone's doing all right. I ask him how he feels about having killed those two men in the ambush.

"It's a funny paradox," he says. "I would have done anything to save that shepherd kid. But I couldn't give a fuck about those guys I just killed. It's like you're supposed to feel fucked-up after killing people. I don't."

Espera says, "We've been brainwashed and trained for combat. We must say 'Kill!' three thousand times a day in boot camp. That's why it's easy." But ever mindful of the priest's admonishment not to enjoy killing, Espera hastily adds, "That dude I saw crawling last night, I shot him in the grape. Saw the top of his head bust off. That didn't feel good. It makes me sick."

BY NINE A.M. the weary Marines are again on the move, making life-and-death decisions. The first guy they almost kill is a young man identified by Captain America as a possible Fedayeen. Captain America spots the young man standing in the field several hundred meters back from the road. He thinks the guy is talking on a radio, working as an enemy observer. The convoy stops. Snipers are called out. They report that the "radio" Captain America saw him holding close to his mouth and speaking into is a cigarette that he's trying to smoke in the wind. They move on without shooting him.

Within a couple of hours, First Recon reaches the alternate route into Muwaffaqiyah. There are farmhouses and bermed fields on either side of the road. The battalion slows to a bump-and-stop crawl, while armored units from RCT-1 move a few kilometers ahead into the town, to clear out the rubble blocking the main road.

While we wait, mortars begin to fall. But the fire is intermittent—one or two concussions every ten minutes—and inaccurate, landing hundreds of meters away in the surrounding fields.

There's a lot of civilian traffic pulled over by the side of the road. Many of the cars seem to have been surprised by the arrival of the Marine convoy. Parked at careless angles just off the road, the cars seem to have pulled over hastily, perhaps when they saw the Marines rolling up on them in their rearview mirrors. In the space of a few kilometers, we pass more than a dozen such vehicles. Clean-shaven young men in urban apparel, similar to that worn by the Syrian ambushers, stand outside the cars and pickup trucks. They flash nervous smiles or throw their hands up when the Marine vehicles pass by. Others who have their shirts off—indicating they've probably just changed out of military uniforms—hide inside the cars. Several of the young men we pass have blue eyes and light or even reddish hair, which are traits not uncommon among Syrians.

The Marines are convinced these guys are foreign jihadi warriors. They're dying to do "snatch missions"—pull over and grab some of them and find out who they are. But their requests are denied. The Marines' objective is to enter Al Muwaffaqiyah and push north as soon as possible. They're at the tip of the spear of Maj. Gen. Mattis's fast-moving invasion, and they don't have time to dally. Nevertheless, letting these guys go creates a baffling situation in the minds of the Marines. In their view, these two opposing armies—of Marines and of foreign jihadis—are passing by within meters of each other on the same road.

During one of our stops, Gunny Wynn walks over to Colbert's vehicle, pissed off. "Isn't stopping terrorists what this war is supposed to be about? Here we are surrounded by them, and all we're doing is waving and smiling."

First Recon's convoy begins to take increasingly concentrated mortar fire. Unseen enemy snipers take potshots with AKs. Marines in Bravo are ordered to sweep the surrounding berms on foot. They find no armed men but piles of mortars, mortar tubes and RPG rounds prepositioned in holes on both sides of the road.

In Charlie Company at the front of the convoy, Graves and Jeschke are ordered on a sniper mission. Despite the trauma of their experience a couple of nights ago of pulling the girl out of the car with her brains shot out, they are eager for their new mission. An enemy mortar landed within 150 meters of their vehicle, and Marines notice a man behaving suspiciously in a nearby field. He keeps popping up and down from behind a berm after the mortars hit, watching the Marines. They think he's an observer, and Graves and Jeschke set up a sniper position by the road to kill him.

With Graves on the M-40 rifle and Jeschke spotting, they see him 175 meters off. They're not absolutely sure he's an observer—the man has no radio or weapon visible—but they've been cleared hot to hit him. Graves fires a shot. The man drops out of view. Neither is sure if they hit him until a few minutes later when several women file out of a nearby hut and go over to the berm. They are joined by two men dressed like farmers, who drag the man out of the dirt and load him into a pickup truck. In the process, Graves observes an AK rifle tumble out of his victim's robes. He believes he made a good kill.

Up the road, Saucier isn't so sure of the military value of his next kill. Saucier is manning the .50-cal for his team on a hasty roadblock when a white car approaches on the highway. Saucier fires high warning shots. The car accelerates. When it comes within 200 meters of his position he lowers his weapon at it and blips off two rounds. Though the .50-cal is an extremely powerful weapon, it's not the most accurate gun used by Marines. The gun employs old-fashioned iron sights, and the mounts used in Recon's Humvees are notoriously wobbly. Nevertheless, Saucier's marksmanship is another testament to Marine Corps training. Of the two rounds he fires into the speeding car, one strikes the head of the driver. The car stops. Three young men jump out. One of them, who had apparently been sitting behind the driver, is covered in gore. They throw themselves down by the road. Marines who examine the driver report that Saucier's hit was perfect—hitting the guy in the center of his head and scooping it out in a V shape. No weapons are discovered on the young men or in the car. But by the Marines' roadblock rules, this kill was legit. The car wouldn't stop.

When I talk to Saucier about this shooting later, he says

he never in his life imagined he would be called on to fire on unarmed people. "Words can't describe how I feel about it," he says. "When we came over here, I expected we would do what you would read in history books. We would go through the desert and fight armies. But all we're seeing are random tactics, guys shooting at us with civilians everywhere, which makes sense from their point of view. Their guerrilla tactics don't make me feel better about or justify the civilian deaths we're causing, but these Marines are my brothers. I'll do anything to defend them. All I try to do is put this bad stuff out of my mind."

AT ABOUT THREE in the afternoon, Colbert's team finally creeps into Al Muwaffaqiyah. The rubble has been pushed to the sides of the road by tanks in RCT-1, which entered earlier. A hundred meters back, partially destroyed buildings yawn open. Beds hang off their upper floors. Marines from RCT-1 report seeing an undetermined number of bodies on rooftops—people killed by the DPICM artillery rounds, which spray shrapnel down from the sky. The Marines fired 100 such rounds into the town, saturating it with a total of about 7,000 submunitions. Statistically, about 15 percent of these submunitions fall to the earth without exploding, which means there are approximately 1,000 unexploded bombs scattered throughout the town and buried in the rubble. They are highly unstable and will blow up if stepped on or picked up. The town is a lethal place.

Colbert's vehicle is ordered to stop part of the way into Al Muwaffaqiyah. We're within view of the bridge and the eucalyptus trees across the river where we almost got killed the night before. Now, in the glare of the midday sun, the rubbled town looks deserted. Everyone's nerves are hinky. Colbert leans out the window, observing likely sniper positions through his rifle scope, and starts singing that Gordon Lightfoot song again.

Originally, the Marines in Bravo were told they were going to speed through the town, but there is a delay. While we wait, young adolescent boys trickle out of the deadly ruins. They come to within thirty meters or so of the Humvees and wave. One kid, probably about eleven, stands in the wreckage of a building destroyed by the Marines. He blows kisses and shouts, "I love you, America!"

Colbert's team is ordered to advance farther into the town. In sections that are not destroyed you can see how it had been a nice place until eighteen hours ago. There are walled gardens with metal gates painted bright colors. To our right there's a wrecked café, decorated with azure highlights around its smashed windows. Lying along the waterfront of the broad canal, the town almost has the Mediterranean feel of a Greek fishing village.

Colbert orders most of his men out of the Humvee. The Marine Corps has spent years studying the Russian experience in Afghanistan and Chechnya. Among the mistakes they made was to stay inside their vehicles when they entered urban terrain. As Colbert says, "If you cocoon in your vehicle, you get schwacked. Even if it's a tank, they'll find a way to blow it up."

Colbert and his men stalk through the streets, peering over walls and around corners. Even though increasing numbers of civilians are straying out, the Marines are tense. It's a hot day, and the Marines' faces—recessed behind puffy MOPP suits, helmets and radio mics—have that throbbing, blotchy look people get after running a marathon.

Colbert stands on the corner by a building, scanning an

alley. An old man in brown robes, sitting cross-legged in front of a building, smiles at him. Colbert smiles back, while still mumbling the words "Sometimes I think it's a sin/When I feel like I'm winnin' when I'm losin' again." He pauses. "I wish I knew the rest of the words."

WE REMAIN IN AL MUWAFFAQIYAH because engineers attached to First Recon have discovered a large cache of weapons in the town. One of the few public buildings not destroyed by Marine artillery in Al Muwaffaqiyah is the schoolhouse. It's an L-shaped, two-story brick building with a basketball court in the middle.

The schoolhouse was taken over by the Iraqi military sometime after Valentine's Day. Marine engineers know this because the walls of one classroom are covered in childish drawings of pink hearts, some with the words "Happy Valentine's" scrawled in English. The fact that schoolchildren in an Arab dictatorship commemorate Valentine's Day comes as a surprise to the Marines, but previously, in a rural school south of Al Hayy, they found drawings done by children depicting girls with blue eyes and blond hair—suggesting that somehow Western pop culture and its idealization of blondness had seeped into the minds of kids living in primitive hamlets. You find surprising things about the private life of a country when you invade it. It's not unlike breaking into someone's home, ransacking the occupants' possessions and learning the ordinary secrets of their lives.

Sometime after the schoolchildren of Al Muwaffaqiyah celebrated Valentine's Day, a battalion-size force of Republican Guard soldiers moved into the town and turned their school into a military headquarters. They shoved all the desks into one room and filled the others with military supplies. Marines find maps, uniforms, gas masks, as well as recently cooked, partially consumed bowls of rice, peanut shells and chicken bones. Apparently, the Republican Guard soldiers stayed back here eating peanuts and chicken while the Syrian jihadis were sent out to the bridge to delay the Americans.

The Marines also find several classrooms piled to the ceilings with weapons and munitions, including 600 mortar shells, 10,000 AK rounds and a couple dozen launchers and rifles. They rig the weapons caches with explosives and prepare to blow the school complex sky-high.

WATCHING THE TOWN'S only school blow up—which we see as a funnel of black smoke jetting up from the western side of the town—comes as a relief to Colbert's team. Its destruction means they can finally roll north and get out of Al Muwaffaqiyah. The atmosphere in the town has changed markedly. Locals have warned Marines in other teams that foreign jihadis have infiltrated the area and plan to attack the Americans with suicide car bombs. The civilians who'd come out earlier to greet the Marines have fled.

Colbert's team is ordered to move to the front of the battalion and set up a roadblock at the north end of the town. We stop near a large industrial complex that looks like a cement factory or machine shop. There are some houses beyond that, then open fields.

Espera pulls his vehicle up beside Colbert's on the road. The two of them orient their guns north. With the battalion and all of RCT-1 behind them, their two Humvees constitute the northernmost Marine unit in central Iraq. Their job is to turn away any cars that come down the road from the north. It's a little before six in the evening. There are tall, leafy trees to our left casting blue shadows over us in the fading daylight.

In the past few hours Colbert and other team leaders in the battalion have developed what they hope will be less lethal means of stopping cars at roadblocks. Instead of firing warning shots from machine guns, they will launch colored smoke grenades. The hope is that drivers will be more likely to heed billowing clouds of colored smoke blocking the road than warning shots fired over their vehicles. Fick and other commanders had initially opposed this kinder, gentler method to halting traffic, with Fick arguing, "Marines are supposed to be an aggressive force. If our stance is less aggressive, we're more likely to be challenged by bad guys." But the enlisted Marines, tired of shooting unarmed civilians, fought to be allowed to use smoke grenades.

Now, when the first vehicle, a white pickup truck, approaches, Colbert strides into the road, ahead of the Humvees.

"Do not engage this truck!" he shouts to his men.

He fires a smoke grenade from his 203 launcher. It makes a plunking sound almost like a champagne cork popping, then bounces into the road, spewing green smoke. Three or four hundred meters down the road, the white pickup truck turns around and drives off.

A couple of cars arrive. The second is a taxi. It speeds up after the launching of the smoke grenade. The Marines by the Humvees hunch lower on their weapons, getting ready to fire.

"Do not engage!" Colbert shouts. He fires another smoke grenade.

The taxi drives through the smoke; then moments before the Marines are about to light it up, the driver cuts a tight, wheel-squealing U-turn. Even on good days, Arab motorists tend to drive like kamikaze pilots. It's not easy for a Marine to differentiate between run-of-the-mill reckless Arab driving and erratic behavior that would indicate a suicide bomber.

The Marines discuss the taxi—debating whether the driver's nearly fatal game of chicken with them was a result of his poor judgment, or the possibility that he's a Fedayeen scouting Marine lines. Their conversation distracts them from the next car's approach.

The blue sedan seems to appear out of nowhere. Perhaps it came from a side street behind the cement factory. In any case, Colbert doesn't step into the road to launch his first smoke grenade until the car is less than 200 meters away.

"Do not engage!" Colbert repeats.

As soon as Colbert fires his smoke grenade, a Marine SAW roars to life, spitting out a short burst. The car, maybe a hundred meters away now, rolls to a stop, green smoke blowing past it. The windshield is frosted. Two men in white robes jump out. One, who looks to be a young man in his early twenties, has blood streaming from his shoulder. The men run hastily toward a mud-brick house by the road and disappear behind a wall.

Hasser stands to the left of Colbert, with the butt of his SAW pressed to his shoulder. It was his gun that fired.

"That was a wounding shot, motherfucker!" Colbert yells, uncharacteristically pissed. "What the fuck were you doing? I said, 'Do not engage'!"

Hasser remains frozen on his SAW.

Colbert walks around to him. He lowers his voice. "Walt, you okay?"

Hasser lowers his SAW and stares at the car.

Colbert squeezes his arm. "Walt, talk to me."

"The car kept coming," Hasser says, mechanically.

The smoke disperses in the breeze, and Marines make out the outline of a man's head behind the shattered windshield. He is sitting upright, as if still holding the wheel. Passenger doors on the right side of the car hang open. The driver seems to be alive, rolling his head from side to side.

None of the Marines say anything for a moment. Colbert looks at the car, then down. He breathes deeply, as if struggling to put his emotions aside. Having watched him cry a few days ago after the shooting of the shepherd, I suspect it's not always easy being the Iceman.

"It's okay, Walt," Colbert says. "You were doing your job."

Since the Marines on these vehicles are at this moment in history the foremost units of the American invasion here, there's a burden that comes with that. They're not allowed to simply run up to the car and see if they can help the guy. Colbert radios Fick, who's a couple hundred meters behind, and tells him there's a man shot in the car ahead. He requests permission to go up to it and render aid to the driver.

"Negative," Fick tells him. The battalion has ordered the platoon to advance a few hundred meters past the car.

We drive toward the blue car. The shot man behind the wheel appears to be in his forties. He sits upright with good posture, his hands on his lap as if they slipped off the steering wheel. He wears a white shirt. His right eye stares ahead; his left eye is covered in blood dripping down from the crown of his head. He's alive. When we pass within about a meter of him, we hear his rapid breathing—a shushing sound.

Due to a temporary rotation in the team, Trombley is on the Mark-19 and Hasser is in the seat to the left of me.

He rides closest to the man he just shot, and stares ahead, refusing to look as we drive past, listening to his dying gasps: *Shhhh! Shhhh! Shhhh!*

Nobody in the Humvee says anything.

As Team Three rolls behind us, Doc Bryan raises his M-4 and tries to get a bead on the man. Without telling anyone else, he has decided to shoot the man in the head and give him a mercy execution. But his Humvee bounces, and he misses his chance for a clean shot.

We stop several hundred meters up the road and get out. There are some huts ahead. Fick and I see a pregnant woman walking toward them. Fick gets a bright yellow pack of humrats from his truck to give to her, and we walk toward her, with Fick holding the humrats high. The woman sees us and veers toward the huts. We walk faster. She starts running, and we do too. Then Fick stops abruptly. "This is ridiculous," he says. "We're terrorizing a pregnant woman."

We watch her flee. "Given the way things are going," Fick says, "it's probably wise of her to run when she sees Americans."

ABOUT TWENTY MINUTES LATER, First Recon's head-quarters units roll past the blue car with the wounded man it. Navy Lieutenant Aubin, the battalion physician, insists on stopping so he can examine the driver.

What Aubin finds is yet another testament to the skills of the Marine Corps rifleman. Of the three rounds Hasser fired, one hit an occupant in the shoulder (whom we saw jump out), one skimmed into the hood and the third entered the driver's left eye. The 5.56mm round then did a ninety-degree turn through the man's brain and went straight up, exiting through the top of his skull. Basically, the man has been lobotomized. Aubin pokes and pinches the skin on the man's upper body and finds he is totally unresponsive, a vegetable. But no arteries were hit. The light, venous bleeding from the entry and exit wounds is not enough to kill him. His breathing and heart rate are good.

Aubin concludes that in a hospital a man with these wounds could live indefinitely. Here, without care, he will die of starvation, infection or swelling of the brain. Unlike Doc Bryan, who was ready to shoot the man, acting as a vigilante mercy killer falls outside of everything Aubin believes in as a doctor. He administers morphine and Valium to quell any pain in case the victim comes to (which is medically possible), but not enough to kill him. He is torn by the dilemma posed by this patient. Aubin later tells me, "In the States we don't practice euthanasia. If we remove someone from life support, I don't make that decision. We have committees of doctors, lawyers, family members, clergy who all debate it."

Aubin knows that to leave the man is a death sentence, but he decides not to call in a medevac. Marine resources are stretched thin. He leaves the man in the care of medical personnel with RCT-1, who will be holding the town. The wounded man dies, unclaimed by anyone, a day later. Marines don't know anything about him other than that he was unarmed, behind the wheel of a blue car, when he drove onto a narrow, blacktop road where an American shot him in the eye.

TWENTY-SIX

○

WALTER HASSER, who shot the man in the blue car, is one of the most well-liked Marines in the platoon. He's twenty-three years old, six feet two inches tall and knows the lyrics to just about every hit country song recorded between 1960 and 1974. Waylon Jennings and Johnny Cash are his heroes. He has a beautiful country singing voice, and in his case Colbert makes a special exemption to his "no country music" rule. Following the ZSU AAA gun attack south of Al Hayy during which Hasser had climbed into the turret under fire and had taken out the enemy gun position, the team had seized the bridge north of the town to the accompaniment of his singing Glen Campbell's "Rhinestone Cowboy."

Raised in a rented farmhouse in Louden County, Virginia, by a single mom who, he says, "didn't have no college," Hasser grew up working on farms and hunting. He seems like your basic country good old boy, but what he enjoys most about the Marine Corps is both the brotherhood and the diversity. "Back home you pal around with your own kind," he says. "I never thought my best friends would be Mexicans. Here, we're brothers, and we all look out for each other. That's the best part of being in a war. We all get to be together."

Earlier in the morning, when everyone had been complaining about the sorry state of MREs, Hasser had explained his basic philosophy of life. "Every chance you have, you should try to hook people up. People in the MRE factory don't understand that. Hell, if I worked there I'd be sneaking in extra pound cakes, jalapeño cheese packs, Tootsie Rolls. You gotta throw things to people when you can."

Now, driving out of Al Muwaffaqiyah, with the sound of that dying man's gasping still fresh in everyone's mind, Hasser stares out the window into a blazing sunset. The SAW is loose on his lap. His wrists are draped across the top of the weapon, but his fingers aren't touching it, almost like he's ignoring it.

"How are you doing?" I ask him.

"Just taking it all in," he says.

THE OBJECTIVE TONIGHT on April 2 is to reach the outskirts of Al Kut, the Marine Corps' goal in central Iraq. It's about thirty kilometers north of Al Muwaffaqiyah. Before the Marines set out from Al Muwaffaqiyah, several old men on the road stopped Second Platoon, offering detailed information about ambushes ahead. Fick, Meesh and I talked to them for several minutes. One of the old men caught my eye. He pointed up the road and dragged his finger across his neck, making a throat-slashing gesture to indicate danger ahead.

Now, as we drive up the route in convoy with the battalion, Colbert picks up reports of sporadic gunfire from the radio. "We're expecting enemy contact at the intersection two clicks up the road," he says. "Person, get your NVGs out. This could go past dark."

"One thing about the Marines," Person says. "We always know how to wrap up a day."

"Small-arms fire to the rear," Colbert says.

"Yeah. Game on!" Trombley says excitedly from the turret. It's his first time on the Mark-19, and he's eager for the chance to blow stuff up with it.

"Stay frosty, Walt," Colbert says.

"Yeah," Hasser says.

I look over at him next to me. He's still not touching the SAW. He's just listlessly staring out the window. I'm glad of his humanity. The fact that he's clearly so broken up by his shooting of that civilian just confirms what a decent guy he is. But I wish he wasn't showing it right now.

We hit the intersection—the suspected ambush point, with berms on the left, a stand of palm trees on the right. No shots are fired.

"Stop!" Colbert says.

We halt between the trees and the berms in the suspected kill zone.

"What are we doing?" Person asks, his voice betraying a hint of nervousness.

"They want us to stop," Colbert says. "I guess we're trying to flush 'em out."

We sit for several minutes, trying to bait the ambushers into shooting. Nobody says anything. It's that leaden silence of old action movies where all you hear are heartbeats and watches ticking (though no one's actually wearing a mechanical watch).

"Move up fifty meters," Colbert says.

Again we sit in silence, broken abruptly when Trombley cuts a loud fart.

Everyone jumps. Nerves are so wired in the vehicle, some mistook it for the blast of a distant mortar.

"Jesus!" Colbert says.

"Sorry," Trombley apologizes.

We creep forward. AKs crackle in the distance. We pick up speed, clearing the suspected ambush spot. We pass two black dogs humping in the ditch by the road. Then a billboard of a grinning Saddam.

"Hey, anybody got a Sharpie?" Person asks. "We should do some bathroom art on him, like draw a cock and balls going into his mouth. I'm serious, let's stop and do it." He starts laughing.

"Shush, Person. Take a deep breath," Colbert says indulgently, like a kindergarten teacher with an unruly child.

"I can't help it," Person says. "I'm running solely on Ripped Fuel tonight."

The sun is now a red disk perched just atop the horizon to the left. Several kilometers ahead, a massive fireball erupts, sending a mushroom cloud into the sky. The radios come to life, everyone debating what it is.

We stop, and for several moments the distant fireball burns more brightly than the setting sun. Now the feeling of being on a 1950s sci-fi movie is complete. Surrounded by the red, bermed fields, strange huts and now what look like two suns setting simultaneously, it's like we've arrived on the alien planet.

A FEW MINUTES after the double sunset, the Marines are ordered to be on the lookout for a downed American aircraft. Later, the BBC reports that a Navy F-18 was shot down, leading Fick and others to surmise that the brilliant fireball we'd seen had been that jet crash.

We drive for several hours in the darkness, dogged by sporadic mortar fire and enemy forces that keep lighting up the sky with illume flares.

Around midnight the battalion stops a few kilometers south of Al Kut and digs in. The canal is a couple hundred meters to our right, and the ground here is saturated. Boots sink ankle-deep in the mud. It takes twenty minutes just to find a spot dry enough to dig a hole. With enemy mortars and illume flares still going off nearby, Colbert's team excavates a massive hole, big enough for everyone, in the event of a bad artillery attack.

Machine-gun fire across the canal is heavy at times. RCT-1 is on the other side, and they are moving into position to assault into Al Kut. Low-flying American jets crisscross overhead. Bombs and artillery rumble.

I sit in the mud, eating an MRE ration I saved for dinner. After squeezing the contents from the foil pack into my mouth, I'm too tired to discern what it tastes like—a spaghetti dinner, chicken breast or chunked beefsteak. There's not enough light to read the packaging and figure out what these chunks of food in my mouth are. It's the first time existing in total darkness has bothered me.

The dark and sleepless conditions under which Marines operate have already caused several fatalities. Two men sleeping near their Humvee in another unit were crushed to death by a tracked vehicle, and a third was paralyzed. An infantry Marine crawled into his hole after watch and fatally shot himself in his sleep with his SAW.

Nearby in the darkness, Marines in Bravo pass around these stories. Some of them now bring up another night-time activity: "combat jacks." They're trying to tally who's masturbated the most since the invasion started. During long, fatiguing hours of watch, some Marines beat off just to keep awake and pass the time. "Dog, after that first ambush," one of the men says, referring to a fevered night of combat jacks after the attack at Al Gharraf, "I get into my hole, and I had to go three times, bam, bam, bam!

Couldn't stop. Hadn't happened like that since I was seventeen. I thought something was broken."

ON THIS NIGHT, April 2, five kilometers south of Al Kut, First Recon is alone on the western side of the canal. Given the fact that Al Kut is home to thousands of Republican Guard forces and is now being bombed from above by American aircraft while being attacked on the ground by RCT-1 (as well as other Marine units from the west), commanders in First Recon are concerned that enemy forces, fleeing the city, might overrun its encampment on this night of chaos. The battalion pushes foot patrols out beyond the perimeter in order to set up observation posts and watch for approaching Iraqis. Kocher, who spent the previous night reconnoitering the ruins of Al Muwaffaqiyah, now leads a patrol out.

The moon hasn't risen yet. Creeping through a field in near-absolute darkness, Kocher and two of his men spot an Arab through their NVGs about twenty meters away. The Arab, wearing a robe, is sitting cross-legged in a low spot between some broad, undulating berms.

Kocher's first impulse is to shoot him. He's upset about Pappy being hit the night before and wouldn't mind exacting some revenge. But as he later explains, Kocher doesn't shoot for fear of giving away his position. Iraqi soldiers are still launching illume flares less than a kilometer away, presumably looking for Americans.

With two of his men covering him, Kocher approaches the lone Arab, confident the guy can't see him in the darkness. Speaking rudimentary Arabic, learned from his Marine cheat sheets, Kocher tells him to put his hands up and stand.

The Arab complies. As he rises, an AK slides out from

under his robes and clatters to the ground. Kocher draws nearer. Then he hears footsteps, someone shouting *"Ahhh!"*

Captain America runs past, making a bayonet charge for the Arab. He slams him in the chest, and the two of them tumble over with a meaty thud.

"I fucked that guy up!" Captain America shouts, rising triumphantly.

Kocher is pissed. It's not just that his commanding officer is running around in the darkness, screaming and bayoneting a prisoner who had in Kocher's opinion been completely under control. Now Kocher figures he's going to have to get out his medical kit and render aid to the Arab if he's not dead.

He rolls the Arab, zip-cuffing his hands behind his back, then spins him around to examine his chest for wounds. He's unharmed. The Arab wears a chest rig beneath his robe, loaded with ammo. Captain America's bayonet smashed apart a rifle magazine in the Arab's vest but failed to penetrate his chest.

"Nice going, Captain," Kocher says. "You missed him."

"That guy was resisting," Captain America says. "I just wanted to jab him."

Kocher strips off the Arab's ammo vest and pulls him to his feet. Captain America curses and tries kicking the Arab in the groin. Instead, he hits Kocher in the stomach.

"Fuck! Did I hit you?"

"Yeah," Kocher says. He doesn't say anything else. Kocher finds that speaking with his commander just adds to the aggravation. Following this night's latest escapade, some of Kocher's men begin fantasizing about capping their captain, talking about it openly among themselves. Kocher doesn't. He tries to maintain a balanced view of his commander. "He's got personal problems," he says.

"I've got no problem with being aggressive, but he's aggressive toward the wrong people."

THE BOMBARDMENT OF AL KUT continues into the morning of April 3. RCT-1's advance into the city is well under way on the other side of the canal. We hear Amtracs clanking past, machine guns, explosions. Some are less than a kilometer away, but from where we're sitting the nearby action has a remote feel, similar to being in a cheap multiplex where you hear sounds of a war movie seeping out from the next theater. First Recon is sitting out this assault.

Within a couple of hours, the Marines in RCT-1 blast their way to the main bridge over the Tigris. But as soon as they reach it, they will pull back and depart the city. Their mission and First Recon's in Central Iraq will be over. After having sent them all the way here, Maj. Gen. Mattis has decided not to seize Al Kut. First Recon and RCT-1 are ordered to turn around and leave.

First Recon's entire campaign since leaving Nasiriyah has been part of a feint—a false movement designed to convince the Iraqi leadership that the main U.S. invasion would be coming through Al Kut. The strategy has been a success. The Iraqis left a key division and other forces in and around Al Kut in order to fight off a Marine advance that now has been abruptly called off. With so many Iraqi forces tied down near Al Kut, Baghdad has been left relatively undefended for the combined Army and Marine assault now gathering on the outskirts.

Mattis, a key architect of this grand diversion, later boasts to me, "The Iraqis expected us to go all the way through Al Kut—that the 'dumb Marines' would fight their way through the worst terrain to Baghdad." While the plan worked brilliantly, Mattis adds, with characteristic modesty, "I'm not a great general. I was just up against other generals who don't know shit."

The Marines have known nothing about this feint strategy until the past couple of days, when Fick began guessing that this was his platoon's purpose, based on hints he'd received from other officers.

Now, midmorning on April 3, while RCT-1 is still pulling back from its diversion into Al Kut, Fick gathers the men by Colbert's vehicle in their muddy encampment and explains what's going on. "By coming up here, we've tied down two Republican Guard divisions," he says. The swagger he had up on the bridge outside of Al Hayy is back. "And for most of the way we were out in front, rolling into these villages and towns ahead of every other American. Often, it was you guys in this platoon at the absolute tippity-tip of the spear. Not to rest on our laurels now, but every one of you should be proud."

"But what about Al Kut?" Garza asks. "After coming all this way we ain't going to Al Kut?"

"No," Fick says. "The feint's over. We're pulling out of here later today."

Garza, sitting by a hole, etching lines in the mud with his boot heels, digests the news. He twists his head up, annoyed. "We just spent a week getting shot at, bombing everything, all based on a fucking wrong turn?"

TWENTY-SEVEN

○

EVEN THOUGH THE IRAQIS have been beaten in Al Kut, they're still dropping mortars around First Recon's encampment, where it has remained through the morning of April 3. In the opinion of the Marines, Iraqis don't fight very hard, but the men are beginning to notice that Iraqis never really seem to completely surrender, either.

"Damn," Person says after another blast. "Didn't RCT-1 already kick their ass once today?"

Everyone is waiting for orders to begin the march to Baghdad to join the final assault. It's grown into a hot day. Earlier, Marines were ordered into their rubber MOPP boots in case of a gas attack. Still, nobody minds the added hardship too much. The platoon was resupplied with food today. Colbert's team sits around their Humvee in the mud, gorging themselves on MREs.

Hasser is still not talking. He leans against the front wheel, writing an after-action summary on the shooting of the man in the blue car, which Fick told him to hand in in case there's an investigation. Person walks over to him and starts dry-humping his shoulder like a dog.

"How you doing, Walt?"

"Get out of here."

Fick walks up. "Walt, when you finish that, we're going to see if there's a better way to stop these cars."

"Walt's got a great way to stop cars," Person says. "Shoot the driver." Behind Hasser's back, his buddies all talk about him in worried, hushed tones, trying to figure out if he's okay. To his face, they tease him unmercifully. For the Marines, this is their attempt at therapy.

Espera comes to Hasser's defense. "Maybe you were a hair too aggressive yesterday, but these motherfuckers are trying to kill us. We can't get soft now because of a few mistakes. I'm lighting up any motherfucker who comes within one hundred meters."

SIGNS OF THE REGIME'S unraveling greet the Marines as they pull south, away from Al Kut, later in the afternoon. We drive on a straight, narrow asphalt road through an utterly flat, thinly populated area of croplands. On the way, we pass a truck full of naked Iraqi men, waving underwear as surrender flags. They say they were robbed of their clothes by fleeing soldiers. Farther along there's a car with two fatally shot men in it. A guy cowering by the road tells a translator the men were killed by rampaging Iraqi soldiers, who in defeat have become bandits.

First Recon sets up a camp twenty kilometers south of Al Kut. The next morning, April 4, the men confront a new, ugly side of war. Refugees begin streaming up to their roadblock on the northern end of the highway.

Second Platoon is tasked with escorting the refugees through First Recon's lines, along a three-kilometer stretch between their roadblocks on the highway. About fifty refugees are gathered by the roadblock when Colbert's team rolls up.

Many of the refugees have been on the road for three

days now, walking and hitchhiking all the way from Baghdad, about 250 kilometers from here. The men wear Western clothes—dusty suits and sleek loafers, shredded from three days of walking. The women, mostly in black, carry infants and are surrounded by small children. Many carry sacks of grain, bags of clothing and other household possessions. There's one little boy, maybe six, in a black and gold-lamé suit with a bow tie that makes him look like a miniature Las Vegas lounge singer. It was probably the most expensive thing he owned, and his family had likely dressed him up in it as a means of transporting it out of Baghdad. He smiles at the Marines, almost self-consciously proud to be greeting them in his finest suit. They laugh and give him candy—unlucky Charms, of course.

When the men begin to escort the first group, with the Marines on foot and in Humvees creeping behind, the little cavalcade has an almost carefree air. There's an extremely beautiful woman among the refugees, who wears a bright green scarf. In her later twenties, she's a biologist from Baghdad who speaks fluent English. Her name is Manal, and her beauty isn't something that's entirely objective. In the squalor of her current circumstances, she radiates calm and high spirits that seem almost mischievous. She accosts one of the Marine escorts with a beguiling smile and asks, "Why did you Americans come here?"

"We want to help you, ma'am," the Marine answers.

"I love my city very much," Manal says, referring to Baghdad. "You are bombing it, and it will be worse."

"Why do you think we came here?" the Marine asks.

"Our country is very rich, and our president is very stupid," Manal says. "Maybe you came for the liberation. I am not so sure."

The exchange is cut short when the Marine notices one of the babies being carried by another woman has blood streaming out of its mouth. A little horror has returned to the war.

"Can you ask her what's wrong?" the Marine says to Manal.

She turns to the woman, who's shushing the bleeding baby even though it isn't crying. She and the baby's mother exchange a few words. Then Manal reports. "Her baby is sick." She scolds the Marine. "All the mothers have been walking for a long time with no water or food."

Colbert comes over to help. He instructs the mother with the bleeding baby to sit by the road, and summons a corpsman over. The bleeding, the corpsman believes, is a result of dehydration. Several other mothers come over with their sick babies. It's already in the low nineties. Colbert dabs the infants with water, trying to cool them down. Soon, more mothers are handing him their babies, perhaps thinking he's a doctor. One baby has chicken pox. Colbert takes the infant, kneels down and rocks him. "Is there anything we can do?" he asks the corpsman.

"Nothing, man," he answers. "They just need lots of water."

Colbert now wears an expression that I've come to see more frequently. He looks helpless. When confronted with these small human tragedies up close, some Marines shut down. Their faces go blank. Despite his Iceman reputation, Colbert doesn't hide his feelings very well. In combat he looks almost ecstatic; now he appears over-whelmed, though still trying to deal with this situation. He hands the baby back to the mother, along with a water bottle. "Put water on the little one," he says, speaking English into the mother's uncomprehending face. She nods gratefully, perhaps thinking he's done more than he actually has to help. Despite the water the Marines hand out, Doc Bryan estimates that a quarter of the infants may die in the next twenty-four hours.

In the space of an hour, two to three hundred refugees show up at the northern roadblock. Marines, who initially vowed to keep their distance, now load rotund old ladies in black robes into the backs of their Humvees and drive them the three kilometers through their lines. Others carry sacks of rice and bedrolls on their heads and shoulders. One of the men on Espera's team, twenty-three-year-old Lance Corporal Nathan Christopher, walks down the road, crying, while carrying a baby. He later tells me what got to him was seeing the mother, weakened from days of walking, almost drop the infant. Despite bawling his eyes out, Christopher tells me helping the refugees has afforded him his best moment in Iraq. "After driving here from Kuwait, shooting every house, person, dog in our path, we finally get to do something decent."

Lt. Col. Ferrando makes an appearance by the northern roadblock. Greater numbers of refugees are flowing in. "We're going to have a fucking humanitarian disaster on our hands if we stay here," he says. "We don't have enough food and water for ourselves."

An hour later, First Recon clears out of its position. Ferrando has finally received orders. First Recon Battalion is instructed to hightail it to Baghdad for the final assault. To get there, the Marines will backtrack down Route 7, then cut west on a circuitous path that covers nearly 300 kilometers.

THE BATTALION SPENDS two days on the road. Huge, cheering crowds turn out in towns Marines smashed through just days ago. Kids run around in muddy lots beside the road, playing soccer, screaming "Bush! Bush! Bush!" or "America! America!" It's the Marines' moment to be hailed as conquerors, or liberators or heroes. No one's really sure what they are. Adoring as the crowds are, Marines know that at any moment seriously bad things can happen. As we drive past the insanely chanting mobs, Colbert waves at them, repeating in a mechanical voice, "You're free now. Good luck. Time for us to go home."

During the two-day journey the men continue to wrestle with the issue of deadly roadblocks. Marines in Alpha Company have also instituted what they hope will be a less lethal approach to warding off traffic by firing smoke grenades. In one of their early attempts to employ the new technique, a team in Alpha successfully stops a civilian passenger by launching a smoke grenade. Before they can call the effort a success, however, the Marines watch in horror as a second smoke grenade fired by the team skips off the pavement and, against all odds, slams into the face of an Arab walking by the road carrying a white flag. He goes down hard, dropping from their view. The men are ordered forward without having a chance to examine the guy or render aid. Later, men in the unit are told by their superiors that the man they hit in the face with the smoke grenade was okay and was even observed eating a meal when they left him. After hearing this good news, one of the Marines says, "That probably just means someone threw an MRE next to the guy's body as we drove past."

First Recon reaches the outskirts of Baghdad early in the morning of April 6. Hastily erected oil pipelines zigzag along the highway. They were built by Saddam to flood adjacent trenches with oil so they could be set ablaze. As a result, smoke hangs everywhere. Saddam intended these flaming oil trenches as some sort of half-assed defense, but their only effect is to add to the general state of pollution and despair. The dust storm caused by thousands of vehicles rolling past has coated all of the wrecked buildings with a thick layer of tan powder. Even the dogs running through the ruins are the color of dust.

Dead cows, bloated to twice their normal size, lie in ditches. Human corpses are scattered about as well. It's the now familiar horrorscape of a country at war. Just before reaching the final Marine camp outside Baghdad, Espera's vehicle swerves to avoid running over a human head lying in the road. When the vehicle turns, he looks up to see a dog eating a human corpse. "Can it get any sicker than this?" he asks.

Person, however, has an entirely different reaction. Set back from the highway, gleaming like some sort of religious shrine, there is a modern-looking glass structure with bright plastic signs in front. It's an Iraqi version of a 7-Eleven. Though looted and smashed, it gives Person hope. "Damn!" he says. "It looks almost half-civilized here."

BY THE EARLY HOURS of April 6, some 20,000 Marines have begun gathering on the outskirts of the city for their assault. The Army has already begun breaking off pieces of Baghdad to the south and west. Two days earlier, elements of the Army's 101st Airborne Division seized Baghdad Airport, fifteen kilometers south of the city. The Marines, now moving to within about ten kilometers of the eastern edge of Baghdad, are gearing up for their assault to begin within the next forty-eight hours.

First Recon settles into a field of tall grass next to some blown-up industrial buildings. Marines stretch out in the greenery, resting after their two days of nonstop movement. American artillery booms continuously, a distant, throbbing rhythm. Towers of smoke rise over Baghdad in the distance. Following this last stretch of the journey, where everyone had seen the wild dogs chewing on the entrails of dead humans and livestock alike, Marines now discuss their rechristening of Iraq. They call it "Dog Land."

Reyes explains, "For the wild dogs, war is a feast."

It's a feast for some commanders as well. Later in the day, after the teams have set up their positions on the perimeter and dug their holes, Ferrando circulates among the men. He drops in on Colbert's team and offers rare praise. "They're speaking pretty highly of First Recon at division headquarters," Ferrando says. "The general thinks we're slaying dragons."

"I'm pleased to hear it, sir," Colbert says.

Ferrando turns to leave, then hesitates. He has something to confide in Colbert, one of his top team leaders.

"Ferrando thinks tanks are going to lead the way into Baghdad," he says, reverting to a habit he has of speaking of himself in the third person. "But we want to get in the game, too. That's the million-dollar question. How do we get into Baghdad?"

Ferrando walks off, working on this puzzle.

After he leaves, Espera offers his own assessment of the battalion's performance thus far in the war. "Do you realize the shit we've done here, the people we've killed? Back home in the civilian world, if we did this, we would go to prison."

TWENTY-EIGHT

○

THE MEN SLEEP WELL outside of Baghdad. It is late in the morning of April 7, and Colbert is sitting in the sun behind his Humvee, staring at the grass, which in the center of the encampment is more than a meter tall. Like everyone else, Colbert is required to wear his helmet and flak vest at all times, unless he is underneath the cammie nets by his Humvee. There are times like today—when the sky is clear, the sun is shining and enemy mortars are only falling about once every couple hours—that the requirement to always wear a helmet and flak vest seems a crime. Some Marines routinely flout the rule, but not Colbert. Suddenly, he stands up, throwing his helmet down, ripping off his flak vest and stripping down to his T-shirt. "You know what?" he announces. "I'm going to run through that field waving my arms like I'm an airplane."

Colbert runs through the grass, making jet sounds, banks into a loose turn and flies back to his Humvee. He quickly dons his gear. "Better now," he says, strapping his helmet on again.

The men don't have any orders today. Lt. Col. Ferrando is still working on his plan to get the battalion in on the final assault on Baghdad. Colbert, however, assembles his team for a special briefing beside his Humvee.

"There's something I've been keeping from you," Colbert says. "I wasn't sure we were going to live to share this moment." He produces a dusty plastic bag, reaches in and pulls out several cans of Chef Boyardee ravioli, one for each man on the team. "To celebrate," he says.

"What the fuck is that?" Person says, spotting something else in the bag.

"Easy there, partner," Colbert says, sliding out a virgin copy of *Juggs* magazine, still in its shrink-wrap.

"Fuck!" Person says. "How the fuck did you hide that from me?" Person tries to grab it.

Colbert yanks it away. "Not yet," Colbert says. "I need some time with this alone. Just calm down. You'll get your sloppy seconds."

They cook the Chef Boyardee on a C-4 fire, in the cans, cutting them open with Ka-Bar knives. The team is more closely knit than it's ever been. Even Trombley has found acceptance. In the wake of the incident in which he accidentally machine-gunned the shepherds, the men have honored him with a nickname: "Whopper." I don't get it when they first reveal it to me. "We call him the Whopper," one of them explains, "because they're sold at Burger King." When I look up, still not understanding, the nearby Marines shake their heads at my ignorance. "Like, Whoppers, Burger King, BK—Baby Killer," one of them says, spelling it out. "Trombley's our little Whopper BK."

They call him this to his face, and Trombley laughs appreciatively. He admits, "When I shot those kids I felt the same way as when I shoot a deer. I felt lucky, like I got the Easter egg." Then adds, "I wanted to look at the kid I shot. It felt weird."

Lilley nudges him affectionately. "That's because you're the Whopper, our little BK Baby Killer."

Person, sitting shirtless partway underneath the cammie netting, slurps the ravioli juice from the jagged can and starts babbling about his NAMBLA-conspiracy theories behind the war.

Hasser, who has maintained his distant silence for days since shooting the man in the blue car, breaks into laughter. "Look at you, Ray," he says, pointing at Person. "You're a fucking mess, man."

Person's face is smeared with ravioli sauce, fluorescent orange in the sunlight. More of it's splattered down his pale white chest, with drippings on his toes. "What?" Person asks, perplexed.

"You're a fucking messed-up hick who can't even eat ravioli." Hasser doubles over, facedown in the grass, laughing.

LATER THAT DAY, the Marines in Bravo are reunited with an old friend, Gunnery Sergeant Jason Swarr. A thirty-two-year-old Recon Marine who works as the battalion's parachute rigger, Swarr nearly missed the war. He only arrived outside Baghdad a couple of days ago. Now, he comes over to Colbert's position with a tale of his strange odyssey through Iraq and his remarkable first experience of combat.

Swarr is one of the more eccentric characters in the battalion. Tall and square-jawed, he looks like your average Marine, but in his off-hours Swarr is an artist who writes and directs ultra-low-budget videos. "I'm like the Ed Wood of my generation," he says. "My goal in life is, people will go in the video store and find my movies in the Cult Film section by *Toxic Avenger*."

Swarr is also a warrior. He served in Somalia, and when this war came along, he vowed he wasn't going to miss it.

But the battalion had other plans. When the invasion began, Swarr and two other Marines from First Recon were ordered to remain behind at the Al Jabar airfield in Kuwait to serve as liaisons to the Marine Corps Air Wing. Within a few days, he and his two comrades figured out their assignment was a bullshit job. "They didn't give a fuck about us at Jabar," Gunny Swarr says. "There was nothing to do."

They pulled some strings, got permission to leave and hitchhiked up to Camp Mathilda with some Pakistani laborers. The battalion had already left for the invasion, but Swarr and his cohorts found out there was a company of reservist Recon Marines still in the camp, who were getting ready to enter Iraq and link up with the battalion in a few days. Swarr and the others figured they'd get a ride with the reservists.

The reservist unit is called Delta Company, and it has three platoons with a total of about ninety Marines and commanders. It's made up of guys who work regular jobs in civilian life, some as software engineers or teachers, but the majority in law enforcement—from LAPD cops to DEA agents to air marshals. In Swarr's opinion, "Delta was the most unorganized thing I've ever seen in my life."

The reservists' problems weren't necessarily caused through any fault of their own. Due to its low standing in the pecking order as a reserve unit, Delta Company was short on trucks, guns, food, flak vests, radios. Nevertheless, the reservists crossed into Iraq nearly a week after the war started. "It was madness from day one," Swarr says. They had no idea where the battalion was and no ability to reach it on comms. Their navigation gear was so poor they nearly bumbled into Nasiriyah at the height of the fighting there. Many of the reservists in Delta had never fired the heavy weapons on their Humvees prior to entering Iraq.

Wandering around highways in southern Iraq, unable to find out where the battalion was, the reservists began running low on food. They were assigned convoy escort duty by the division and, according to Swarr, they turned this into a gold mine. At the time, lightly armed supply convoys were rolling through the area, their drivers terrified of being ambushed. So, Swarr says, "We put a sign out: 'Need Convoy Security? Stop Here.' As soon as they'd stop, we'd bullshit the drivers, tell 'em, 'Hey, two hours ago a convoy passing through here got ambushed.' Then we'd ask 'em, 'What do you got for us? Any MREs, flak vests, water? Hand it over, and we'll escort you.' "

According to Swarr, Delta Company made out pretty well for a while. Then, in his opinion, the company started going out of control. "Some of the cops in Delta started doing this cowboy stuff. They put cattle horns on their Humvees. They'd roll into these hamlets, doing shows of force—kicking down doors, doing sweeps—just for the fuck of it. There was this little clique of them. Their ringleader was this beat cop, who's like a corporal back home and a commander out here. He's like five feet tall, talks like Joe Friday and everyone calls him 'Napoleon.' We started to get the idea these guys didn't want to find the battalion. They knew they'd get their balls stepped on. They were having too much fun being cowboys.

"Some of the other reservists were coming up to us, saying, 'You've got to help us find the battalion. These guys are going to get us killed.' But there was nothing we could do."

Finally, it all came to a head a couple of days ago. "We're guarding an airfield for chow and water," Swarr says. "These kids come up selling soda and cigarettes. The ringleaders in Delta decide it would be funny to trade them some porn magazines, which these Iraqi kids had never seen. About an hour later, this elder comes out of a hamlet 400 meters away, yelling and shaking his fist. The kids all scatter. One of them tells us the old man is pissed. He didn't like kids having porn magazines. The kid says he's going to get an RPG. Sure enough, the old man comes out of this hut with an RPG, just kind of waving it around."

Swarr takes a deep breath. "Delta fucking freaks! They lob like twenty-six Mark-19 rounds at the guy. He's two hundred meters away, and they all miss him. Instead, they light up this friendly village behind him that's been passing us information.

"I'm just watching this. I didn't have nothing to shoot at, and I see this old dude dressed like a Marine running past with a flak vest and camera, huffing and puffing. 'What are they lighting up?' he asks. 'Nothing,' I say. 'Just some pissed-off Iraqi with an RPG.' Then I look at the guy I'm talking to, and it's Ollie North." (North served as a correspondent for Fox News in Iraq.)

"I'm like, 'Ollie, how you doing?'" Swarrs continues.

" 'Fucking great.' He takes a dip and says, 'This war's going to be over in seventy-two hours. Saddam's dead.'

"I'm like, 'Good to go, Ollie.'

"He huffs off, and this colonel comes out who's in charge of the airfield, and he's mad. He's like, 'You guys just lit up a friendly village.'

"I don't think Delta killed any of the villagers, but they blew up a few of their huts. We gave 'em a few cases of humrats and got out of there."

When Colbert hears the story, he just shakes his head. "This is so colossally retarded I can't even say anything about it."

I'm not convinced that Gunny Swarr is the most

reliable source. I set out to find other people who were there. One of the men from First Recon who was with him is a captain in the battalion, with a reputation for being levelheaded and forthright. He tells me Gunny Swarr's tale is "on the money." Later, I talk to Ferrando, who admits, "There was a comm problem for about a week with Delta." I go over to Delta's position in the camp and talk to more than a half dozen of the reservists, including the Mark-19 gunner, Lance Corporal Bryan Andrews, twenty-two, who fired on the village. They corroborate essential details of Swarr's story. Andrews adds, "I guess it worked out okay. I scared off the old man. He ran away."

KOCHER SPENDS his free day outside Baghdad, sitting in the shade of his vehicle's cammie nets, writing a journal intended for his wife, who's also in the Marines. He doesn't indulge in the open vilification of his commander, Captain America, the way some of the men do, but he tells me when I stop by that he is disturbed by Captain America's behavior, especially his treatment of the Iraqi prisoner the other night. "I could be a lot more personal about my feelings toward the Iraqis," Kocher says. "My wife is here. Her civil affairs unit is in Nasiriyah. I think about her every day and the things that could happen to her. But I don't lose control over it."

Against his powerful forearms, the pen Kocher holds looks puny. The log he writes in is an account of the war he calls his "Bitter Journal."

"If something happens to me, I want my wife to know the truth," he says. "If they say we fought valiantly here, I want her to know we fought retarded. They haven't used us right—sending us into these towns, onto the airfield, with no observation."

Captain America approaches. One of the men by Kocher's vehicle shouts a warning: "Here comes Dumbass."

Captain America's within easy earshot of their comment, but he sticks his head under the cammie netting and greets the men with a forced, though somewhat wobbly, smile. "Everyone enjoying the day off?" he asks.

The Marines freeze him out with blank stares.

"We're fine, sir," Kocher says.

The truth is, I feel sort of bad for Captain America. The way his men treat him reminds me of seeing a kid hazed and picked on on the playground. I sit down with him in the grass a few meters from Kocher's vehicle. One on one, he seems likable but possesses an unfocused intensity that's both charismatic and draining. When he stares at you, he doesn't blink; his pupils almost vibrate.

I ask him about complaints voiced by his men that he's been a little too zealous in his shooting from the vehicle and in his treatment the other night of the EPW (it's technically a war crime to strike, threaten or bayonet a man once he's been captured). Captain America denies any wrongdoing. He asserts to me that in each instance where he's employed violence, it's always been in response to a threat, which perhaps his Marines didn't perceive. "Each man sees things differently in combat," he says.

Then Captain America veers into Nietzschean speculation on the deadly nature of battle. "Some of us are not going to make it out of here. Each of us has to test the limits of his will to survive in this reality." He leans forward and speaks in grave tones. "Right now, at any time, we could die. It almost makes you lose your sanity." His pupils quiver with increased intensity. "The fear of dying will make you lose your sanity. But to remain calm and stay in a place where you think you will die, that is the definition of insane, too. You must become insane to survive in combat."

LATE IN THE DAY, Marines are told to expect warning orders for their mission in the assault on Baghdad. Ferrando has figured out a way to get into the game. But other news circulating among the Marines has taken priority.

Horsehead is dead. The beloved former first sergeant in First Recon, a powerfully built 230-pound African American named Edward Smith, was felled by an enemy mortar or artillery blast while riding atop an armored vehicle outside Baghdad on April 4. He died in a military hospital the next day. Horsehead, thirty-eight, had transferred out of First Recon to an infantry unit before the war started. News of his death hits the battalion hard.

Marines in Bravo Company gather under the cammie nets, trading Horsehead stories. Reyes repeats a phrase Horsehead always used back home at Camp Pendleton in San Diego. Before loaning anyone his truck, which had an extensive sound-equalizer system, Horsehead would always say, "You can drive my truck. But don't fuck with my volumes." For some reason, repeating the phrase makes Reyes laugh almost to the verge of tears.

Just before sundown, the Marines hold a memorial for Horsehead in their camp. About fifteen of them gather in the grass, next to an M-4 rifle planted upright in the dirt with a helmet on it. It's drizzling in a gray, humid twilight. One of them reads a brief eulogy.

Then they put their hands together, and their voices scream in unison as they chant the First Recon cheer in Horsehead's memory: "Kill!"

TWENTY-NINE

○

By EARLY MORNING on April 8, Army and Marine
armored units have maneuvered into Baghdad's suburbs
to the west, south and east. Under a ceaseless American
artillery and aerial bombardment, they are getting ready
for the final assault into the city center, set to begin after
dark. Maj. Gen. Mattis is deeply concerned about the lack
of American forces to the north of Baghdad. With his
Marines oriented toward the center of the city, their
northern flanks are exposed. His fear is that Iraqi
Republican Guard units may be massing for a counter-
attack in a town called Baqubah, fifty kilometers north of
Baghdad, getting ready to roll down and hit the Marines'
northern flanks.

The problem is, Mattis doesn't know what the Iraqis are
doing north of Baghdad. For the past thirty-six hours, a
low cover of dust and rain clouds has hampered American
surveillance efforts. The farthest Marine checkpoint north
of Baghdad sits about ten kilometers outside the city on
the road to Baqubah. Marines have dubbed the checkpoint
the "magic line." Every time they've sent units to probe
above the magic line in the past few days, the Marines
have been hit by heavy fire. Recently, a platoon of about

forty-five Iraqis attacked the Marine checkpoint and were repulsed after a short gun battle. After that, Iraqis tried to drive a car bomb into the checkpoint. It seems the Iraqis are up to something above the magic line, though it's uncertain exactly what it might be.

The weakness in the Marines' northern flanks gives Lt. Col. Ferrando his opening to get First Recon back into the game. After consulting with Mattis, Ferrando has volunteered to take First Recon north of the magic line, assault through the enemy ambushes and push on to Baqubah.

If the worst-case fears of Mattis are true, the Marines in First Recon will be confronting several thousand Iraqis in tanks. Baqubah is home to a Republican Division with a strength, on paper at least, of 20,000 soldiers equipped with 600 armored vehicles. Mattis knows that if the Iraqis come down in tanks, First Recon will be unable to stop them, but as he later tells me, "I knew that at least the Marines could slow them down for a few hours."

Even in the best-case scenario—if the Iraqi tanks aren't active—First Recon will be dashing through forty kilometers of known ambush positions. They will be the only Americans operating in the region, and by the time they reach Baqubah, they will have gone beyond the range of Marine artillery.

When Fick briefs his men on the mission early in the afternoon of the eighth, he tells them, "Once again, we will be at the absolute tippity-tip of the spear, going into the unknown. As soon as we step off, be prepared to engage and destroy targets of opportunity."

First Recon assembles a mixed force for the mission. Some 120 Marines in its best-equipped platoons will be joined by the ninety reservist Marines in Delta Company.

In addition, First Recon will be accompanied by an LAR unit of some 100 Marines in twenty-four vehicles. This unit's call sign is "War Pig."

Even though it's clear to the Marines that on this mission they might be serving more or less as human speed bumps—to slow down a much larger Iraqi advance—the men are quietly excited. After a couple of days of rest, most are sick of being in the camp. It's a hot, muggy afternoon, nearly 100 degrees in the shade. Flies breeding in Marine latrine trenches inside the camp, as well as on the dead livestock and human corpses outside the perimeter, infest the air. Several Marines in the platoon are suffering from the fever and dysentery that has plagued the unit since leaving Nasiriyah. But spirits are high as they load their vehicles. "I'm scared as fuck," Lilley tells me. "But I started getting anxious here in this camp. It's weird. I feel better knowing we're going to go shoot things again and fuck shit up again."

"Fuck, yeah!" Person says. "It beats sitting around doing nothing while everybody else gets to have fun attacking Baghdad."

One thing the Marine Corps can bank on is the low tolerance for boredom among American youth. They need constant stimulation, more than late-night bull sessions, ravioli fiestas and Colbert's now shredded, dog-eared copy of *Juggs* can provide. They need more war.

COLBERT'S HUMVEE is ordered into the lead of First Recon's convoy of about fifty vehicles as we leave the camp near five p.m. on April 8. Colbert stares out his window at the fading light, then mumbles something I can't quite make out. I ask him to repeat it. "It was nothing," he says. "I was just thinking about Horsehead.

He was one hell of a man. Takes shrapnel to the head and winks out."

We enter the eastern outskirts of Baghdad, an industrial district of factories and warehouses. The streets are filled with newly liberated Iraqis in the throes of celebration. Though the city center will not fall for another twenty-four hours, freedom fills the air, along with the stench of rotting corpses, uncollected garbage and overflowing sewers. Trash piles and pools of fetid water line the edges of the road. Old women in black kneel in the puddles gathering, in jugs, water that their families will boil and drink later.

Smoke pours from bombed, burning buildings on both sides of the road. Ashes fall like snowflakes. Iraqis stream through the haze, hauling random looted goods—ceiling fans, pieces of machinery, fluorescent lights, mismatched filing-cabinet drawers. As we pass by, the looters wave and give us the thumbs-up—thanking the Marines for making all this possible. Some stand in clusters, chanting the words everyone in Iraq now uses to hail the American liberators, "Bush! Bush! Bush!"

The bedlam continues for about ten kilometers. Explosions from the American assault now under way in the city center boom steadily. Kids crawl around twisted, blown-up Iraqi tanks by the road, playing on them or gathering scrap.

Hundreds, if not thousands, of American military vehicles stream past us going south. First Recon's convoy is about the only unit headed north.

We roll into open mudflats and link up with the twenty-four LAVs of First LAR Battalion's Charlie Company, call sign War Pig. With their eight wheels and upside-down bathtub shape, LAVs are among the strangest-looking war machines in the American arsenal.

Designed to swim on the surface of the ocean as well as cruise on land, they have small propellers protruding from their rears, punctuating the oddness of their appearance. Because of their advanced optics and the devastating firepower, derived from the Bushmaster rapid-fire cannon each has mounted on its turret, Iraqis have nicknamed LAVs "the Great Destroyers."

For the Marines in First Recon, this is the first time they've started a mission with an armored escort. "Damn! That's fucking awesome," Person says. "We've got the Great Destroyers with us."

"No, the escort is not 'awesome,'" Colbert says. "This just tells us how bad they're expecting this to be."

As we pull out, following War Pig toward the magic line, Colbert's mood shifts from darkly brooding to grimly cheerful. "Once more into the great good night," he says in a mock stage voice, then quotes a line from *Julius Caesar.* "Cry 'Havoc,' and let slip the dogs of war."

Hunched over the wheel, his helmet weighted down with his NVGs, Person says, "Man, when I get home, I'm gonna eat the fuck out of my girlfriend's pussy."

"Enemy contact," Colbert says, passing on word from radio. "LAVs report enemy contact ahead."

JUST AFTER DARKNESS FALLS, War Pig's lead LAV reaches the magic line and the Marine checkpoint, where coils of concertina wire block the narrow, asphalt highway. War Pig's twenty-four LAVs are spaced about fifty meters apart in a single-file line stretching for more than a kilometer. Colbert's Humvee is directly behind the rear LAV, with First Recon's vehicles stretched behind his in a line that extends for another two kilometers.

Minutes after the guards at the checkpoint pull the

concertina wire aside to let the convoy through, a white pickup truck speeds toward the lead LAV in War Pig. Its crew observes the truck through thermal nightscopes as it comes to within a couple hundred meters of them, executes a screeching 180-degree turn and hauls ass north. Iraqis in the back of the truck open up on the LAVs with AKs. It's nothing but harassing fire. The Marines guess the truck is acting as a "rabbit vehicle," trying to entice them into a chase and, they expect, an ambush.

The LAVs hesitate to cross the magic line. According to War Pig's executive officer, twenty-seven-year-old First Lieutenant William Wennberg, thus far in the war when working with other units they've occasionally had to go through red tape in order to get cleared hot to engage enemy forces. They've never worked with First Recon's Ferrando before, whom they refer to by his call sign, Godfather, and are uncertain how he will respond to the appearance of the rabbit vehicle shooting at them on the road.

When War Pig contacts Godfather and tells him about the harassing fire, he immediately clears them hot to pursue. "Godfather was awesome," Wennberg later says. "Some commanders get so caught up worrying about the politics of being too aggressive—destroying too much property, hurting innocent civilians—that they put your own forces at risk. Godfather told us to do what we needed to do, and it was good to go."

The LAVs lunge across the magic line in pursuit. Colbert's vehicle follows directly behind the rear LAV, as reports flow over the radio of the initial enemy contact. Everyone is quiet, waiting for the ambush. It's so dark inside Colbert's Humvee I can barely see my hands. I can't see the LAV through the front windshield ahead of us. I can't see what's out my window to the right, other than dim outlines of farm huts along the road in the flat landscape. A strong wind is starting to whip against the side of the vehicle. Above it, all I hear is the rumbling of the Humvee's diesel.

Colbert calls out to Hasser, who stands in the turret wearing NVGs. "See anything, Walt?"

"Nope," he shouts down.

"Look alert!" Colbert shouts, his voice cracking slightly.

Sitting to my left, Trombley says, his voice barely audible, "I hope I get to use her tonight." He's referring to his SAW machine gun. Though I can't see him, I can picture him caressing the top of his SAW as he sometimes does during tender moments before a firefight.

We drive this way for about ten minutes.

Then, after proceeding five kilometers north of the magic line, machine guns, rockets and mortars flash ahead of us in the darkness. The enemy has opened fire on the LAVs in front of us. Now I can see their outlines in the strobe-light effect of bombs and tracers going off around them. The blasts sound like hammers beating on the sides of Colbert's Humvee.

In the first moments, enemy ambushers who are entrenched alongside the road launch approximately forty RPGs at War Pig's column. In Wennberg's LAV, shrapnel from the RPGs immediately shreds four of his vehicle's tires. He estimates about 120 Iraqis are attacking from the west. Their ambush was coordinated enough that they held their fire until all of the LAVs had rolled into their kill box. As the enemy fire from the west intensifies, more Iraqis dug in to the east start to open up. They "bracket" the convoy by dropping heavy 82mm mortars on both ends of it, north and south (where Colbert's Humvee is positioned). These Iraqis have apparently figured out that the LAVs use thermal sights, and many of them are concealed beneath blankets to minimize their heat signatures.

The convoy halts. Through the windshield in Colbert's vehicle we can see the outlines of the LAVs as bombs flash all around. The LAVs open up with everything they have. Their cannons stutter explosively, spewing out tracer lines like red ropes that lash the ground for hundreds of meters on either side of the convoy. Pom-poms of fire bounce up from their targets. Iraqi tracers stream in toward them. The opposing lines of tracer fire tangle around one other, making it look almost like the two sides are dueling each other with glow-in-the-dark Silly String.

"I have no targets, no targets," Colbert shouts. The fire just ahead of us makes a steady roar. We could be standing at the edge of Niagara Falls.

Hasser shouts down from the turret. "I don't see nothing!"

There's nothing close enough for the team to engage. We watch the gun battle go on in front of us several minutes. Then the Iraqi fire into the LAV column drops precipitously. A lone Iraqi machine gun continues to spit tracers toward the LAVs. A half dozen of them pour fire onto it, but every time it looks like they've silenced it, the enemy machine gun starts up again. This duel continues on and off for another five minutes.

In the relative quiet that follows, Colbert leans out his window, using his nightscope to observe a small hamlet of four to eight mud huts perhaps twenty-five meters to our immediate right. In the window of the closest hut there's an amber light from a lantern or a candle.

"There's nothing there," Colbert says after studying the hamlet for a long time. "Just civilians behind a wall in back."

"Small-arms fire to our rear," Person says, passing on a report from the radio.

Then we hear AKs—they make a sharper, more substantial cracking sound than Marine M-4s—directly behind our vehicle. Fick reports over the radio that enemy fire is coming directly in on his Humvee about 100 meters behind us. Several rounds snap close to his head.

Recon Marines behind us return fire. It's not heavy yet, just intermittent crackling, like branches snapping in the woods.

"I have no targets, no targets!" Colbert repeats.

All at once, Marines in vehicles far to the rear of Fick's seemingly open up with every weapon they possess. Their gunfire sounds like a torrential rain. It's Delta Company, the reservist Marines. They're blazing away with machine guns and Mark-19s.

"Jesus Christ," Colbert shouts, laughing. "Those guys are putting down FPF." FPF—or final protective fire, shooting every weapon you have—is what Marines are trained to do only as a last-ditch measure. "They must think they've got the Chinese coming at them across the frozen Chosin," Colbert says, referring to the epic Korean War battle.

The village to our immediate right now comes under heavy machine-gun and Mark-19 fire from the Marines in Delta. As dozens of their grenades bounce off the huts and flash, exploding just thirty meters from us, a few Marines in Bravo open up. They mistake the sparkling Mark-19 bursts for enemy muzzle flashes—a common problem.

"I have no targets! No targets!" Colbert repeats. But our vehicle rocks as Hasser begins lobbing rounds from the Mark-19.

"Cease fire!" Colbert shouts.

"I got muzzle flashes, for sure," Hasser shouts.

"Easy there, buddy," Colbert yells. "You're shooting a goddamn village. We've got women and children there."

The reservists behind us have already poured at least a hundred grenades into the village. Colbert continues scanning it through his scope. "We're not shooting the village, okay?" he says. In times like these, Colbert often assumes the tone of a schoolteacher calling a timeout during a frenzied playground scuffle. Mortars explode so close we feel the overpressure punching down on the Humvee. But Colbert will not allow his team to give in to the frenzy and shoot unless the men find clear targets.

The fire from Delta Company continues unabated. One of First Recon's air officers riding near them looks back and sees a Mark-19 gunner in Delta standing at his weapon, burning through cans of ammunition, and he's not wearing NVGs, meaning he can't even see what he's shooting at. The reservists now make another classic mistake of nervous, undisciplined Marines: They fire down the axis of the convoy, their rounds skipping and exploding next to the friendly vehicles in front of them. A platoon commandeer in Alpha gets on the comms, shouting, "Get those assholes to cease fire. They're shooting at us!"

Their wild fire continues. Then the voice of Captain America comes over the radio, quavering and cracking. "Enemy, enemy! They've got us on both sides!"

"Oh, my God!" Person says. "Is he crying?"

"No, he's not," Colbert replies, cutting off what will likely be a bitter tirade about Captain America. In recent days, Person has pretty much forgotten his old hatreds for pop stars such as Justin Timberlake—a former favorite subject of long, tedious rants about everything that's wrong with the United States—and now he complains almost exclusively about Captain America.

"He's just nervous," Colbert says. "Everyone's nervous. Everyone's just trying to do their job."

"We're going to die if we don't get out of here!" Captain America screams over the radio. "They've sent us to die here!"

"Okay," Colbert says. "Fuck it. He is crying."

The firing drops off behind us. In front, LAVs pop off quick bursts. We hear their diesels grinding as they maneuver.

"LAVs are breaking contact," Person reports from the radio. It's a relief. It means we're turning around, pulling back. Mortars are still bursting steadily, while AKs crackle intermittently.

"Person, move forward," Colbert says. "We're covering the LAVs while they pull back."

"Is that right?" Person asks, startled.

"They want us to envelop them," Colbert says. "Just move up the road."

The wisdom of driving into a column of twenty-four LAVs while they pull beside us, some still firing their weapons, escapes the Marines. Colbert's team has no radio contact with the LAVs, nor much experience practicing an enveloping maneuver.

Person deals with the order by simply flooring it. We speed up alongside the LAVs as their guns pop off rounds in front and behind us. Their diesels growl past us as they retreat. Soon all of War Pig and First Recon are behind us. Second Platoon sits out alone on the highway for several minutes.

"Turn around," Colbert says.

"Roger that!" Person says, evidently relieved.

"We're moving three clicks south and punching out patrols," Colbert says.

We draw past the hamlet lit up so heavily by Delta.

"That was a civilian target," Colbert says. "I saw them."

He sounds tired. I think this war has lost its allure for him. It's not that he can't take it. During the past hour or so of shooting, he still seemed excited by the action. But I think after mourning the loss of his friend Horsehead, trying to care for dehydrated, sick babies among the refugees the other day, the shot-up kids by the airfield before that, and having seen so many civilians blown apart, he's connected the dots between the pleasure he takes in participating in this invasion and its consequences. He hasn't turned against the aims of this war; he still supports the idea of regime change. But the side of him that loves war—his inner warrior—keeps bumping against the part of him that is basically a decent, average suburban guy who likes bad eighties music and Barry Manilow and believes in the American Way.

THIRTY

○

THE BATTALION spends the night of April 8 in a bermed field by the road just two kilometers north of the magic line. Because of the low cloud cover, it's an especially dark night. On the horizon, lightning competes with bomb bursts from mortars War Pig is dropping on suspected enemy positions. The rolling berms we occupy are rock-hard. Walking around in the darkness, unable to see my own feet, I feel like I'm in a curved, concrete skateboard park. The Marines were ordered out of their MOPP suits a couple of days ago—the military no longer believes there is any chance of WMDs being used. But I put mine on tonight. I've reached a point where I feel calm during shooting, but afterward I tend to get a little spun. I'm convinced there's going to be a chemical attack tonight. Even though my MOPP suit has a hole in it and wouldn't do me much good, I wear it along with my rubber boots—eliciting amused laughter from Fick. I find a ditch to lie in for the night and wrap myself up in a poncho.

F-18s make repeated low passes. It's too cloudy for them to bomb anything, but according to Fick, it's hoped they'll scare off any tanks from approaching. Some of the passes the F-18s make are so low, the sonic forces they exert feel like a crushing weight on your skull.

Marines on the perimeter talk among themselves, as they observe for enemy movement. They pass around different optical devices, debating whether different shapes they see in the surrounding fields might be weapons or enemy positions. Their voices are quietly excited, cheerful. They like this part of war, being a small band out here alone in enemy territory, everyone focused on the common purpose of staying alive and killing, if necessary.

The high winds pick up. But instead of dust, they carry rain. It pours for about twenty minutes, and two hours later the sun comes up.

Standing in the early-morning mist, Fick gives his team leaders the order for the day. "We are clearing and killing enemy, moving north through hostile areas. We made two kilometers yesterday. We have thirty-eight to go."

THE BATTALION devotes the morning of April 9 to creeping up the road to Baqubah at a walking pace. Marines on foot clear the surrounding fields, with War Pig's LAVs sometimes joining them, sporadically firing into huts and ditches. The enemy drops mortars continuously, but with the Marine lines stretched across several kilometers, they present a diffuse target. In Colbert's vehicle, we sometimes get a flurry of mortars falling within a few hundred meters, then nothing for twenty minutes.

The Iraqis' tactics today seem clear: They let off some harassing fire with AKs and light machine guns, then retreat while dropping mortars. None of their fire is particularly accurate. While the Marine advance is dangerous, tedium sets in.

Colbert and Person are beginning to have personal

problems. There's no particular reason for the strain; it's more like they're two rock stars who have been touring a little bit too long together.

About noon, when a salvo of six to eight enemy mortars lands a few hundred meters from the Humvee, Colbert begins harping on Person's driving. The platoon is ordered to scatter into a berm by the road and wait out further mortar strikes. The idea is for Person to pull between two high berms for cover, but Colbert is not satisfied. As the next salvo begins to blow up in the vicinity, Colbert starts giving Person a driving lesson, ordering him to back up and maneuver the Humvee repeatedly.

"You see that pile of dirt by the trail we're on?" Colbert says, his voice cracking. "That is a berm, Person. Berms make me feel warm and fuzzy inside because they protect me from shrapnel. So when I say, 'Pull up next to the god-damn berm,' I mean pull the fucking Humvee up next to the fucking berm. Don't leave it sitting in the middle of the fucking field."

Person responds by alternately pumping the gas and brakes. We slam into the berm. Cans of ammo and AT-4 rockets piled in the rear shoot forward through the compartment. "Sorry about that," Person mumbles, not sounding very sorry.

A Hellfire missile blows up something 500 meters across the field. Mortars boom. Person begins belting out his latest song, one he and Hasser have been composing. It's a country song, which he sings in flagrant violation of Colbert's ban. Colbert doesn't even try to shut him up anymore. It's tough to reach Person these days. He's had a severe allergic reaction to Iraq. His eyes have swollen to red slits. They ooze tears constantly, which mix with the snot pouring from his nose. Doc Bryan has put him on a regimen of antihistamines and other medications to combat the allergies. God only knows how these medications interact with the Ripped Fuel and other stimulants Person uses. The whole morning, Person has been babbling about his latest scheme. He and Hasser are going to change their last names to "Wheaten" and "Fields," respectively, in order to put out a country music album, eponymously titled *Wheaten Fields.*

Now, as the explosions continue, he shares their first song, much of which they composed last night on watch. It's called "Som' Bitch," and its aim, according to Person, is to hit every theme of the country-music lifestyle. Person sings:

Som' bitch an' goddamn and fuck
All I ever seem to do is cuss
About how life's a' fuckin' treatin' me
To save my one last shred of sanity.

Som' bitch and goddamn an' fuck
The price of Copenhagen just went up
My NASCAR won't come in on rabbit ears
My broken fridge won't even chill my beer.

When he finishes, he turns to Colbert. "You like that?"
"Why don't you just quit while you're ahead," Colbert says.

MINUTES AFTER Person's performance, we drive back onto the road. Colbert stays behind, leading Garza and other Marines in a foot patrol of fields edging the highway. Several minutes later, they come under fire from Marines in Alpha Company, who rake their position with

.50-cal machine-gun rounds. The Marines in Alpha are specifically trying to hit Garza. With his brown Mexican skin, they've mistaken him for an Arab.

Person floors the Humvee toward Alpha's truck while screaming out the window, "You're shooting Marines!"

The men on the truck continue firing for another thirty seconds, until Capt. Patterson catches their error and orders them to stop. Colbert and Garza emerge from the field unscathed. Garza approaches the Humvee, shaking his head. "I figured it was those LAPD cops from Delta lighting us up. They love shooting Mexicans."

"Mistakes happen," Colbert says, climbing into the Humvee. Despite his attempt to slough it off, his face appears almost silver from the perspiration drenching it.

BY EARLY AFTERNOON the Marines have advanced more than twenty-five kilometers past the magic line and are fifteen kilometers south of their destination, Baqubah. In keeping with the poor judgment the Iraqis have shown in other situations, they only start to move their armor down to attack toward the middle of the day. But by now the clouds have burned off, and waves of British and American jets and Marine Cobras simultaneously bomb, rocket and strafe targets in all directions. Trucks, armor, homes and entire hamlets are being attacked from the air, blown up and set on fire. The Iraqis' one chance to wipe out the Marines with a mass formation of armor evaporated with the vanishing cloud cover.

Right now, the world's attention is focused on televised pictures of American Marines in the center of Baghdad, pulling down a statue of Saddam Hussein. Meanwhile, where we are, enemy mortars start exploding within fifty meters of Bravo Company's position. From a raw-fear standpoint, this is among the worst moments for the platoon.

The Marines in Second Platoon have been ordered to hold a position in a barren field by the highway. Their five Humvees are bunched within a few meters of one another when the mortars begin to land.

"We are receiving accurate mortar fire," Fick informs his commander over the radio.

"Remain in position," his commander, Encino Man, radios back.

Unlike earlier in the day, when Marines rolled back during close encounters with enemy mortars, Lt. Col. Ferrando doesn't want to lose his momentum. Now, having the benefit of robust air support, he's divided his Marines into two columns a few kilometers apart. His plan is to rush toward Baqubah as quickly as possible, while conditions remain favorable.

When Fick passes the word that the men in Second Platoon are to remain in place, Espera turns to his men in the next Humvee over from ours and says, "Stand by to die, gents."

The twenty-two Marines in the platoon sit in their vehicles, engines running, as per their orders, while blasts shake the ground beneath them. Everyone watches the sky. A mortar lands ten meters from Espera's open-top Humvee, blowing a four-foot-wide hole in the ground. It's so close, I see the column of black smoke jetting up from the blast area before I hear the boom. I look out and see Espera hunched over his weapon, his eyes darting beneath the brim of his helmet, watching for the next hit. His men appear frozen in the vehicle as the smoke rises beside them.

Before leaving on this mission, many of the men in Colbert's platoon had said good-bye to one another by shaking hands or even by hugging. The formal farewells seemed odd considering that everyone was going to be shoulder-to-shoulder in the cramped Humvees. The good-byes almost seemed an acknowledgment of the transformations that take place in combat. Friends who lolled around together during free time talking about bands, stupid Marine Corps rules and girlfriends' fine asses aren't really the same people anymore once they enter the battlefield.

In combat, the change seems physical at first. Adrenaline begins to flood your system the moment the first bullet is fired. But unlike adrenaline rushes in the civilian world—a car accident or bungee jump, where the surge lasts only a few minutes—in combat, the rush can go on for hours. In time, your body seems to burn out from it, or maybe the adrenaline just runs out. Whatever the case, after a while you begin to almost lose the physical capacity for fear. Explosions go off. You cease to jump or flinch. In this moment now, everyone sits still, numbly watching the mortars thump down nearby. The only things moving are the pupils of their eyes.

This is not to say the terror goes away. It simply moves out from the twitching muscles and nerves in your body and takes up residence in your mind. If you feed it with morbid thoughts of all the terrible ways you could be maimed or die, it gets worse. It also gets worse if you think about pleasant things. Good memories or plans for the future just remind you how much you don't want to die or get hurt. It's best to shut down, to block everything out. But to reach that state, you have to almost give up being yourself. This is why, I believe, everyone said good-bye to each other yesterday before leaving on this mission. They would still be together, but they wouldn't really be seeing one another for a while, since each man would, in his own way, be sort of gone.

After the platoon holds its position under close mortar fire for about fifteen minutes, the attacks cease. The platoon is ordered to move a couple more kilometers north, toward an intersection where locals have warned of an ambush.

We drive to within a kilometer of the intersection and stop. There's a cluster of barracks-like structures, a water tower and high-tension power lines ahead where the road forks into a Y. To the left there's a thick stand of palm trees extending west for about a kilometer. Several minutes earlier, Cobras had come under AAA fire from the buildings near the intersection. They and other aircraft decide to prep the area before the Marines roll through on the ground.

We sit back and watch them bomb and strafe the intersection for about ten minutes. Colbert tunes in the Air Wing's radio channels. We listen as the pilots call in intended targets—from Iraqi military personnel hiding behind garden walls and in berms to trucks and armored vehicles—then watch as the aircraft nose down and destroy them. Orange rosettes flash ahead of us from powerful bombs dropped by jets.

"We've never had this much air," Colbert says, eyes gleaming, pleased with all the destruction we are witnessing. "It's all about having some air and LAV escorts," he concludes with a grand smile.

Pilots over the radio now discuss their next move, doing a "recon by fire" on the palm grove to the left of the intersection. The pilots can't see what's in the palm grove, nor have they taken any hostile fire from positions inside it. Nevertheless, they request permission to do a recon by fire, which simply means they're going to rocket and machine-gun the fuck out of it and see if anything shoots back. The battalion's forward air controller on the ground approves the plan. Helicopters skim low over the trees, stitching the ground with machine guns, setting off a storm of white fire with their rockets. It's a real *Apocalypse Now* moment.

Colbert's team and the rest of the platoon are ordered to drive up to the intersection, take the Y left and enter the palm grove while it's still burning.

We drive into a bank of smoke, glimpsing a succession of small horrors. There's a truckful of shot-up cows in the field, nearby several slaughtered sheep, their guts smeared out around them. Two charred human corpses by the road are still smoking. There's a dog with his head buried up to his ears in the stomach of a cow he's eating. We are again in Dog Land.

We come alongside the palm grove on our left. Fences made of dried reeds crackle and burn outside the vehicle. We continue on, pull upwind of the smoke and now see there's a hamlet nestled between the trees—a series of farmhouses, interconnected by walls, animal pens and grape arbors. Thatched roofs and fences burn. These are what were reconned by fire.

"I hope there's no people in there," Colbert says. The gleam that had been in his eyes moments earlier during the bombing has been replaced with his worried, helpless look.

Republican Guard berets, uniforms and other pieces of military gear are scattered by the road across from the palm grove. Iraqi forces—legitimate military targets—have obviously been in the area. Colbert stops the Humvee. He and other Marines get out. Iraqi military communications lines—cables from field phones—lie by the side of the road. Colbert's men cut them apart with their Leatherman tools.

While standing outside, we hear a babble of voices. Men whom we can't see are chanting something. Their voices come from ditches by the road across from the burning hamlet. An old man now rises from behind a berm ten meters away. His hands are up. His eyes are wild and his face covered with tears as he shrieks, "No Saddam! No Saddam!"

A couple of other men rise behind him, all of them chanting the same words. One has his shirt off and is waving it as a surrender flag. Another man climbs out of a ditch carrying a small frightened girl, about five or six. She stares at the Marines in shock. They're all civilians— probably residents of the hamlet reconned by fire.

The Marines lift their rifles high and gesture for the now-homeless villagers to step forward. The men keep chanting.

"Okay, okay!" Fick shouts. He gives them an exaggerated smile, trying to reassure them.

The eldest man approaches, still chanting insanely. Fick pats his arm. The man begins to shout. "George Bush! George Bush!" he says, pronouncing the first name like "Jor." The Marines offer the little girl some candy but she turns away in mute fear.

Fick grabs the old man's shoulder, steadying him. "Yes, George Bush," Fick says. "No problem. Okay?"

The old man finally stops shouting. He stares at Fick, perhaps finally recognizing that this American is not going to kill him. He breaks down sobbing, grabs Fick's face and smothers him in kisses.

THIRTY-ONE

○

By three o'clock in the afternoon of April 9, First
Recon and War Pig have come to within about ten kilometers of Baqubah, advancing in two columns spaced
several kilometers apart. While Bravo Company clears
through the burning hamlets reconned by fire to the
west, Alpha Company, led by Patterson, is pushing north
on a trail that follows a canal to the east. The canal runs
north-south, and the Marines in Alpha are pushed up
against the edge of it to their right. Ahead of them is an
expanse of bermed fields. Even as they creep forward—
eighty Marines in about fifteen Humvees and
trucks—shepherds dot the fields around them, tending
flocks of sheep.

While the company is halted, a volley of mortars lands
in their midst. A blast detonates so close to Capt.
Patterson, standing beside his Humvee, that it knocks him
against the side of his vehicle and rips up his pack with
shrapnel but misses him. Then his column comes under
machine-gun fire from a lone hut 200 meters ahead.
Beyond the hut, Iraqis concealed in ditches, some fortified
with sandbags, begin firing at them with AKs.

The lead Marines in Alpha begin to take fire from

heavy, 73mm guns on BMPs—light Iraqi tanks—that seem to be about a kilometer ahead of them. The Marines in Alpha dive for cover. Patterson estimates there are as many as 150 Iraqi soldiers entrenched in the fields. With his unit hemmed in by the canal on the right side and by Iraqis to the left and in front, for the first time of the war, Patterson thinks, as he later tells me, "We are really on the brink here."

Fawcett, whose team is near the front of Alpha's position, takes cover behind a berm. The enemy BMP continues blasting at his men with its main gun, which fires shells about half the size of a Marine heavy artillery round. Fawcett and Sutherby, the sniper, peek up and observe more enemy troops pouring into the fields ahead of them. The Iraqi soldiers are being ferried in aboard military trucks, hopping out, then scrambling behind berms to fire on the Marines, whom they will soon out-number about three to one.

Battalion forward air controllers contact an Air Force F-15 Strike Eagle in the vicinity to take out the BMPs. Marines are wary of working with jets, especially those flown by the Air Force. The fear is that jet pilots, moving too fast and far removed from Marines on the ground, will end up striking friendly positions. This fear is borne out when the F-15 drops its first 500-pound bomb intended to hit the BMP. The pilot misses by nearly a kilometer. The bomb lands fewer than 200 meters from Fawcett's position. The men are buffeted by the shock wave, and temporarily deafened by the blast, but unharmed.

The pilot drops a second bomb directly on the BMP, destroying it, then moves on to take others farther north. Cobras linger to wipe out enemy machine-gun positions with Hellfire missiles.

Alpha's Marines climb into their Humvees and advance on the Iraqis in the fields ahead. The Iraqis put out a lot of AK fire but seem incapable of hitting the Marines. Many put their rifles over their heads and shoot indiscriminately, without looking. Marine snipers steadily pick them off, while the .50-cal and Mark-19 gunners saturate their positions with lethal fire. The thing that amazes Sutherby is seeing shepherds run onto the field amidst the shooting, to drag off wounded sheep caught in the crossfire.

Alpha's pace quickens. Marine gunners begin competing with one another to cut down the enemy fighters. Over the course of the next two hours, they advance approximately ten kilometers, destroying or routing all hostile forces ahead of them. When I run into Fawcett a short while later, he greets me with a blissed-out, ashram grin. After weeks of complaining about the war, fretting over its moral implications, he enthuses about slaughtering squads of uniformed Iraqi soldiers in the fields with the nearly 250 Mark-19 rounds he fired. "I feel invincible," he tells me. "I had rounds skipping in the dirt right next me, a BMP shooting straight at us, Cobras lighting stuff up all around, a five-hundred-pound bomb blow up almost on top of us, and nothing hit me. Maybe it's karma."

On its western approach to Baqubah, Bravo Company stops outside a two-story, pale-yellow stucco building that appears to be an abandoned military post. Two hundred meters behind us, Kocher leads his team into the field, advancing just thirty meters into it from the highway. While picking their way through dried brush, waist-high in places, they encounter a group of Marines from Delta Company, the reserve unit. Several of the reservists surround a dead enemy fighter, a young man in a ditch, still clutching his AK, lying with his brains spilled out of his head. While the reservists gawk at the corpse, a man on Kocher's team notices a live, armed Iraqi hiding in a trench nearby.

Kocher and his men turn on the armed Iraqi with their weapons ready to fire. They shout at him to drop his AK. It's a tense moment for the Marines. Strictly speaking, this armed Iraqi had gotten the drop on them and could have easily taken them out had he fired. There's gunfire all around, and the Marines are worried more Iraqis are hidden nearby.

But the Iraqi complies, drops his weapon and rises. One of the reservist Marines, First Sergeant Robert Cottle, a thirty-seven-year-old SWAT team instructor with the LAPD, jogs over, takes out a pair of zip cuffs and binds the Iraqi's hands behind his back—so tightly that his arms later develop dark-purple blood streaks all the way to his shoulders.

The prisoner, a low-level Republican Guard volunteer in his late forties, is overweight, dressed in civilian clothes—a sleeveless undershirt and filthy trousers—and has a droopy Saddam mustache. He looks like a guy so out of shape he'd get winded driving a taxicab in rush hour. Surrounded by Marines, the man begins to blubber and cry.

Kocher hands his rifle to another Marine, pulls out his 9mm sidearm and approaches the prisoner. With combat raging around them, this enemy takedown begins in a highly charged manner. Kocher slams the Iraqi to the ground, puts the pistol to his head and shouts, "If you move, I'll blow your fucking head off!" Pinning the guy with his knee in his back, he pulls AK magazines and a military ID out of his pockets. The prisoner starts pleading in English, "I have a family."

Kocher hauls him to his feet and frog-marches him to

the highway. In the surrounding fields, enemy mortars continue to boom amidst the crackling of Marine machine guns. Kocher knocks the prisoner over. He falls facedown in the dirt, with his hands still bound behind his back. In Kocher's mind, his aggressiveness fits with his philosophy of handling prisoners. "I try to keep a prisoner off-balance so he knows I'm in control."

The Marines bring Meesh over, and he barks at the man in Arabic, repeatedly asking him where the enemy mortars are positioned. The prisoner begs for his life. They conclude he knows nothing. They tie a sack over his head—a precaution taken since they are on a battlefield and don't want this guy to shout or signal his comrades in any way should he see them—and wait to load him onto a truck.

Cottle, from the reservist unit, walks up to Kocher and shakes his hand, saying, "Thanks for saving my life."

The situation seems pretty much wrapped up when Captain America makes a dramatic appearance, jogging up the road, screaming, with his bayonet out. He brandishes his bayonet toward the prisoner and shouts, "We ought to cut his throat like the Chechnyans in the video." It's a reference to a gore video circulating on the Internet, which many of the troops had seen before the invasion. It consisted of choppy MPEG-file footage that purported to show live Russian soldiers having their throats slashed by Chechnyan guerrillas.

Whether he was serious we never discovered because Captain America then jabs the prisoner several times in his ribs and neck with the tip of his bayonet. The man starts screaming through the bag on his head, pleading again about his family. "Shut up!" Captain America yells. "Shut the fuck up!"

Watching this bizarre drama, Kocher orders Redman to

step off the Humvee and guard the prisoner. They both figure the move will be a way of calming down Captain America. Redman picks up his M-4 and approaches the prisoner. He says to Captain America, "Dude, I've got him."

Redman stands over the prisoner, placing his boot heel on his neck. Captain America shouts at the guy a few more times, then backs off.

Fick arrives. He exchanges a few words with Captain America, who's now smiling and chuckling nervously, as he often does after a good outburst. Fick has no idea that anything out of the usual just occurred. He loads the prisoner into his Humvee and drives off.

A while later some of the reservist Marines approach Kocher and Redman. Cottle, who'd thanked Kocher a few minutes earlier for saving his life, now says, "You guys abused that prisoner. I should never have let you take custody of him. I ought to kick your fucking ass."

Within twenty-four hours, the reservists file a report charging Kocher, Redman and Captain America with assaulting the prisoner. Captain America is temporarily suspended from command. Kocher is relieved of his job as team leader and ordered to ride with a support unit. Redman, who's allowed to remain on the team, is dismayed. "Dude, when I put my boot on the prisoner's neck, there were people out there still shooting at us. I wanted to control the prisoner and still be able to see what was happening." He adds, "Kocher and I were trying to calm the situation down. I didn't stomp or kick the guy. Dude, we just wanted Captain America to go away."

Even Cottle later confesses, "I feel bad for the enlisted guys. They weren't really the problem. It was the officer." One of Cottle's fellow reservists, a senior enlisted man who also witnessed the events, says, "From what I saw, that officer's got problems. There's something wrong with him."

Captain America denies committing a misdeed. He later tells me he simply thinks his accusers in the reserve unit were insufficiently acquainted with the realities of the battlefield. "The prisoner was handled properly, even though they didn't like the way it looked," Captain America says. "They saw the beast that day, and they didn't know how to handle it."

BY FIVE O'CLOCK in the afternoon, the Iraqis who had earlier put up determined-though-inept resistance have either fled or been slaughtered. Colbert's team, along with the rest of the platoon, speeds up the road toward the outskirts of Baqubah. Headless corpses—indicating well-aimed shots from high-caliber weapons—are sprawled out in trenches by the road. Others are charred beyond recognition, still sitting at the wheels of burned, skeletized trucks. Some of the smoking wreckage emits the odor of barbecuing chicken—the smell of slow-roasting human corpses inside. An LAV rolling a few meters in front of us stops by a shot-up Toyota pickup truck. A man inside appears to be moving. A Marine jumps out of the LAV, walks over to the pickup truck, sticks his rifle through the passenger window and sprays the inside of the vehicle with machine-gun fire.

Watching this apparent execution unfold, I wonder if shooting the Iraqi in the truck ahead of us was an act of barbarity or a mercy killing along the lines of the one Doc Bryan had tried to perform on the wounded man outside Al Muwaffaqiyah. There's no time to sort this out.

We advance a few more kilometers, and Colbert's team sets up a roadblock. We are now within four kilometers of

Baqubah. My first encounter with the enemy prisoner whom Captain America had taunted and abused earlier takes place in the back of Fick's Humvee parked nearby.

The prisoner is squirming on the truck bed, the burlap sack tied over his head, when I approach. A few Marines have gathered around and are taunting him. "What do you think you'd be doing to us if we were your prisoner?" a nineteen-year-old Marine rails at him.

Fick walks over. "Hey, I don't want any war crimes in the back of my truck." He says this lightly, having no idea yet of the brewing controversy surrounding the man's capture. "Untie him and give him some water."

The man's arms are swollen and purple when the Marines cut off the zip cuffs. The angry nineteen-year-old Marine helps give him a bottle of water and a package of MRE pound cake. The prisoner, snuffling his tears away, eyes the offerings suspiciously for a moment, then eats hungrily.

"Just 'cause we're feeding you doesn't mean I don't hate you," the young Marine says, still trying to keep up his edge of hostility. "I hate you. Do you hear me?"

I study the man closely while he eats. He wears a torn, grimy wife-beater undershirt with his fat belly protruding. I look for bleeding or bayonet marks on his body—to see if Captain America penetrated his skin—but see no evidence of this. The worst signs of mistreatment on his body are gruesome bruises on his arms from the zip cuffs. While eating, the man periodically grabs his shoulders and winces in pain. I ask him how badly he hurts. He speaks English reasonably well.

"I need medicine," he says, then bursts into tears, sniffling loudly.

"For your wounds?" I ask.

"No, I need medicine for my heart," he says. "It is bad."

He tells me his name is Ahmed Al-Khizjrgee. Despite his suffering, the more we talk he gives the impression of being both buffoonish and crafty. With his considerable girth, he brings to mind Sergeant Schultz in the old *Hogan's Heroes* series. He tries to convince me that he is not actually a soldier. "It is your imagination that I am a fighter," he says.

When I point out that he was found with military ID documents, carrying a loaded rifle in an enemy-ambush position, he finally admits, shrugging and stroking his Saddam mustache, "I am a very low soldier."

Al-Khizjrgee says he is forty-seven years old, with two sons and five daughters. He claims he was originally a shoemaker and joined the Republican Guard late in life. His brother is a cabdriver in Baghdad. He is a peace-loving man. One of the Marines points out that a lot of other Iraqis threw down their weapons and fled. "You were waiting to kill us," the Marine says. "You didn't put your weapon down until we made you."

"It is not true," Al-Khizjrgee protests. "I am afraid. If I put my gun down, the police come and beat us." He says he and the other men in his unit received no outside information on the state of the world. They could be shot for listening to a radio.

I ask him how he thinks the war is going. He tells me his superiors told him and the other men in the unit that Iraq was winning the war. He says he and the other men holed up in Baqubah had their doubts but kept these to themselves. "Everybody under Saddam is silent," he says. "If Saddam say we have war with America, we say, 'Good!' If he say no war, we say, 'Good!' "

The Marines, who were so angry with the man a moment ago, have now warmed up to him. One of them says, "We can't put our weapons down, either."

"He was just doing his job," another Marine adds, now sounding almost impressed with the guy's tenacity in hanging on to his rifle.

The Marines smile at him and feed him more pound cake.

Al-Khizjrgee fails to catch on to the newly festive atmosphere. He leans forward and confides in me that he is desperately afraid. "How can I go home now? What if my sergeant finds me? He will know I did not fight."

About half an hour earlier, Colbert tuned in the BBC and picked up the report that Baghdad had fallen. I pass this information on to Al-Khizjrgee. "There is no Saddam. There is no Iraqi army. You have no sergeant anymore."

Al-Khizjrgee stares in disbelief. "It's true," I tell him.

He begins to cry again, only now he smiles. "I am so happy!"

The news is only getting better for Al-Khizjrgee.

Fick walks up and tells Al-Khizjrgee he will be driving him to a detention facility near Baghdad tonight.

"For free?" he asks, as if unable to believe his good fortune.

THE BATTALION'S final enemy contact outside Baqubah occurs an hour before sunset, when the men in Alpha's Second Platoon spot a T-72 tank near their roadblock south of the city. T-72s are the most formidable tanks in the Iraqi arsenal. As soon as the Marines call it in to their platoon commander, he orders them to attack it with an AT-4 missile. Ordinarily, Marines would call in an air strike on a T-72, but no aircraft are immediately available, and Second Platoon's commander wants this tank stopped now. One T-72 could wreak havoc on the whole battalion.

Burris, whose team led the way through the ambush at Al Gharraf, volunteers to lead the AT-4 strike on the tank. It's potentially a highly risky mission. The shoulder-fired AT-4 missile isn't really designed to defeat a T-72. At best, Marines believe an AT-4 can score a "mobility kill"— blowing a track off the tank—and to do this Burris will have to get in close to the tank, within 150 meters.

Nearly every engagement Burris has been in since the invasion started has somehow turned into his own personal, comic mishap. From the time he tripped on his rifle stock at Nasiriyah, giving himself a shiner, to the ambush at Al Gharraf, where he was sprayed from head to toe with human excrement when his Humvee plowed into the town's open sewer puddle, Burris has concluded almost every firefight he's been in knocked on his ass, laughing.

Now he approaches the T-72, with several Marines and his platoon commander by his side. They reach the stepping-off point, where Burris will continue on alone to get in close to his target, and his platoon commander, Capt. Kintzley, slaps him on the back. "Burris," he says. "Don't miss."

Burris ducks down, runs across the road, dives into a berm and creeps up behind the tank. He gets even closer to the monster T-72 than his superiors had ordered him to go, crawling to within 125 meters. He sees an auxiliary fuel pod on the back of the tank and aims for it, figuring it will multiply the effects of his relatively puny AT-4 missile. He fires the missile.

Initially, Burris sees only a small flash where the missile hits. He's worried that perhaps the missile glanced off the armor (believed to be nearly invincible on the T-72) and berates himself for not aiming at the track. An instant later, it feels like a giant fist comes out of the sky and pounds Burris on his back, slamming him to the ground. The tank erupts in a massive explosion.

Down the road, his platoon commander can actually see individual pieces of the tank—flywheels and gears—flying overhead. Several hundred meters farther back from the blast, twenty-three-year-old Corporal Steven Kelsaw, standing by a headquarters vehicle, is struck in the helmet by a piece of the tank and knocked down. It feels to him like someone just hurled a bowling ball at him. His Kevlar helmet is partially shattered, but all he suffers is a bad headache.

Burris's hit on the T-72 produces one of the biggest explosions many Marines have seen in the entire war.

When Burris walks back to rejoin his team, Capt. Patterson, his company commander, walks up to congratulate him. Patterson wants to commend "this kid"—as he refers to each of his Marines—for going out there all by himself against the T-72. But as soon as he sees Burris's dirty face and his dazed, somewhat confused-looking smile, Patterson is seized by a fit of laughter. Finally, he manages to say, "Burris, I was worried sick about you."

"Sir, what's so funny?" Burris asks, still shaken up, his ears still ringing from the explosion.

"Nothing, Burris," Patterson says. "Good job."

AFTER THE DESTRUCTION of the T-72 tank, ten Humvees from Charlie Company race into Baqubah, with A-10s flying overhead as escorts. The roads are blockaded with rubble and concertina wire. Abandoned Iraqi military positions are everywhere. The Humvees snake through the barricades and make their way toward two military command centers—headquarters for a Republican Guard division and a brigade. The division headquarters is in ruins from repeated American airstrikes. The brigade headquarters is still partially standing. A team of Recon Marines speeds up to the building. They jump out, run inside and steal the Iraqi "colors"—the enemy's flag.

The Marines have reclaimed, in part, their honor, sullied after the loss of their own colors in their truck burned outside Ar Rifa. The Americans hightail it out of the city, and the battalion prepares to drive back to Baghdad. With hundreds of Iraqis killed or wounded during the operation, the most serious injury sustained among Marines in First Recon is Kelsaw's headache. For the Marines it feels as if the entire mission to Baqubah has ended as an extremely bloody game of capture the flag. Weeks later, Baqubah emerges as a key center in the "Sunni Triangle" insurgency against the American occupation. But for the Marines pulling out, the mission stands as one of their more clear-cut triumphs. They seized forty kilometers of highway, probably killed more soldiers than civilians and captured the enemy's flag.

We drive back to Baghdad in darkness. Person, at the wheel, navigating with NVGs on his helmet, begins to sing, "Mamas, don't let your babies grow up to be cowboys."

"Hold on, buddy!" Colbert shouts. "No goddamn country music."

"That's not country," Person insists. "It's a cowboy song."

"I hate to break it to you, but there are no cowboys," Colbert says.

"Yeah, there are," Person says, his voice simultaneously flat yet defiant. "There's tons of cowboys."

"A cowboy isn't some dipshit with a ten-gallon hat and a dinner plate on his belt," Colbert says. "There haven't been any real cowboys for almost a hundred years. Horse raising is a science now. Cattle raising is an industry."

A report comes over the radio of enemy fire on the column. "Hold on," Colbert says, reluctantly putting the argument aside. "I'd like to hear about this firefight."

War Pig, driving ahead of us on the same highway the battalion fought its way up earlier, is again taking fire from both sides of the road. Tracers stream through the night sky. We drive into the gunfire. Enemy muzzle flashes jet toward us from the right side of the road no more than five meters from my window. Colbert opens up on the position, his rifle clattering. Spent shell casings ejected from the side of his M-4 rain down inside the Humvee. If his past performances in these types of situations are any guide, there's a strong likelihood he hit his target. I picture an enemy fighter bleeding in a cold, dark ditch and feel no remorse—at this time.

We drive the next ten kilometers in near silence, while the Marines search for additional targets, until we leave the ambush zone. Colbert pulls his weapon back in from the window and resumes his discussion with Person. "The point is, Josh, people that sing about cowboys are annoying and stupid."

THIRTY-TWO

○

By the night of April 9, offensive U.S. military operations in Baghdad have ceased. The city is taken. Crowds have toppled Saddam statues. American military units are pouring into the city to begin the occupation.

We reach the outskirts of Baghdad at about eleven o'clock, having driven straight from Baqubah. We arrive in the same industrial suburbs we passed through the day before. The looters are gone, the streets are empty, the city is black. A few fires rage in the distance, sending columns of flame over Baghdad, but given the level of destruction Marines have witnessed recently, the place seems relatively tranquil. The American artillery that was pounding continuously for the past several days is silent. We pass construction sites where military bulldozers, with floodlights mounted on them, are laboring in the night. The military machine that crushes everything in its path is quickly followed by armies of worker-ant battalions, who've already marched up and begun smoothing out the rubble and building infrastructure. We drive into a sprawling supply depot and fueling station erected in the past several hours to service thousands of American vehicles. There's a sense in the air tonight that

Baghdad is pacified, the Americans are now quietly, efficiently in control. It's perhaps the only time things will ever appear this way to the men in First Recon.

FIRST RECON enters central Baghdad on April 10, at about three in the afternoon. Colbert's team drives with Hasser at the wheel, singing the hobo classic "King of the Road." We approach the city from the east. The striking thing about the outskirts of Baghdad is how green everything is. We pass through a wealthy neighborhood of spacious stucco homes perched atop small hills, shaded beneath palms, sycamores and eucalyptus trees. Occupants of some homes sit outside in gardens, watching convoys belonging to the American invaders rumble past on streets below.

We cut down a dirt embankment and approach a temporary pontoon bridge over the Diyala River, the eastern crossing point into the city. When we reach the other side, Fick reports over the radio that American forces in Baghdad are experiencing "intermittent sniper fire and attacks from Fedayeen in trucks."

The eastern side of Baghdad is a shantytown. We drive on dirt roads past corrugated tin and mud-brick huts jumbled together amidst a patchwork of open spaces, with cows and chickens roaming everywhere. We round a corner and two enormous bulls, each seeming more powerful than the Humvee we're in, stand in the road. Hasser gingerly veers around them.

We pass donkey carts pulled over on the side of the road, intermixed with Toyotas, ancient Chevys and BMWs. Barefoot, scruffy kids line the edges of the shantytown. Some shout, "Go! Go! Go!" while pointing toward the city center and dancing like cheerleaders. One kid we pass comes right to the point: "Money! Money! Money!" he chants.

The battalion drives onto a massive berm, about five meters wide by five meters high. The Marines laugh. There are berms even in Baghdad. The battalion stops. Marines get out. The berm offers a commanding view of the city—a sprawl of low-slung apartment blocks, homes, offices, avenues, canals, freeways that stretch beyond the vanishing point. It spreads across nearly 800 square kilometers and has a population of about six million people.

"Jesus Christ!" Colbert says. "That's a lot of city."

Gunny Wynn walks over to Colbert's vehicle. The two of them study maps and detailed satellite images of the city, marveling at the thousands of streets and alleyways. Gunny Wynn shakes his head. "And we thought those little towns a kilometer long were tough. I don't know how we're going to control this."

Person stands by the Humvee, urinating on the berm. "Hey!" He calls out triumphantly. "I wrote U.S.A. with my piss."

FIRST RECON'S DESTINATION in Baghdad is a working-class slum called Saddam City (since renamed Sadr City). More than two million Iraqis live here in an expanse of vaguely Stalinist-looking apartment blocks spread out over several kilometers. We drive down the main road that edges Saddam City and are greeted with a blend of enthusiasm tinged with violence. Thousands of people line the street, pressing up against the sides of Colbert's Humvee. Sniper rounds periodically crack in the air. The side streets into Saddam City are barricaded with rubble, trunks of palm trees and scorched cars.

When Colbert's Humvee momentarily stops, along with the rest of First Recon's convoy, we're swamped by young men in threadbare clothes who zombie-shuffle up to the windows. Many smile, but their faces have a hungry, vacant look. They resemble a crowd from *Night of the Living Dead*. Several grab at the Marines' gear hanging off the sides of the Humvee—canteens, shovels and rucksacks. Colbert pushes his door open, jumps out and cows the crowd of perhaps 300 people into backing away from the vehicle. He paces from side to side, weapon out, establishing his territory.

Colbert is ordered back into the vehicle. The convoy circles around, driving over some traffic islands, and snakes into a gated industrial complex across from Saddam City. Inside, vast warehouses are spread across several acres. Most of them are bomb-smashed, with smoke and flames curling out of missing roofs. Piles of bright silver paper flutter on the ground like leaves. A familiar aroma wafts from the smoldering warehouses: tobacco. Someone in the Humvee figures out the silver paper on the ground is from cigarette packs. We have rolled into Iraq's central cigarette factory. Hundreds of thousands, if not millions, of burning cigarettes fill the air with what is likely the world's biggest-ever cloud of secondhand smoke.

The convoy stops by a loading dock next to a warehouse untouched by bombs, the battalion's first camp in Baghdad. Nicotine-addict Marines immediately loot the nearby structure. Inside, cases of Iraq's "Sumer" brand of filter cigarettes are stacked ten meters high. Marines emerge with cartons of them, then lie back by their Humvees and smoke the spoils of conquest.

Gunny Wynn paces uneasily up to Fick. "Do you realize how fucking weird this is?" he says. "When we set up in Mogadishu, we spent our first night in a cigarette factory. I hope this turns out better."

There's a ten-story glass-and-steel office tower on the west side of the complex, perhaps 500 meters from the warehouse where we've stopped. Every few minutes, loud bangs emanate from the upper floors of the office tower. Navy SEAL snipers occupy the top of the building, and are busy taking out targets across the city. Judging by the pace of their shooting, they're killing Iraqis at a rate of about one every five to ten minutes. We on the ground below them have no idea who they're shooting at. Only later do we discover there are Iraqis spread out around this complex, taking random shots at American troops, and the SEALs are attempting to eliminate them.

Fick gathers the men for a briefing. "Marines have been here for more than twenty-four hours," he says. "They're set up on the other side of this warehouse. They've had one killed and one wounded from sniper or mortar fire." He then adds, "Compared to where we've been, I think it's pretty safe here. We should all get a good rest tonight."

A few minutes after his pronouncement, the complex is rocked by a powerful explosion. Someone has set off a car bomb outside the main gate. A furious firefight ensues outside, involving Marines from other units. The gun battle is only a couple hundred meters away, but the complex is surrounded by a three-meter-high cement fence so we can't see anything. We just hear a torrent of shots.

Fick walks up to me and smiles, deeply amused by the crescendo of gunfire. "I was wrong about that good night's rest," he says. Moments later, a random bullet falls from the sky and skips onto the concrete, sparking behind Fick's back. He laughs. "This is definitely not good."

We both watch a casevac helicopter flying past the

complex. Skimming low over rooftops, it suddenly rears up to avoid enemy tracer rounds fired at it from the ground. We watch the life-and-death drama playing out in the sky for several moments. The helicopter escapes. "Not good at all," Fick says.

But to the men, racking out on pavement—no holes to dig here—surrounded by concrete walls, with all the gun-fighting being handled by Marines from other units, this war-torn complex represents five-star luxury. They lie back, eating, talking, smoking. For many, it's the first time they've rested since the mission to Baqubah started seventy-two hours ago.

WHILE MOST GOT TO SLEEP, Espera leans against the wheel of his Humvee parked by Colbert's, composing a letter to his wife back home in Los Angeles. He uses a red lens flashlight, which emits a dim glow, not easily spotted by potential enemy shooters, to write on a tattered legal pad. Espera's wife was a sophomore at Loyola Marymount College when they met. At the time, he was a nineteen-year-old laborer with no future. They married shortly after she got pregnant, and much of Espera's life since has been an effort to better himself in order to meet her high standards. "You see, dog," he explains, "my wife is smart, but she fucked up big-time when she married me. I was a piece of shit. I remember my wife talking about all the books she'd read, and it hit me there was a whole world I'd missed. Before I met her I used to think, I've got a shitload of hand skills—welding, pipe-fitting—any pussy can read a book. See, I didn't grow up with no understanding. My mom tried, but my dad is a psycho ex-Marine Vietnam vet."

Espera uses the term "psycho ex-Marine Vietnam vet"

with the utmost respect. He aspires to possess warrior skills equal to those of his father, who won a bronze star in Vietnam, and believes if he's lucky, he himself will retire one day as a "proud, psycho ex-Marine." Despite his reverence for his father's combat valor, the man abandoned him at a young age (after an incident, according to Espera, in which his dad was shot in their home by a jealous girlfriend), and their relationship remains rocky.

Espera bitterly recalls a past incident. Several years ago, when his father tried to patch things up by taking him on a fishing trip, his old man ended up stopping off at a porn shop on their way to the lake. While Espera waited outside for his dad to finish his business in the private viewing booths, he got into an altercation with a man he believed was trying to cruise him in the parking lot, and Espera threw a brick through the windshield of the man's car. "That was our father-son trip," he says.

Since meeting his wife, Espera has become an avid reader, voraciously consuming everything from military histories to Chinese philosophy to Kurt Vonnegut (his favorite author). In the Middle East, he spends every free moment either reading or writing long letters to his wife, who works at an engineering firm in the San Fernando Valley. Tonight, at the cigarette factory, Espera reads me the beginning of a letter to his wife. "I've learned there are two types of people in Iraq," he reads, "those who are very good and those who are dead. I'm very good. I've lost twenty pounds, shaved my head, started smoking, my feet have half rotted off, and I move from filthy hole to filthy hole every night. I see dead children and people everywhere and function in a void of indifference. I keep you and our daughter locked away deep down inside, and I try not to look there." Espera stops reading and looks up at me. "Do you think that's too harsh, dog?"

Gun battles rage all night long in Baghdad. Marines sleep soundly on either side of me. I watch tracer rounds rising almost gracefully over the city. Some of this is probably just celebratory fire. But every fifteen minutes or so, powerful explosions go off, followed by furious bouts of weapons fire. During the lulls, ambulance sirens wail through the streets.

Occasionally rounds snap into the complex. You hear them zinging, then cracking as they strike nearby buildings.

After one of them hits, I hear a Marine in darkness say, "Is that all you've got?"

Ripples of laughter erupt. Between the gun battles and ambulance sirens, we hear singsong Arabic blaring through loudspeakers. It's either muezzins calling prayers—unlikely after dark—or American psychological operations units trying to calm the people down by playing messages urging them to stop fighting. It's not doing much good.

At around midnight I decide to use the toilet facilities. About 200 meters from where we sleep, Marines have set up a designated "shitter"—a grenade box perched over the open storm drain that encircles the cigarette factory complex. I creep over to it in the darkness. A solitary Marine is perched on the shitter. I wait a long time. As my eyes adjust to the darkness, I finally make out what's keeping him. His right arm is moving up and down. He's getting in a late-night combat jack.

I leave him in peace and go over to another section of the storm drain. As I'm about to settle over it, I notice that on this side of the complex the wall separating us from the street is an open-stake fence. Marines had been told the complex was surrounded by a solid concrete wall, but in this corner you can look through to the street and shops just a few meters beyond. I decide to perch down anyway, but as I'm about to do so, a gun battle erupts on the street, maybe ten meters in front of me. Red lines of tracer rounds zoom past, skipping low over the pavement on the street directly before my eyes. You can't see who's shooting, how far away they are or what they're aiming at. I retreat back to the Humvees.

I fall asleep to the sound of pitched street battles in Free Baghdad.

THIRTY-THREE

○

Early the next morning, April 11, at the cigarette factory, Fick gathers his Marines to brief them on their mission in Baghdad. He reads from the official statement: "First Recon will conduct military operations in and around Saddam City to include patrols establishing the American presence, stop the looting, and restore a sense of security in order to allow critical, life-sustaining functions to take place. The intent is to locate key facilities in our zones, such as schools and hospitals, to collect intelligence on Fedayeen and Baath loyalists who are still at large and to prevent lawlessness and to disarm the populace. The end state is a humble, competent force occupying this area, ensuring security and mutual trust between us and the local populace."

After reading the official statement, Fick adds, "We have rolled through this country fucking things up. Now we have to show these people what we liberated them from."

Fick radiates quiet confidence, mixed with purpose. He tells me after the briefing, "What we did up to now was the easy part. This is where the work really begins." Fick is under the impression that Marines will stay in this cigarette factory for at least a month, maybe longer. They will be given sectors to patrol. They will set up nighttime observation posts in neighborhoods in order to capture or stop looters, paramilitary forces or jihadis who are still active. They will come to know the people in the neighborhoods they patrol, rendering them assistance and serving as liaisons for the nation-builders—engineers, doctors, civil-affairs specialists—who are no doubt on their way.

"This is going to be tough," Fick tells me. "But I think for my men it will give them a sense of purpose about all the terrible things they've seen and been through."

A SHORT WHILE after Fick's briefing, he invites his team leaders and me to accompany him on a tour of their new home, the cigarette-factory complex. As soon as we near the open-stake fence I discovered the night before, a crowd of civilians on the other side rushes forward. They stick their faces between the bars and begin shouting at the Marines, several of them in English. "Please, stop the looting," two of them plead.

Fick approaches the fence, telling them, "Order will be restored very soon."

More civilians mob the fence, shouting in Arabic, gesticulating. Fick and the others retreat from the babble. We walk into an open area between looming warehouse structures, cross about fifty meters of barren ground and approach another section of fence—this one with no people on the other side. We're looking out at the city when there's a loud cracking sound, followed by a zing. A few more follow. Smoke puffs pop up from the ground a few meters behind us.

"Sniper," several of the Marines say at once.

Lovell, who's also an expert sniper, says the rounds are coming from close by, and that we are directly in front of the barrel of whatever gun is shooting at us. I ask him how he knows this. "You can tell by the sound," he says. He explains that the type of cracking we're hearing isn't the gun-powder blast of the bullet being fired but the sonic boom the bullet makes as it crosses the sound barrier. You only hear it so clearly when you're pretty much directly in front of the barrel. The zinging sound we also hear, he says, is something you only pick up if the bullet's passing within a few meters of your ears. This is all more information than I wanted.

The five of us have fifty meters of open ground to cross before we can reach cover. We sprint back one at a time under fire from the sniper. For some reason, as I make the dash all I can think of is the scene from the Peter Falk comedy, *The In-Laws*, in which Falk absurdly urges his sidekick to run in a "serpentine" pattern when they come under fire from a band of guerrillas while stuck in a Central American dictatorship. In my fear, this scene comes to me when I run through the sniper fire. Following Peter Falk's advice, I zig-zag in a serpentine pattern as the shots ring out. It takes me twice as long to reach safety as it takes the Marines. After everyone gathers behind a building, we stand for a moment, panting heavily, collecting ourselves. Finally, Fick looks at his team leaders and they all burst out laughing. Lovell asks me why I was running back and forth. When I tell him, he suggests, "Next time we come under fire, just run in a straight line. You might live longer."

FIRST RECON BATTALION only launches one patrol on its first full day in Baghdad. The problem is, the battalion has just one translator, Meesh. While looting and burning continues unabated in the city, the Marines, with nothing to do in First Recon's "occupation force," kill the day by exploring the factories, warehouses and offices in the complex.

I follow along with several on a mission to ratfuck the main office tower. Marines are hoping to find cool souvenirs to bring home. On the way in, the Marines grab giant crescent wrenches from one of the cigarette-factory buildings to break down doors.

The main office tower has already been claimed by the First Battalion, Fourth Marines. They guard the front entrances, but the ratfuck crew I'm with smashes through some of the side windows with their monkey wrenches and circumvents the sentries. We take stairs up to the eighth floor. Some of the outer offices are occupied by the SEAL sniper teams, still busily shooting Iraqis every few minutes.

We sneak into rooms containing vast rows of low cubicles. The Marines are simultaneously freaked out and disappointed. It looks like any boring American office. You can see some workers have gone to a lot of trouble to decorate the drab cubicle walls with family photos, framed kitschy pictures of peaceful sunsets, beaches, forests, as well as Christmas and Valentine's cards with holiday sentiments written on them in English.

Marines rifle through everything, looking for souvenirs, but all they find are colored pens and coffee mugs. "It's all stupid crap," one of them says, slamming his wrench into a computer screen.

The Marines kick down the door to what looks like the boss's office in the corner. One of them sits behind the expansive wooden desk, punches buttons on the speaker-phone and plays boss. "Have my secretary send in my next appointment," he says in an obnoxiously official voice.

Then he starts smashing the phone and the desk apart with his wrench. The Marines destroy the boss's office with gleeful vengeance, throwing stuff at the walls, pissing in the corner, all of them maniacally laughing. In a weird way, they're living out the fantasy Carazales often talks about—in which one day a year the blue-collar man gets to go into rich neighborhoods and smash apart expensive homes.

AFTER TWO DAYS of aimless waiting, the Marines in Second Platoon finally get a mission in Baghdad. Their job is to enter a neighborhood north of Saddam City and drive through the streets. The goals are simple: to talk to locals who've never seen Americans before and to not get into any gunfights. Before leaving, Fick briefs his men. "If we take a potshot, don't open up with a machine gun on a crowd. The days of running and gunning through towns are over."

His precautionary briefing seems unnecessary when the Marines roll into the neighborhood. Compared to Saddam City, the place they enter seems almost bucolic. Broad, unpaved roads lead to large stucco homes that would not be out of place in San Diego. Lush gardens grow from vacant lots. Young men line the street and greet the Marines in halting, yet formal English. "Good morning, sir," they say.

The Humvees drive for about 500 meters until a cluster of residents blocks the road. They stream out of their homes bearing jugs of water and hot tea, which they offer the Marines. Small girls emerge carrying roses for the Americans.

The neighborhood men gather around the Humvees, puffing cigarettes and bitching about life under Saddam. Most of their complaints are economic—the lack of jobs, the bribes that had to be paid to get basic services. "We have nothing to do but smoke, talk, play dominoes," a wiry chain-smoking man in his late thirties tells me. "Saddam was an asshole. Life is very hard." He asks if the Marines can provide him with Valium. He pleads, "I cannot sleep at night, and the store to buy liquor has been closed since the war started."

Aside from the complaints of the idle men, the most striking feature of the neighborhood is the hard labor performed by women. Covered in black robes, they squat beneath the sun in the empty-lot gardens, harvesting crops with knives, while children crawl at their feet. Others trudge past carrying sacks of grain on their heads. The division of labor exists even among children. Small boys run around playing soccer while little girls haul water. "Damn, the women are like mules here," Person observes.

"If we'd have fought these women instead of men," another Marine comments, "we might have got our asses kicked."

The other culture shock for the Marines is that several of the men seem to be hitting on them. One asks Garza to lift up his glasses. When he does so, the man leans forward and says, "You have pretty eyes."

Another of them asks a Marine if he likes boys or girls. When the Marine says, "Girls," the man makes a face and says, "Girls. Blah!" Then he points to a young man standing nearby, makes an intercourse gesture with his fingers and says, "You go with my friend, you like."

The Marines are amused. Soon Marines and Iraqis stand around the Humvees in a big, noisy klatch, laughing, trying to communicate through gestures and fractured English. They trade Marine gear, like their soft-cover hats, which Iraqis seem to universally prize, for Muslim prayer beads, which Marines all covet. After worrying that his Marines were going to indiscriminately shoot civilians, Fick has to wade in and break up the party.

The neighborhood is filled with unexploded munitions—mostly mortars and RPGs, fired by Iraqi forces, that failed to detonate. Fick roams around the area, scrupulously recording the locations of unexploded munitions in a handheld computer for a future removal effort.

Residents assail him with a list of other problems—lack of electricity and running water, broken phone lines, ransacked hospitals, bandits coming in at night and robbing homes, even the dearth of jobs. They expect the Americans, who so handily beat Saddam, will take care of everything. The Marines shake their hands, promise to see them again soon, and drive off, heroes for the day.

They never return to the neighborhood.

THE ORIGINAL PLAN Fick had briefed his men on executing—restoring stability to Baghdad by patrolling specific neighborhoods and rooting out Fedayeen and Baathists—never materializes. Instead, over the next several days, First Recon's plans shift, as the city plunges further into chaos. The battalion moves from the cigarette factory to a wrecked children's hospital north of the city to a looted power plant. Each time they change locations, Second Platoon is assigned new sectors to patrol. Within a few days, Fick admits to me the whole endeavor is so haphazard it seems to him at times like a "pointless exercise."

The basic problem with the American occupation of

liberated Baghdad is that the fighting is so heavy at night, most U.S. forces decide not to go out after dark. On their third day in Baghdad, Fick tells his men, "We're not going out at night. There are too many revenge killings going on in the city. Mostly it's Shias doing a lot of dirty work, taking out Fedayeen and Sunni Baathists."

Lt. Col. Ferrando takes this even further, telling his senior men that the Shias are wiping out paramilitary forces through "a sort of an agreement" with the American occupiers. "We have to be careful about night-time operations," he tells his men, "because the Shias will be out doing the same things you are. They might want to engage you."

An internal Marine intelligence report I come across, dated April 12, confidently predicts that the ability of hostile forces in Baghdad "to successfully and continually engage our forces will be complicated by the local Shias' intolerance for regime paramilitary forces hiding out in their neighborhoods."

The Americans' assumption seems to be that all they need to do in Baghdad is sit back and let the Shias clean house. Not only do the Americans tolerate this bloodshed, but at least one Marine commander in an infantry unit working in Saddam City allegedly distributes stocks of confiscated AKs to Shia leaders who promise to use them to rout out the "bad guys."

FLAWS IN THE American occupation plan become apparent to the Marines in Fick's platoon when they mount their first patrol into a vast, predominantly Shia slum on the northeast side of Baghdad. On the morning of April 13, Colbert's Humvee leads the rest of the platoon into the slum known as Seven Castles. We roll in atop a high berm overlooking about a square kilometer of ramshackle, two-story apartment blocks. According to the translator with us, 100,000 people live here. The twenty-two Marines in Second Platoon are the first Americans to enter this neighborhood since Baghdad fell four days ago. The platoon stops in the crest of the berm overlooking the neighborhood.

Within minutes hundreds of children run up and surround the Humvees, chanting, "Bush! Bush! Bush!" They are soon joined by elders from the neighborhood.

The translator helping Fick today is a local Iraqi, Sadi Ali Hossein, a courtly man in his fifties who used to work at the factory the Marines occupy. He showed up yesterday to offer his services to the Americans as a translator. (An exceedingly polite man who wears a rumpled yet dignifying brown suit, Hossein vanishes the day after this patrol; other Iraqis who work at the factory later claim he's a Baathist agent.) With his help as a translator today, Fick tries to find out what the neighborhood requires. Initially, elders who emerge from the mob tell Fick they need just two things: water and statues of George Bush, which they plan to erect up and down the streets as soon as the Americans help them pump out the sewage currently flowing in them.

Fick turns to the translator with a puzzled expression on his face. Hossein explains, "They think Bush is a ruler like Saddam. They don't understand the idea of a president who maybe the next year will go out."

The streets below not only run with sewage but are filled with uncollected garbage. In the midst of this, there are pools of stagnant rainwater. Somehow, locals differentiate between pools of stagnant rainwater and sewage, since they dip buckets into the former and drink it.

They say they haven't had water or electricity in the

neighborhood for a few years now. What the elders urgently need help with is security at night. All of them have the same story: As soon as the sun goes down, bandits roam the streets, robbing people and carrying out home invasions. Residents in the neighborhood have set up barricades on the streets to keep them out. Everyone is armed. The locals claim that since armories and police stations were overrun at the end of the war, an AK now costs about the same as a couple of packs of cigarettes.

"They kill our houses," one of the men says.

"The Americans have let Ali Baba into Baghdad," his friend adds.

Another man claims enemies from an outlying neighborhood have set up a mortar position behind a mosque and are randomly shelling them at night.

Even late in the morning, you can still smell cordite in the streets from all the gunfire of the previous night. What's striking about the residents' complaints is the fact that Marine commanders have been claiming that all the gunfire at night is a result of Shias removing Fedayeen and other enemies they share with the Americans. But this is a 100-percent Shia neighborhood, and these people are clearly distraught by the violence. They ask Fick if his Marines will stay for the night.

He tells them that is not possible, but that his men will try to bring water some other day.

Hossein tells me he has a grim view of Iraq's future. "You have taken this country apart," he says. "And you are not putting it together." He believes that the violence the Americans are allowing to go on at night will only fuel conflicts between the Sunni and Shia factions. "Letting vigilantes and thieves out at night will not correct the problems of Saddam's rule," he says. He gestures toward the crowded slum below, teeming with people. "This is a bomb," he says. "If it explodes, it will be bigger than the war."

Espera, who's been listening to Hossein's analysis, offers his own take on the situation. "Let a motherfucker use an American toilet for a week and they'll forget all about this Sunni-Shia bullshit."

Doc Bryan sets up a medical station under some ponchos in front of his Humvee. Mothers bring children sick with giardia caused by drinking dirty water, feverish infants, a girl whose legs were burned when a cooking fire exploded. Men start pushing to the front of the line, complaining of headaches and sleeplessness. Like the guy we met in the first neighborhood, they want Valium. Another family brings a son who can't walk, hoping that Doc Bryan can cure him like a faith healer. A fight nearly breaks out between a Marine and men in Doc Bryan's line who are stealing candy the Marines are giving to the sick children. By this time, hundreds of people throng the Marines' position, just trying to get a look at the Americans.

The Marines are driven out as the pandemonium grows. Farther into the neighborhood, hundreds of people descend on the Humvees. What Marines had initially viewed as jubilation begins to feel increasingly like hysteria. The mob's incessant chanting starts to drive the men crazy. Everyone who approaches is dirty, scared and desperately in need of help, which the Marines are incapable of giving. They nearly run over children who fall in front of the Humvees while running beside them. At one stop, Fick and I get out and see kids rocking on an unexploded artillery shell, gleefully bouncing on it like a hobbyhorse. "This is madness," Fick concludes.

As the Marines gather around their concrete sleeping area that night, some are disgusted by the behavior of the

Iraqis. "What American man," Doc Bryan asks, "would cut in a line of children with life-threatening illnesses to try to get Valium for a headache, then steal their fucking candy? I have no respect for these men."

"Bro, it's not that bad here," a Marine says in the darkness. "Just think if someone invaded Los Angeles. Americans would fucking riot if their cable went out for three days. These people don't have water, electricity, hospitals, sewers, nothing, and they're waving and smiling."

"They won't be for long," Espera says. "Iraqis have a short attention span just like the American public. As soon as they stop celebrating that we got rid of Saddam and we cut 'em off at the titty—they figure out we're not going to be pouring money into this motherfucker, giving everyone a new car and a color TV—they'll turn on us."

IN AN EFFORT to reach out to community leaders, Bravo Company sends Meesh to meet with the imam at a Shia mosque during a patrol. This neighborhood in north Baghdad is marginally better off than others. There's no sewage in the streets, and the low apartment blocks and shops near the mosque look tidy. The mosque itself is a squat, stucco building, with a small dome and a minaret not much bigger than a telephone pole. There are loudspeakers hanging from it for the prayers broadcast through the neighborhood.

Meesh enters the mosque early in the afternoon. Several young men who serve as the imam's bodyguards train their AKs on him the moment Meesh sets foot in the gloomy anteroom. After twenty minutes of negotiating with these characters, one of them leads him into the imam's office in the back.

The imam, a man in his early fifties who studied in Iran, looks to Meesh almost exactly like a younger version of the late Ayatollah Khomeini, with a long, pointed white beard and dark-black eyebrows. Though Meesh is a Sunni—as well as a beer-drinking dope smoker—he and the imam kneel and perform a prayer together. Then, according to Meesh, the imam tells him he welcomes the Americans, so long as they don't expose the Iraqi people to corrupting Western influences. Meesh tells the imam the Marines will try to bring some water the next day to distribute from the grounds of the mosque. He asks for the imam's help in controlling the people who invariably mob the Marines' vehicles. According to Meesh, the imam tells him, "If they come too close, the Americans should hit them. These people are used to being pushed around. You have to threaten them."

Within hours of Meesh's meeting, the loudspeakers from the minaret blare a message from the imam: "It is against your religion to harm Americans." Then the imam's guards go through the neighborhood, painting messages in red on the stucco walls lining the streets. They say, "An AK used after sunset is a tool of damnation." At least this is what Meesh claims happens as a result of his meeting with the imam.

The next morning Second Platoon returns to the mosque, escorting a military tanker truck to distribute 2,000 gallons of fresh water to the residents. The Marines park the truck beside the mosque in an open dirt lot and wait beneath overcast skies. Unlike the day before, when crowds had turned out cheering the Marines, this morning there's almost no one on the streets. The few adults and children who are out hang back, staring vacantly. The Marines stand around the truck, holding a hose up, beckoning people to come and get the free water, but in twenty minutes only two or three venture forward. "All week people have been asking for water," Fick says. "We finally bring it to them, and nobody fucking wants it."

Though Meesh vows to me that the messages blared from the mosque and painted on the walls by the imam's followers were all pro-American, something has dramatically changed in the neighborhood. The people seem almost frightened of the Marines. I press Meesh about this. "Are you sure the imam said he wanted the Americans to come here?" I ask him.

"Dude, the meeting was totally cool," Meesh assures me.

Whatever really transpired with the imam, only Meesh knows. As has been the case since the invasion began, First Recon Battalion is almost entirely dependent on Meesh for all its Arabic intelligence gathering. It's not that Meesh is a bad guy, but it's astonishing to me that in an elite unit of American forces, among the first to occupy the capital city of a conquered country, there's no one within the command structure who fluently speaks the local language.

ONE WEEK after arriving in Baghdad, Second Platoon finally receives orders for a night mission. There's a park in Baghdad that Fedayeen are suspected of using as an operations base. Second Platoon is ordered to set up observation posts near the park overnight, then move in and sweep it for signs of hostile forces in the morning.

An hour before sunset, the platoon moves into position on a high berm near the park. When the sun drops, the vast city, without any electricity, goes nearly black. Then tracers light up the sky from the gun battles raging on all sides of the berm we occupy.

What makes the spectacle of these nocturnal gun battles even stranger is the fact that a kilometer to our east, a freeway is filled with cars streaming into Baghdad. We watch the fire course over the string of headlights.

Fick and I are taking this all in when he receives a call on his radio from his commander, Encino Man, who suggests he send foot patrols out tonight into the neighborhoods below. Encino Man tells him that Lt. Col. Ferrando has decided, after a week of keeping the men off the streets at night, that it's time for the Marines to become "more aggressive."

Fick resists the order, telling Encino Man he's going to keep his men in a defensive position on the berm and not move until dawn. He sits down next to Gunny Wynn and vents. "Look at this," he says, gesturing to the hundreds of tracer lines zipping through the sky. "They want me to be 'more aggressive,' to send the men into this? For what? Just to be out there waving the American flag? So I can come home with nineteen men instead of twenty?"

Fick watches the ongoing destruction in the city, then adds, "If Iraq stays a flaming cesspool until the end of time, does anyone really care? Does it fucking matter?"

Fick's talk a week earlier at the cigarette factory of giving his men a purpose by restoring order in Iraq seems like ancient history. Fick appears to have lost his belief in his mission here. The problem is not so much that the city has unraveled before his eyes in the past week—he pretty much expected Baghdad to be in total chaos. Instead, what's come undone is his belief that the Americans have any kind of occupation plan to remedy the situation. "Our impact on establishing order is just about zero," he says. "As far as I can see, there's no American plan for Baghdad. Maybe it's coming, but I don't see any signs of it." But he adds, leaving room for optimism, "A platoon commander's situational awareness doesn't extend very far."

In the morning the platoon drives down to the entrance of the park. There's a road bridge leading into it, with a tower sort of like Seattle's Space Needle rising beyond. It turns out this is Baghdad's amusement park, complete with roller coasters, hot-dog stands and buildings with giant pictures of Disney characters painted on them (no doubt in fiendish violation of international trademark law). The platoon stops by the bridge outside the park. Cars are driving in and out. Meesh finds out that there's a fuel depot in the park, and citizens are entering to steal gasoline. The Marines block off the bridge, turning away traffic in preparation for moving into the park.

A beat-up red Volkswagen Passat speeds toward them. Marines aim their weapons at it. The car stops nearby. There's a woman at the wheel with a fifteen-year-old girl in the passenger seat. The girl looks out at the Marines, smiling almost flirtatiously.

The driver gets out. A worried-looking middle-age woman in a brightly colored shawl, she's the girl's mother. Her name is Mariane Abas, and she tells Meesh that eight days ago while playing outside their house north of Baghdad, her daughter, Suhar, was hit in the leg by shrapnel from a bomb that seemed to come out of no-where—perhaps from a high-flying U.S. plane. Doc Bryan opens the door. Suhar smiles at him. Her leg is in a cast. Doc Bryan and Colbert turn the girl sideways, extending her leg out of the car.

"Doc, you've got fifteen minutes," Fick says. "We've got to move into the park."

Doc Bryan cuts away the cast. The girl screams. Her mother climbs in on the driver's side and wraps her arms around her daughter's head and chest, holding her in place as she writhes in agony. Whatever hit the girl's leg ripped chunks of flesh off from her calf to her thigh. The bones were broken as well. Whoever treated her stuffed the wounds with cotton, which Doc Bryan now must rip out. Pus oozes out. She has a high fever, a bad septic infection. On top of this, her foot was set in the cast with the toes pointing down, so if she lives and her bones heal, she'll walk with a lame foot.

"We've got to get her to a hospital," Doc Bryan says. "This infection is going to kill her."

Fick radios the battalion, requesting permission to medevac the girl. It's denied. The platoon delays its mission for two hours, while Doc Bryan does his best to clean the wounds out. The girl wails and sobs most of the time. Her mother holds her head. Doc Bryan curses softly.

Fick walks away, turning his back on the girl. "This is fucking up our mission," he says, pissed off at the girl for showing up with her horrific wounds. "A week after liberating this city, the American military can't provide aid to a girl probably hit by one of our bombs," he says, pissed off at the war.

DESPITE AN APATHY that's set in among many Marines over the futility of their missions in Baghdad, Colbert remains committed. When a resident of one neighborhood comes forward complaining of an unexploded bomb in a garden where children play, Colbert enlists Espera's (grudging, extremely reluctant) aid to destroy it with a C-4 charge, though neither of them is specifically trained in ordnance removal, and the platoon is under orders to avoid handling unexploded rounds. Later, Colbert climbs into a five-foot-deep hole in a risky effort to locate and destroy an unexploded artillery round next to a home.

Fick, concerned that he might kill himself, orders him to cease the operation.

Colbert despairs when he hears reports of other units accidentally firing on civilians. One episode reported on the BBC enrages him. U.S. soldiers, newly arrived in Iraq to begin the occupation, accidently slaughtered several Iraqi children playing on abandoned tanks. Under the ROE, the children were technically "armed" since they were on tanks, so the GIs opened fire. Maj. Gen. Mattis would later call this shooting "the most calamitous engagement of the war." After he hears of it, Colbert rails, "They are screwing this up. Those fucking idiots. Don't they realize the world already hates us?"

Espera tries to console him by sharing some wisdom he learned on the streets of L.A. Espera explains that if he were writing a memoir of his days as a car repo man before joining the Marines, he would title it *Nobody Gives a Fuck*. According to Espera, the ideal place and time to repossess or steal an automobile is a crowded parking lot in the middle of the afternoon. "Jump in, drive that bitch off with the car alarm going—nobody's going to stop you, nobody's going to even look at you," he says. "You know why? Nobody gives a fuck. In my line of work, that was the key to everything. The only people that will fuck you up are do-gooders. I can't stand do-gooders."

As Colbert continues to fulminate over mounting civilian casualties and their effect on undermining the American victory, Espera throws his arm over his shoulder. "Relax, Devil Dog," Espera says. "The only thing we have to worry about are the fucking do-gooders. Luckily, there's not too many of those."

* * *

EARLY ON APRIL 18, the men in First Recon are told they will be departing Baghdad. Though they haven't completed their mission to "restore a sense of security," few regret the order to leave.

Their final night in Baghdad is spent camped in the playing field of the soccer stadium that once belonged to Saddam's son Uday. Tonight, the usual gun battles fought by locals start before sunset. Recon Marines keeping watch high up on the bleachers come under fire. As rounds zing past, one of the men up in the bleachers, caught by surprise, stumbles as he tries to pull his machine gun off the fence and take cover. His arms flail while he tries to regain his balance. More gunshots ring out. Marines watching on the grass below burst into laughter.

Later, several Marines in First Recon gather in a dark corner of the stadium to drink toasts to a one-armed Iraqi man in Baghdad who sold them locally distilled gin for five American dollars per fifth. Generally, it doesn't require any alcohol to lower the Marines' inhibitions. But now, with the gin flowing, a Marine brings up a subject so taboo I doubt he'd ever broach it sober among his buddies. "You know," he says, "I've fired 203-grenade rounds into windows, through a door once. But the thing I wish I'd seen—I wish I could have seen a grenade go into someone's body and blow it up. You know what I'm saying?" The other Marines just listen silently in the darkness.

THIRTY-FOUR

○

AT FIRST LIGHT ON APRIL 19, the battalion leaves Baghdad on a deserted super-highway and sets up camp sixty kilometers south of the city. The encampment offers a familiar setting—Humvees nestled beneath cammie nets in a barren field surrounded by low berms. The next morning, April 20, is Easter Sunday. It's almost like Florida weather this morning. It's humid and bright, but there are clouds in the sky as well, and it rains periodically through the sunlight.

Navy Lieutenant Commander Bodley, the chaplain, consecrates this day by pounding a crude wooden cross into the mud. He drapes it with an olive-drab rag to symbolize Christ's body on the cross.

At nine in the morning, the chaplain gathers about fifty faithful Marines—predominantly officers and personnel from battalion support units—who sit in the dirt in front of the cross, rifles propped up beside them, and leads them in a mumbling version of the hymn "He Rose from the Dead." Then the chaplain tells them, "I have good news." He announces that a Marine has chosen this special day to be baptized.

When Colbert hears of the good news after watching

the service from his Humvee in the distance, he cannot conceal his outrage. To him, religion is right up there with country music as an expression of collective idiocy. "Give me a break," he says. "Marines getting baptized? This used to be a place of men with pure warrior spirit. Chaplains are a goddamn waste."

But Colbert's disgust this morning isn't merely about religion. He and others in the platoon are annoyed by continued threats from Encino Man and Casey Kasem to punish Fick and Gunny Wynn for disobeying orders. Encino Man remains angry at Fick and Gunny Wynn for questioning his plan to call in an artillery strike nearly on top of their position at Ar Rifa. Since that episode, Fick and Gunny Wynn have persisted in questioning Encino Man's orders, most recently in Baghdad when Fick declined to send a patrol out at night.

Casey Kasem has complained vociferously about the "lack of obedience to orders" displayed by the leaders of Second Platoon. "Their job is to execute whatever the commander tells them," he's fumed, "and they don't."

While following orders is at the heart of good military discipline, the men have no faith in the layer of command above Fick, starting with Encino Man and his loyal enlisted helper, Casey Kasem. "Those two are dangerous out here," one of Colbert's friends in the platoon says. " 'Obedience to orders' to them means they don't want to look bad to their commanders. They're afraid to question orders. Fick and Gunny Wynn are great men because they have the courage to do the right thing."

THE DEBATE over questioning orders from superiors becomes far less abstract the evening of April 22, at First

Recon's camp south of Baghdad. This night a battalion watch officer, whose job is to sit in for Lt. Col. Ferrando and, in effect, babysit the battalion when he's indisposed, mistakenly issues an order for Marines to go out in the darkness and mark the location of a minefield by the highway north of the camp. The watch officer radios Capt. Patterson and asks him to send some of his men in Alpha to escort combat engineers on the mission.

The mines were discovered a few days earlier by Patterson's men along the highway a kilometer north of the camp. Combat engineers have been removing mines all day, but hundreds remain. The watch officer erroneously believes there's an order to mark the location of the remaining mines with chemlites. Patterson tells him that he must be mistaken. There's a division-wide order banning Marines from operating in minefields at night. Besides, thousands of American military vehicles have passed by the mines in recent weeks without incident. The job can wait until morning, Patterson tells him, declining to execute the order.

But the watch officer persists. He radios Encino Man and asks him to send Marines out in the dark to mark the minefield. Encino Man promises to push Marines out immediately. He later tells me, "I didn't want to send Marines out there, but the watch officer is the voice of the battalion commander [Ferrando]. I couldn't say no."

The operation gets into full swing when Encino Man contacts Captain America and issues the command for his men to accompany three engineers into the minefield. In the wake of the episode in which Captain America taunted an EPW with his bayonet, he was reinstated to command of his platoon following a brief suspension but is still awaiting final disposition on possible disciplinary action from Ferrando. The enlisted men, Kocher and Redman, were cleared of wrongdoing in that matter, and Captain America now orders their team and another to transport the engineers up the road to the minefield.

The Marines reach the minefield at about nine-thirty that night, parking two Humvees on the highway, leaving their headlights on. Kocher steps onto the road with three engineers, among them Gunnery Sergeant David Dill and Staff Sergeant Ray Valdez. The plan tonight is simply for the engineers to stand on the road and toss chemlites into the minefield that runs along the side of it.

The engineers earlier spent the day in the field removing more than 150 mines. Dill, a compactly built twenty-seven-year-old with a tattoo on his right calf that says MINEFIELD MAINTENANCE is passionate about land mines. Before he was attached to First Recon he spent a year at Guantánamo in Cuba removing mines from the fields the U.S. sowed there in the 1960s. Other engineers who work with him consider Dill an inspirational figure. "He makes everybody excited about our jobs," says a Marine who serves under him.

Combat engineers tend to be fanatical about their profession. Perhaps it's a prerequisite. De-mining, which is usually done completely by touch—probing the earth with plastic rods, then feeling each mine to check for antihandling booby traps and removing it by hand—is highly stressful. According to their own guidelines, engineers are not supposed to pull more than twelve anti-tank mines a day, given the toll it takes on their nerves.

During the afternoon of April 22, Dill removed more than thirty mines from the field beside the road (with his team gathering an additional 120, which they detonated in a terrific explosion just before reentering the field after dark). Now, standing on the road in the glare of the Humvees' headlights, Dill observes what appears to be a mine in a portion of the field believed to have been cleared. He and Valdez, twenty-eight, step off the road to investigate.

A third engineer standing far back on the road, twenty-three-year-old Sergeant Randy Weiss, sees Dill and Valdez walk off the road and is about to caution them but decides against it. Weiss later tells me, "If anyone knows what he's doing, it's Gunny Dill." Not only is Dill Weiss's mentor within the Marines, they are good friends. Both of them married, each with a young child, they live near each other off-base, and their wives are close.

There's a tremendous blast as Dill steps on a mine at the edge of the road. Weiss is temporarily blinded by spraying debris, even though he's nearly ten meters back from the explosion.

Kocher, standing directly behind Dill on the road, is thrown onto his back. He goes temporarily deaf from the blast, and his eyes reflexively shut. In the immediate aftermath, only his olfactory sense still functions. He smells burning flesh. Kocher opens his eyes and sees Dill lying a few meters out in the field, thrown there by the explosion.

When Kocher rises to his feet, the ringing in his ears subsides. He hears Dill yelling, "I'm bleeding out! Throw me a tourniquet."

Kocher and his team's corpsman, forty-six-year-old Navy Hospitalman First Class George Graham, walk about four meters into the minefield. Dill screams, "Get the fuck out of here!"

Kocher sees that Dill's foot hangs from his leg at a weird angle. The boot is shredded. His toes are exposed, dangling by some skin. His heel is blown off, and his tib-fib bones are sticking out, the ends charred and smoking. He stepped on the smallest mine in the field, a BS-50

Italian "toe-popper." He and Graham tourniquet him off and carry him back to the road. (The next day, when engineers return to the field, they find two other mines a few inches from the footprints made by Kocher and Graham.)

Redman leaps into the front of the Humvee and joins Carazales, the driver. They try to radio the battalion for medical assistance. First Recon's camp is only one or two kilometers distant, but the radios aren't functioning.

Redman jumps onto the highway. He sees Valdez wandering beside the road, holding his hands over his eyes, moaning.

Redman pulls Valdez onto the pavement. They kneel facing each other and Redman grabs him by the shoulders to steady him. "Dude, you're gonna be okay," Redman says. "Let go of your eyes."

Redman gently pulls Valdez's hands away from his face.

"Are my eyelids there?" Valdez asks.

"Yeah," Redman says, not really certain if they are there. He shines a flashlight into his face.

"Are my eyes there?" Valdez asks. "I can't see nothing."

Redman suppresses the urge to vomit. Both of Valdez's eyes are filled with pebbles and debris. His left eye is packed. Bloody tissue puffs out around it like a blossom.

"Dude, your eye is gone," Redman says.

Redman carefully plucks out the debris from the mangled hole that used to be Valdez's left eye. As he shines the light into it in order to put a dressing on it, Valdez says, "I can see your light. My eye must be okay."

"I guess I was wrong," Redman says. "I'm really sorry."

But Valdez's eye is gone. The nerves are sending false signals to his brain, fooling him into thinking he can see the light.

They load the two men into the Humvees, one in each. Getting Valdez in is easy. He can sit upright. Loading Dill in with his toes and foot hanging by the skin, and charred bones sticking out, is not so easy. They have to drape him sideways across the backseats in Kocher's Humvee, while trying not to jiggle his loose foot too much. Dill curses steadily, "Fuck, fuck, fuck it hurts."

"Give him morphine," Captain America says.

Everyone ignores him. Even the most boot Marine knows you don't give morphine to a guy with an un-stabilized, bleeding wound. It can make his blood pressure drop and kill him.

Captain America jumps in Kocher's vehicle. The camp is about a kilometer due south on the perfectly straight highway. Driving back there should be a simple pro-position. But Captain America manages to screw this up.

"Turn off here," he says. "I know a shortcut."

"Let's take the road we know," Kocher says.

After weeks of having his authority mocked and stripped away by his men, Captain America decides to assert himself. He orders Carazales to make the turn. "Do what I say," he says. "I know this shortcut."

Fifty meters into Captain America's shortcut, the Humvee drops into a sabka patch. Carazales tries rocking the vehicle out from the tar and quicksand, but it only sinks deeper. Dill, lying in the back with his partially connected foot and toes bouncing around, howls in agony.

The Marines are forced to carry him out to the second Humvee. They make it back to the camp and medevac the two engineers. Dill loses his right leg up to the knee, including his tattoo. Valdez loses his left eye.

The next morning, April 23, Weiss, whose face is polka-dotted with cuts from the blast but who is other-wise fine, returns to the minefield with another engineer.

He clears twelve more mines, and they finish marking the field.

When I ask Encino Man about this episode a few days later, he insists he did the right thing in not questioning the order to send the men out there. "Gunny Dill was the mistake in the whole thing," he says. "He's the one that stepped off the road."

THIRTY-FIVE

○

AT TEN IN THE MORNING on April 23, First Recon drives south on Highway 8 to its final camp in Iraq outside of Ad Diwaniyah, 180 kilometers from Baghdad. The battalion joins about 18,000 other Marines from the First Division occupying a former Iraqi military complex—barracks, supply depots and training fields spread across fifteen square kilometers. While most of First Recon's Marines wind up occupying brick barracks, through the luck of the draw those in Bravo Company end up in a former tank repair yard in a windswept corner of the camp. For the next six weeks, they will sleep in the open on a four-by-forty-meter concrete strip.

Surveying this infernal spot with an almost satisfied smile the afternoon he arrives, one of the men in Second Platoon says, "One universal fact of being in the Marine Corps is that no matter where we go in the world, we always end up in some random shitty place."

Bravo's Second and Third platoons spend most of their daytime hours here, as well as their nights, as if they're living on a ship. The camp's burn pits and latrines are located adjacent to this sleeping/living area. Plastic MRE wrappings and human excrement, mixed with diesel fuel in steel barrels, are burned round the clock just ten meters from the men. When the wind is still, they live in a haze of flies, mosquitoes and pungent, black smoke. When it blows, they're inundated with dust. Shamal storms, with fifty-mile-per-hour winds, strike every day, usually lasting three to six hours. During them, Marines just lie on the concrete pad with ponchos wrapped around their heads. Daytime temperatures now typically hover around 115 degrees. Wild dogs are kept at bay by a Marine gunnery sergeant who roams the camp with a shotgun, blasting away at them.

According to Navy Commander Kevin Moore, the division surgeon, injuries among Marines at the camp are running high from guys picking up the unexploded ordnance littering the place. Numerous cases of malaria have occurred, and everyone is becoming ill with what Moore calls "ass-to-hand" disease. A few Marines have undergone psychotic episodes and have been picked up running around the wire, screaming at imaginary Fedayeen. Moore attributes most of these cases to temporary psychosis induced by overuse of stimulants like Ripped Fuel.

One Marine in First Recon's support unit freaks out early in the stay at this camp. The episode is prompted after a Game Boy (which he brought into Iraq in violation of battalion regulations) disappeared from his rucksack. Early one afternoon following the battalion's arrival at Ad Diwaniyah, he runs into the warehouse serving as a chow hall with his M-16, puts it to the head of the suspected thief, racks a round into the chamber and screams, "Give me back my Game Boy!" Other Marines talk him out of pulling the trigger. The battalion isolates him for a few days, then returns him to his unit. The Game Boy is never recovered.

On my third morning here, I'm sitting with Colbert's team, eating an MRE breakfast. Most Marines still haven't had a proper shower since they left Camp Mathilda more than a month ago. A few rinsed off by spraying themselves with a fire hose in a warehouse they occupied in Baghdad, but not everyone had a chance to use it. Fick washes up for breakfast by spitting in his hands and wiping them on his dirty fatigues.

Colbert says, "You know, I don't miss anything from home. The only exception is my bike. I miss that. Speed, solitude and no one can touch me."

"You mean you're out here in the middle of nowhere, and you miss being alone?" Person laughs quietly. He doesn't say anything else, which is kind of amazing. After a month of insane, nonstop chattering in the Humvee, he barely talks now. When Person detoxes from Ripped Fuel, endless days of mortar fire, ambushes and sleepless nights behind the wheel of the Humvee, he turns into a soft-spoken guy from Nevada, Missouri, pop. 8,607. He now admits to me, despite his relentless mockery of the Corps, "When I get out of the Marines in November, I'm going to miss it."

In spite of the austerities at the platoon's encampent, spirits are high. The men build an open-air gym. They scavenge gears and drive shafts from wrecked Iraqi tanks and turn them into free weights and chin-up bars they hang from concrete pilings. They run for kilometers in the 115-degree heat. They practice hand-to-hand combat in the dirt. They pace back and forth barefoot through gravel to build calluses on their feet. The Marines sleep through each night for the first time in weeks, boil coffee every morning on fires started with C-4 explosive, play cards, dip tin after tin of Copenhagen and spend days, when they are not working out, engaging in endless bull sessions.

"Man, this is fucking awesome," Second Platoon's twenty-two-year-old Corporal James Chaffin declares one morning. "I can't believe I'm getting paid to work out, dip and hang out with the best guys in the world."

Up until now, no one has known the name of the war they've been fighting. Gunny Wynn passes on the rumor that he thinks they might be calling it "Iraqi Freedom." Hearing the news, Carazales scoffs. "Fuck that. I'll tell you what 'freedom' was, Phase Three Iraq," he says, referring to the military's term for the combat-operations phase of the invasion. "That was fucking Iraqi freedom. Rip through this bitch shooting anything that moves from your window. That's what I call freedom."

THE SENIOR OFFICERS, set up in nicer quarters across the camp, are basking in the glow of victory. First Recon, one of the smallest, most lightly armed battalions in the Corps, led the way for much of the Marines' blitzkrieg to Baghdad. "No other military in the world can do what we do," Ferrando tells me. "We are America's shock troops."

I meet Lt. Col. Ferrando in a small office that formerly belonged to an Iraqi officer. The one-story building is shaded by sycamore trees and has thick adobe walls, keeping it relatively cool even on this hot afternoon. One of the issues still dogging the battalion is Captain America's behavior. After a lengthy investigation into the incident in which he taunted an EPW with his bayonet, Ferrando returned him to command but hesitated to fully exonerate him. He finally does in late April, about the time I meet with him. He tells me he thinks Captain America walked a fine line but was still "within the box" of acceptable behavior. But he adds, "In my mind, when you allow that behavior to progress, you end up with a

My Lai Massacre." Then he leans across his desk and asks me if I think he should have taken harsher action toward Captain America.

I honestly can't answer him. In the past six weeks, I have been on hand while this comparatively small unit of Marines has killed quite a few people. I personally saw three civilians shot, one of them fatally with a bullet in the eye. These were just the tip of the iceberg. The Marines killed dozens, if not hundreds, in combat through direct fire and through repeated, at times almost indiscriminate, artillery strikes. And no one will probably ever know how many died from the approximately 30,000 pounds of bombs First Recon ordered dropped from aircraft. I can't imagine how the man ultimately responsible for all of these deaths—at least on the battalion level—sorts it all out and draws the line between what is wanton killing and what is civilized military conduct. I suppose if it were up to me, I might let Captain America keep his job, but I would take away his rifle and bayonet and give him a cap gun.

As I'm about to leave his office, Ferrando stops me. "Something I'm struggling with internally is it's exciting to get shot at," he says, sounding almost confessional. "It's an excitement that I hadn't thought about before." He hastily adds, "But at the same time it's a terrible feeling to be the man sending other people into combat."

Earlier, in a talk to his men, Ferrando referred to his order to send them onto the airfield at Qalat Sukhar with no preparation as "reckless." Many of his men feel the whole campaign of rushing into ambushes was characterized by recklessness. But in the end, he's been vindicated. He became, in a sense, Maj. Gen. Mattis's go-to guy in central Iraq. While Col. Dowdy, commander of the much larger regimental force in the region, sometimes appeared to hesitate, as he had in entering Nasiriyah, and was removed from command in early April, Ferrando seldom if ever turned down a chance to race his forces into another hairy situation. Much of the time during the dash to Al Kut, Ferrando's battalion set the pace. He shrugged off the fact that his men weren't adequately equipped or specifically trained for the kinds of assaults they were doing. (By contrast, after Dowdy was relieved of his command he was reportedly castigated in a subsequent fitness report for being "overly concerned about the welfare" of his men, with the idea being that this concern got in the way of mission accomplishment.) In the end, Ferrando's battalion exemplified the virtues of maneuver warfare, employing speed over firepower to throw Iraqi defenders off balance.

As much as some of the enlisted men despise Ferrando for what they saw as his dangerous haste (not to mention his obsession with the Grooming Standard), Fick praises him. "He got the job done for Major General Mattis, and in the Marine Corps that's all that matters. It's mission accomplishment first, troop welfare second. Ferrando has no problem with that."

When I talk to Mattis the next day at Ad Diwaniyah, he heaps praise on the courage and initiative displayed by the men in First Recon, to whom he credits with a large measure of the invasion's success. "They should be very proud," he says.

After I return to Second Platoon's squalid encampment and pass on the general's praise, the men stand around in the dust, considering his glowing remarks. Finally, Garza says, "Yeah? Well, we still did a lot of stupid shit."

"War doesn't change anything," Doc Bryan says. "This place was fucked up before we came, and it's fucked up now. I personally don't believe we 'liberated' the Iraqis. Time will tell."

"The American people ought to know the price we pay to maintain their standard of living," Espera says. Despite his avowals of being a complete cynic, he continually turns back to the incident at Al Hayy, where he shot and killed three unarmed men fleeing a truck at the Marines' roadblock. "I wish I could go back in time and see if they were enemy, or just confused civilians," he says.

"It could have been a truckful of babies, and with our Rules of Engagement you did the right thing," Fick says.

"I'm not saying I care," Espera says. "I don't give a fuck. But I keep thinking about what the priest said. It's not a sin to kill with a purpose, as long you don't enjoy it. My question is, is indifference the same as enjoyment?"

"All religious stuff aside," Colbert cuts in. "The fact is people who can't kill will be subject to those who can."

Despite their moral qualms—or lack thereof—about killing, most Marines unabashedly love the action. "You really can't top it," Redman says. "Combat is the supreme adrenaline rush. You take rounds. Shoot back, shit starts blowing up. It's sensory overload. It's the one thing that's not overrated in the military."

"The fucked thing," Doc Bryan says, "is the men we've been fighting probably came here for the same reasons we did, to test themselves, to feel what war is like. In my view it doesn't matter if you oppose or support war. The machine goes on."

EPILOGUE

○

I LEAVE First Recon's camp at Ad Diwaniyah in a Navy helicopter at dawn on May 4. We fly low and fast to avoid enemy ground fire. Our flight path takes us directly over the tank repair yard, where I see the men of Second Platoon stirring from their sleep on the concrete pad. They will remain here for more than a month, returning to Camp Pendleton on June 3, 2003.

Pappy, shot in the foot at Al Muwaffaqiyah, returned to duty at Camp Pendleton before his platoon's home-coming. Despite having received a "lucky" wound in an extremity, Pappy had to undergo intensive physical therapy to overcome a limp. Still walking with a cane when he returned to duty, he was roused one evening in his barracks room by a surprise visit from the ladies of the Key Wives Club—a spouse support group headed by Encino Man's wife. She and Lt. Col. Ferrando's wife offered him a heartfelt Key Wives' welcome home and gifts of fresh baked goods and a new toothbrush, then left a few minutes later. Pappy's bloody boot, worn the night he was shot, had been out on his floor when the Key Wives dropped in, but they made no mention of it. Pappy thought nothing of the visit, until June 3, when he went to March Air Force base to greet First Recon on its return. The first man he encountered off the plane was Ferrando, who walked up to him on the tarmac and chewed Pappy out for having left his tattered boot on the floor of his room when the Key Wives visited. "I don't like you showing your bloody boot to my wife," Ferrando had rasped, then brushed past, without further ado. "At least he didn't bitch about my mustache," Pappy later said. Pappy was awarded a Bronze Star for his actions in the invasion.

Upon his return, Colbert received one of the highest honors in the Marine Corps, a combat meritorious promotion to staff sergeant. He was nominated to enter a two-year exchange program with the British Royal Marines, with whom he is now serving.

Person got out of the Marines and moved to Kansas City, Missouri, to pursue his career as a rock star while working at the front desk of a twenty-four-hour fitness club.

After being promoted to the rank of captain, Fick left the Marine Corps in August to pursue graduate degrees in business and foreign relations at Harvard. For several months he debated whether he had been a good officer, or whether his concern for his men colored his judgment. He concluded, "My feelings made me a more conflicted officer. There was no celebratory cigar smoking on the battlefield for me. But we achieved every mission objective. I did my job." Under his command, the men in Second Platoon received more combat citations and awards than any other platoon in First Reconnaissance Battalion.

Capt. Patterson also left the Marine Corps, after being promoted to major, in order to study environmental engineering at the University of Washington. After more than ten years of distinguished military service, Patterson

departed following a loss of control in front of his men—
one that only raised their opinion of him. In my last
conversation with Patterson, he confessed that he was still
troubled by the episode in which Encino Man had
mistakenly followed an incorrect order to send men out to
mark a minefield at night. One of the engineers injured,
Valdez, who lost an eye, had served with Patterson's
company. "Valdez was my man," Patterson said to me.
"What the fuck happened?" Despite his anger, he refused
to cast blame on any individual. "It happened as a result
of dysfunction in the battalion, not because of what a
single officer did."

Patterson's eruption—and it could be called that given
the fact that ordinarily he is so mild-mannered it almost
makes him seem diminutive—happened midday on May
3, when the men in the companies were racing in a com-
petition whose winners would receive a phone call home.
Encino Man checked a corporal from Alpha Company
who was pulling ahead in an obstacle race, and Patterson
exploded, rushing Encino Man, throwing him into a head-
lock and slamming him against a wall. The enlisted men
were forced to break the two officers apart. Later,
Patterson laughed off the assault, claiming it was done in
the spirit of fun. Whatever his motives, Patterson
achieved hero status within the ranks.

Captain America departed from his command a few
weeks after the battalion's return. Some thought the
move was a demotion, until he was reassigned to a
prestigious command staff position in another unit.

Doc Bryan had a sad parting from the Middle East.
While waiting at a desert camp in Kuwait to fly home, he
was on hand at a football game held among Marines in
other units when one of the players went berserk with his
M-16 and shot a young man on the opposing team,

hitting him in the chest and neck. Doc Bryan and other corpsmen were unable to save the Marine. The incident only added fuel to Doc Bryan's bitter complaints about war. Later, Doc Bryan had been engaging in one of his typical bitch sessions about the incompetence of superiors when, he says, he suddenly heard his voice as if it belonged to someone else. Something snapped in him, and he realized, "You know what, I'm just not cut out for the military." But the feeling didn't last. His first week home, he was happily recruited out of First Recon into a secretive Special Forces unit. He has been training for a mission he is not at liberty to talk about.

Trombley finally completed the Basic Reconnaissance Course and is now a full-fledged Recon Marine. In the autumn he also participated in an LAPD training program. He's thinking of joining the LAPD when he gets out in a year.

Reyes achieved the dream of a lifetime when his temporary promotion to team leader after Pappy's wounding at Muwaffaqiyah was made permanent at Camp Pendleton. A week later, he was suspended following a hazing incident that occurred under his supervision. While training a Marine new to First Recon, one who was having trouble keeping up on a fitness run, Garza ordered the kid to dig a Ranger grave. Then Garza and others buried him, leaving only a small breathing space. Reyes had approved of the disciplinary measure, telling me later, "That was the kind of hard training we did under Horsehead." Reyes was immediately docked a month's pay. The rest of the men in the platoon took money from their paychecks to make up the difference in his lost salary, while he awaited formal punishment proceedings.

A few weeks after Espera returned from Iraq he had an eerie experience while driving with his family down

Ventura Boulevard in Los Angeles. Espera was at the wheel of a new SUV, purchased to celebrate his homecoming, when he glimpsed a man on the street who looked exactly like an Iraqi civilian the platoon had fatally shot at a roadblock in Iraq. In an instant he realized it wasn't the pedestrian on the street who had reminded him of the dead man; the light was glancing off the windshield of his new SUV the same way it had in his Humvee when he'd witnessed the shooting. A short while after this flashback, Espera was invited to a party at a gated community in Malibu where residents wanted to toast a war hero. In civilian clothes, with his hair grown out, and having gained the weight that he'd lost in Iraq, Espera cut a handsome figure. As the guests repeatedly praised his heroism in serving his country, Espera hung his head with an almost embarrassed smile. Then, after his fifth or sixth glass of wine, he rose to his feet. "I'm not a hero," he said. The guests nodded, their smiles stretching even wider at this hero's show of humility. "Guys like me are just a necessary part of things," Espera continued. "To maintain this way of life in a fine community like this, you need psychos like us to go out and drop a bomb on somebody's house."

In November the men were told First Recon would be returning to Iraq. Reyes was reinstated as team leader. Gunny Wynn, who was still facing disciplinary action for his disobedience to Encino Man in Iraq, was also cleared. "In the end," Reyes says, "they need bodies for the war." Reyes adds, "This is the way the Corps is. You join for the idealism, but eventually you see the flaws in it. You might fight this for a while. Then you accept that one man isn't going to change the Marine Corps. If you love the Corps, you give up some of the ideals which motivated you to join in the first place."

When Person heard through the grapevine that his unit was going back, he called Gunny Wynn at home, drunk, from Kansas City, and told him he was reenlisting. Gunny Wynn told him to shut up, go to bed and stay a civilian.

As this book goes to press, the men in Bravo Second Platoon, along with the rest of First Recon, are in Fallujah, Iraq.

ACKNOWLEDGMENTS

○

This book would not have been possible without the bravery of the United States Marine Corps, which in its mission to defend the U.S. Constitution allowed a reporter in its midst. Thanks to all of the men of First Recon, from Godfather on down, who helped in providing access, interviews and support. Special thanks to Nate for his wisdom, to Josh for his exceptional driving and to Brad, James, Gabe and Walt for their warm hospitality and accurate shooting. This effort was backed by Jann S. Wenner and began with the help of these mentors: Allan MacDonell, Michael Louis Albo, Dylan Ford, Janet Duckworth, Karl Taro Greenfeld, Will Dana, Gunnery Sergeant Mark Oliva, Rex Bowman, Sean Woods, Richard Abate, Rob McMahon and David Highfill.

A SELECTED LIST OF RELATED TITLES
AVAILABLE FROM CORGI AND BANTAM BOOKS